Gertrude Moller

The Standard Operas

By GEORGE P. UPTON

MUSICAL HANDBOOKS
THE STANDARD OPERAS
New revised edition from new plates. 12mo. Illustrated. $1.75

THE STANDARD CONCERT GUIDE
A Handbook of the Standard Symphonies, Oratorios, Cantatas, and Symphonic Poems, for the Concert Goer. Profusely Illustrated 12mo. $1.75

THE STANDARD CONCERT REPERTORY
Uniform in style with above. Illustrated with numerous portraits. Indexed. 12mo. $1.75

THE STANDARD ORATORIOS
THE STANDARD CANTATAS
THE STANDARD SYMPHONIES
THE STANDARD LIGHT OPERAS
12mo. Yellow edges. Per volume, $1.50

WOMAN IN MUSIC
16mo. $1.00

MUSICAL PASTELS: A Series of Essays on Quaint and Curious Musical Subjects.
Large 8vo. With ten full-page illustrations from rare wood engravings. $1.50

A. C. McCLURG & COMPANY · CHICAGO

Lilli Lehmann as *Isolde*

Copyright, Aimé Dupont

The Standard Operas

*Their Plots, Their Music, and
Their Composers*

By George P. Upton
Author of
"Standard Handbooks on Music," "Life of Theodore
Thomas," etc., etc.

New Edition, Enlarged and Revised

Profusely Illustrated

Chicago
A. C. McClurg & Co.
1911

COPYRIGHT

BY JANSEN, MCCLURG & CO., 1885
BY A. C. MCCLURG & CO., 1896, 1906

ENTERED AT STATIONERS' HALL, LONDON, ENGLAND

All rights reserved

This illustrated edition, published October, 1906, is the twentieth printing of this book

Second printing of this edition, December, 1906
Third printing of this edition, May, 1907
Fourth printing of this edition, February, 1908
Fifth printing of this edition, December, 1908
Sixth printing of this edition, March, 1909
Seventh printing of this edition, July, 1909
Eighth printing of this edition, February, 1910
Ninth printing of this edition, August, 1910
Tenth printing of this edition, August, 1911

THE UNIVERSITY PRESS, CAMBRIDGE, U.S.A.

TO THE MEMORY
OF
THEODORE THOMAS
MASTER OF MUSIC

PREFACE

THE object of the compiler of this Handbook is to present to the reader a brief but comprehensive sketch of the operas contained in the modern repertory. To this end he has consulted the best authorities, adding to the material thus collected his own observations, and in each case has presented a necessarily brief sketch of the composer, the story of each opera, the general character of its music, its prominent scenes and numbers, — the latter in the text most familiar to opera-goers, — the date of first performances, with a statement of the original cast wherever it has been possible to obtain it, and such historical information concerning the opera and its composition as will be of interest to the reader. As many new operas have been produced since "The Standard Operas" was first published, these have been included in the new edition, although it is as yet uncertain whether some of them will become "standard" in the strict sense of the word. In a work of this kind, indeed, the selection of "standard" operas must be somewhat arbitrary. It is difficult to say where the line should be drawn. The writer's aim has been to acquaint his reader with the prominent operas of the past and the present, assuming that it may be well to know their story and musical construction whether they retain their places upon the stage or not. The work has

PREFACE

been prepared for the general public rather than for musicians; and with this purpose in view, technicalities have been avoided as far as possible, the aim being to give musically uneducated lovers of opera a clear understanding of the works they are likely to hear, and thus heighten their enjoyment. To add to their pleasure and recall delightful memories, the new edition has been illustrated generously with portraits of leading artists in their most favorite roles. In a word, the operas are described rather than criticised, and the work is presented with as much thoroughness as was possible, considering the necessarily brief space allotted to each opera. In the preparation of the Handbook the compiler acknowledges his indebtedness to Grove's "Dictionary of Music," Baker's "Biographical Dictionary of Musicians," Champlin and Apthorp's "Cyclopedia of Music and Musicians," and Ramann's "Opern Handbuch" for dates and other statistical information; and he has also made free use of standard musical works in his library for historical events connected with the performance and composition of the operas. He has sought to obtain accuracy of statement by verification after consultations of the best authors, and to make "Standard Operas" a popular reference for opera-goers. It only remains to submit this work to them with the hope that it may add to their enjoyment and prove a useful addition to their libraries.

G. P. U.

CHICAGO, June, 1906.

CONTENTS

	PAGE
ADAM	1
THE POSTILION OF LONGJUMEAU	2
AUBER	5
FRA DIAVOLO	6
MASANIELLO	9
THE CROWN DIAMONDS	12
BALFE	17
THE BOHEMIAN GIRL	18
THE ROSE OF CASTILE	22
BEETHOVEN	25
FIDELIO	26
BELLINI	30
NORMA	31
LA SONNAMBULA	34
I PURITANI	36
BENEDICT	39
THE LILY OF KILLARNEY	39
BIZET	43
CARMEN	44
BOIELDIEU	48
LA DAME BLANCHE	49
BOITO	52
MEPHISTOPHELES	53
BRÜLL	56
THE GOLDEN CROSS	56

CONTENTS

	Page
CHERUBINI	59
The Water Carrier (Les deux journées)	59
DAMROSCH	62
The Scarlet Letter	62
DE KOVEN	64
Robin Hood	64
Maid Marian	66
DELIBES	69
Lakme	69
DONIZETTI	73
The Daughter of the Regiment	74
La Favorita	76
Don Pasquale	79
Lucia di Lammermoor	81
L'Elisir d'Amore	84
Lucrezia Borgia	86
Linda de Chamouni	88
FLOTOW	91
Martha	92
Stradella	95
GENÉE	98
Nanon	98
GLUCK	101
Orpheus	102
GOETZ	106
The Taming of the Shrew	106
GOLDMARK	110
The Queen of Sheba	110
Merlin	113
GOUNOD	117
Faust	118
Roméo et Juliette	121
Philémon and Baucis	123

CONTENTS

	PAGE
HALÉVY	126
The Jewess	127
L'Eclair	129
HEROLD	132
Zampa	132
Le Pré aux Clercs	135
HUMPERDINCK	137
Hansel and Gretel	138
JAKOBOWSKI	142
Erminie	142
LECOCQ	144
Giroflé-Girofla	144
La Fille de Madame Angot	147
LEONCAVALLO	150
I Pagliacci	151
LÖRTZING	154
Czar and Carpenter	154
MARSCHNER	157
Hans Heiling	158
MASCAGNI	161
Cavalleria Rusticana	162
Iris	165
L'Amico Fritz	166
MASSÉ	169
Paul and Virginia	169
La Reine Topaze	171
The Marriage of Jeanette	172
MASSENET	174
Le Roi de Lahore	175
Le Cid	177
Manon	180
Esclarmonde	182

CONTENTS

	PAGE
MEYERBEER	185
THE HUGUENOTS	186
THE STAR OF THE NORTH	190
ROBERT THE DEVIL	194
DINORAH	198
THE PROPHET	201
THE AFRICAN	205
MILLÖCKER	209
THE BEGGAR STUDENT	209
MOZART	212
THE MARRIAGE OF FIGARO	213
DON GIOVANNI	218
THE MAGIC FLUTE	223
NESSLER	229
THE TRUMPETER OF SÄKKINGEN	229
NICOLAI	233
THE MERRY WIVES OF WINDSOR	233
OFFENBACH	236
THE GRAND DUCHESS OF GEROLSTEIN	237
LA BELLE HÉLÈNE	239
ORPHÉE AUX ENFERS	241
PADEREWSKI	244
MANRU	244
PLANQUETTE	248
THE CHIMES OF NORMANDY	248
PONCHIELLI	251
LA GIOCONDA	251
PUCCINI	256
LA BOHÈME	256
LA TOSCA	259
REYER	262
SIGURD	262

CONTENTS

xiii

	PAGE
RICCI	266
Crispino	266
ROSSINI	269
The Barber of Seville	270
Semiramide	273
William Tell	277
RUBINSTEIN	281
Nero	282
The Demon	285
SAINT-SAËNS	287
Samson and Delila	288
Henry VIII	290
Proserpine	293
STRAUSS, JOHANN	296
The Merry War	297
The Bat (Die Fledermaus)	298
The Queen's Lace Handkerchief	299
The Gypsy Baron	301
STRAUSS, RICHARD	303
Feuersnot	304
SULLIVAN	308
The Sorcerer	309
H. M. S. Pinafore	311
The Pirates of Penzance	314
Patience	316
Iolanthe	319
Princess Ida	321
The Mikado	324
Ruddygore	326
The Yeomen of the Guard	328
The Gondoliers	330
SUPPÉ	333
Fatinitza	333
Boccaccio	336
The Beautiful Galatea	337

CONTENTS

	PAGE
THOMAS	340
Mignon	340
Hamlet	345
TSCHAIKOWSKY	347
Eugen Onégin	347
VERDI	350
Ernani	351
Rigoletto	354
La Traviata	358
Il Trovatore	361
The Masked Ball	365
Aïda	368
Othello	372
Falstaff	375
WAGNER	379
Rienzi	380
The Flying Dutchman	386
Tannhäuser	389
Lohengrin	393
Tristan und Isolde	398
The Mastersingers	401
The Ring of the Nibelung	406
Das Rheingold	414
Die Walküre	417
Siegfried	422
Die Götterdämmerung	426
Parsifal	430
WAGNER (SIEGFRIED)	437
Der Bärenhäuter	437
Der Kobold	439
WALLACE	441
Maritana	442
Lurline	446

CONTENTS

	Page
WEBER	449
DER FREISCHÜTZ	450
OBERON	456
EURYANTHE	460
PRECIOSA	463
APPENDIX	467
APPENDIX TO NEW EDITION	471
ALBERT, D'	
TIEFLAND	472
BRETON	
LA DOLORES	475
BRUNEAU	
L'ATTAQUE DU MOULIN	478
CATALANI	
LA WALLY	481
CHARPENTIER	
LOUISE	484
CONVERSE	
THE PIPE OF DESIRE	487
DEBUSSY	
PELLÉAS AND MÉLISANDE	491
FRANCHETTI	
GERMANIA	494
GIORDANO	
ANDREA CHENIER	496
GOLDMARK	
CRICKET ON THE HEARTH	498
LEHAR	
THE MERRY WIDOW	500
MANCINELLI	
ERO E LEANDRO	503
MASSENET	
GRISELIDIS	505
HERODIADE	506
WERTHER	509
CENDRILLON	511

CONTENTS

	Page
Sapho	511
Thaïs	513
Le Jongleur de Notre Dame	515
Don Quixote	516

NEVIN
Poia 518

OFFENBACH
Les Contes de Hoffmann 520

PUCCINI
Madame Butterfly 522
Manon Lescaut 524
Le Villi 525

SMETANA
The Bartered Bride 527

STRAUSS, R.
Salome 529
Elektra 531
Der Rosenkavalier 533

TSCHAIKOWSKY
Dame de Pique 536

INDEX 539

LIST OF PORTRAITS

LILLI LEHMANN AS ISOLDE . . . . *Frontispiece*

ADAM PAGE
    THE POSTILION OF LONGJUMEAU: Wachtel, creator of the
        title-role 2

AUBER
    FRA DIAVOLO: Santley as *Fra Diavolo* 8

BELLINI
    NORMA: Grisi as *Norma* 32

BIZET
    CARMEN: Calvé as *Carmen* 44
        Journet as *Escamillo* 46
        Caruso as *Don José* 46

BOITO
    MEPHISTOPHELES: Marie Roze as *Helen* 54

DONIZETTI
    THE DAUGHTER OF THE REGIMENT: Jenny Lind as *Marie* 74
    LUCIA DI LAMMERMOOR: Saleza as *Edgardo* 82
    L'ELISIR D'AMORE: Sembrich as *Adina* 84
    LUCREZIA BORGIA: Mme. de Moschi as *Lucrezia Borgia* . 86

FLOTOW
    MARTHA: Sembrich as *Martha* 94

GLUCK
    ORPHEUS: Schalchi as *Orpheus* 104

xviii LIST OF PORTRAITS

GOUNOD   PAGE
  FAUST: Melba as *Marguerite* 118
    Saleza as *Faust* 120
    Plançon as *Mephistopheles* 120
  ROMÉO ET JULIETTE: Geraldine Farrar as *Juliet* 122

HALÉVY
  THE JEWESS: Falcon as *Rachel* 128

LECOCQ
  LA FILLE DE MADAME ANGOT: Soldene as *Mdlle. Lange* 148

LEONCAVALLO
  I PAGLIACCI: Fritzi Scheff as *Nedda* 152
    Alvarez as *Canio* 152

MASCAGNI
  CAVALLERIA RUSTICANA: Calvé as *Santuzza* 164

MASSENET
  LE CID: Breval as *Chimène* 178

MEYERBEER
  THE HUGUENOTS: Nilsson as *Valentin* 186
    Jean de Reszke as *Raoul* 190
    Plançon as *St. Bris* 190
  THE PROPHET: Schumann-Heink as *Fides* 202
    Alvarez as *The Prophet* 202
  L'AFRICAINE: Dippel as *Vasco di Gama* 206

MOZART
  THE MARRIAGE OF FIGARO: Sigrid Arnoldson as *Cherubino* 214
  DON GIOVANNI: Sontag as *Donna Anna* 218
    Scotti as *Don Giovanni* 220
    Edouard de Reszke as *Leporello* 220
  THE MAGIC FLUTE: Gadski as *Pamina* 224
    Dippel as *Tamino* 224

OFFENBACH
  THE GRAND DUCHESS OF GEROLSTEIN: Hortense
    Schneider as *La Grande Duchesse* 238
  ORPHÉE AUX ENFERS: Jeanne Granier as *Eurydice* . . . 242

LIST OF PORTRAITS

PADEREWSKI

   Manru: Sembrich as *Ulana* 246
       Bispham as *Urok* 246
       Bandrowski as *Manru* 246

PONCHIELLI

   La Gioconda: Louise Homer in " La Gioconda " . . . 252
       Caruso as *Enzo* 252

PUCCINI

   La Bohème: Saleza as *Rodolfo* 256
       Group of *Rodolfo*, *Colline*, *Marcel*, and *Schaunard* . . 256
   La Tosca: Adelaide Norwood as *Tosca* 258
       Scotti as *Scarpia* 260

ROSSINI

   The Barber of Seville: Sembrich as *Rosina* 270
       Campanari as *Figaro* 270
   Semiramide: Group of *Semiramide*, *Arsace*, and *Assur* . 276

SAINT-SAËNS

   Samson and Delila: Tamagno as *Samson* 288

STRAUSS, JOHANN

   The Bat: Sembrich as *Rosalind* 298

THOMAS

   Mignon: Ambré as *Mignon* 340
   Hamlet: Calvé as *Ophelia* 340

VERDI

   Ernani: Sembrich as *Elvira* 352
   Rigoletto: Louise Homer as *Gilda* 354
       Caruso as *The Duke* 354
   La Traviata: Geraldine Farrar as *Violetta* 358
   Il Trovatore: Campanini as *Manrico* 362
   The Masked Ball: Eames as *Amelia* 366
   Aïda: Gadski as *Aïda* 368
       Marie Brema as *Amneris* 370
   Othello: Tamagno as *Othello* 374

WAGNER

	Page
The Flying Dutchman: Hiedler as *Senta*	386
Muhlmann as *The Flying Dutchman*	386
Tannhäuser: Ternina as *Elizabeth*	390
Adams as *Tannhäuser*	390
Lohengrin: Eames as *Elsa*	394
Kraus as *Lohengrin*	394
Schumann-Heink as *Ortrud*	396
Tristan und Isolde: Lehmann as *Isolde* (frontispiece)	
Jean de Reszke as *Tristan*	400
Edouard de Reszke as *King Mark*	400
Bispham as *Kurwenal*	400
Die Meistersinger: Van Rooy as *Hans Sachs*	402
Bispham as *Beckmesser*	402
Winklemann as *Walter*	404
Das Rheingold: Mme. Materna	414
Louise Homer as *Erda*	416
Die Walküre: Nordica as *Brünnhilde*	418
Gadski as *Brünnhilde*	418
Fremstad as *Sieglinde*	420
Burgstaller as *Siegmund*	420
Van Rooy as *Wotan*	422
Siegfried: Alvary as *Siegfried*	424
Bispham as *Alberich*	426
Reiss as *Mime*	426
Die Götterdämmerung: Jean de Reszke as *Siegfried*	428
Parsifal: Dippel as *Parsifal* (First Act)	434
Dippel as *Parsifal* (Third Act)	434
Fremstad as *Kundry*	436
Perron as *Amfortas*	438
Goritz as *Klingsor*	438

The Standard Operas

THE STANDARD OPERAS

THEIR PLOTS, THEIR MUSIC, AND THEIR COMPOSERS

ADAM

ADOLPHE CHARLES ADAM was born in Paris, July 24, 1803, and died in that city, May 3, 1856. He entered the Conservatoire in 1817, where he studied the organ and harmonium with Benoit. His success as composer, however, was largely due to Boieldieu, with whom he was not only a favorite pupil but close friend. Boieldieu's confidence in his ability is shown by the fact that Adam wrote the overture to the latter's "La Dame Blanche." It was upon his advice also that he devoted himself to the composition of light operas, some of which proved very successful. His first production was a one-act operetta, "Pierre and Catherine" (1829), which was followed by many others, the best of which are "Le Chalet" (1834); "Le Postillion de Longjumeau," the most successful of his works (1836); "Le Brasseur de Preston" (1838); "Le Roi d'Yvetot" (1842), and "Cagliostro" (1844). In 1847 he started a new theatre, called the "Théâtre Nationale," which proved a disastrous undertaking and involved him heavily in debt. He recovered his losses, however, by composition and contributions to literary and musical periodicals, for he was a ready and very attractive writer. His life of Boieldieu, for instance, is a notable addition to musical biographies. His music, though not of the highest order, is always bright and gay, and some of his melodies have attained a widespread popularity.

THE POSTILION OF LONGJUMEAU

"The Postilion of Longjumeau," opera comique, in three acts, text by De Leuven and Brunswick, was first produced at the Opéra Comique, Paris, October 13, 1836. This sprightly opera is characterized by grace and elegance of treatment, fascinating rhythm, and odd contrasts in effects. Its plot is very dramatic, and affords ample scope for humorous action. The opening scene of the first act, which is laid in Longjumeau, a French village, time of Louis the Fifteenth, introduces us to the wedding of Chapelou, the postilion, and Madeleine, mistress of the inn. During the merriment which follows, the Marquis de Courcy, superintendent of the Paris Grand Opera, whose carriage has broken down, makes his appearance, seeking the aid of a wheelwright. He hears Chapelou singing, and is so pleased with his voice that he offers him a position in the opera. Chapelou, after some persuasion, accepts, entreats Bijou, the village blacksmith, to look after Madeleine, and goes off with the Marquis in quest of artistic glory. Bijou informs Madeleine of Chapelou's baseness, and the act closes with her denunciations of him, in which she is enthusiastically assisted by the female members of the wedding-party.

The second act opens in Paris. Madeleine has inherited a fortune from an aunt, and makes her appearance in the gay city as a rich and noble lady, under the assumed name of Madame de la Tour. The Marquis de Courcy, who is in love with her, at her request brings Chapelou, who is now a famous tenor known as St. Phar, Bijou, the Longjumeau blacksmith, who is primo basso under the name of Alcindor, and the operatic chorus to her chateau for a

Herr Wachtel
Famous as the creator of The Postilion of Longjumeau

rehearsal. St. Phar not wishing to sing, pleads a cold, but when he learns that he is in the apartments of Madame de la Tour he consents, and the rehearsal goes off finely. Left alone with his hostess, he proposes to her and is accepted, but as he is already married he arranges that Boudon, the chorus leader, shall play the part of priest. The Marquis, who overhears the conspiracy, informs Madame de la Tour, who sends for a real priest and accompanies St. Phar to the altar, where they are married for the second time.

In the third act, St. Phar, who fears that he will be hanged for committing bigamy, finds a happy escape from his troubles. The Marquis, furious because he has been rejected by Madame de la Tour in favor of an opera singer, seeks revenge, but his plans are thwarted. A humorous scene ensues, in which St. Phar is tormented by Alcindor and the wedding-party, as well as by the Marquis, who is now reconciled. Finally, upon being left alone in a darkened room with Madame de la Tour, she also aggravates him by personating two characters, singing from different sides of the apartment in the voice of the Madame and that of Madeleine. The denouement ensues when she appears to him as the veritable Madeleine of Longjumeau, whither the joyous pair return and are happy ever after.

The principal music of the first act is a romanza for soprano, "Husband ever dear," leading into a dance chorus; the famous Postilion's Song with whip-snapping accompaniment; and a balcony serenade by Madeleine. The second act opens with a long and well-written aria for soprano, which is followed by the rehearsal scene,— a clever bit of humorous musical writing. In the course of this scene the tenor has a characteristic aria, preceded by a clarinet obbligato, and the basso also has one running down to G, in which he describes with much gusto the immunities of a basso with a "double G." A duet follows for soprano and tenor with a cadenza of extraordinary length, the act closing with a finale in the conventional Italian style.

The third act opens with a long clarinet solo, the refrain of which is heard in the close of the act. This is followed by a "Good Night" chorus in mazurka time. The tenor then has an aria followed by a comic trio, which in reality is a duet, as the soprano is personating two singers with different voices. A duet and finale close the opera, the music of which is of just the class to be popular, while the action is so sustained in its humor as to make the bright little opera a favorite wherever heard. The success of the "Postilion of Longjumeau" in the United States was largely due to Wachtel's remarkable dramatic as well as vocal presentation of the role of Chapelou.

AUBER

DANIEL FRANÇOIS ESPRIT AUBER, one of the most prominent representatives of the opera comique, was born at Caen, in Normandy, January 29, 1784. He first attracted attention in the musical world by his songs and ballads, written when a mere boy. Young as he was, they were great favorites in French and English drawing-rooms, and their success diverted him from his commercial intentions to that profession in which he was destined to achieve such popularity. His debut was made as an instrumental composer in his twentieth year, but before he had reached his thirtieth he was engrossed with operatic composition. His first two works were unsuccessful; but the third, "La Bergère Châtelaine," proved the stepping-stone to a career of remarkable popularity, during which he produced a large number of dramatic works, which not only secured for him the enthusiastic admiration of the Parisians, with whom he was always a favorite, but also carried his name and fame throughout the world, and obtained for him marks of high distinction from royalty, such as the office of Director of the Conservatoire from Louis Phillippe, and that of Imperial Maître de Chappelle from Louis Napoleon. He died May 13, 1871, amid the fearful scenes of the Paris Commune. His best-known operas are: "Masaniello" (1828); "Fra Diavolo" (1830); "The Bronze Horse" (1835); "The Black Domino" (1837); "The Crown Diamonds" (1841); and "Zerline" (1851), — the last-named written for the great contralto, Mme. Alboni. Of these, "Fra Diavolo," "Masaniello," and "The Crown

FRA DIAVOLO

"Fra Diavolo," opera comique, in three acts, words by Scribe, was first produced at the Opera Comique, Paris, January 28, 1830; in English, at Drury Lane, London, November 3, 1831; in Italian at the Lyceum, London, July 9, 1857, for which occasion the spoken dialogue was converted into accompanied recitative. The composer himself also, in fitting it for the Italian stage, made some changes in the concerted music and added several morceaux. The original Italian cast was as follows:

Zerlina	Mme. BOSIO.
Lady Allcash	Mlle. MARAI.
Fra Diavolo	Sig. GARDONI.
Lord Allcash	Sig. RONCONI.
Beppo	Sig. TAGLIAFICO.
Giacomo	Sig. ZELGER.

The original of the story of "Fra Diavolo" is to be found in Lesueur's opera, "La Caverne," afterwards arranged as a spectacular piece and produced in Paris in 1808 by Cuvellier and Franconi, and again in Vienna in 1822 as a spectacle-pantomime, under the title of "The Robber of the Abruzzi." In Scribe's adaptation the bandit, Fra Diavolo, encounters an English nobleman and his pretty and susceptible wife, Lord and Lady Allcash, at the inn of Terracina, kept by Matteo, whose daughter Zerlina is loved by Lorenzo, a young soldier, on the eve of starting to capture Fra Diavolo when the action of the opera begins. In the first scene the English couple enter in great alarm, having narrowly escaped the robbery of all their valuables by Fra Diavolo's band. The bandit himself, who has followed them on their journey in the disguise of a marquis, and has been particularly attentive to the lady, enters the inn just as Lord Allcash has been reproving his wife for her familiarity with a stranger. A quarrel ensues in a duet of a very humorous character ("I don't object"). Upon the entrance of Fra Diavolo, a quintet ("Oh, Rapture unbounded!") occurs, which is one of the most effective and admirably harmonized ensembles Auber has ever written. Fra Diavolo learns the trick by which they saved the most of their valuables, and, enraged at the failure of his band, lays his own plan to secure them. In an interview with Zerlina, she, mistaking him for the Marquis, tells him the story of Fra Diavolo in a romanza ("On yonder Rock reclining"), which is so fresh, vigorous, and full of color, that it has become a favorite the world over. To further his schemes, Fra Diavolo makes love to Lady Allcash and sings an exquisitely graceful barcarole to her ("The Gondolier, fond Passion's Slave"), accompanying himself on the mandolin. Lord Allcash interrupts the song, and the trio, "Bravi, Bravi," occurs, which leads up to the finale of the act. Fra Diavolo eludes the carbineers, who have returned, and they resume their search for him, leaving him unmolested to perfect his plans for the robbery.

The second act introduces Zerlina in her chamber about to retire. She first lights Lord and Lady Allcash to their room, a running conversation occurring between them in a trio ("Let us, I pray, good Wife, to rest"), which by many good critics has been considered as the best number in the work. Before Zerlina returns to her chamber, Fra Diavolo and his companions, Beppo and Giacomo, conceal themselves in a closet, and, somewhat in violation of dramatic consistency, Fra Diavolo sings the beautiful serenade, "Young Agnes," which had been agreed upon as a signal to his comrades that the coast was clear. Zerlina enters and after a pretty cavatina ("'T is To-morrow") and a prayer, charming for its simplicity ("Oh, Holy Virgin"), retires to rest. The robbers in attempting to cross her room partially arouse her. One of them rushes to the bed to stab her, but falls back awestricken as she murmurs her prayer and sinks to rest again. The trio which marks this scene, sung pianissimo, is quaint and simple and yet very dramatic. The noise of the carbineers returning outside interrupts the plan of the robbers. They conceal themselves in the closet again. Zerlina rises and dresses herself. Lord and Lady Allcash rush in *en déshabillé* to find out the cause of the uproar. Lorenzo enters to greet Zerlina, when a sudden noise in the closet disturbs the company. Fra Diavolo, knowing he will be detected, boldly steps out into the room and declares that he is there to keep an appointment with Zerlina. Lorenzo challenges him, and he promises to give him satisfaction in the morning, and coolly effects his escape. One of his comrades, however, is captured, and to secure his own liberty agrees to betray his chief.

The third act introduces Fra Diavolo once more among his native mountains, and there is the real breath and vigor of the mountain air in his opening song ("Proudly and wide my Standard flies"), and rollicking freedom in the rondeau which follows it ("Then since Life glides so fast away"). He exults in his liberty, and gleefully looks forward to a meeting with Lord and Lady Allcash, which he anticipates will redound to his personal profit. His exultation is interrupted by the entrance of the villagers arrayed in festival attire in honor of the approaching wedding ceremonies, singing a bright pastoral chorus ("Oh, Holy Virgin! bright and fair"). The finale of the act is occupied with the development of the scheme between Lorenzo, Beppo, and Giacomo, to ensnare Fra Diavolo and compass his death; and with the final tragedy, in which Fra Diavolo meets his doom at the hands

Santley as *Fra Diavolo*

of the carbineers, but not before he has declared Zerlina's innocence. This finale is strong and very dramatic, and yet at the same time simple, natural, and unstudied. The opera itself is a universal favorite, not alone for its naturalness and quiet grace, but for the bright and even boisterous humor, which is displayed by the typical English tourist, who was for the first time introduced in opera by Scribe. The text is full of spirit and gayety, and these qualities are admirably reflected in the sparkling music of Auber. Not one of the books which the versatile Scribe has supplied for the opera is more replete with incident or brighter in humor. How well it was adapted for musical treatment is shown by the fact that "Fra Diavolo" made Auber's reputation at the Opera Comique.

MASANIELLO

"Masaniello," or "La Muette de Portici," lyric opera in five acts, words by Scribe and Delavigne, was first produced at Paris, February 29, 1828; in English, at London, May 4, 1829; and in Italian, at London, March 15, 1849. The original cast included Mme. Damoreau-Cinti as Elvira, Mlle. Noblet as Fenella, and M. Massol as Pietro. In the Italian version, Sig. Mario, Mme. Dorus-Gras, and Mlle. Leroux, a famous mime and dancer, took the principal parts; while in its English dress, Braham created one of the greatest successes on record, and established it as the favorite opera of Auber among Englishmen.

The scene of the opera is laid near Naples. The first act opens upon the festivities attending the nuptials of Alphonso, son of the Duke of Arcos, and the Princess Elvira. After a chorus of rejoicing, the latter enters and sings a brilliant cavatina ("O, bel Momento") expressive of her happiness. In the fourth scene the festivities are interrupted by the appearance of Fenella, the dumb girl, who implores the princess to save her from Selva, one of the Duke's officers, who is seeking to return her to prison, from which she has escaped, and where she has been confined at the orders of some unknown cavalier who has been persecuting her. The part of Fenella is of course expressed by pantomime throughout. The remainder of the act is intensely dramatic. Elvira promises to protect Fenella, and then, after some spirited choruses by the soldiers, enters the chapel with Alphonso. During the ceremony Fenella discovers that he is her betrayer. She attempts to go in, but is prevented by the soldiers. On the return of the newly wedded pair Fenella meets Elvira and denounces her husband, and the scene ends with a genuine Italian finale of excitement.

The second act opens on the seashore, and shows the fishermen busy with their nets and boats. Masaniello, brother of Fenella, enters, brooding upon the wrongs of the people, and is implored by the fishermen to cheer them with a song. He replies with the barcarole, " Piu bello sorse il giorno," — a lovely melody, which has been the delight of all tenors. His friend Pietro enters and they join in a duet (" Sara il morir ") of a most vigorous and impassioned character, expressive of Masaniello's grief for his sister and their mutual resolution to strike a blow for freedom. At the conclusion of the duet he finds Fenella preparing to throw herself into the sea. He calls to her and she rushes into his arms and describes to him the story of her wrongs. He vows revenge, and in a magnificent, martial finale, which must have been inspired by the revolutionary feeling with which the whole atmosphere was charged at the time Auber wrote (1828), incites the fishermen and people to rise in revolt against their tyrannical oppressors.

In the third act, after a passionate aria ("Il pianto rasciuga") by Elvira, we are introduced to the marketplace, crowded with market-girls and fishermen disposing

AUBER

of their fruits and fish. After a lively chorus, a fascinating and genuine Neapolitan tarantella is danced. The merry scene speedily changes to one of turmoil and distress. Selva attempts to arrest Fenella, but the fishermen rescue her and Masaniello gives the signal for the general uprising. Before the combat begins, all kneel and sing the celebrated prayer, "Nume del Ciel," taken from one of Auber's early masses, and one of his most inspired efforts.

The fourth act opens in Masaniello's cottage. He deplores the coming horrors of the day in a grand aria ("Dio! di me disponesti") which is very dramatic in its quality. Fenella enters, and after describing the tumult in the city sinks exhausted with fatigue. As she falls asleep he sings a slumber song ("Scendi, o sonno dal ciel"), a most exquisite melody, universally known as "L'Air du Sommeil." It is sung by the best artists mezza voce throughout, and when treated in this manner never fails to impress the hearer with its tenderness and beauty. At its close Pietro enters and once more rouses Masaniello to revenge by informing him that Alphonso has escaped. After they leave the cottage, the latter and Elvira enter and implore protection. Fenella is moved to mercy, and a concerted number follows in which Masaniello promises safety and is denounced by Pietro for his weakness. In the finale, the magistrates and citizens enter, bearing the keys of the town and the royal insignia, and declare Masaniello king in a chorus of a very inspiriting and brilliant character.

The last act is very powerful, both dramatically and musically. It opens in the grounds of the Viceroy's palace, and Vesuvius is seen in the distance, its smoke portending an eruption. Pietro and companions enter with wine-cups in their hands, as from a banquet, and the former sings a barcarole ("Ve' come il vento irato"). At its close other fishermen enter and excitedly announce that troops are moving against the people, that Vesuvius is about to burst into flame, and that Masaniello, their leader, has lost his reason. This is confirmed by the appearance of the hero in disordered attire, singing music through which fragments of the fishermen's songs as they rise in his disturbed brain are filtered. This scene, the third in the act, is one not only of great power but of exquisite grace and tenderness, and requires an artist of the highest rank for its proper presentation. Fenella rouses him from his dejection, and he once more turns and plunges into the fight, only to be killed by his own comrades. On learning of her brother's death she unites the hands of Alphonso and Elvira, and then in despair throws herself into the burning lava of Vesuvius.

"Masaniello" made Auber's fame at the Grand Opéra, as "Fra Diavolo" made it at the Opera Comique, but it has no points in common with that or any other of his works. It is serious throughout, and full of power, impetuosity, and broad dramatic treatment. Even Richard Wagner conceded its vigor, bold effects, and original harmonies. Its melodies are spontaneous, its instrumentation full of color, and its stirring incidents are always vigorously handled. In comparison with his other works it seems like an inspiration. It is full of the revolutionary spirit, and its performance in Brussels in 1830 was the cause of the riots that drove the Dutch out of Belgium.

THE CROWN DIAMONDS

"The Crown Diamonds" ("Les Diamants de la Couronne"), opera comique, in three acts, words by Scribe and St. George, one of the most charming of Auber's light operas, was first produced in Paris in 1841, but its reputation has been made on the English stage. It was first performed in London, at the Princess Theatre, May 2, 1844, with Mme. Anna Thillon, a charming singer and most fascinating woman, as Catarina; but its real success was made at Drury Lane in 1854 by Louisa Pyne and Harrison, who took the parts of Catarina and Don Henrique. The other roles, Count de Campo Mayor, Don Sebastian, Rebolledo, and Diana, were filled by Mr. Horncastle, Mr. Reeves, Mr. Borrani, and Miss Pyne, sister of the preceding, and with this cast the opera ran a hundred nights.

The story of the opera is laid in Portugal, time, 1777. The opening scene discloses the ruins of a castle in the mountains, near the monastery of St. Huberto, where Don Henrique, nephew of the Count de Campo Mayor, Minister of Police at Coimbra, overtaken by a storm, seeks shelter. At the time of his misfortune he is on his way to take part in the approaching coronation, and also to sign a marriage contract with his cousin Diana, daughter of the Minister of Police. He solaces himself with a song ("Roll on, roll on"), during which he hears the blows of hammers in a distant cavern. Looking about he discovers Rebolledo, the chief of the coiners, and two of his comrades examining the contents of his trunk which is in their possession. Don Henrique conceals himself while Rebolledo is singing a rollicking muleteer's song ("O'er Mountain steep, through Valley roaming"). At its conclusion Rebolledo, about to summon the other coiners to their secret work, discovers Don Henrique, and thinking him a spy rushes upon him. He is saved by the sudden entrance of Catarina, the leader of the gang, who tells the story of her life in a concerted number that reminds one very strikingly of the bandit song in "Fra Diavolo." After examining Don Henrique, and, to his surprise, showing an intimate acquaintance with his projects, she returns him his property, and allows him to depart on condition that he shall not speak for a year of what he has seen. He consents; and then follows another of the concerted numbers in which this opera abounds, and in which occurs a charming rondo ("The young Pedrillo"), accompanied by a weird, clanging chorus. Before he can effect his departure the gang find that they are surrounded by troops led by Don Sebastian, a friend of Don Henrique. The coiners, in company with the latter, however, make their escape in the disguise of monks on their way to the neighboring monastery, singing a lugubrious chorus ("Unto the Hermit of the Chapel"), while Catarina and Rebolledo elude the soldiers by taking a subterranean passage, carrying with them a casket containing some mysterious jewels.

The second act opens in the Château de Coimbra, and discovers the Count, Don Henrique, Don Sebastian, and Diana. The first scene discloses that Don Henrique is in love with the mysterious Catarina, and that Diana is in love with Don Sebastian. In a sportive mood Diana requests Don Henrique to sing with her, and chooses a nocturne called "The Brigand," which closes in gay bolero time ("In the deep Ravine of the Forest"). As they are singing it, Don Sebastian announces that a carriage has been overturned and its occupants desire shelter. As the duet proceeds, Catarina and Rebolledo enter, and a very flurried quintet ("Oh, Surprise unexpected!") occurs, leading up to an ensemble full of humor, with a repetition of the brigand song, this time by Catarina and Diana, and closing with a bravura aria sung by Catarina ("Love! at once I break thy Fetters"). Catarina and Rebolledo accept the proffered hospitality, but the latter quietly makes his exit when Diana begins to read an account of a robbery which contains a description of himself and his companion. Catarina remains, however, in spite of Don Henrique's warning that she is in the house of the Minister of Police. In a moment of passion he declares his love for her and begs her to fly with him. She declines his proffer, but gives him a ring as a souvenir. A pretty little duet ("If I could but Courage feel") ensues between Diana and Don Henrique, in which she gently taunts him with his inattention to her and his sudden interest in the handsome stranger. At this juncture the Count enters in wild excitement over the announcement that the crown jewels have been stolen. Don Henrique's ring is recognized as one of them, and in the excitement which ensues, Catarina finds herself in danger of discovery, from which she is rescued by Diana, who promises Don Henrique she will send her away in the Count's carriage if he will agree to refuse to sign the marriage contract. He consents, and she departs upon her errand. At this point in the scene Don Henrique sings the beautiful ballad, "Oh, whisper what thou feelest!" originally written for Mr. Harrison. This song leads up to a stirring finale, in which Don Henrique refuses to sign the contract and Catarina makes her escape.

The last act opens in the anteroom of the royal palace at Lisbon, where Diana is waiting for an audience with the Queen. She sings another interpolated air, originally written for Louisa Pyne ("When Doubt the tortured Frame is rending"), and at its close the Count, Don Henrique, and Don Sebastian enter. While they are conversing, Rebolledo appears, announced as the Count Fuentes, and a quintet occurs, very slightly constructed, but full of humor. An usher interrupts it by announcing that the Queen will have a private audience with the Count. While awaiting her, the latter, in a monologue, lets us into the secret that the real crown jewels have been pledged for the national debt, and that he has been employed to make duplicates of them to be worn on state occasions until the real ones can be redeemed. The Queen enters, and expresses her satisfaction with the work, and promotes him to the position of Minister of Secret Police. On his departure she sings a charming cavatina ("Love, dwell with me"), and at its close Count de Campo Mayor enters with the decision of the Council that she shall wed the Prince of Spain. She protests that she will make her own choice. The Count seeks to argue with her, when she threatens to confiscate his estate for allowing the crown jewels to be stolen, and commands him to arrest his daughter and nephew for harboring the thieves. Diana suddenly enters, and an amusing trio ensues, the Queen standing with her back to Diana lest she may be discovered. The latter fails to recognize her as Catarina, and implores pardon for assisting in her escape. The situation is still further complicated by the appearance of Don Henrique, who has no difficulty in recognizing Catarina. Bewildered at her presence in the Queen's apartments, he declares to Diana that he will seize her and fly to some distant land. His rash resolution, however, is thwarted by his arrest, on the authority of the Queen, for treason. A martial finale introduces us to the Queen in state. Don Henrique rushes forward to implore mercy for Catarina. The Queen reveals herself at last, and announces to her people that she has chosen Don Henrique, who has loved her for herself, for her husband and their king. And thus closes one of the most sparkling, melodious, and humorous of Auber's works. What the concerted numbers lack in solidity of construction is compensated for by their grace and sweetness.

BALFE

MICHAEL WILLIAM BALFE was born at Dublin, Ireland, May 15, 1808. Of all the English opera composers, his career was the most versatile, as his success, for a time at least, was the most remarkable. At seven years of age he scored a polacca of his own for a band. In his eighth year he appeared as a violinist, and in his tenth was composing ballads. At sixteen he was playing in the Drury Lane orchestra, and about this time began taking lessons in composition. In 1825, aided by the generosity of a patron, he went to Italy, where for three years he studied singing and counterpoint. In his twentieth year he met Rossini, who offered him an engagement as first baritone at the Italian Opera in Paris. He made his debut with success in 1828, and at the close of his engagement returned to Italy, where he appeared again on the stage. About this time (1829–1830) he began writing Italian operas, and before he left Italy had produced three which met with considerable success. In 1835 he returned to England; and it was in this year that his first English opera, the "Siege of Rochelle," was produced. It was played continuously at Drury Lane for over three months. In 1836 the "Maid of Artois"; in 1837, "Catharine Grey" and "Joan of Arc"; and in 1838, "Falstaff" were produced. During these years he was still singing in concerts and opera, and in 1840 appeared as manager of the Lyceum. His finest works were produced after this date, — "The Bohemian Girl" in 1843; "The Enchantress" in 1844; "The Rose of Castile," "La Zingara," and "Satanella" in 1858, and "The Puritan's Daughter" in

1861. His last opera was "The Knight of the Leopard," known in Italian as "Il Talismano," which has also been produced in English as "The Talisman." He married Mlle. Rosen, a German singer, whom he met in Italy in 1835; and his daughter Victoire, who subsequently married Sir John Crampton, and afterwards the Duc de Frias, also appeared as a singer in 1856. Balfe died October 20, 1870, upon his own estate in Hertfordshire. The analyses of his two operas which are best known in this country — "The Bohemian Girl" and "The Rose of Castile" — will contain sufficient reference to his ability as a composer.

THE BOHEMIAN GIRL

"The Bohemian Girl," grand opera in three acts, words by Bunn, adapted from St. George's ballet of "The Gypsy," which appeared at the Paris Grand Opera in 1839, — itself taken from a romance by Cervantes, — was first produced in London, November 27, 1843, at Drury Lane, with the following cast:

Arline	Miss ROMER.
Thaddeus	Mr. HARRISON.
Gypsy Queen	Miss BETTS.
Devilshoof	Mr. STRETTON.
Count Arnheim	Mr. BORRANI.
Florestein	Mr. DURNSET.

The fame of "The Bohemian Girl" was not confined to England. It was translated into various European languages, and was one of the few English operas which secured a favorable hearing even in critical Germany. In its Italian form it was produced at Drury Lane as "La Zingara," February 6, 1858, with Mlle. Piccolomini as Arline; and also had the honor of being selected for the state performance connected with the marriage of the Princess Royal. The French version, under the name of "La

Bohémienne," for which Balfe added several numbers, besides enlarging it to five acts, was produced at the Théâtre Lyrique, Paris, in December, 1869, and gained for him the Cross of the Legion of Honor.

The scene of the opera is laid in Austria, and the first act introduces us to the chateau and grounds of Count Arnheim, Governor of Presburg, whose retainers are preparing for the chase. After a short chorus the Count enters with his little daughter Arline and his nephew Florestein. The Count sings a short solo ("A Soldier's Life"), and as the choral response by his retainers and hunters dies away and they leave the scene, Thaddeus, a Polish exile and fugitive, rushes in excitedly, seeking to escape the Austrian soldiers. His opening number ("'T is sad to leave your Fatherland") is a very pathetic song. At its end a troop of gypsies enter, headed by Devilshoof, singing a blithe chorus ("In the Gypsy's Life you may read"). He hears Thaddeus's story and induces him to join them. Before the animated strains fairly cease, Florestein and some of the hunters dash across the grounds in quest of Arline, who has been attacked by a stag. Thaddeus, seizing a rifle, joins them, and rescues the child by killing the animal. The Count overwhelms him with gratitude, and urges him to join in the coming festivities. He consents, and at the banquet produces a commotion by refusing to drink the health of the Emperor. The soldiers are about to rush upon him, when Devilshoof interferes. The gypsy is arrested for his temerity, and taken into the castle. Thaddeus departs and the festivities are resumed, but are speedily interrupted again by the escape of Devilshoof, who takes Arline with him. The finale of the act is very stirring, and contains one number, a prayer ("Thou who in Might supreme"), which is extremely effective.

Twelve years elapse between the first and second acts,

and during this time Count Arnheim has received no tidings of Arline, and has given her up as lost forever. The act opens in the gypsy camp in the suburbs of Presburg. Arline is seen asleep in the tent of the Queen, with Thaddeus watching her. After a quaint little chorus ("Silence, Silence, the Lady Moon") sung by the gypsies, they depart in quest of plunder, headed by Devilshoof, and soon find their victim in the person of the foppish and half-drunken Florestein, who is returning from a revel. He is speedily relieved of his jewelry, among which is a medallion, which is carried off by Devilshoof. As the gypsies disappear, Arline wakes and relates her dream to Thaddeus in a joyous song ("I dreamed I dwelt in Marble Halls"), which is a favorite with every one. At the close of the ballad Thaddeus tells her the meaning of the scar upon her arm, and reveals himself as her rescuer, but does not disclose to her the mystery of her birth. The musical dialogue, with its ensemble, "The Secret of her Birth," will never lose its charm. Thaddeus declares his love for her just as the Queen, who is also in love with Thaddeus, enters. Arline also confesses her love for Thaddeus, and, according to the custom of the tribe, the Queen unites them, at the same time vowing vengeance against the pair.

The scene now changes to a street in the city. A great fair is in progress, and the gypsies, as usual, resort to it. Arline enters at their head, joyously singing, to the accompaniment of the rattling castanets, "Come with the Gypsy Bride"; her companions, blithely tripping along, responding with the chorus, "In the Gypsy's Life you may read." They disappear down the street and reappear in the public plaza. Arline, the Queen, Devilshoof, and Thaddeus sing an unaccompanied quartet ("From the Valleys and Hills"), a number which for grace and flowing harmony deserves a place in any opera. As they mingle among the people an altercation occurs between Arline and Florestein, who has attempted to insult her. The Queen recognizes Florestein as the owner of the medallion, and for her courage in resenting the insult maliciously presents Arline with it. Shortly afterwards he observes the medallion on Arline's neck, and has her arrested for theft. The next scene opens in the hall of justice. Count Arnheim enters with a sad countenance, and as he observes Arline's portrait, gives vent to his sorrow in that well-known melancholy reverie, "The Heart bowed down," which has become famous the world over. Arline is brought before him for trial. As it progresses he observes the scar upon her arm and asks its cause. She tells the story which Thaddeus had told her, and this solves the mystery. The Count recognizes his daughter, and the act closes with a beautiful ensemble ("Praised be the Will of Heaven").

The last act opens in the salon of Count Arnheim. Arline is restored to her old position, but her love for Thaddeus remains. He finds an opportunity to have a meeting with her, through the cunning of Devilshoof, who accompanies him. He once more tells his love in that tender and impassioned song, "When other Lips and other Hearts," and she promises to be faithful to him. As the sound of approaching steps is heard, Thaddeus and his companion conceal themselves. A large company enter, and Arline is presented to them. During the ceremony a closely veiled woman appears, and when questioned acknowledges she is the Gypsy Queen. She reveals the hiding-place of her companions, and Thaddeus is dragged forth and ordered to leave the house. Arline declares her love for him, and her intention to go with him. She implores her father to relent. Thaddeus avows his noble descent, and boasts his ancestry and deeds in battle in that stirring martial song, "When the fair Land of Poland." The Count finally yields and gives his daughter to Thaddeus. The Queen, filled with rage and despair, induces one of the tribe to fire at him as he is embracing Arline; but by a timely movement of Devilshoof the bullet intended for Thaddeus pierces the breast of the Queen. As the curtain falls, the old song of the gypsies is heard again as they disappear in the distance with Devilshoof at their head.

Many of the operas of Balfe, like other ballad operas, have become unfashionable; but it is doubtful whether "The Bohemian Girl" will ever lose its attraction for those who delight in song-melody, charming orchestration, and sparkling, animated choruses. It leaped into popularity at a bound, and its pretty melodies are still as fresh as when they were first sung.

THE ROSE OF CASTILE

"The Rose of Castile," comic opera in three acts, the text by Harris and Falconer, was first produced at the Lyceum Theatre, London, October 29, 1857. The scene is laid in Spain; time, last century. At the opening of the opera, Elvira, Queen of Leon, has just ascended the throne, and her hand has been demanded by the King of Castile for his brother, Don Sebastian, the Infant. The latter, with the design of satisfying his curiosity about her, is on the eve of entering the city disguised as a muleteer. Elvira hears of this, and adopts the same expedient, by starting with Carmen, one of her attendants, disguised as peasants, to intercept him. In the opening of the first act the two appear at an inn where the peasants are dancing. The innkeeper is rude to them, but Don Sebastian, disguised as Manuel, the muleteer, protects them, and offers his services as escort, which the Queen willingly accepts, for she has recognized him and he has fulfilled the motive of the story by falling in love with her. At this point Don Pedro, who has designs upon the throne, enters with his fellow-conspirators, Don Sallust and Don Florio. Observing Elvira's likeness to the Queen, they persuade her to personate Her Majesty, which, after feigned reluctance, she consents to do. She also accepts their services as escorts, and all the more unhesitatingly because she knows Manuel will follow her.

The second act opens in the throne-room of the palace. Don Pedro enters, somewhat dejected by the uncertainty of his schemes. The Queen, who has eluded the surveillance of the conspirators, also appears and grants an audience to Manuel, in which he informs her of the meeting with the peasant girl and boy and declares his belief that they are the Queen and Carmen. He also informs her of the conspirators' plot to imprison her, which she thwarts by inducing a silly old Duchess to personate the Queen for one day and ride, closely veiled, to the palace in the royal carriage. Her scheme succeeds admirably. The Duchess is seized and conveyed to a convent. In the next scene, while Don Pedro and Don Florio are mourning over the loss of their peasant girl, she appears. Their mourning turns to desperate perplexity when the Queen reveals herself and announces her intention of marrying the muleteer.

In the last act Carmen and Don Florio agree to marry. The Queen and her ladies now enter, and a message is delivered her from Don Sebastian announcing his marriage. Enraged at the discovery that the muleteer is not Don Sebastian, the Queen upbraids him and yet declares she will be true to him. This pleases Don Pedro, as he believes he can force her to abdicate if she marries a muleteer; but in the last scene Manuel mounts the throne, and announces he is King of Castile. Elvira expresses her delight, and all ends happily.

The story of the opera is exceedingly involved, but the music is well sustained and ranks with the best that Balfe has written. The principal numbers of the first act are the lively chorus, "List to the gay Castanet"; the vocal scherzo by Elvira, "Yes, I 'll obey you"; Manuel's rollicking song, "I am a simple Muleteer"; the buffo trio, which ends in a spirited bacchanale, "Wine, Wine, the Magician thou art"; and Elvira's pleasing rondo, "Oh! were I the Queen of Spain." The second act contains the expressive conspirators' chorus, "The Queen in the Palace"; the beautiful ballad, "Though Fortune darkly o'er me frowns," sung by Don Pedro; the ballad, "The Convent Cell," sung by Elvira, which is one of Balfe's happiest inspirations; the buffo trio, "I 'm not the Queen, ha, ha"; and Elvira's characteristic scena, "I 'm but a simple Peasant Maid." The leading numbers of the last act are the bravura air, "Oh! joyous, happy Day," which was intended by the composer to show the vocal ability of Eliza Pyne, who first appeared in the role of Elvira; Manuel's fine ballad, "'T was Rank and Fame that tempted thee"; Don Pedro's martial song, "Hark, hark, methinks I hear"; the stirring song by Manuel, when he mounts the throne, which recalls "The fair Land of Poland" in "The Bohemian Girl"; and Elvira's second bravura air, "Oh! no, by Fortune blessed."

BEETHOVEN

LUDWIG VAN BEETHOVEN, the greatest of composers, was born December 17, 1770, at Bonn, Germany, his father being a court singer in the chapel of the Elector of Cologne. He studied in Vienna with Haydn, with whom he did not always agree, however, and afterwards with Albrechtsberger. His first symphony appeared in 1801, his earlier symphonies, in what is called his first period, being written in the Mozart style. His only opera, "Fidelio," for which he wrote four overtures, was first brought out in Vienna in 1805; his oratorio, "Christ on the Mount of Olives," in 1812; and his colossal Ninth Symphony, with its choral setting of Schiller's "Ode to Joy," in 1824. In addition to his symphonies, his opera, oratorios, and masses, and the immortal group of sonatas for the piano, which were almost revelations in music, he developed chamber music to an extent far beyond that reached by his predecessors, Haydn and Mozart. His symphonies exhibit surprising power, and a marvellous comprehension of the deeper feelings in life and the influences of nature, both human and physical. He wrote with the deepest earnestness, alike in the passion and the calm of his music, and he invested it also with a genial humor as well as with the highest expression of pathos. His works are epic in character. He was the great tone-poet of music. His subjects were always lofty and dignified, and to their treatment he brought not only a profound knowledge of musical technicality, but intense sympathy with the innermost feelings of human nature, for he was a humanitarian in the broadest sense. By the common consent of the musical world he stands at the head of all composers, and has always been their guide and inspiration. He died March 26, 1827, in the midst of a raging thunder-storm, one of his latest utterances being a recognition of the "divine spark" in Schubert's music.

FIDELIO

"Fidelio, oder die eheliche Liebe" ("Fidelio, or Conjugal Love"), grand opera in two acts, words by Sonnleithner, translated freely from Bouilly's "Léonore, ou l'Amour Conjugal," was first produced at the Theatre An der Wien, Vienna, November 20, 1805, the work at that time being in three acts. A translation of the original programme of that performance, with the exception of the usual prices of admission, is appended:

IMPERIAL AND ROYAL THEATRE AN DER WIEN.
NEW OPERA.

To-day, Wednesday, 20 November, 1805, at the Imperial and Royal Theatre An der Wien, will be given for the first time.

FIDELIO;
Or, CONJUGAL LOVE.

Opera in three acts, translated freely from the French text by JOSEPH SONNLEITHNER.
The music is by LUDWIG VAN BEETHOVEN.

Dramatis Personæ.

Don Fernando, Minister	Herr WEINKOFF.
Don Pizarro, Governor of a State Prison	Herr MEIER.
Florestan, prisoner	Herr DEMMER.
Leonora, his wife, under the name of *Fidelio*	Fräulein MILDER.
Rocco, chief jailer	Herr ROTHE.
Marcellina, his daughter	Fräulein MÜLLER.
Jacquino, turnkey	Herr CACHE.
Captain of the Guard	Herr MEISTER.

Prisoners, Guards, People.

The action passes in a State prison in Spain, a few leagues from Seville.
The piece can be procured at the box-office for fifteen kreutzers.

During its first season the opera was performed three times and then withdrawn. Breuning reduced it to two acts, and two or three of the musical numbers were sacrificed, and in this form it was played twice at the Imperial Private Theatre and again withdrawn. On these occasions it had been given under Beethoven's favorite title, "Léonore." In 1814 Treitschke revised it, and it was produced at the Kärnthnerthor Theatre, Vienna, May 23, of that year, as "Fidelio," which title it has ever since retained. Its first performance in Paris was at the Théâtre Lyrique, May 5, 1860; in London, at the King's Theatre, May 18, 1832; and in English at Covent Garden, June 12, 1835, with Malibran in the title role. Beethoven wrote four overtures for this great work. The first was composed in 1805, the second in 1806, the third in 1807, and the fourth in 1814. It is curious that there has always been a confusion in their numbering, and the error remains to this day. What is called No. 1 is in reality No. 3, and was composed for a performance of the opera at Prague, the previous overture having been too difficult for the string section of the orchestra. The splendid "Leonora," No. 3, is in reality No. 2, and the No. 2 is No. 1. The fourth, or the "Fidelio" overture, contains a new set of themes, but the "Leonora" is the grandest of them all.

The entire action of the opera transpires in a Spanish prison, of which Don Pizarro is governor and Rocco the jailer. The porter of the prison is Jacquino, who is in love with Marcellina, daughter of Rocco, and she in turn is in love with Fidelio, Rocco's assistant, who has assumed male disguise the better to assist her in her plans for the rescue of her husband, Florestan, a Spanish nobleman. The latter, who is the victim of Don Pizarro's hatred because he had thwarted some of his evil designs, has been imprisoned by him unknown to the world, and is slowly starving to death. Leonora, his wife, who in some way has discovered that her husband is in the prison, has obtained employment from Rocco, disguised as the young man Fidelio.

The opera opens with a charming, playful love scene between Jacquino and Marcellina, whom the former is teasing to marry him. She puts him off, and as he sorrowfully departs, sings the Hope aria, "Die Hoffnung," a fresh, smoothly flowing melody, in which she pictures the delight of a life with Fidelio. At its close Rocco enters with the despondent Jacquino, shortly followed by Fidelio, who is very much fatigued. The love episode is brought out in the famous canon quartet, "Mir ist so wunderbar," one of the most beautiful and restful numbers in the opera. Rocco promises Marcellina's hand to Fidelio as the reward of her fidelity, but in the characteristic and sonorous Gold song, "Hat man nicht auch Geld daneben," reminds them that money as well as love is necessary to housekeeping. In the next scene, while Don Pizarro is giving instructions to Rocco, a packet of letters is delivered to him, one of which informs him that Don Fernando is coming the next day to inspect the prison, as he has been informed it contains several victims of arbitrary power. He at once determines that Florestan shall die, and gives vent to his wrath in a furious dramatic aria ("Ha! welch ein Augenblick!"). He attempts to bribe Rocco to aid him. The jailer at first refuses, but subsequently, after a stormy duet, consents to dig the grave. Fidelio has overheard the scheme, and, as they disappear, rushes forward and sings the great aria, "Abscheulicher!" one of the grandest and most impassioned illustrations of dramatic intensity in the whole realm of music. The recitative expresses intense horror at the intended murder, then subsides into piteous sorrow, and at last breaks out into the glorious adagio, "Komm Hoffnung," in which she sings of the immortal power of love. The last scene of the act introduces the strong chorus of the prisoners as they come out in the yard for air and sunlight, after which Rocco relates to Fidelio his interview with Don Pizarro. The latter orders the jailer to return the prisoners to their dungeons and go on with the digging of the grave, and the act closes.

The second act opens in Florestan's dungeon. The prisoner sings an intensely mournful aria ("In des Lebens Frühlingstagen"), which has a rapturous finale ("Und spür' Ich nicht linde"), as he sees his wife in a vision. Rocco and Fidelio enter and begin digging the grave, to the accompaniment of sepulchral music. She discovers that Florestan has sunk back exhausted, and as she restores him recognizes her husband. Don Pizarro enters, and after ordering Fidelio away, who meanwhile conceals herself, attempts to stab Florestan. Fidelio, who has been closely watching him, springs forward with a shriek, and interposes herself between him and her husband. He once more advances to carry out his purpose, when Fidelio draws a pistol and defies him. As she does so the sound of a trumpet is heard outside announcing the arrival of Don Fernando. Don Pizarro rushes out in despair, and Florestan and Leonora, no longer Fidelio, join in a duet ("O namenlose Freude") which is the very ecstasy of happiness. In the last scene Don Fernando sets Florestan and the other prisoners free in the name of the king. Pizarro is revealed in his true character, and is led away to punishment. The happy pair are reunited, and Marcellina, to Jacquino's delight, consents to marry him. The act closes with a general song of jubilee. As a drama and as an opera, "Fidelio" stands almost alone in its perfect purity, in the moral grandeur of its subject, and in the resplendent ideality of its music.

BELLINI

VINCENZO BELLINI was born November 3, 1802, at Catania, Sicily, coming of musical parentage. He was sent to Naples by a generous patron and studied at the Conservatory under Zingarelli. His first opera was "Adelson e Salvino," and its remarkable merit secured him a commission from the manager, Barbaja, for an opera for San Carlo. The result was his first important work, "Bianca e Fernando," written in 1826. Its success was moderate; but he was so encouraged that he at once went to Milan and wrote "Il Pirata," the tenor part for Rubini, which met with such favor that the managers of La Scala commissioned him for another work. In 1828 "La Straniera" appeared, quickly followed by "Zaira," in 1829 (which failed at Parma), and "I Capuletti ed i Montecchi," a version of "Romeo and Juliet," which made a great success at Venice in 1830. A year later he composed "La Sonnambula," unquestionably his best work, for La Scala, and it speedily made the tour of Europe, and gained for him an extended reputation. A year after its appearance he astonished the musical world with "Norma," written, like "Sonnambula," for Mme. Pasta. These are his greatest works. "Norma" was followed by "Beatrice di Tenda," and this by "I Puritani," his last opera, written in Paris for the four great artists, Grisi, Rubini, Tamburini, and Lablache. Bellini died September 24, 1835, in the thirty-fourth year of his age, preserving his musical enthusiasm to the very last. He was a close follower of Rossini, and studied his music diligently, and though without a very profound knowledge of harmony or orchestration, succeeded in producing at least three works, "Norma," "Sonnambula," and "I Puritani," which were the delight of the opera-goers of his day, and still hold the stage.

NORMA

"Norma," serious opera in two acts, words by Romani, was first produced during the season of Lent, 1832, at Milan, with the principal parts cast as follows:

Norma . . . . Mme. PASTA.
Adalgisa . . . . Mme. GRISI.
Pollione . . . . Sig. DONZELLI.

It was first heard in London in 1833, and in Paris in 1855, and Planché's English version of it was produced at Drury Lane in 1837. The scene of the opera is laid among the Druids, in Gaul, after its occupation by the Roman legions. In the first scene the Druids enter with Oroveso, their priest, to the impressive strains of a religious march which is almost as familiar as a household word. The priest announces that Norma, the high priestess, will come and cut the sacred branch and give the signal for the expulsion of the Romans. The next scene introduces Pollione, the Roman proconsul, to whom Norma, in defiance of her faith and traditions, has bound herself in secret marriage, and by whom she has had two children. In a charmingly melodious scena ("Meco all' altar di Venere") he reveals his faithlessness and guilty love for Adalgisa, a young virgin of the temple, who has consented to abandon her religion and fly with him to Rome. In the fourth scene Norma enters attended by her priestesses, and denounces the Druids for their warlike disposition, declaring that the time has not yet come for shaking off the yoke of Rome, and that when it does she will give the signal from their altar. After cutting the sacred mistletoe, she comes forward and invokes peace from the moon in that exquisite prayer, "Casta diva," which electrified the world with its beauty and tenderness, and still holds its place in popular favor, not alone by the grace of its embellishments, but by the pathos of its melody. It is followed by another cavatina of almost equal beauty and tenderness ("Ah! bello a me ritorno"). In the next scene Adalgisa, retiring from the sacred rites, sings of her love for Pollione, and as she closes is met by the proconsul, who once more urges her to fly to Rome with him. The duet between them is one of great power and beauty, and contains a strikingly passionate number for the tenor ("Va, crudele"). Oppressed by her conscience, she reveals her fatal promise to Norma, and implores absolution from her vows. Norma yields to her entreaties, but when she inquires the name and country of her lover, and Adalgisa points to Pollione as he enters Norma's sanctuary, all the priestess's love turns to wrath. In this scene the duet, "Perdoni e ti compiango," is one of exceeding loveliness and peculiarly melodious tenderness. The act closes with a terzetto of great power ("O! di qual sei tu"), in which both the priestess and Adalgisa furiously denounce the faithless Pollione. In the midst of their imprecations the sound of the sacred shield is heard calling Norma to the rites.

The second act opens in Norma's dwelling, and discovers her children asleep on a couch. Norma enters with the purpose of killing them, but the maternal instinct overcomes her vengeful thought that they are Pollione's children. Adalgisa appears, and Norma announces her intention to place her children in the virgin's hands, and send her and them to Pollione while she shall expiate her offence on the funeral pyre. Adalgisa pleads with her not to abandon Pollione, who will return to her repentant; and the most effective number in the opera ensues, — the grand duet containing two of Bellini's most

Grisi as *Norma*

BELLINI

beautiful inspirations, the "Deh! con te li prendi" and the familiar "Mira, O Norma," whose strains have gone round the world and awakened universal delight. Pollione, maddened by his passion for Adalgisa, impiously attempts to tear her from the altar in the temple of Irminsul, whereupon Norma enters the temple and strikes the sacred shield summoning the Druids. They meet and she declares the meaning of the signal is war, slaughter, and destruction. She chants a magnificent hymn ("Guerra, guerra"), which is full of the very fury of battle. Pollione, who has been intercepted in the temple, is brought before her. Love is still stronger than resentment with her. In a very dramatic scena ("In mia mano alfintu sei") she informs him he is in her power, but she will let him escape if he will renounce Adalgisa and leave the country. He declares death would be preferable; whereupon she threatens to denounce Adalgisa. Pity overcomes anger, however. She snatches the sacred wreath from her brow and declares herself the guilty one. Too late Pollione discovers the worth of the woman he has abandoned, and a beautiful duet ("Qual cor tradisti") forms the closing number. She ascends the funeral pyre with Pollione, and in its flames they are purged of earthly crime. It is a memorable fact in the history of this opera, that on its first performance it was coldly received, and the Italian critics declared it had no vitality; though there are few operas in which such intense dramatic effect has been produced with simple melodic force, and no Italian opera score to-day is more alive or more worthy of living than that of "Norma."

La Sonnambula

"La Sonnambula," opera in two acts, words by Romani, was first produced in Milan, March 6, 1831, with the following cast:

Amina	Mme. PASTA.
Elvino	Sig. RUBINI.
Rodolfo	Sig. MARIANO.
Lisa	Mme. TOCCANI.

It was brought out in the same year in Paris and London, and two years after in English, with Malibran as Amina. The subject of the story was taken from a vaudeville and ballet by Scribe. The scene is laid in Switzerland. Amina, an orphan, the ward of Teresa, the miller's wife, is about to marry Elvino, a well-to-do landholder of the village. Lisa, mistress of the inn, is also in love with Elvino, and jealous of her rival. Alessio, a peasant lad, is also in love with the landlady. Such is the state of affairs on the day before the wedding. Rodolfo, the young lord of the village, next appears upon the scene. He has arrived incognito for the purpose of looking up his estates, and stops at Lisa's inn, where he meets Amina. He gives her many pretty compliments, much to the dissatisfaction of the half-jealous Elvino, who is inclined to quarrel with the disturber of his peace of mind. Amina, who is subject to fits of somnambulism, has been mistaken for a ghost by the peasants, and they warn Rodolfo that the village is haunted. The information, however, does not disturb him, and he quietly retires to his chamber. The officious Lisa also enters, and a playful scene of flirtation ensues, during which Amina enters the room, walking in her sleep. Lisa seeks shelter in a closet. Rodolfo, to escape from the embarrassment of the situation, leaves the apartment, and Amina reclines upon the bed as if it were her own. The malicious Lisa hurries from the room to inform Elvino of what she has seen, and thoughtlessly leaves her handkerchief. Elvino rushes to the spot with other villagers, and finding Amina, as Lisa had described, declares that she is guilty, and leaves her. Awakened by the noise, the unfortunate girl, realizing the situation, sorrowfully throws herself into Teresa's arms. The villagers implore Rodolfo to acquit Amina of any blame, and he stoutly protests her innocence; but it is of no avail in satisfying Elvino, who straightway offers his hand to Lisa. In the last act Amina is seen stepping from the window of the mill in her sleep. She crosses a frail bridge which yields beneath her weight and threatens to precipitate her upon the wheel below; but she passes it in safety, descends to the ground, and walks into her lover's arms amid the jubilant songs of the villagers. Elvino is convinced of her innocence, and they are wedded at once, while the discovery of Lisa's handkerchief in Rodolfo's room pronounces her the faithless one.

Such is the simple little pastoral story to which Bellini has set some of his most beautiful melodies, the most striking of which are the aria, "Sovra il sen," in the third scene of the first act, where Amina declares her happiness to Teresa; the beautiful aria for baritone in the sixth scene, "Vi ravviso," descriptive of Rodolfo's delight in revisiting the scenes of his youth; the playful duet between Amina and Elvino, "Mai piu dubbi!" in which she rebukes him for his jealousy; the humorous and very characteristic chorus of the villagers in the tenth scene, "Osservate, l' uscio è aperto," as they tiptoe into Rodolfo's apartment; the duet, "O miō dolor," in the next scene, in which Amina asserts her innocence; the aria for tenor in the third scene of the second act, "Tutto e sciolto," in which Elvino bemoans his sad lot; and that joyous ecstatic outburst of birdlike melody,

"Ah! non giunge," which closes the opera. In fact, "Sonnambula" is so replete with melodies of the purest and tenderest kind, that it is difficult to specify particular ones. It is exquisitely idyllic throughout, and the music is as quiet, peaceful, simple, and tender as the charming pastoral scenes it illustrates.

I Puritani

"I Puritani," grand opera in two acts, text by Count Pepoli, was first produced at Paris, January 25, 1835, with the following cast:

Elvira	Mme. GRISI.
Arturo	Sig. RUBINI.
Ricardo	Sig. TAMBURINI.
Giorgio	Sig. LABLACHE.

The story of the opera is laid in England during the war between Charles II and his Parliament, and the first scene opens in Plymouth, then held by the parliamentary forces. The fortress is commanded by Lord Walton, whose daughter, Elvira, is in love with Lord Arthur Talbot, a young cavalier in the King's service. Her hand had previously been promised to Sir Richard Forth of the parliamentary army; but to the great delight of the maiden, Sir George Walton, brother of the commander, brings her the news that her father has relented, and that Arthur will be admitted into the fortress for the celebration of the nuptials. Henrietta, widow of Charles I, is at this time a prisoner in the fortress, under sentence of death. Arthur discovers her situation and seeks to effect her escape by shrouding her in Elvira's bridal veil. On their way out he encounters his rival; but the latter, discovering that the veiled lady is not Elvira, allows them to pass. The escape is soon discovered, and Elvira, thinking her lover has abandoned her, loses her reason. Arthur is proscribed by the Parliament and sentenced to death, but Sir Richard, moved by the appeals of Sir George Walton, who hopes to restore his niece to reason, promises to use his influence with Parliament to save Arthur's life should he be captured unarmed. Arthur meanwhile manages to have an interview with Elvira; and the latter, though still suffering from her mental malady, listens joyfully to his explanation of his sudden flight. Their interview is disturbed by a party of Puritans who enter and arrest him. He is condemned to die on the spot; but before the sentence can be carried out, a messenger appears with news of the King's defeat and the pardon of Arthur. The joyful tidings restore Elvira to reason, and the lovers are united.

The libretto of "I Puritani" is one of the poorest ever furnished to Bellini, but the music is some of his best. It is replete with melodies, which are not only fascinating in their original setting, but have long been favorites on the concert stage. The opera is usually performed in three acts, but was written in two. The prominent numbers of the first act are the pathetic cavatina for Ricardo, "Ah! per sempre io ti perdei," in which he mourns the loss of Elvira; a lovely romanza for tenor ("A te o cara"); a brilliant polacca ("Son vergin vezzosa") for Elvira, which is one of the delights of all artists; and a concerted finale, brimming over with melody and closing with the stirring anathematic chorus, "Non casa, non spiaggia." The first grand number in the second act is Elvira's mad song, "Qui la voce," in which are brought out not only that rare gift for expressing pathos in melody for which Bellini is so famous, but the sweetest of themes and most graceful of embellishments. The remaining numbers are Elvira's appeal to her lover ("Vien, diletto"), the magnificent duet for basses ("Suoni la tromba"), known as the "Liberty Duet," which in sonorousness, majesty, and dramatic intensity hardly has an equal in the whole range of Italian opera; a tender and plaintive romanza for tenor ("A una fonte aflitto e solo"); a passionate duet for Arthur and Elvira ("Star teco ognor"); and an adagio, sung by Arthur in the finale ("Ella è tremante").

BENEDICT

JULIUS BENEDICT was born at Stuttgart, November 27, 1804, and died in London, June 5, 1885. In his early life he studied with Abeille and Hummel, and was fortunate in having Weber for a patron, by whose influence he secured the position of conductor at the Kärnthnerthor Theatre in Vienna. He held this post from 1823 to 1825, and in the latter year secured a similar appointment at the San Carlo in Naples, where he brought out his first opera, "Giacinta ed Ernesto," in 1829. In 1834 he went to Paris and thence, upon the advice of Malibran, to London in the next year. He remained in the latter city the rest of his life and brought out there the best of his operas, "The Brides of Venice" (1843), "The Crusaders" (1846), and the "Lily of Killarney" (1862), besides some beautiful cantatas, among them "Undine" (1860), "Richard Cœur de Lion" (1863), and the oratorios, "St. Cecilia" (1866), and "St. Peter" (1870). He also composed a large number of songs, fantasies, operettas, and piano and orchestral works. He was conductor of the Norwich Festivals from 1845 to 1878 and of many societies, and accompanied Jenny Lind as director during her concert tour in this country. He was distinguished as composer, conductor, and performer, and was knighted in 1871 as a tribute to the important service he had rendered to music.

THE LILY OF KILLARNEY

"The Lily of Killarney," romantic opera in three acts, text by Oxenford and Boucicault, is a musical setting of the latter's "Colleen Bawn." It was first produced at Covent

Garden Theatre, London, February 8, 1862. The scene is laid at Killarney, Ireland; time, last century.

The first act opens with the festivities of Hardress Cregan's friends at the hall at Tore Cregan. During their temporary absence to witness a horse race, Corrigan, "the middle-man," calls upon Mrs. Cregan and suggests the marriage of her son to the heiress, Anne Chute, as the only chance of securing the payment of a mortgage he holds upon the place. Failing in this, he expresses his own willingness to accept Mrs. Cregan's hand, but the hint meets with no favor. At this point Danny Mann, Hardress's boatman, is heard singing, and Corrigan informs Mrs. Cregan he is about to take her son to see Eily, the Colleen Bawn, Anne Chute's peasant rival. Danny and Hardress set off on their errand, leaving Mrs. Cregan disconsolate and Corrigan exultant. In the second scene Corrigan and Myles na Coppaleen, the peasant lover of the Colleen Bawn, have an interview in which Corrigan tells him she is the mistress of Hardress. The next scene introduces us to Eily's cottage, where Father Tom is seeking to induce her to persuade Hardress to make public announcement of his marriage to her. When Hardress appears he asks her to give up the marriage certificate and conceal their union; but Myles prevents this, and Father Tom makes Eily promise she will never surrender it.

In the second act Hardress is paying court to Anne Chute, but is haunted by remorse over his desertion of Eily. Danny Mann suggests putting her on board a vessel and shipping her to America, but Hardress rejects the scheme. Danny then agrees that Eily shall disappear if he will send his glove, a token secretly understood between them. This also he rejects. Meanwhile Corrigan is pressing his alternative upon Mrs. Cregan, but is interrupted by Hardress, who threatens to kill him if he does not desist. Corrigan retires, uttering threats of revenge. Danny Mann

BENEDICT

then intimates to Mrs. Cregan that if she will induce Hardress to send the glove, he can bring happiness to the family again. She secures the glove and gives it to Danny, who promptly takes it to Eily with the message that her husband has sent for her. Eily, in spite of Myles's warnings, gets into Danny's boat and trusts herself to him. Danny rows out to a water cave, and ordering her to step upon a rock, demands the certificate. She refuses to give it up, and Danny pushes her into the water. Myles, who uses the cave for secret purposes, mistakes Danny for another and shoots him, and then, espying Eily, plunges in and saves her.

The denouement of the story is quickly told in the last act. Hardress is arrested for murder, but Danny, who was fatally wounded, makes a dying confession of his scheme against the life of the Colleen Bawn. Corrigan brings soldiers to the house of Anne Chute at the moment of Hardress's marriage with her, but is thwarted in his revenge when Myles produces Eily Cregan, Hardress's lawful wife. Mrs. Cregan also confesses her part in the plot, and absolves her son from intentional guilt. Everything being cleared up, Eily rushes into Hardress's arms, and the chorus declares

> "A cloudless day at last will dawn
> Upon the hapless Colleen Bawn."

The music is very elaborate for light opera purposes, and is written broadly and effectively, especially for the orchestra. Many Irish melodies sprinkled through the work relieve its heaviness. The principal numbers are the serenade and duet, "The Moon has raised her Lamp above"; Myles's song, "It is a charming Girl I love"; Eily's song, "In my wild Mountain Valley he sought me," and the well-known original Irish melody, "The Cruiskeen Lawn," also sung by Eily; the "Tally-ho" chorus, introducing the second act; Danny Mann's recitative and airs, "The Colleen Bawn" and "Duty? Yes, I'll do my Duty," the dramatic finale to the second act; Myles's serenade in the third act, "Your Slumbers, och! Soft as your Glance may be"; Hardress's beautiful song, "Eily Mavourneen, I see thee before me"; and the fine concerted trio which closes the act.

BIZET

GEORGES BIZET was born at Paris, October 25, 1838, and in an artistic atmosphere, as his father, an excellent teacher, was married to a sister of Mme. Delsarte, a talented pianist, and his uncle, a musician, was the founder of the famous Delsarte system. He studied successively with Marmontel and Benoist, and subsequently took lessons in composition from Halevy, whose daughter he afterwards married. His first work was an operetta of not much consequence, "Docteur Miracle," written in 1857, and in the same year he took the Grand Prix de Rome. On his return from Italy he composed "Vasco de Gama" and "Les Pecheurs de Perles," neither of which met with much success. In 1867 "La Jolie Fille de Perth" appeared, and in 1872, "Djamileh." During the intervals of these larger works he wrote the Patrie overture and the interludes to "L'Arlesienne," a very poetical score which Theodore Thomas introduced to this country, and both works were received with enthusiasm. At last he was to appreciate and enjoy a real dramatic success, though it was his last work. "Carmen" appeared in 1875, and achieved a magnificent triumph at the Opera Comique. It was brought out in March, and in the following June he died of acute heart disease. He was a very promising composer, and specially excelled in orchestration. During his last few years he was a close student of Wagner, whose influence is apparent in portions of this last work of his life.

Carmen

"Carmen," opera in four acts, words by Meilhac and Halevy, adapted from Prosper Merimée's romance of "Carmen," was first produced at the Opera Comique, Paris, March 3, 1875, with Mme. Galli-Marie in the title role and Mlle. Chapuy as Michaela. The scene is laid in Seville; time, 1820. The first act opens in the public square, filled with a troop of soldiers under command of Don José, and loungers who are waiting the approach of the pretty girls who work in the cigar-factory near by, and prettiest and most heartless of them all, Carmen. Before they appear, Michaela, a village girl, enters the square, bearing a message to Don José from his mother, but not finding him departs. The cigar-girls at last pass by on their way to work, and with them Carmen, who observes Don José sitting in an indifferent manner and throws him the rose she wears in her bosom. As they disappear, Michaela returns and delivers her message. The sight of the gentle girl and the thoughts of home dispel Don José's growing passion for Carmen. He is about to throw away her rose, when a sudden disturbance is heard in the factory. It is found that Carmen has quarrelled with one of the girls and wounded her. She is arrested, and to prevent further mischief her arms are pinioned. She so bewitches the lieutenant, however, that he connives at her escape and succeeds in effecting it, while she is being led away to prison by the soldiers. In the second act Carmen has returned to her wandering gypsy life, and we find her with her companions in the cabaret of Lillas-Pastia, singing and dancing. Among the new arrivals is Escamillo, the victorious bull-fighter of Grenada, with whom Carmen is at once fascinated. When the inn is closed, Escamillo and the soldiers depart, but Carmen waits with two of the

Calvé as *Carmen*

Copyright, Falk

gypsies, who are smugglers, for the arrival of Don José. They persuade her to induce him to join their band, and when the lieutenant, wild with passion for her, enters the apartment, she prevails upon him to remain in spite of the trumpet-call which summons him to duty. An officer appears and orders him out. He refuses to go, and when the officer attempts to use force Carmen summons the gypsies. He is soon overpowered, and Don José escapes to the mountains. The third act opens in the haunt of the smugglers, a wild, rocky, cavernous place. Don José and Carmen, who is growing very indifferent to him, are there. As the contrabandists finish their work and gradually leave the scene, Escamillo, who has been following Carmen, appears. His presence and his declarations as well arouse the jealousy of Don José. They rush at each other for mortal combat, but the smugglers separate them. Escamillo bides his time, invites them to the approaching bull-fight at Seville, and departs. While Don José is upbraiding Carmen, the faithful Michaela, who has been guided to the spot, begs him to accompany her, as his mother is dying. Duty prevails, and he follows her as Escamillo's taunting song is heard dying away in the distance. In the last act the drama hurries on to the tragic denouement. It is a gala-day in Seville, for Escamillo is to fight. Carmen is there in his company, though her gypsy friends have warned her Don José is searching for her. Amid great pomp Escamillo enters the arena, and Carmen is about to follow, when Don José appears and stops her. He appeals to her and tries to awaken the old love. She will not listen, and at last in a fit of wild rage hurls the ring he had given her at his feet. The shouts of the people in the arena announce another victory for Escamillo. She cries out with joy. Don José springs at her like a tiger, and stabs her just as Escamillo emerges from the contest.

"Carmen" is the largest and best-considered of all Bizet's works, and one of the best in the modern French repertoire. The overture is short but very brilliant. After some characteristic choruses by the street lads, soldiers, and cigar-girls, Carmen sings the Habanera ("Amor, misterioso angelo"), a quaint melody in which the air is taken from an old Spanish song by Iradier, called "El Aveglito." A serious duet between Michaela and Don José ("Mia madre io la rivedo") follows, which is very tender in its character. The next striking number is the dance tempo, "Presso il bastion de Seviglia," a seguidilla, sung by Carmen while bewitching Don José. In the finale, as she escapes, the Habanera is heard again.

The second-act music is peculiarly Spanish in color, particularly that for the ballet. The opening song of the gypsies in the cabaret, to the accompaniment of the castanets ("Vezzi e anella scintillar"), is bewitching in its rhythm, and is followed in the next scene by a stirring and very picturesque aria ("Toreador, attento"), in which Escamillo describes the bull-fight. A beautifully written quintet ("Abbiamo in vista"), and a strongly dramatic duet, beginning with another fascinating dance tempo ("Voglio danzar pel tuo piacer"), and including a beautiful pathetic melody for Don José ("Il fior che avevi"), close the music of the act.

The third act contains two very striking numbers, the terzetto of the card-players in the smugglers' haunt ("Mischiam! alziam!"), and Michaela's aria ("Io dico no, non son paurosa"), the most effective and beautiful number in the whole work, and the one which shows most clearly the effect of Wagner's influence upon the composer. In the finale of the act the Toreador's song is again heard as he disappears in the distance after the quarrel with Don José.

The last act is a hurly-burly of the bull-fight, the

Caruso as *Don José*
Copyright, Aimé Dupont

Journet as *Escamillo*
Copyright, Aimé Dupont

Toreador's taking march, the stormy duet between Don José and Carmen, and the tragic denouement in which the "Carmen" motive is repeated. The color of the whole work is Spanish, and the dance tempo is freely used and beautifully worked up with Bizet's ingenious and scholarly instrumentation. Except in the third act, however, the vocal parts are inferior to the orchestral treatment.

BOIELDIEU

FRANÇOIS ADRIEN BOIELDIEU was born December 16, 1775, at Rouen, France. Little is known of his earlier life, except that he studied for a time with Broche, the cathedral organist. His first opera, "La Fille Coupable," appeared in 1793, and was performed at Rouen with some success. In 1795 a second opera, "Rosalie et Myrza," was produced in the same city; after which he went to Paris, where he became acquainted with many prominent musicians, among them Cherubini. His first Paris opera was the "Famille Suisse" (1797), which had a successful run. Several other operas followed, besides some excellent pieces of chamber music which secured him the professorship of the piano in the Conservatory. He also took lessons at this time of Cherubini in counterpoint, and in 1803 brought out a very successful work, "Ma Tante Aurore." We next hear of him in St. Petersburg, as conductor of the Imperial Opera, where he composed many operas and vaudevilles. He spent eight years in Russia, returning to Paris in 1811. The next year one of his best operas, "Jean de Paris," was produced with extraordinary success. Though he subsequently wrote many operas, fourteen years elapsed before his next great work, "La Dame Blanche," appeared. Its success was unprecedented. All Europe was delighted with it, and it is as fresh to-day as when it was first produced. The remainder of Boieldieu's life was sad, owing to operatic failures, pecuniary troubles, and declining health. He died at Jarcy, near Paris, October 8, 1834.

LA DAME BLANCHE

"La Dame Blanche," opera comique in three acts, words by Scribe, adapted from Walter Scott's novels, "The Monastery" and "Guy Mannering," was first produced at the Opera Comique, December 10, 1825, and was first performed in English under the title of "The White Maid," at Covent Garden, London, January 2, 1827. The scene of the opera is laid in Scotland. The Laird of Avenel, a zealous partisan of the Stuarts, was proscribed after the battle of Culloden, and upon the eve of going into exile intrusts Gaveston, his steward, with the care of the castle, and of a considerable treasure which is concealed in a statue called the White Lady. The traditions affirmed that this lady was the protectress of the Avenels. All the clan were believers in the story, and the villagers declared they had often seen her in the neighborhood. Gaveston, however, does not share their superstition nor believe in the legend, and some time after the departure of the Laird he announces the sale of the castle, hoping to obtain it at a low rate because the villagers will not dare to bid for it through fear of the White Lady. The steward is led to do this because he has heard the Laird is dead, and knows there is no heir to the property. Anna, an orphan girl, who had been befriended by the Laird, determines to frustrate Gaveston's designs, and appears in the village disguised as the White Lady. She also writes to Dickson, a farmer, who is indebted to her, to meet her at midnight in the castle of Avenel. He is too superstitious to go, and George Brown, a young lieutenant who is sharing his hospitality, volunteers in his stead. He encounters the White Lady, and learns from her he will shortly meet a young lady who has saved his life by her careful nursing after a battle, — Anna meanwhile recognizing George as the person she had saved. When the day of sale comes, Dickson is empowered by the farmers to purchase the castle, so that it may not fall into Gaveston's hands. George and Anna are there; and the former, though he has not a shilling, buys it under instructions from Anna. When the time comes for payment, Anna produces the treasure which had been concealed in the statue, and, still in the disguise of the White Lady, reveals to him the secret of his birth during the exile of his parents. Gaveston approaches the spectre and tears off her veil, revealing Anna, his ward. Moved by the zeal and fidelity of his father's *protégée*, George offers her his hand, which, after some maidenly scruples, she accepts.

The opera is full of beautiful songs, many of them Scotch in character. In the first act the opening song of George ("Ah, what Pleasure a Soldier to be!") is very poetical in its sentiment. It also contains the characteristic ballad of the White Lady, with choral responses ("Where yon Trees your Eye discovers"), and an exquisitely graceful trio in the finale ("Heavens! what do I hear?"). The second act opens with a very plaintive romanza ("Poor Margaret, spin away!"), sung by Margaret, Anna's old nurse, at her spinning-wheel, as she thinks of the absent Laird, followed in the fifth scene by a beautiful cavatina for tenor ("Come, O gentle Lady"). In the seventh scene is a charming duet ("From these Halls"), and the act closes with an ensemble for seven voices and chorus, which has hardly been excelled in ingenuity of treatment. The third act opens with a charmingly sentimental aria for Anna ("With what Delight I behold"), followed in the third scene by a stirring chorus of mountaineers, leading up to "the lay ever sung by the Clan of Avenel," — the familiar old ballad, "Robin Adair," which loses a little of its local color under French treatment, but gains an added grace. It is stated on good authority that two of Boieldieu's pupils, Adolph Adam and

Labarre, assisted him in the work, and that the lovely overture was written in one evening, — Boieldieu furnishing the andante and the two others the remaining movements. Though a little old-fashioned in some of its phrasing, the opera still retains its freshness and beautiful sentiment. Its popularity is best evinced by the fact that up to June, 1875, it had been given 1340 times at the theatre where it was first produced.

BOITO

ARRIGO BOITO was born in 1840, and received his musical education in the Conservatory at Milan, where he studied for nine years. In 1866 he became musical critic for several Italian papers, and about the same time wrote several poems of more than ordinary merit. Both in literature and music his taste was diversified; and he combined the two talents in a remarkable degree in his opera of "Mephistopheles," the only work by which he is known to the musical world at large. He studied Goethe profoundly; and the notes which he has appended to the score show a most intimate knowledge of the Faust legend. His text is in one sense polyglot, as he has made use of portions of Marlowe's "Doctor Faustus," as well as excerpts from Blaze de Bury, Lenau, Widmann, and others who have treated the legend. He studied Wagner's music also very closely, and to such purpose that after the first performance of this opera at La Scala, in 1868, the critics called him the Italian Wagner, and, in common with the public, condemned both him and his work. After Wagner's "Lohengrin" had been produced in Italy and met with success, Boito saw his opportunity once more to bring out his work. It was performed at Bologna in 1875, and met with an enthusiastic success. Its introduction to this country is largely due to Mme. Christine Nilsson, though Mme. Marie Roze was the first artist to appear in it here.

MEPHISTOPHELES

"Mephistopheles," grand opera in a prologue, four acts, and epilogue, words by the composer, was first performed at La Scala, Milan, in 1868. The "Prologue in the Heavens" contains five numbers, a prelude, and chorus of the mystic choir; instrumental scherzo, preluding the appearance of Mephistopheles; dramatic interlude, in which he engages to entrap Faust; a vocal scherzo by the chorus of cherubim; and the Final Psalmody by the penitents on earth and chorus of spirits. The prologue corresponds to Goethe's prologue in the heavens, the heavenly choirs being heard in the background of clouds, accompanied by weird trumpet-peals and flourishes in the orchestra, and closes with a finale of magnificent power.

The first act opens in the city of Frankfort, amid the noise of the crowd and the clanging of holiday bells. Groups of students, burghers, huntsmen, and peasants sing snatches of chorus. A cavalcade escorting the Elector passes. Faust and Wagner enter, and retire as the peasants begin to sing and dance a merry waltz rhythm ("Juhé! Juhé!"). As it dies away they reappear, Faust being continually followed by a gray friar (Mephistopheles in disguise), whose identity is disclosed by a motive from the prologue. Faust shudders at his presence, but Wagner laughs away his fears, and the scene then suddenly changes to Faust's laboratory, whither he has been followed by the gray friar, who conceals himself in an alcove. Faust sings a beautiful aria ("Dai campi, dai prati"), and then, placing the Bible on a lectern, begins to read. The sight of the book brings Mephistopheles out with a shriek. When questioned by Faust, he reveals his true self in a massive and sonorous aria ("Son lo spirito"). He throws off his disguise, and appears in the garb of a knight, offering to serve Faust on earth if he will serve the powers of darkness in hell. The compact is made, as in the first act of Gounod's "Faust," and the curtain falls as Faust is about to be whisked away in Mephistopheles's cloak.

The second act opens in the garden, with Faust (under the name of Henry), Marguerite, Mephistopheles, and Martha, Marguerite's mother, strolling in couples. The music, which is of a very sensuous character, is descriptive of the love-making between Faust and Marguerite, and the sarcastic passion of Mephistopheles for Martha. It is mostly in duet form, and closes with an allegretto quartet ("Addio, fuggo"), which is very characteristic. The scene then suddenly changes to the celebration of the Witches' Sabbath on the summits of the Brocken, where, amid wild witch choruses, mighty dissonances, and weird incantation music, Faust is shown a vision of the sorrow of Marguerite. It would be impossible to select special numbers from this closely interwoven music, excepting perhaps the song ("Ecco il mondo") which Mephistopheles sings when the witches, after their incantation, present him with a globe of glass which he likens to the earth.

The third act opens in a prison, where Marguerite is awaiting the penalty for murdering her babe. The action is very similar to that of the last act of Gounod's "Faust." Her opening aria ("La' altra notte a fondo al maro") is full of sad longings for the child and insane moanings for mercy. Faust appeals to her to fly with him, and they join in a duet of extraordinary, sensuous beauty blended with pathos ("Lontano, lontano!"). Mephistopheles urges Faust away as the day dawns, and as Marguerite falls and dies, the angelic chorus resounding in the orchestra announces her salvation.

In the fourth act a most abrupt change is made, both in a dramatic and musical sense. The scene changes to the "Night of the Classical Sabbath" on the banks of

Marie Roze as *Helen*

the Peneus, amid temples, statues, flowers, and all the loveliness of nature in Greece. The music also changes into the pure, sensuous Italian style. Faust, still with Mephistopheles, pays court to Helen of Troy, who is accompanied by Pantalis. The opening duet for the latter ("La luna immobile") is one of exceeding grace and loveliness, and will always be the most popular number in the work. With the exception of a powerfully dramatic scena, in which Helen describes the horrors of the destruction of Troy, the music is devoted to the love-making between Helen and Faust, and bears no relation in form to the rest of the music of the work, being essentially Italian in its smooth, flowing, melodious character.

At the close of the classical Sabbath another abrupt change is made, to the death-scene of Faust, contained in an epilogue. It opens in his laboratory, where he is reflecting upon the events of his unsatisfactory life, and contemplating a happier existence in heaven. Mephistopheles is still by his side as the tempter, offers him his cloak, and urges him to fly again. The heavenly trumpets which rang through the prologue are again heard, and the celestial choirs are singing. Enraged, Mephistopheles summons the sirens, who lure Faust with all their charms. Faust seizes the Sacred Volume, and declares that he relies upon its word for salvation. He prays for help against the demon. His prayer is answered; and as he dies a shower of roses falls upon his body. The tempter disappears, and the finale of the prologue, repeated, announces Faust has died in salvation.

The opera as a whole is episodical in its dramatic construction, and the music is a mixture of two styles, — the Wagnerian and the conventional Italian; but its orchestration is bold and independent in character, and the voice-parts are very striking in their adaptation to the dramatic requirements.

BRÜLL

IGNAZ BRÜLL, who is known both as pianist and composer, was born at Prossnitz, Moravia, November 7, 1846. He first came into notice by his piano concertos and some minor works, among them a serenade, for orchestra, which were played in 1864. He made several concert tours as a pianist, playing his own compositions with great success. From 1872 to 1878 he was regularly engaged in teaching at the Horak Institute in Vienna. His first opera, "Der Bettler von Samarkand" (1864), was not very successful, but his second, "Das Goldene Kreuz" ("The Golden Cross"), speedily became popular in Austria, Germany, and England, Carl Rosa bringing it out in the latter country. Among others of his operas are "Der Landfriede" (1877), "Bianca" (1879), Königin Mariette" (1883), "Das Steinerne Herz" (1888), "Gringoire" (1892), "Schach dem König" (1893), and "Der Husar" (1898). He has also written several concertos and sonatas for piano and violin, besides many songs.

The Golden Cross

"Das Goldene Kreuz" ("The Golden Cross"), two-act opera, text by Mosenthal, was first produced in Berlin, December 22, 1875. The scene is laid at the village of Melun, not far from Paris, and its time is 1812 and 1815. The libretto is an adaptation of the French comedy, "Croix d' Or," by Brazier and Melville.

The story of "The Golden Cross" is quite simple. In the opening scene, Nicholas, a mill-owner in the village, is summoned by Bombardon, the sergeant, to join the army, — his name being on the conscription list, — upon the very day fixed for his marriage to his cousin Theresa. His sister Christine vainly implores some of the young men of the village, who have been protesting their love for her, to go as his substitute, and offers her hand to any one who will go to the war and bring back the golden cross which she takes from her neck. No one is willing to go and Nicholas is about to follow Bombardon, when the latter declares he has found a substitute, a young French nobleman, who will accept her cross upon her conditions. Three years are supposed to have elapsed when the second act opens at the same locality. Among those at the tavern is Goutrau l'Ancre, who is recovering from a serious wound received in the war. Christine has tenderly nursed him through his long illness and fallen in love with him, but she feels it her duty to await the return of the unknown substitute with her cross. At last he informs her he is the substitute but he is unable to produce the cross, as he gave it to a comrade, when he thought he was dying, to return to her. Bombardon appears at this juncture, and, supposing Goutrau to be dead, shows the cross and jestingly demands her hand; upon hearing Goutrau's voice, however, Bombardon bears witness to the truth of his comrade's statement and all ends happily.

As the dialogues are spoken the musical numbers can be readily denoted. The first scene opens with a lively and graceful chorus of village girls congratulating Theresa upon her wedding day ("Rosmasin mit bunten Bändern"), which is followed by a romanza for Christine, ("Die Eltern Starben frühe"), leading up to a very pretty duet for Theresa and Christine ("Man soll's nicht verschevören"). The principal number in the third scene is an effective duet for Bombardon and Goutrau, ("Halt, Front, Gewehr bei Fuss"), and in the fourth, a song for Goutrau with its haunting refrain, "Jugendgluck, Jugendtraum," which is reproduced several times in the progress of the work. A tender and impassioned quintet for Christine, Theresa, Goutrau, Nicholas, and Bombardon is in strong contrast with the lively rataplan song of Bombardon, which follows ("Bom, bom, bom, trara, trara"). In the finale of the first act there is a graceful waltz measure, the soldiers sing a spirited rataplan behind the scenes as the recruits march off, and the curtain falls as Goutrau repeats his farewell refrain.

The second act opens with a duet for Theresa and Nicholas ("Schau, schau, mein Männchen"), followed by a pretty aria for Theresa ("Der Mäuner muss man sich dressiren") and a romanza for Goutrau ("Nein, nein, ich will ihr Herz nicht zwingen"), these in turn followed by the charming supper-table quartet ("Da ist sie, zu Tische!"). The fourth scene opens with one of the most effective numbers in the opera, a love duet for Christine and Goutrau ("Durf ich's glauben"), which beginning softly and tenderly closes with a fine climax. The remaining numbers of importance are Bombardon's fine song ("Wie anders war es"), the repetition of Goutrau's delightful refrain, the chorus of rejoicing, and Bombardon's rataplan summons to the altar —

"Allons! Vorwärts, junges Paar!
Grenadier! — Marsch, Zum Altar!
Bom plan, plan, trara, trara."

The story is simple and charming and the music is of a character which admirably fits it.

CHERUBINI

MARIA LUIGI CARLO ZENOBIO SALVATORE CHERUBINI was born in Florence, September 14, 1760, and died March 15, 1842. His musical talent was displayed at an early age, and at sixteen he had already composed many works for the church, which made him well known. By the aid of royal patronage he went to Bologna in 1778 and studied polyphony, acquiring such proficiency that he soon excelled nearly every musician of his time. It was not until 1780 that his first opera, "Quinto Fabio," appeared, and for the next fourteen years he was almost continuously engaged in operatic composition. He did a great work for the development of opera in France and was made a Chevalier of the Legion of Honor by Napoleon and afterwards elected a member of the Institute under Louis XVIII. In 1822 he became Director of the Paris Conservatoire. The catalogue of his works is a long one, including both vocal and instrumental, secular and sacred music. His most important operas are "Démophon" (1788); "Lodoïska" (1791); "Ali Baba" (1794); "Medea" (1797); "Anacreon" (1803); "Faniska" (1806); and "Les deux journées" (1800), known in Germany as "Der Wasserträger," and in England as "The Water Carrier." It is this opera which, in Beethoven's estimation, placed Cherubini at the head of all living operatic composers.

LES DEUX JOURNÉES

"Les deux journées," popularly known in England and in this country as "The Water Carrier," opera comique in three acts, text by Bouilly, was first produced in Paris,

January 16, 1800. The first scene opens at the house of Michele, a water carrier of Paris, whose son, Antonio, is about to wed Angeline, a young peasant lass living at Genesse. Michele has a daughter, Marcelline, and from motives of gratitude for past benefits is interested in a Count Armand, who is persecuted by Cardinal Mazarin. The city gates are watched so that he shall not escape, and no one is allowed to leave without a pass. As Michele has passes for his son and daughter, he devises a plan for the escape of Armand and his wife Costanza. He induces Marcelline to give up going to her brother's wedding and arranges that Costanza shall personate her and get out of the city, escorted by Antonio. Costanza effects her departure with little trouble, and then Michele has to arrange the union of Armand with his wife. The Count is carried past the gates in Michele's water-barrel, but at one time during the trip he has to hide in a hollow tree. When the coast is clear it is planned that Costanza shall clap her hands thrice as a signal to her husband. Soldiers, however, concealed among the rocks, seize Costanza, whereupon Armand rushes to her rescue and confronts her assailants with a brace of pistols. As the murder now is out, Armand proclaims himself, and is about to be carried away when Michele comes forward with the news that the persecution has ceased and that the Count's title, estates, and liberty are restored to him.

The principal numbers in the first act are the romanza for Antonio (" Da casa il princo, mio signor "); the aria (" Deh so m'ascolti ") in Michele's couplet; the aria for Costanza (" No se donessi "), and the trio for Armand, Costanza, and Michele (" O mio liberator "), one of the most beautiful numbers in the opera, followed by a charming duet for Armand and Costanza. The second act opens with an intensely dramatic ensemble for Costanza, Antonio, and the soldiers (" Via ! cedete ull' evidenza "), which is one of those masterpieces in dramatic writing for which Cherubini was famous. The trio in the finale of this act, with its effective march, is also very dramatic. The conspicuous numbers of the last act are the Wedding Chorus ("La pastorella"), which is full of rustic color and freshness, and merges into a picturesque soldiers' chorus ("Nulla pieta de omai"), the finale of the act reaching its climax in a brilliant quartet and double chorus.

"Les deux journées" is designated by some writers as grand opera, but from its general character and especially from the use of spoken dialogue it is more correct to class it as opera comique. It is a work characterized by simplicity in treatment and absence of all sensation, great dignity, and strong dramatic effect, and by exceedingly rich instrumentation, although Cherubini had not the advantage of modern resources. Its beautiful overture is still a frequent number on orchestral programmes. It is to be regretted that the whole work is not more frequently given.

DAMROSCH

WALTER J. DAMROSCH, son of Dr. Leopold Damrosch, was born in Breslau, Silesia, January 30, 1862, and inherited musical ability from his father, with whom he studied, as well as with Rischbieter, Draeseke, Von Inten, Bockelmann, and Max Pinner. He also took lessons in the art of conducting from his father and Von Bülow. He is conductor of the New York Oratorio and Symphony Society, founded the New York Symphony Orchestra in 1892, and the Damrosch Opera Company in 1894. He occupies a prominent position before the public at present as a conductor, and is also performing a very important educational work by his lectures and piano illustrations of Wagner's operas. His most important compositions are the opera, "The Scarlet Letter," and the "Manila Te Deum." He has also written several songs which are great favorites in the concert room.

THE SCARLET LETTER

"The Scarlet Letter," opera in three acts, text by George Parsons Lathrop, was first produced in Boston, Mass., February 10, 1896, with the following cast of the principal characters:

Hester Prynne	JOHANNA GADSKI.
Arthur Dimmesdale	BARRON BERTHOLD.
Gov. Bellingham	CONRAD BEHRENS.
Rev. John Wilson	GERHARD STEHMAN.
Roger Chillingworth	WILHELM MERTEN.

The text is an original poem upon the theme developed by Hawthorne in his well-known romance, "The Scarlet

Letter." Mr. Lathrop himself calls it a poem "after Hawthorne's romance," though many liberties are taken with the original story, especially in the tragic and, in some respects, inconsistent denouement. The first act discloses Hester brought from prison, amid the jeers of the crowd, her condemnation to wear the scarlet letter "A," and her unwitting disclosure of her lover as he is brought fainting out of church. The second act is occupied with interviews between the governor and Chillingworth and the two lovers, who in the finale make their plans to escape to England. These plans are frustrated in the third act, which is mainly devoted to the tragedy. The minister ascends the pillory with Hester, makes his confession and dies while Hester, declaring "Thou shalt not go alone," poisons herself and dies to the melody of the final chorus, "The Flower of Sacrifice," sung by those who have just been jeering her.

In "The Scarlet Letter" Mr. Damrosch has made the first attempt, since the days of Fry and Bristow, to write a serious work upon the lines of grand opera, and he has measurably succeeded. Much of the music indeed is so effective that it is to be regretted he has not made further attempts in the same direction. The most successful numbers are the Brook solo, followed by the May Day madrigal, sung by the newly arrived Pilgrims at the opening of the second act; the chorus of Pilgrims interrupted by the Shipmaster's song — one of the best of modern sea songs; the scenes between Hester and Chillingworth, and at the pillory, with the final chorus, "Hush, hush, their Souls are fled," in the third act.

DE KOVEN

REGINALD DE KOVEN, the American composer, was born at Middletown, Conn., April 3, 1859. He was educated in Europe and took his degree at Oxford in 1879. Meanwhile he had studied the piano, and after his graduation went to Germany where he studied the piano and harmony with various teachers; to perfect himself in his work he also studied singing with Vanuccini in Italy and operatic composition with Genée and Délibes. The most of his time has been devoted to operettas and in this line he has been very successful. The best of them are "The Begum" (1887); "Don Quixote" (1889); "Robin Hood" (1889); "The Algerian" (1893); "Rob Roy" (1894); "Maid Marian" (1901); and "Happy Land" (1905).

Robin Hood

"Robin Hood," comic opera in three acts, text by Harry B. Smith, was first produced in Chicago, June 9, 1890. The scene is laid in England, time of Richard the First. The first act opens in the market-place of Nottingham, where the villagers are holding a fair and at the same time celebrating May Day with a blithe chorus, for Robin Hood's name is often associated with that day. The three outlaws, Allan-a-Dale, Little John, and Will Scarlet, enter, and most lustily sing the praises of their free life in Sherwood Forest, the villagers joining in chorus. The tantara changes to a graceful and yet hilarious dance chorus ("A Morris Dance must you entrance"), sung fortissimo. The second number is a characteristic and lively song by Friar

Tuck, in which he offers at auction venison, ale, and homespun, followed by the third number, a humorous pastoral, the milkmaid's song with chorus ("When Chanticleer crowing"). This leads up to the entrance of Robin Hood in a spirited chorus ("Come the Bowmen in Lincoln Green"), in which the free life of the forest is still further extolled. Another and still more spirited scene introduces Maid Marian, which is followed by an expressive and graceful duet for Maid Marian and Robin Hood ("Though it was within this Hour we met"), closing in waltz time. This is followed by the Sheriff's buffo song with chorus ("I am the merry Sheriff of Nottingham"), and this in turn by a trio introduced by the Sheriff ("When a Peer makes Love to a Damsel fair"), which, after the entrance of Sir Guy and his luckless wooing, closes in a gay waltz movement ("Sweetheart, my own Sweetheart"). In the finale Robin Hood demands that the Sheriff shall proclaim him Earl. The Sheriff declares that by his father's will he has been disinherited, and that he has the documents to show that before Robin Hood's birth his father was secretly married to a young peasant girl, who died when the Earl's first child was born. He further declares that he reared the child, and that he is Sir Guy, the rightful heir of Huntington. Maid Marian declares she will suppress the King's command and not accept Sir Guy's hand, and Robin Hood vows justice shall be done when the King returns from the Crusades.

The second act opens with a brisk hunting-chorus ("Oh! cheerily soundeth the Hunter's Horn"), sung by Allan-a-Dale, Little John, Scarlet, and the male chorus, in the course of which Scarlet tells the story of the tailor and the crow, set to a humming accompaniment. This is followed by Little John's unctuous apostrophe to the nut-brown ale ("And it's will ye quaff with me, my Lads"). The next number is a tinker's song ("'T is merry Journeymen we are"), with characteristic accompaniment, followed by an elaborate sextet ("Oh, see the Lambkins play"). Maid Marian sings a joyous forest song ("In Greenwood fair"), followed by Robin Hood's serenade ("A Troubadour sang to his Love"), and a quartet in which Maid Marian declares her love for Robin Hood and Allan-a-Dale vows revenge. In the finale, opening in waltz time, the Sheriff is placed in the stocks by the outlaws, who jeer at him while Dame Durden flouts him, but he is finally rescued by Sir Guy and his archers. The outlaws in turn find themselves in trouble, and Maid Marian and Robin Hood are in despair.

The last act opens with a vigorous armorer's song ("Let Hammer on Anvil ring"), followed by a pretty romance, ("The Legend of the Chimes"), with a ding-dong accompaniment. A graceful duet follows ("There will come a Time"), in which Robin Hood and Maid Marian plight their troth. In strong contrast with this, Annabel, Dame Durden, Sir Guy, the Sheriff, and Friar Tuck indulge in a vivacious quintet ("When Life seems made of Pains and Pangs, I sing my Too-ral-loo-ral-loo"). A jolly country dance and chorus ("Happy Day, Happy Day") introduce the finale, in which Maid Marian is saved by the timely arrival of Robin Hood at the church door with the King's pardon, leaving him free to marry.

MAID MARIAN

"Maid Marian," comic opera in three acts, text by Harry B. Smith, was first produced at Chestnut Street Opera House, Philadelphia, Pa., November 4, 1901. The scene is laid in England and Palestine, time of Richard the First. The story of "Maid Marian" introduces most of the familiar characters in "Robin Hood" and some new ones and is intended as a sequel to the latter opera.

DE KOVEN

The plot begins at the point where Maid Marian and Robin Hood were betrothed. Robin has joined the Crusaders and left Marian on the eve of the wedding. He also leaves a letter for Marian in Little John's charge, directing her in case of trouble to apply to him for help. This letter is stolen by the Sheriff of Nottingham, who substitutes for it a forged missive calculated to make her believe that Robin is false. The first act closes with the arrival of Little John and the forest outlaws, who leave for the holy war. Marian joins them to seek for Robin.

The second act opens in the camp of the Crusaders, near the city of Acre. Maid Marian has been captured by the Saracens and sold into slavery, but is rescued by Robin Hood. Then the Sheriff of Nottingham and Guy of Gisborne, the latter still intent upon marrying Marian, appear in the disguise of merchants and betray the camp into the hands of the Saracens. Dame Durden's encounter with the Sheriff and Friar Tuck's antics as an odalisque add merriment to the story.

In the last act all the principals are back in England and the scene opens with a Christmas revel in Huntington Castle. Robin thwarts all the schemes of the Sheriff, comes into his rights, and is reunited to Maid Marian.

While the story lacks in interest as compared with that of "Robin Hood," the music gains in dramatic power and seriousness of purpose, and at the same time is full of life and vivacity. The overture is notable for being in genuine concert form, — the first instance of the kind in comic opera for many years past, — and thus naturally sets the pace, as it were, for the opera, and gives the clew to its musical contents. The most noticeable numbers in the first act are the Cellarer's Toast, "The Cellar is dark and the Cellar is deep," a rollicking song for Scarlet, Friar Tuck, and chorus; the charmingly melodious "Song of the Falcon," "Let one who will go hunt the Deer," for

Maid Marian; the Sheriff's song, "I am the Sheriff mild and good," which is always popular; and a delightful madrigal, the quintet, "Love may come and Love may go." The second act contains many pleasing and characteristic songs, among them "The Monk and the Magpie," sung by Scarlet and chorus; the "Song of the Outlaw," a spirited ballad by Robin Hood; the Sheriff's serenade, a popular tune, "When a Man is in Love"; "The Snake Charmer's Song," by Maid Marian; and the vigorous "Song of the Crusader" by Robin; but the two most effective numbers are a graceful song, "Tell me again, Sweetheart," sung by Allan-a-Dale, and the duet in waltz manner, "True Love is not for a Day," by Robin and Marian. The third act is largely choral, the introductory Christmas carolling and dance rhythms being especially effective, and it contains one of the best solo numbers in the work, the dainty song with chorus, "Under the Mistletoe Bough." The music throughout is dramatic, strong, and well written. While the opera has not been as popular as its predecessor, yet the music is of a higher order, and occasionally approaches grand opera in its breadth and earnestness.

DELIBES

LEO DELIBES, the French composer, was born at St. Germain du Val in 1836, and was graduated at the Paris Conservatory, where he reached high distinction. His first work, written in 1855, was an operetta entitled " Deux Sous de Carbon"; but he did not make his mark until his " Maitre Griffard" was produced at the Théâtre Lyrique in 1857. In 1865 he was appointed chorusmaster at the Opera, and there his real career began. His first great triumph was in ballet music, which he afterwards made his specialty. His first ballet, " La Source," was produced at the Opera, November 12, 1865, and delighted all Paris. It was followed by a divertissement for the revival of Adam's " Corsaire" (1867), the ballet "Coppelia" (1870), a three-act opera, " Le Roi l'a dit" (1873), and the exquisite ballet in three acts and five tableaux, " Sylvia" (1876), with the music of which Theodore Thomas has made American audiences familiar. His opera " Lakme" was written in 1879.

LAKME

The romantic opera, " Lakme," written in 1879, was first performed in this country by the American Opera Company in 1886, Mme. L'Allemand taking the title role. The principal characters are Lakme, daughter of Nilakantha, an Indian priest; Gerald and Frederick, officers of the British Army; Ellen and Rose, daughters of the Viceroy; and Mrs. Benson, governess. The scene is laid in India. Nilakantha cherishes a fond hatred of all foreigners. The two English officers, Gerald and Frederick, accompanied by a bevy of ladies, intrude upon his sacred grounds. They stroll about and gradually retire, but Gerald remains to sketch some jewels, which Lakme has left upon a shrine while she goes flower-gathering with her slave Mallika, and evidently also to await developments when she returns. Lakme soon approaches in her boat, and there is a desperate case of love at first sight. Their demonstrations of affection are interrupted by the appearance of the priest, whose anger Gerald escapes by fleeing, under cover of a convenient thunder-storm. In the next act Lakme and her father appear in the public market-place, disguised as penitents. He compels his daughter to sing, hoping that her face and voice will induce her lover to disclose himself. The ruse proves successful. Nilakantha waits his opportunity, and stealing upon his enemy stabs him in the back and makes good his escape. In the third act we find Gerald in a delightful jungle, where Lakme has in some manner managed to conceal him, and where she is carefully nursing him with the hope of permanently retaining his love. She saves his life; but just at this juncture, and while she is absent to obtain a draught of the water which, according to the Indian legend, will make earthly love eternal, Gerald hears the music of his regiment, and Frederick appears and urges him back to duty. His allegiance to his queen, and possibly the remembrance of his engagement to a young English girl, prove stronger than his love for Lakme. The latter returns, discovers his faithlessness, gathers some poisonous flowers, whose juices she drinks, and dies in Gerald's arms just as the furious father appears. As one victim is sufficient to appease the anger of Nilakantha's gods, Gerald is allowed to go unharmed.

The first act opens with a chorus of Hindoos, oriental in its character, followed by a duet between Lakme and her father; the scene closing with a sacred chant. The Hindoos gone, there is a charming oriental duet ("'Neath yon Dome where Jasmines with the Roses are blooming") between Lakme and her slave, which is one of the gems of the opera. The English then appear and have a long, talky scene, relieved by a pretty song for Frederick ("I would not give a Judgment so absurd"), and another for Gerald ("Cheating Fancy coming to mislead me"). As Lakme enters, Gerald conceals himself. She lays her flowers at the base of the shrine and sings a restless love-song ("Why love I thus to stray?"). Gerald discovers himself, and after a colloquy sings his ardent love-song ("The God of Truth so glowing"), and the act closes with Nilakantha's threats.

The second act opens in the market square, lively with the choruses of Hindoos, Chinamen, fruit venders, and sailors, and later on with the adventures of the English party in the crowd. Nilakantha appears and addresses his daughter in a very pathetic aria ("Lakme, thy soft Looks are over-clouded"). Soon follows Lakme's bell-song ("Where strays the Hindoo Maiden?"), a brilliant and highly embellished aria with tinkling accompaniment, which will always be a favorite. The recognition follows; and the remaining numbers of importance are an impassioned song by Gerald ("Ah! then 't is slumbering Love"), with a mysterious response by Lakme ("In the Forest near at Hand"). A ballet, followed by the stabbing of Gerald, closes the act.

In the third act the action hastens to the tragic denouement. It opens with a beautiful crooning song by Lakme ("'Neath the Dome of Moon and Star") as she watches her sleeping lover. The remaining numbers of interest are Gerald's song ("Tho' speechless I, my Heart remembers"), followed by a pretty three-part chorus in the distance and Lakme's dying measures, "To me the fairest

Dream thou 'st given " and " Farewell, the Dream is over."
Though the opera is monotonous from sameness of color
and lack of dramatic interest, there are many numbers
which leave a charming impression by their grace, refinement, and genuine poetical effect.

DONIZETTI

GAETANO DONIZETTI was born at Bergamo, Italy, September 25, 1798. He studied music both at Bologna and Naples, and then entered the army rather than subject himself to the caprice of his father, who was determined that he should devote himself to church music. While his regiment was at Naples he wrote his first opera, "Enrico di Borgogna" (1818), which was soon followed by a second, "Il Falegname de Livonia." The success of the latter was so great that it not only freed him from military service but gained him the honor of being crowned. The first opera which spread his reputation through Europe was "Anna Bolena," produced at Milan in 1830, and written for Pasta and Rubini. Two years afterwards, "L'Elisir d' Amore" appeared, which he is said to have written in fifteen days. He wrote with great facility. "Il Furioso," "Parisina," "Torquato Tasso," "Lucrezia Borgia," and "Gemma di Vergi," rapidly followed one another. In 1835 he brought out "Marino Faliero," in Paris, but its success was small. Ample compensation was made, however, when in the same year "Lucia" appeared and was received with acclamations of delight. In 1840 he revisited Paris and produced "Il Poliuto," "La Fille du Regiment," and "La Favorita." Leaving Paris he visited Rome, Milan, and Vienna, bringing out "Linda di Chamouni" in the latter city. Returning to Paris again, he produced "Don Pasquale" at the Théâtre des Italiens, and "Don Sebastien" at the Académie, the latter proving a failure. His last opera, "Catarina Comaro," was brought out at Naples in 1844. This work also was a failure. It was evident that his capacity for work was over. He grew sad and melancholy, and during the last three years of his life was attacked by fits of abstraction which gradually intensified and ended in insanity and physical paralysis. He died at Bergamo, April 8, 1848.

THE DAUGHTER OF THE REGIMENT

"The Daughter of the Regiment" ("La Fille du Regiment"), opera comique in two acts, words by Bayard and St. Georges, was first produced at the Opera Comique, Paris, February 11, 1840, with Mme. Anna Thillon in the role of Marie. Its first performance in English was at the Surrey Theatre, London, December 21, 1847, under the title of "The Daughter of the Regiment," in which form it is best known in this country. In 1847 it was performed as an Italian opera in London, with added recitatives, and with Jenny Lind in the leading part.

The music of the opera is light and sparkling, the principal interest centering in the charming nature of the story and its humorous situations, which afford capital opportunities for comedy acting. The scene is laid in the Tyrol during its occupation by the French. Marie, the heroine, and the *vivandière* of the Twenty-first Regiment of Napoleon's army, was adopted as the Daughter of the Regiment, because she was found on the field, after a battle, by Sergeant Sulpice. On her person was affixed a letter written by her father to the Marchioness of Berkenfeld, which has been carefully preserved by the Sergeant. At the beginning of the opera the little waif has grown into a sprightly young woman, full of mischief and spirit, as is shown by her opening song ("The Camp was my Birthplace"), in which she tells the story of her life, and by the duet with Sulpice, known the world over as "The Rataplan," which is of a very animated, stirring, and martial

Jenny Lind as *Marie*

DONIZETTI 75

character, to the accompaniment of rattling drums and sonorous brasses. She is the special admiration of Tony, a Tyrolean peasant, who has saved her from falling over a precipice. The soldiers of the regiment are profuse in their gratitude to her deliverer, and celebrate her rescue with ample potations, during which Marie sings the Song of the Regiment ("All Men confess it"). Poor Tony, however, who was found strolling in the camp, is placed under arrest as a spy, though he succeeds in obtaining an interview with Marie and declares his love for her. The declaration is followed by a charming duet ("No longer can I doubt it"). Tony manages to clear up his record, and the soldiers decide that he may have Marie's hand if he will consent to join them. He blithely accepts the condition and dons the French cockade. Everything seems auspicious, when suddenly the Marchioness of Berkenfeld appears and dashes Tony's hopes to the ground. The Sergeant, as in honor bound, delivers the letter he has been preserving. After reading it she claims Marie as her niece, and demands that the regiment shall give up its daughter, while Tony is incontinently dismissed as an unsuitable person to be connected in any capacity with her noble family. Marie sings a touching adieu to her comrades ("Farewell, a long Farewell"), and the act closes with smothered imprecations on the Marchioness by the soldiers, and protestations of undying love by Tony.

The second act opens in the castle of Berkenfeld, where Marie is duly installed, though she does not take very kindly to her change of surroundings. The old Sergeant is with her. Grand company is expected, and the Marchioness desires Marie to rehearse a romance, "The Light of Early Day was breaking," which she is to sing to them. Before she finishes it she and the Sergeant break out into the rollicking Rataplan and go through with the military evolutions, to the horror of the

Marchioness. While regret for the absent Tony keeps her in a sad mood, she is suddenly cheered up by the sound of drums and fifes, announcing the approach of soldiers. They are the gallant Twenty-first, with Tony, now a colonel, at their head. He sues once more for Marie's hand. The soldiers also put in a spirited choral appeal, "We have come, our Child to free." The Marchioness again refuses. Tony proposes an elopement, to which Marie, in resentment at her aunt's cruelty, consents. To thwart their plans, the Marchioness reveals to Marie that early in life she had been secretly married to an officer of lower family position than her own, and that this officer was Marie's father. Unable to dispute the wishes of her mother, she renounces Tony in an agony of grief. At last Marie's sorrow arouses old associations in the mind of the Marchioness, and she consents to the union of Tony and Marie.

While the music of the opera is light, it is none the less very attractive, and the work is nearly always popular when performed by good artists, owing to the comedy strength of the three leading parts, Marie, Tony, and the Sergeant. The role of the heroine, small as it is, has always been a favorite one with such great artists as Jenny Lind, Patti, Sontag, and Albani, while in this country Miss Kellogg and Mrs. Richings-Bernard made great successes in the part. The latter singer, indeed, and her father, whose personation of the Sergeant was very remarkable, were among the first to perform the work in the United States.

La Favorita

"La Favorita," grand opera in four acts, words by Royer and Waëtz, the subject taken from the French drama, "Le Comte de Commingues," was first produced at the Académie, Paris, December 2, 1840, with Mme. Stolz as Leonora, Duprez as Fernando, and Baroelhst as Balthasar.

Its success in England, where it was first produced February 16, 1847, was made by Grisi and Mario. The scene of the opera is laid in Spain, and the first act opens in the monastery of St. James, of Compostella, where the young novice, Fernando, is about to take his vows. Before the rites take place he is seized with a sudden passion for Leonora, a beautiful maiden who has been worshipping in the cloisters. He confesses his love to Balthasar, the superior, who orders him to leave the monastery and go out into the world. Leonora, meanwhile, is beloved by Alphonso, king of Castile, who has provided her a secret retreat on the island of St. Leon. Though threatened by the pontiff with excommunication, he has resolved to repudiate his queen, in order that he may carry out his intention of marrying the beautiful Leonora. To her asylum a bevy of maidens conducts Fernando. He declares his passion for her and finds it reciprocated. He urges her to fly with him, but she declares it impossible, and, giving him a commission in the army signed by the King, urges him to go to the wars and win honors for her sake.

In the second act Balthasar, in the name of the pontiff, visits their retreat and pronounces the papal anathema upon the guilty pair. The same curse is threatened to all the attendants unless Leonora is driven from the King, and the act closes with their vengeful menaces.

In the third act Fernando returns victorious from the war with the Moors. Already beginning to fear the result of the papal malediction, and having learned of Leonora's passion for the victor, Alphonso heaps rewards upon him, even to the extent of giving him Leonora's hand. Fernando, who is ignorant of her past relations to the King, eagerly accepts the proffer; but Leonora, in despair, sends her attendant, Inez, to inform him of the real nature of the situation and implore his forgiveness. The King intercepts her, and the marriage takes place at once, Fernando not discovering Leonora's shame until it is revealed by the courtiers, who avoid him. He flies from the world to the monastery once more for shelter and consolation, followed by Leonora, who dies in his arms after she has obtained forgiveness.

The music of the work is very dramatic in its character, some of the finales being the strongest Donizetti has written. In the first act there is a beautifully melodious aria ("Una Vergine"), in which Fernando describes to Balthasar the vision of Leonora which had appeared to him at his orisons, and a very tender duet ("Deh, vanne! deh, parti") between Fernando and Leonora, in which they sorrowfully part from each other. In the second act the King has a very passionate aria, where he curses his courtiers for leaguing against him at Rome, followed by a very dramatic duet with Leonora ("Ah! l' alto ardor"). The third act contains the beautiful aria, "O mio Fernando!" which is a favorite with all contraltos. It is remarkable for its warmth and richness, as well as its dramatic spirit, and the act closes with a concerted finale of splendid power, in which Fernando breaks his sword, and once more Balthasar anathematizes the King. The fourth act is the most beautiful of all in its music and the most powerful in dramatic effect. The chorus of monks in the first scene ("Scaviam l' asilo") is remarkable for its religious character and solemnity. In the third scene occurs one of the tenderest and loveliest romanzas ever written ("Spirto gentil"), which Donizetti transferred to this work from his opera, "Le Duc d'Albe," which had not been performed, the libretto of which was originally written by Scribe for Rossini. The closing duet between Fernando and Leonora is full of pathos and beauty, and forms a fitting close to an act which, in one sense at least, is an inspiration, as the whole act was composed in four hours, — a proof of the marvellous ease and facility with which Donizetti wrote.

Don Pasquale

"Don Pasquale," opera buffa in three acts, was first produced at the Théâtre des Italiens, in Paris, January 4, 1843, with the following extraordinary cast:

Norina	Mme. GRISI.
Ernesto	Sig. MARIO.
Dr. Malatesta	Sig. TAMBURINI.
Don Pasquale	Sig. LABLACHE.

The scene of this brilliant and gay little opera is laid in Rome. Don Pasquale is in a rage with Ernesto, his nephew, because he will not marry to suit him. Dr. Malatesta, his friend and physician, who is also very much attached to the nephew, contrives a plot in the latter's interest. He visits the Don, and urges him to marry a lady, pretending that she is his sister, though in reality she is Norina, with whom Ernesto is in love. He then calls upon Norina, and lets her into the secret of the plot, and instructs her how to play her part. She is to consent to the marriage contract, and then so harass the Don that he will not only be glad to get rid of her, but will give his consent to her marriage with Ernesto. The second act opens in Don Pasquale's house, where Ernesto is bewailing his fate. The Don enters, magnificently dressed, and ready for the marriage. Norina appears with Malatesta, and feigns reluctance to enter into the contract; but when the notary arrives she consents to sign. No sooner, however, has she signed it than she drops her assumed modesty. Ernesto, who is present, is bewildered at the condition of affairs, but is kept quiet by a sign from the Doctor. Norina refuses all the Don's amatory demonstrations, and declares Ernesto shall be her escort. She summons the servants, and lays out a scheme of housekeeping so extravagant that the Don is enraged, and declares he will not pay the bills. She insists he shall, for she is now mistress of the house. In the third act we find Norina entertaining milliners and modistes. Don Pasquale enters, and learning that she is going to the theatre forbids it, which leads to a quarrel, during which Norina boxes his ears. As she leaves the room she drops a letter, the reading of which adds the pangs of jealousy to his other troubles. The Doctor at this juncture happens in and condoles with him. The Don insists that Norina shall quit his house at once. In the next scene he taxes her with having a lover concealed in the house, and orders her to leave. The Doctor counsels him to let his nephew marry Norina; and in the course of explanations the Don discovers that the Doctor's sister and Norina are one and the same person, and that the marriage was a sham. He is only too glad of an escape to quarrel with the Doctor for his plot, and the young couple are speedily united, and have the old man's blessing.

The charm of the opera lies in its comic situations, and the gay, cheerful music with which they are illustrated. It is replete with humor and spirit, and flows along in such a bright stream that it is almost impossible to cull out special numbers, though it contains two duets and a quartet which are of more than ordinary beauty, and the exquisite serenade in the last act, "Com' e gentil," which has been heard on almost every concert stage of the world, and still holds its place in universal popular esteem. For brilliant gayety it stands in the front rank of all comic operas, though Donizetti was but three weeks in writing it. It is said that when it was in rehearsal its fate was uncertain. The orchestra and singers received it very coldly; but when the rehearsal was over, Donizetti merely shrugged his shoulders and remarked to his friend, M. Dormoy, the publisher: "Let them alone; they know nothing about it. I know what is the matter with 'Don Pasquale.' Come with me." They went to the composer's house. Rummaging among a pile of manuscripts, Donizetti pulled out a song. "This is what 'Don Pasquale' wants," he said. "Take it to Mario and tell him to learn it at once." Mario obeyed, and when the opera was performed sang it to the accompaniment of a tambourine, which Lablache played behind the scenes. The opera was a success at once, and no song has ever been more popular.

In strange contrast with the gay humor of "Don Pasquale," it may be stated that in the same year Donizetti wrote the mournful "Don Sebastien," which has been described as "a funeral in five acts." Crowest, in his "Anecdotes," declares that the serenade is suggestive of Highland music, and that many of his other operas are Scottish in color. He accounts for this upon the theory that the composer was of Scotch descent, his grandfather having been a native of Perthshire, by the name of Izett, and that his father, who married an Italian lady, was Donald Izett. The change from Donald Izett to Donizetti was an easy one. The story, however, is of doubtful authenticity.

LUCIA DI LAMMERMOOR

"Lucia di Lammermoor," opera seria in three acts, words by Cammarano, was first produced at Naples in 1835, with Mme. Persiani and Sig. Duprez, for whom the work was written, in the principal roles of Lucia and Edgardo. Its first presentation at Paris was August 10, 1839; in London, April 5, 1838; and in English, at the Princess Theatre, London, January 19, 1843. The subject of the opera is taken from Sir Walter Scott's novel, "The Bride of Lammermoor," and the scene is laid in Scotland; time, about 1669.

Sir Henry Ashton, of Lammermoor, brother of Lucy, the

heroine, has arranged a marriage between her and Lord Arthur Bucklaw, in order to recover the fortune which he has dissipated, and to save himself from political peril he has incurred by his participation in movements against the reigning dynasty. Sir Edgar Ravenswood, with whom he is at enmity, is deeply attached to Lucy, who reciprocates his love, and on the eve of his departure on an embassy to France pledges herself to him. During his absence Edgar's letters are intercepted by her brother, who hints to her of his infidelity, and finally shows her a forged paper, which she accepts as the proof that he is untrue. Overcome with grief at her lover's supposed unfaithfulness, and yielding to the pressure of her brother's necessities, she at last consents to her union with Lord Arthur. The marriage contract is signed with great ceremony, and just as she has placed her name to the fatal paper, Edgar appears. Learning from Lucy what she has done, he tramples the contract under foot, hurls an imprecation upon the house of Lammermoor, and bursts out of the room in a terrible rage. Sir Henry follows him, and a fierce quarrel ensues, which ends in a challenge. Meanwhile, at night, after the newly wedded couple have retired, a noise is heard in their apartment. The attendants rush in and find Lord Arthur dying from wounds inflicted by Lucy, whose grief has made her insane. When she returns to reason, the thought of what she has done and the horror of her situation overcome her, and death shortly puts an end to her wretchedness. Ignorant of her fate, Edgar goes to the churchyard of Ravenswood, which has been selected as the rendezvous for the duel with Sir Henry. While impatiently waiting his appearance, the bell of the castle tolls, and some of the attendants accosting him bring the news of her death. The despairing lover kills himself among the graves of his ancestors, and the sombre story ends.

Saleza as *Edgardo*

Copyright, Aimé Dupont

DONIZETTI

The popular verdict has stamped "Lucia" as Donizetti's masterpiece, and if the consensus of musicians could be obtained, it would unquestionably confirm the verdict. It contains incomparably the grandest of his arias for tenor, the Tomb song in the last act, and one of the finest dramatic concerted numbers, the sextet in the second act, that can be found in any Italian opera. Like the quartet in "Rigoletto," it stands out in such bold relief, and is so thoroughly original and spontaneous, that it may be classed as an inspiration. The music throughout is of the most sombre character. It does not contain a joyous phrase. And yet it can never be charged with monotony. Every aria, though its tone is serious and more often melancholy, has its own characteristics, and the climaxes are worked up with great power. In the first act, for instance, the contrasts are very marked between Henry's aria, "Cruda, funesta smania," the chorus of hunters, "Come vinti da stanchezza," Henry's second aria, "La pietade in suo favore," in which he threatens vengeance upon Edgar, the dramatic and beautifully written arias for Lucy, "Regnava nel silenzio" and "Quando rapita in estasi," and the passionate farewell duet between Lucy and Edgar, which is the very ecstasy of commingled love and sorrow. The second act contains a powerful duet ("Le tradirmi tu potrai") between Lucy and Henry; but the musical interest of the act centres in the great sextet ("Chi mi frena"), which ensues when Edgar makes his unexpected appearance upon the scene of the marriage contract. For beauty, power, richness of melody, and dramatic expression, few concerted numbers by any composer can rival it. The last act also contains two numbers which are always the delight of great artists, — the mad song of Lucy ("Oh! gioja che si senti"), and the magnificent tomb scena ("Tomba degl' avi miei"), which affords even the most accomplished tenor ample scope for his highest powers.

L'Elisir d'Amore

"L'Elisir d'Amore," opera buffa in two acts, words by Romani, was first produced in Milan, in 1832, and in English, at Drury Lane, in 1839, as "The Love Spell." The heroine of this graceful little opera is Adina, a capricious country girl, who is loved by Nemorino, a young farmer, whose uncle lies at the point of death, and by Belcore, a sergeant, whose troops are billeted upon the neighboring village. While Adina keeps both these suitors in suspense, Dr. Dulcamara, a travelling quack, arrives at the village in great state to vend his nostrums. Nemorino applies to him for a bottle of the Elixir of Love, — with the magical properties of which he has become acquainted in a romance Adina has been reading that very morning. The mountebank, of course, has no such liquid, but he passes off on the simple peasant a bottle of wine, and assures him that if he drinks of it he can command the love of any one on the morrow. To thoroughly test its efficacy, Nemorino drinks the whole of it. When he encounters Adina he is half tipsy, and accosts her in such disrespectful style that she becomes enraged, and determines to give her hand to the sergeant, and promises to marry him in a week. Meanwhile an order comes for the departure of the sergeant's detachment, and he begs her to marry him the same day. She gives her consent, and the second act opens with the assembling of the villagers to witness the signing of the marriage contract. While the sergeant, Adina, and the notary have retired to sign and witness the contract, Nemorino enters in despair, and finding Dulcamara enjoying a repast, he implores him to give him some charm that will make Adina love him at once. Having no money, the quack refuses to assist him, and Nemorino is again plunged into despair. At this juncture the sergeant enters, not in the best of humor, for Adina has declined to sign the

Sembrich as *Adina*

Copyright, Aimé Dupont

contract until evening. Discovering that Nemorino wants money, he urges him to enlist. The bonus of twenty crowns is a temptation. Nemorino enlists, takes the money, hurries to the quack, and obtains a second bottle of the elixir, which is much more powerful than the first. In the next scene the girls of the village have discovered that Nemorino's uncle has died and left him all his property, though Nemorino himself has not heard of it. They crowd about him, trying to attract his attention with their charms and blandishments. He attributes his sudden popularity to the effects of the elixir, and even the quack is somewhat bewildered at the remarkable change. Nemorino now determines to pay Adina off in kind, and at last rouses her jealousy. Meanwhile Dulcamara acquaints her with the effects of the elixir and advises her to try some of it, and during the interview inadvertently informs her of Nemorino's attachment for her. Struck with his devotion, she repays the sergeant herself, announces her change of mind, and bestows her hand upon the faithful Nemorino. Like "Don Pasquale," the opera is exceedingly graceful in its construction, and very bright and gay in its musical effects, particularly in the duets, of which there are two, — one between Dulcamara and Nemorino in the first act ("Obbligato, ah ! si obbligato"), and one between Dulcamara and Adina in the second act ("Quanto amore ! ed io spietata"), which are charming in their spirit and humor. There is also an admirable buffo song in the first act, beginning with the recitative, "Udite, udite, o rustici," in which the Doctor describes his wares to the rustics, and a beautiful romanza in the second act for tenor ("Una furtiva lagrima"), which is of world-wide popularity, and bears the same relation to the general setting of the work that the Serenade does to "Don Pasquale."

Lucrezia Borgia

"Lucrezia Borgia," grand opera in three acts, words by Romani, was first produced at La Scala, Milan, in 1834. The subject was taken from Victor Hugo's tragedy of the same name, and its text was freely adapted by Romani. When it was produced in Paris, in 1840, Victor Hugo took steps to suppress any further representations. The libretto was then rewritten, under the title of "La Rinegata," the Italian characters were changed to Turks, and in this mutilated form the performances were resumed. It was in this opera that Signor Mario made his English debut, in 1839, with great success. Its first presentation in English was at London, December 30, 1843.

The history of Lucrezia Borgia, daughter of Rodrigo Borgia, afterwards Pope Alexander VI, and sister of Cæsar Borgia, is too well known to need recapitulation. It is necessary to the comprehension of the story of the opera, however, to state that she had an illegitimate son, named Genarro, who was left when an infant with a fisherman, but who subsequently entered the Venetian army and rose to an eminent rank. The opera opens with a brilliant festival in the gardens of the Barberigo Palace, which is attended by Genarro, Orsini, and others, all of them cordial haters of the detestable Borgias. While they are telling tales of Lucrezia's cruel deeds, Genarro lies down and goes to sleep, and Orsini in a spirited aria ("Nelle fatal di Rimini") relates to his companions the story of Genarro's gallantry at the battle of Rimini. As they leave, Lucrezia approaches, masked, in a gondola, and is received by Gubetta, with whom she has come to Venice on some secret errand. She discovers Genarro asleep, and expresses her delight at his beauty, and at the same time her maternal love, in a brilliant aria, "Com' e bello." As she kisses his hand he wakes, and in the duet which follows tells her the story of

Mme. de Moschi as *Lucrezia Borgia*

Copyright, Aimé Dupont

his early life in an exquisite romanza ("Di pescatore ignobile"), which is one of the most familiar numbers in Italian opera. He begs her to reveal her name, but she refuses. As he continues to implore her, his friends return and denounce her to Genarro as the hated Borgia, in a concerted number ("Chi siam noi sol chiarirla") of great dramatic power, which closes the first act.

The second act opens in the public square of Ferrara, with the palace of the Borgias on the right. The Duke Alphonso, Lucrezia's husband, who has been observant of Lucrezia's attachment to Genarro, vows vengeance in a passionate aria ("Vieni la mia vendetta"). In the next scene Genarro, who has been taunted by his friends with being a victim of Lucrezia's fascinations, recklessly rushes up to the palace door and strikes off the first letter of her name with his dagger. When Lucrezia discovers the insult, she demands of the Duke that the guilty person shall be arrested and condemned to death. The Duke has already seized Genarro, and agrees to carry out his wife's demands. When the prisoner is brought before them for judgment, she is horror-stricken to find he is her son. She implores his life, but the infuriated Duke retaliates upon her with the declaration that she is his paramour. The duet between them ("O! a te bada"), in which Lucrezia passes from humble entreaties to rage and menace, is a fine instance of Donizetti's dramatic power. The Duke, however, is resolute in his determination, and will only allow her to choose the mode of Genarro's death. She selects the Borgia wine, which is poisoned. Genarro is called in, and after a trio ("Le ti tradisce"), which is one of the strongest numbers in the opera, he is given the fatal draught under the pretence of a farewell greeting from the Duke, who then leaves mother and son together. She gives him an antidote, and he is thus saved from the fate which the Duke had intended for him.

The last act opens at a banquet in the palace of the Princess Negroni, which is attended by Genarro and his friends, Lucrezia, meanwhile, supposing that he has gone to Venice. During the repast she has managed to poison their wine. In the midst of the gay revel Orsini sings the popular drinking-song, "Il segreto per esser felici," which is now familiar the world over. The festivities are interrupted, however, by the appearance of Lucrezia, who reveals herself with the taunting declaration: "Yes, I am Borgia. A mournful dance ye gave me in Venice, and I return ye a supper in Ferrara." She then announces that they are poisoned. The music is changed with great skill from the wild revelry of drinking-songs to the sombre strains of approaching death. Five coffins are shown them, when Genarro suddenly reveals himself to Lucrezia and asks for the sixth. The horror-stricken woman again perceives that her son has been poisoned by her own hand. As his companions leave the apartment she implores Genarro to take the antidote once more, and at last reveals herself as his mother. He steadily refuses to save himself, however, since his companions have to die, and expires in her arms just as the Duke and his followers enter. She discloses Genarro's relationship, and then dies with the despairing cry on her lips that Heaven has pronounced its final judgment upon her. Among all of Donizetti's operas, not one, unless it be "Lucia," is more popular than "Lucrezia Borgia," which may be attributed to the fact that while the story itself is one of fascinating dramatic interest, the musical numbers are simple, beautiful, and effective.

Linda de Chamouni

"Linda de Chamouni," grand opera in three acts, text by Rossi, was first produced at the Kärnthnerthor Theatre, Vienna, May 19, 1842. The first act opens in the valley of Chamouni and discloses the home of Antonio Lonstolat, a farmer, and his old wife, Madalina, whose only daughter, Linda, is in love with Carlo, a young painter who has recently come into the valley. Misfortunes have overtaken the old couple, and they are in danger of losing their farm, which is owned by the Marchioness de Sirval. Their anxiety is temporarily relieved when the Marquis of Boisfleury visits them and assures them he will save the farm, his real purpose being to effect the ruin of Linda by ingratiating himself with her parents. The Prefect of the village, however, is aware of his designs, and induces them to allow Linda to accompany a party of villagers to Paris, promising at the same time to place her with his brother, who is supposed to be living in that city. She soon leaves under the protection of Pierotto, the Savoyard.

The second act discloses them on the way to Paris, but Linda unfortunately loses her companion. Upon reaching Paris she finds that the Prefect's brother is dead. Meanwhile Carlo, who has followed her, arrives, and reveals to her that he is the Viscount Sirval, son of the Marchioness, and nephew of the Marquis. He renews his offer of marriage, and places her in a handsome apartment. In these questionable surroundings Pierotto discovers her. Her father, who has had to give up the farm, also finds her, and, distrusting her innocence amid such luxury, curses her. The Marchioness meanwhile, who has learned of her son's attachment, threatens to imprison Linda if he does not marry the lady she has selected for him. He gives his feigned consent, and Linda, thinking he has deserted her, goes insane.

In the last act Pierotto takes her back to her native village. Carlo arrives there in search of her, and finding her with Pierotto sings to her, hoping she will recognize his voice and that her reason may return. The song has the desired effect. Subsequently the Marchioness relents, gives her consent to their union, and all ends happily.

The music of "Linda" is of that serious and dignified kind which justifies its inclusion in the list of grand operas. In the first act the opening aria of Antonio ("We were both in this Valley nurtured") is a touching expression of the sorrow of the aged couple. Linda's farewell, "Oh, Stars that guide my fervent Love," familiar on the concert stage by its Italian title, "O, luce di quest' anima," is an aria of strong dramatic power, and has always been a popular favorite. In this act also are Pierotto's pathetic ballad, "Once a better Fortune seeking," and the passionate duet for Linda and Carlo, "Oh, that the blessed Day were come!" The principal numbers in the second act are the brilliant duet for Linda and Pierotto ("Oh, Linda, at thy happy Fate"), which is highly embellished, and the aria for Linda ("Ah! go, my Love"). The last act contains a mournful aria by Carlo ("If from Heaven the Bolts should reach me"); his charming song in which he appeals to Linda ("Hear the Voice that, softly singing"); and the rapturous duet for Linda and Carlo ("Ah! the Vision of thy Sorrow fades"), which closes the opera.

FLOTOW

FRIEDRICH VON FLOTOW was born April 27, 1812, in the duchy of Mechlenberg-Schwerin, and in 1827 went to Paris, where he studied music under Reicha. His first work was "Stradella," a mere sketch in its original form, which was brought out at the Palais Royal in 1837; but his first public success was made in 1839, with his opera, "Le Naufrage de la Méduse," which had a run, and was afterwards produced in Germany under the title of "Die Matrosen." "L' Esclave de Camoens" appeared in Paris in 1843; "Stradella," rewritten as an opera, in Hamburg (1844); "L' Âme en peine," in Paris (1846); "Martha," in Vienna (1847). The works of his later period, which never equalled his earlier ones in popularity, were "Die Grossfürstin" (1850); "Indra" (1853); "Rubezahl" (1854); "Hilda" (1855); "Der Müller von Meran" (1856); "La Veuve Grapin" (1859); "L'Ombre" (1869); "Naïda" (1873); "Il Flor d' Harlem" (1876); and "Enchanteresse" (1878). Of these later works, "L'Ombre" was the most successful, and was received with favor in France, Italy, Spain, and England, in which latter country it was performed under the title of "The Phantom." In 1856 he received the appointment of Intendant of the theatre of the Grand Duke of Mecklenberg, and entered upon his duties with high hopes of making the theatre exercise the same influence upon music in Germany as the Weimar stage; but court intrigues and rivalries of artists so disgusted him that he resigned in 1863 and went to Paris, and a few years later to Vienna, where he took up his abode.

Outside of a few of his operas his works are little known, though he composed a "Fackeltanz," some incidental music to the "Winter's Tale" of Shakespeare, and several overtures, songs, and chamber-pieces. An interesting episode in his career occurred in 1838, when he brought out an opera in three acts, the "Duc de Guise," at the Théâtre de la Renaissance, the libretto based upon Dumas's "Henri III." The performance was organized by the Princess Czartoryska, for the benefit of the Poles. Mme. de Lagrange made her debut in a leading part, and the parts of the choristers were filled by duchesses and princesses of the Faubourg St. Germain, upon whose persons two million dollars worth of diamonds were blazing, — sufficient evidence that the performance was brilliant in at least one sense. He died at Wiesbaden, January 24, 1883.

Martha

"Martha," opera in three acts, libretto by St. Georges, translated into German by Friedrich, was first produced at Vienna, November 25, 1847, with Mlle. Anna Zerr in the title role, Herr Ander as Lionel, and Carl Formes as Plunkett. It was first produced in English and Italian at London in 1858, and in French at Paris in 1865. The history of its origin is interesting. M. de St. Georges, at the request of the manager of the Paris Grand Opera, wrote, in 1842, the libretto to a ballet entitled "Lady Henrietta, or the Servant of Greenwich," the subject being suggested to him by the adventures of two ladies of his acquaintance who had mingled with servants at a fair. The music was confided to three composers. The first act was given to Herr von Flotow, the second to Herr Burgmuller, and the third to M. Deldeves. The ballet had such a remarkable success, and Flotow was so delighted with the plot, that he entreated St. Georges to rewrite it for an opera. The latter consented, and the result of their collaboration was the appearance of one of the most popular operas which has ever been placed upon the stage.

The scene of the opera is laid at Richmond, England, and the time is during the reign of Queen Anne, though the Italian version places it in the fifteenth century, and the French in the nineteenth. Lady Henrietta, an attendant upon the Queen, tired of the amusements of court life, contrives a plan to visit the servants' fair at Richmond disguised as a servant-girl, and accompanied by Nancy, her maid, and Sir Tristan, her somewhat aged cousin, who is also her devoted admirer. In the first three scenes their plans are laid much to the disgust of Sir Tristan, who is to pass as John, while his fair cousin masquerades as Martha. The duet between the ladies ("Of the Knights so brave and charming") and the trio with Tristan, are in dance time, and full of animation. The fourth scene opens in the market-place at Richmond, where the people are gathering to the fair. Thither also resort Plunkett, a farmer, and Lionel, his brother by adoption, whose parentage is unknown, and who has no souvenir of his father except a ring which has been left for him, with instructions to present it to the Queen if he ever finds himself in trouble. Lionel tells his story in an aria ("Lost, proscribed, an humble Stranger") which is universally popular, and the melody of which has been set to various words. They have come to the fair to procure help for their farm. While the sheriff, according to law, is binding the girls for a year's service, Plunkett and Lionel meet Martha and Nancy, and are so delighted with their appearance that they tender them the customary bonus, or "earnest-money," which secures them. Too late for escape, they find that they are actually engaged, and they are obliged to drive away with the young farmers, leaving Sir Tristan in despair.

The second act opens in the farmhouse, where the four

have arrived. The farmers inquire their names, and seek to find out what they can do, testing them first at the spinning-wheel. The spinning quartet ("When the Foot the Wheel turns lightly") is very gay and full of humor, and is one of the most delightful concerted numbers in the opera. The brothers soon find that their new servants are useless, but they are so pleased with them that they decide to keep them. At last Nancy, in a pet, kicks her wheel over and runs off, followed by Plunkett. Lionel, left alone with Martha, grows very tender to the new servant, and at last finds himself violently in love. He snatches a rose from her bosom, and refuses to return it unless she will consent to sing. She replies with the familiar ballad, "'T is the last Rose of Summer," which Flotow has interpolated in this scene, and in the performance of which he makes a charming effect by introducing the tenor in the close. Her singing only makes him the more desperately enamoured, and he asks her to be his wife on the spot, only to find himself the victim of Martha's sport, although his devotion and sincerity have made a deep impression upon her. Plunkett and Nancy at last return, and another charming quartet follows, "Midnight sounds," better known as the "Good Night Quartet." The two brothers retire, but Martha and Nancy, aided by Tristan, who has followed them and discovered their whereabouts, make good their escape. The next scene opens in the woods, where several farmers are drinking and carousing, among them Plunkett, who sings a rollicking drinking-song ("I want to ask you"). Their sport is interrupted by a hunting-party, composed of the Queen and her court ladies. Plunkett and Lionel recognize their fugitive servants among them, though the ladies disclaim all knowledge of the farmers. Plunkett attempts to seize Nancy, but the huntresses attack him and chase him away, leaving Lionel and Lady Henrietta

Sembrich as *Martha*

Copyright, Aimé Dupont

together again. The scene contains two of the most beautiful numbers in the opera, — the tenor solo, "Like a Dream bright and fair" ("M' appari" in the Italian version), and a romance for soprano ("Here in deepest Forest Shadows"); and the act closes with a beautiful concerted finale, quintet and chorus, which is worked up with great power. In this finale the despairing Lionel bethinks him of his ring. He gives it to Plunkett, desiring him to present it to the Queen. By means of the jewel it is discovered that he is the only son of the late Earl of Derby, and she orders his estates, of which he has been unjustly deprived, to be restored to him.

The last act is not important in a musical sense, for the climax is attained in the previous finale. The dramatic denouement is soon reached, and the Lady Henrietta, who has for some time been seriously in love with Lionel, is at last united to him; and it is almost needless to add that the fortunes of Plunkett and Nancy are also joined. The charm of "Martha" is its liveliness in action and tunefulness in music. Though not a great opera from a musical point of view, it is one of the most popular in the modern repertory, and though few others have been performed so many times, it still retains that popularity. Its melodies, though sung in every country of the civilized world by amateurs and professional artists, have not yet lost their charm.

STRADELLA

"Stradella," romantic opera in three acts, was first written as a lyric drama and produced at the Palais Royal Théâtre, Paris, in 1837, and was subsequently rewritten in its present form under the title of "Alessandro Stradella" and produced at Hamburg, December 30, 1844. The English version, which was somewhat altered by Bunn, was produced in London, June 6, 1846. The story follows the historic narrative of Stradella, the Italian musician, except in the denouement. Stradella woos and wins Leonora, the fair ward of Bassi, a rich Venetian nobleman, with whom the latter is himself in love. They fly to Rome and are married. Bassi hires two bravoes, Barbarino and Malvolio, to follow them and kill Stradella. They track him to his house, and while the bridal party are absent enter and conceal themselves, Bassi being with them. Upon this occasion, however, they do not wait to accomplish their purpose. Subsequently they gain admission again in the guise of pilgrims, and are hospitably received by Stradella. In the next scene Stradella, Leonora, and the two bravoes are together in the same apartment, singing the praises of their native Italy. During their laudations the chorus of a band of pilgrims on their way to the shrine of the Virgin is heard, and Leonora and Stradella go out to greet them. The bravoes have been so moved by Stradella's singing that they hesitate in their purpose. Bassi enters and upbraids them, and finally, by the proffer of a still larger sum, induces them to consent to carry out his design. They conceal themselves. Stradella returns and rehearses a Hymn to the Virgin which he is to sing at the festivities on the morrow. Its exquisite beauty touches them so deeply that they rush out of their hiding-place, and falling at his feet confess the object of their visit and implore his forgiveness. Leonora enters, and is astonished to find her guardian present. Explanations follow, a reconciliation is effected, and the lovers are happy. The denouement differs from the historical story, which, according to Bonnet, Bourdelot, and others, ends with the death of the lovers at Genoa, at the hands of the hired assassins.

The opera is one of the most charming of Flotow's works for its apt union of very melodious music with dramatic interest. Its most beautiful numbers are Stradella's serenade ("Horch, Liebchen, horch!"), the following nocturne ("Durch die Thäler, über Hügel"), the brilliant and animated carnival chorus ("Freudesausen, Jubelbrausen") of the masqueraders who assist in the elopement, in the first act; the aria of Leonora in her bridal chamber ("Seid meiner Wonne"), the rollicking drinking-song of the two bravoes ("'Raus mit dem Nass aus dem Fass") and the bandit ballad ("Tief in den Abruzzen") sung by Stradella, in the second act; an exquisite terzetto ("Sag doch an, Freund Barbarino") sung by Bassi and the two bravoes when they hesitate to perform their work, and Stradella's lovely Hymn to the Virgin ("Jungfrau Maria! Himmlisch verklärte"), in the last act.

GENÉE

FRANZ FRIEDRICH RICHARD GENÉE, a German light opera composer, was born at Danzig, February 7, 1823, and died at Baden, June 15, 1895. His first studies were in medicine, but he soon abandoned them and went to Berlin and studied music. Between the years 1848 and 1867 he was theatre capellmeister in ten different places in Germany, Bohemia, and Holland, and from 1868 to 1878 held the same position at the theatre An der Wien, Vienna. His principal operas are "Der Geiger aus Tirol" (1857); "Die Generalprobe," and "Am Runenstein," — the last with Flotow (1868); "Der Seekadett" (1876); "Nanon," "Die Piraten," and "Die Dreizehn" (1887). Besides his operettas, he wrote several librettos for Millöcker, Suppé, and Strauss, J.

NANON

"Nanon," opera comique, in three acts, text by Zell, was first produced in Vienna in 1877. The scene is laid in Paris in the time of Louis XIV. The first act opens at the inn of the Golden Lamb, near the gates of Paris, kept by Nanon, who has become so famous for her wit and beauty that the Marquis de Marsillac, director of the Royal Theatre, takes his nephew Hector there to see her. Thither also goes Ninon de l'Enclos, the famous beauty, to get a sight of Nanon, who, she suspects, has attracted the attentions of her own lover, the Marquis d'Aubigné. She is told that Nanon is to be married to Grignan, the drummer, and returns to the city with her suspicions allayed. Grignan, however, is in reality the Marquis, who, in the disguise of a drummer, intends to abduct Nanon. After a serenade to her she surprises him with a proposal of marriage; but when everything is ready for the ceremony, the Marquis secures his own arrest by his colonel on account of a duel. While grieving over the arrest, Nanon receives a ring and some friendly assurances from Gaston, the page of Ninon de l'Enclos, and thereupon turns to her for help in rescuing the supposed Grignan from death, which is the penalty for duelling.

The second act opens in Ninon's salon. Marsillac, his nephew, and an abbé, who is one of Ninon's lovers and confessor of Mme. de Maintenon, are present at a ball, likewise D'Aubigné, who is reproached by Ninon for having remained away so long and forgotten her birthday. To escape embarrassment he sings to her the same serenade he had sung to Nanon. Shortly afterwards Nanon arrives to seek Ninon's aid in saving Grignan. In the meantime D'Aubigné, jealous of Hector, because he pays court both to Nanon and Ninon, challenges him, and they hurry into the latter's garden and settle their quarrel with the sword. During their absence Marsillac, who has noted Grignan's serenade, also sings it, accompanied by the musicians of the court chapel, but is only laughed at for his trouble. When D'Aubigné returns from the duel, he is asked to clear up the mystery of this song; but before he can do so the guard, who has seen the duel, enters and arrests Hector, who has been wounded, and refuses to give the name of his opponent.

The third act opens in the private chapel of Mme. de Maintenon, where the Abbé sings to her the same serenade in the form of a hymn. Marsillac appears to ask for Hector's pardon, and receives it, when it appears that D'Aubigné was the challenging party. D'Aubigné thereupon congratulates Ninon upon her birthday with the serenade, and Marsillac repeats it. Ninon and Nanon next appear to intercede for their lovers, D'Aubigné and Grignan. The King presents Nanon with the life of Grignan, and she in turn, recognizing Grignan, presents the pardon to Ninon. Touched by her generosity, Grignan offers Nanon his hand, and Mme. de Maintenon, who is somewhat uneasy at the King's evident admiration for Nanon, gives her consent, and she is made Marquise d'Aubigné.

The music of "Nanon" is gay and brilliant throughout. The principal numbers are the serenade, a minstrel's song, as it is usually designated ("Ah! what a joyful Day is this; I am so full of Glee"), which is heard in various forms in all three acts; the opening drinking-choruses; Nanon's ballad ("Once before this Tavern straying"); the jolly chorus of the country relatives ("Here we come in Troops of Dozens, Uncles, Nephews, Aunts, and Cousins"); Gaston's ballad ("All that Frenchmen now will heed"); Hector's song ("Young appearing"), in the second act; and the lively concerted finale of the last act.

GLUCK

CHRISTOPH WILLIBALD GLUCK, one of the most eminent of German operatic composers, was born at Weidenwang, in the Upper Palatinate, July 2, 1714. He began his musical studies in a Bohemian Jesuits' School at the age of twelve. In his eighteenth year he went to Prague, where he continued his education with Czernhorsky. Four years later he was fortunate enough to secure Prince Melzi for a patron, who sent him to Milan, where he completed his studies with Sammartini. From 1741 to 1745 he produced numerous operas, which were well received, and in the latter year visited London, where he brought out several works, among them "La Caduta de' Giganti." His English experience was far from satisfactory, and he soon returned to Germany, stopping at Paris on the way, where Rameau's operas had a strong influence upon him. From 1746 to 1762 he wrote a large number of operas, with varying success so far as performance was concerned, but with great and lasting benefit to his style and fame, as was shown when his "Orpheus" was first produced, October 5, 1762. Its success determined him at once to acquaint the musical world with his purpose to reform the opera by making it dramatically musical instead of purely lyric, thus paving the way for the great innovator of Baireuth. "Alceste," produced in 1767, was the first embodiment of these ideas. Strong criticism greeted it, to which he replied with "Iphigénie en Aulide," written in 1772, and performed for the first time in Paris two years later, under the auspices of Marie Antoinette, who had once been his pupil. It was followed by "Orpheus and

Eurydice," adapted from his earlier work of the same name, which met with brilliant success. In 1777 he brought out "Armide." It aroused an unprecedented excitement. Piccini was at that time in Paris. He was the representative of the old Italian school. His partisans gathered about him, and a furious war was waged between the Gluckists and Piccinists for three or four years; the combatants displaying a bitterness of criticism and invective even worse than that which Wagner brought down upon his devoted head. When Gluck brought out his great work, "Iphigénie en Tauride," in 1779, however, the Piccinists quitted the field and acknowledged the reformer's superiority. "Echo et Narcisse" was written in the same year, but "Iphigénie en Tauride" was his last great work. He retired shortly afterwards to Vienna, where he died November 15, 1787.

Orpheus

"Orpheus," the libretto by the Italian poet Calzabigi, was first produced at Vienna, October 5, 1762, and for the first time outlined the new ideas which Gluck had advanced for the reform of the lyric stage. Twelve years later the composer revised the work. Several new numbers were added, its acts were extended to three, and the principal role was rewritten for a high tenor in place of the alto, to whom it had been originally assigned. In this form it was brought out at the Paris Académie, August 2, 1774. In 1859 it was revived in Paris, for which occasion Berlioz restored the original alto part for Mme. Viardot-Garcia. With its performances in this country by the American Opera Troupe, during the season of 1885–1886, under the direction of Mr. Theodore Thomas, the American public is familiar. The three soloists during that season were Helene Hastreiter, Emma Juch, and Minnie Dilthey, and its first performance was in New York, January 8, 1886.

The story, except in its denouement, closely follows the antique legend. After performing the funeral rites of Eurydice, Orpheus resolves to seek for her in the world of Shades, having received permission from Zeus upon condition that he will not look upon her until they have safely returned. Orpheus descends to Hades; and though his way is barred by phantoms, his pleading appeals and the tender tones of his lute induce them to make way for him. He finds Eurydice in the Elysian fields, and taking her by the hand leads her on to the upper world. In a fatal moment he yields to her desire to see him, and she sinks back lifeless. Love, however, comes to the rescue, and full of compassion, restores her. Thus the happy lovers are reunited; and the opera closes without the tragic denouement of the old myth. In the American performances the opera was divided into four acts, which is the order followed here.

The short overture is characterized by a grandeur and solemnity that well befit the pathetic story. The curtain rises upon a grotto containing the tomb of Eurydice, against which Orpheus mournfully leans, while upon its steps youths and maidens are strewing flowers as they chant the sombre song, "Ah! in our still and mournful Meadow." The sad wail of Orpheus upon the single word "Eurydice" is heard through its strains, which continually increase in solemnity. At last, as if too much to bear, Orpheus interrupts their threnody with the words, "The Sounds of your Lament increase my bitter Anguish." The chorus in reply resumes its melancholy tribute to Eurydice and then retires, leaving Orpheus alone, who in a monologue full of pathos and sorrow ("My Eurydice! my Eurydice! lost forever"), sings his grief and implores the gods to restore his loved one. In answer to his prayer, Amor, god of love, appears and announces that the gods have been moved to compassion; and if his song and lyre

can appease the phantoms, death shall give back Eurydice
upon the conditions already named. The act closes with
the joyful song of Orpheus, "Will pitying Heaven with
wondrous Favor restore mine own?"

The second act opens in the abysses of the underworld.
Flames shoot up amid great masses of rock and from
yawning caverns, throwing their lurid glare upon the phantoms,
who, writhing in furious indignation, demand in wild
and threatening chorus, as the tones of Orpheus's lyre are
heard, "Who through this awful Place, thinking alive to
pass, rashly dares venture here?" Madly they call upon
Cerberus "to kill thy new Prey here." The barking of the
triple-headed monster is heard in the tones of the orchestra.
They surround Orpheus as he approaches, and with
renewed clamor continue this thrilling chorus. In the
midst of its cruel intensity is heard the appealing voice of
Orpheus ("In Pity be moved by my Grief"). With overwhelming
wrath comes the reiterated monosyllable, "No,"
from the Furies, — one of the most daring and powerful
effects ever made in dramatic music, — followed by another
appalling chorus, as they announce to him, "These
are the Depths of Hell, where the Avengers dwell." At
last they are touched by the charm of his music and the
sorrow of his story; and as their fury dies away, the song
of Orpheus grows more exultant as he contemplates the
reunion with Eurydice.

The gates of the lower world are opened, and in the
third act Orpheus enters Elysium. The scene begins with
a tender, lovely song by Eurydice and her companions
("In this tranquil and lovely Abode of the Blest"), the
melody taken by the flute with string accompaniment.
All is bright and cheerful and in striking contrast with the
gloom and terror of the Stygian scene we have just left.
After a short recitative ("How mild a Day, without a
Noon"), Orpheus seeks her. She is brought to him by a

Schalchi as *Orpheus*

GLUCK

crowd of shadows; and breaking out in joyful song he takes her by the hand and turns his face to the upper world.

The fourth act is almost entirely an impassioned duet between Orpheus and Eurydice. He releases her hand for fear that he may turn and look upon her. Eurydice chides him ("Am I changed or grown old that thou wilt not behold me?"). In vain he urges her to follow him. She upbraids him for his coldness, and demands one glance as a test of his love. He still refuses, and then she sorrowfully bids him farewell. At last, overcome with weariness and sorrow, he gazes upon her; and at that instant she falls lifeless. Then Orpheus breaks out in that immortal song, the "Che faro senz' Eurydice" ("I have lost my Eurydice"), the beauty and pathos of which neither time nor change of musical custom can ever mar. He is about to take his life with his sword; but Amor suddenly appears upon the scene, stays his hand, and tells him the gods are moved by his sufferings. He restores Eurydice to life, and the opera closes with a beautiful terzetto in Love's temple. The denouement is followed by ballet music.

GOETZ

HERMANN GOETZ, to whose life attaches a mournful interest, was born at Königsberg, December 17, 1840. He had no regular instruction in music until his seventeenth year. At that period he began his studies with Köhler, and then passed successively under the tuition of Stern, Ulrich, and Von Bülow. At the age of twenty-three he obtained a position as organist at Winterthur, and also taught at Zurich. It was during this time that he composed his opera, "The Taming of the Shrew," while struggling with actual poverty. For years he attempted to secure a hearing for his opera; but it was not until 1874 that its great merit was recognized, for in that year it was produced at Mannheim with instant success. Its fame travelled all over Germany. It was performed in Vienna in 1875, and the same year in Leipsic and Berlin, and reached London in 1878. It was not heard in this country until the season of 1885–1886, when it was produced by the American Opera Company. The composer did not live long enough, however, to enjoy the fruits of his work, as he died in 1876. He also left behind him an unfinished score of a second opera, "Francesca di Rimini," which was completed by his friend Franke at his request, but proved a failure. His other works include a symphony in F, a suite for orchestra, and many chamber compositions.

THE TAMING OF THE SHREW

"The Taming of the Shrew," as related in the sketch of the composer's life, was written about the year 1863, and first produced at Mannheim in 1872. Its first performance in this country was in January, 1886, when the cast was as follows:

Katharine	PAULINE L'ALLEMAND.
Bianca	KATE BENSBERG.
Petruchio	WILLIAM H. LEE.
Baptista	W. H. HAMILTON.
Lucentio	W. H. FESSENDEN.
Hortensio	ALONZO STODDARD.
A Tailor	JOHN HOWSON.

The libretto is freely adapted from Shakespeare's comedy by Joseph Victor Widmann. The plot is very simple. Baptista, a rich Paduan gentleman, has two daughters, — Katharine, the shrew, and Bianca, of sweet and lovable disposition. Both Hortensio and Lucentio are in love with Bianca; but the obdurate father will not listen to either until Katharine shall have been married. In this apparently hopeless situation a gleam of comfort appears in the suit which the rich gallant Petruchio of Verona pays to Katharine, in disgust with the sycophants who have been manifesting such deference to his wealth. The remainder of the story is occupied with the details of the various processes by which he breaks and tames the shrew, and the ingenious ruse by which Lucentio gains the hand of the lovely Bianca.

The curtain rises upon a night scene in Padua, with Lucentio before Bianca's house singing a melodious serenade. Its strains are interrupted, however, by a hurly-burly in the house, caused by the shrew's demonstrations. The tumult is transferred to the street, and gives occasion for a very vigorous ensemble. When the crowd disperses, Lucentio resumes his serenade, Bianca appears upon the balcony, and the two join in a very pleasing duet. The number is also interrupted by Hortensio, at the head of a band of street musicians, who has also come to serenade his mistress. The encounter of the two lovers brings on a quarrel, which is averted, however, by the interposition of Baptista. A duet follows between them, at the close of which Lucentio retires. Petruchio now appears upon the scene, and learns from Hortensio of Katharine's vixenish disposition, which determines him to woo her. With a stirring song ("She is a Wife for such a Man created"), the act comes to an end.

The second act opens in a chamber in Baptista's house, where Katharine is berating Bianca for accepting serenades from suitors, and abuses her even to blows. The scene closes with a vigorous song for Katharine ("I'll give myself to no one"), which is greeted with cynical applause by Petruchio, Baptista, Lucentio, and Hortensio, who enter, the last two disguised as teachers. In the next scene, Petruchio and Katharine alone, we have the turbulent wooing, which is accompanied throughout by characteristic music. As the others return Petruchio announces his success in the song, "All is well," the theme of which is taken by the quintet, closing the act.

The third is the most interesting act of the three. It opens on the day selected for the wedding of Katharine and Petruchio, in Baptista's garden; the first number being a charming quintet for Katharine, Bianca, Lucentio, Hortensio, and Baptista. The guests are present, but Petruchio is not there. An explanation is made, followed by a chorus as the guests leave; and then Bianca is free to take her lessons, in one of which Lucentio makes his avowal of love to her. The arrangement of the two lessons is both unique and skilful. Lucentio turns the familiar opening lines of the Æneid ("Arma virumque cano," etc.), into a love song by declarations interposed between them; while Hortensio explains the mysteries of the scale to her, each line of his love song beginning with one of its letters. It is soon found, however, that Lucentio is the accepted lover. Baptista now enters and announces Petruchio's return, which leads to a charming quartet. The finale of the opera, which is very spirited, includes the preparations for the marriage feast, the wedding, and the scene in which Petruchio abruptly forces his bride to leave with him for his country house.

GOLDMARK

KARL GOLDMARK was born at Keszthely, Hungary, May 18, 1832. He first studied with the violinist Jansa at Vienna, and in his fifteenth year entered the Conservatory in that city. Little is known of the events of his early life. Indeed, his success in his profession is generally credited more to his native ability and industry than to the influence of teachers or schools. He began composition at an early period, and produced his works in concerts with much success under the encouragement of Hellmesberger and others, who recognized his ability before he had made any impression out of Vienna. Four of his compositions, the "Sakuntala" overture, the operas "The Queen of Sheba" and "Merlin," and "Die ländliche Hochzeit" ("The Country Wedding") symphony have made a permanent reputation for him. The overture and operas have been performed many times in this country. Besides these he has written several pieces of chamber music.

THE QUEEN OF SHEBA

"The Queen of Sheba" was first produced in Vienna, March 10, 1875, and was first heard in this country at New York, December 2, 1885, when the cast was as follows:

King Solomon	Herr ROBINSON.
High Priest	Herr FISCHER.
Sulamith	Frl. LEHMANN.
Assad	Herr STRITT.
Baal Hanan	Herr ALEXI.
Queen of Sheba	Frau KRAMER-WEIDL.
Astaroth	Frl. BRANDT.

The libretto by Mosenthal is one of rare excellence in its skilful treatment of situations and arrangement of scenes with the view to spectacular and dramatic effect. The Biblical story has but little to do with the action of the opera beyond the mere fact of the famous visit of the Queen of Sheba to Solomon. The stirring episodes during the journey and the visit spring from the librettist's imagination. The story in substance is as follows:

King Solomon, learning of the Queen's intention to visit him, sends his favorite courtier Assad to escort her. While she waits outside the gates of Jerusalem, Assad announces her arrival to the King and Sulamith, the daughter of the high priest, to whom the courtier is affianced. Observing his disturbed looks, the King, after dismissing his attendants, inquires the cause. Assad replies that on their journey through the forest he had encountered a nymph bathing whose beauty had so impressed him as to banish even the thoughts of his affianced. The wise Solomon counsels him to marry Sulamith at once. Meanwhile the Queen comes into the King's presence, and as she lifts her veil reveals the unknown fair one. She affects ignorance of Assad's passion; but when she learns that he is to wed Sulamith love for him springs up in her own breast. Upon the day of the wedding ceremony Assad, carried away by his longing for the Queen, declares her to be his divinity, and is condemned to death for profaning the Temple. Both the Queen and Sulamith appeal to the King for mercy. He consents at last to save his life, but banishes him to the desert. The Queen seeks him there, and makes an avowal of her love; but Assad repulses her. As Sulamith comes upon the scene a simoom sweeps across the desert. They perish in each other's arms; while in a mirage the Queen and her attendants are seen journeying to their home.

The first act opens in the great hall of Solomon's palace with a brilliant, joyous chorus ("Open the Halls, adorn the Portals") in praise of the King's glory. After the entrance of the high priest, Sulamith sings a fascinating bridal song ("My own Assad returns"), richly Oriental both in music and sentiment, dreamy and luxurious in its tone, and yet full of joyous expectation, with characteristic choral refrain and dainty accompaniment. The fourth and fifth scenes are full of agitation and unrest, and lead up to Assad's explanation of his perturbed condition ("At Lebanon's Foot I met Arabia's Queen"), a monologue aria of rich, glowing color, and reaching a fine dramatic climax as it progresses from its sensuous opening to the passionate intensity of its finale. It is followed by the entrance of the Queen, accompanied by a brilliant march and a jubilant chorus ("To the Sun of the South our Welcome we bring") and a stirring concerted number, describing the recognition of the Queen by Assad; after which the chorus resumes its jubilant strain, bringing the act to a close.

The second act opens in the gardens of the palace and discloses the Queen, who gives expression to her love for Assad and her hatred of Sulamith in an impassioned aria ("Let me from the festal Splendor"). In the second scene Astaroth, her slave, appears and lures Assad by a weird strain, which is one of the most effective passages in the opera ("As the Heron calls in the Reeds"). After a short arioso by Assad ("Magical Sounds, intoxicating Fragrance"), a passionate duet with the Queen follows, interrupted by the call of the Temple-guard to prayer. The scene changes to the interior of the sanctuary with its religious service; and with it the music changes also to solemn Hebrew melodies with the accompaniment of the sacred instruments, leading up to the stirring finale in which Assad declares his passion for the Queen, amid choruses of execration by the people.

The third act opens in the banquet-hall upon a scene of festivity introduced by the graceful bee dance of the Almas. It is followed by the powerful appeal of the Queen for Assad's life, rising to an intensely dramatic pitch as she warns the King of the revenge of her armed hosts ("When Sheba's iron Lances splinter and Zion's Throne in Ruins falls"). In sad contrast comes the mournful chant which accompanies Sulamith as she passes to the vestal's home ("The Hour that robbed me of him"), and ends in her despairing cry rising above the chorus of attendants as Solomon also refuses her petition.

The last act passes in the desert. Beneath a solitary palm tree Assad laments the destiny which pursues him ("Whither shall I wend my weary Steps?"). In the next scene the Queen appears, and an agitated duet follows, ending with her repulse. Assad in despair calls upon death to relieve him. The sky darkens. Clouds of sand envelop the fugitive. The palm bends before the blast as the simoom sweeps by. The storm at last subsides. The sky grows brighter; and the Queen and her attendants, with their elephants and camels, appear in a mirage, journeying eastward, as Sulamith and her lover expire in each other's arms. As their duet dies away, the chorus of maidens brings the act to a close with a few strains from the love-song in the first act.

MERLIN

The opera of "Merlin" was first performed at Vienna, November 17, 1886, and was heard for the first time in this country at New York, January 3, 1887, under the direction of Mr. Walter Damrosch, with the following cast:

King Arthur	Herr ROBINSON.
Modred	Herr KEMLITZ.
Lancelot	Herr BURSCH.
Gawein	Herr HEINRICH.
Glendower	Herr VON MILDE
Merlin	Herr ALVARY.
Viviane	Frl. LEHMANN.
The Fay Morgana	Frl. BRANDT.
Bedwyr	Herr SIEGLITZ.
The Demon	Herr FISCHER.

The libretto of the opera is by Siegfried Lipiner. The scene is laid in Wales, and the hero, Merlin, is familiar as the wizard. The story is as follows:

The Devil, seeking to banish all good from the world, unites himself to a virgin that he may beget a child who shall aid him in his fell purpose. The child is Merlin, who partakes of the mother's goodness, and instead of aiding his father, seeks to thwart his design. The Devil thereupon consults the Fay Morgana, who tells him Merlin will lose his power if he falls in love. In the opening scene King Arthur sends Lancelot to Merlin for aid and Merlin promises him victory and achieves it by the assistance of his familiar, a demon, who is in league with the Devil. Tired of his service to Merlin, the demon contrives to have him meet the beautiful Viviane, with whom he falls in love. The second act transpires in Merlin's enchanted garden, and reveals his growing passion, and at the same time his waning power of magic; for when once more Arthur summons his aid he attempts to tear himself away from her only to realize his weakness. She seeks to detain him by throwing a magic veil over him which has been given her by the demon; in an instant the scene changes, and Merlin appears confined to a rock by fiery chains, while the demon mocks him from a neighboring eminence, and Viviane gives way to anguish. In the last act Viviane is told by the Fay Morgana that Merlin's release can only be secured by woman's self-sacrifice. Once more an appeal for help comes to him from Arthur, and he promises his soul to the demon in exchange for his freedom. His chains fall off. He rushes into the battle and secures the victory, but is fatally wounded. The demon claims him; but Viviane, remembering the words of the Fay Morgana, stabs herself and thus balks him of his expectant prey.

Like Wagner's operas, "Merlin" has its motives, the principal ones being that of the demon, or the evil principle, and two love motives. In its general treatment it is also Wagnerian. The first scene opens with the spirited message of Lancelot to Glendower, beseeching Merlin's aid for the hard-pressed Arthur. It is followed by the strains of Merlin's harp in the castle and his assurance of victory, and these in turn by very descriptive incantation music summoning the demon and the supernatural agencies which shall compass the defeat of Arthur's enemies. Then comes the interview between the demon and the Fay Morgana, in which he learns the secret of Merlin's weakness. In the next scene Arthur returns from his victory over the Saxons to the tempo of a stirring march, and accompanied by the joyous choruses of women. A vigorous episode, in which Bedwyr, one of Arthur's knights, is charged with treachery, is followed by Merlin's chant of victory with chorus accompaniment. As its strains die away a distant horn announces Viviane, who makes her appearance singing a breezy hunting song with her maidens, leading up to a spirited septet. Then follows the baffled attempt of Viviane to crown Merlin, the scene closing with a repetition of the chant of victory and the choruses of jubilation.

The second act opens in the enchanted gardens of Merlin, the first scene of which reveals a conspiracy to seize the crown during Arthur's absence and proclaim Modred king, and the farewell of Arthur and his suite to Merlin. The magic-veil scene follows with its fascinating dance tempos, and leads with its graceful measures up to the passionate love scene between Merlin and Viviane, which is harshly broken in upon by the clash of arms between Modred and his perfidious companions and the faithful friends of Arthur. A dramatic scene of great energy follows, in which Viviane at last throws the magic veil around Merlin, resulting in the transformation already mentioned.

The last act opens with Viviane's mournful lament for the wretched fate which she has brought upon her lover, and the announcement of the means by which he may be released made to her in slumber by the Fay Morgana. Her maidens seek to rouse her with choral appeals in which phrases of her hunting-song are heard. Meanwhile mocking spirits appear to Merlin and taunt him in characteristic music. Then follows the compact with the Demon which releases him. He rushes into the battle accompanied by Viviane's exultant song, but a funeral march soon tells the story of his fate. A very dramatic ensemble contains the deed of self-sacrifice by which Viviane ends her life to redeem Merlin from the demon, and with this powerful effect the opera closes.

GOUNOD

CHARLES FRANÇOIS GOUNOD was born in Paris, June 17, 1818. He studied music in the Conservatory, under the direction of Halevy, Lesueur, and Paer, in 1839 obtained the first prize, and, under the usual regulations, went to Italy. While at Rome he devoted himself largely to religious music. On his return to Paris he became organist of the Missions Étrangères, and for a time seriously thought of taking orders, but in 1851 he brought out his first opera, "Sappho," which met with success, and at this point his active musical career began. In 1852 he became conductor of the Orphéon, and wrote the choruses for Ponsard's tragedy of "Ulysse." The year 1854 brought a five-act opera, "La Nonne Sanglante," founded on a legend in Lewis's "Monk." In 1858 he made his first essay in opera comique, and produced "Le Médecin malgré lui," which met with remarkable success. The next year "Faust" was performed, and placed him in the front rank of living composers. "Philémon et Baucis" appeared in 1860, and "La Reine de Saba," which was afterwards performed in English as "Irene," in 1862. In 1863 he brought out the pretty pastoral opera, "Mireille." This was succeeded in 1866 by "La Colombe," known in English as "The Pet Dove," and in 1867 by "Roméo et Juliette." In 1877 he produced "Cinq-Mars," and in 1878 his last opera, "Polyeucte." He has also written much church music, the more important works being the "Messe Solennelle," a "Stabat Mater," the oratorios "Tobie" and "The Redemption," a

"De Profundis," an "Ave Verum," and many single hymns and songs, among which "Nazareth" is universally popular. His list of compositions for orchestra is also very large, and includes such popular pieces as the "Saltarello," "Funeral March of a Marionette," and the "Meditation," based on Bach's First Prelude, which is accompanied by a soprano solo. He was elected a member of the Institut de France in 1866.

Faust

"Faust," grand opera in five acts, words by Barbier and Carré, founded upon Goethe's tragedy, was first produced at the Théâtre Lyrique, Paris, March 19, 1859, with the following cast of the principal parts:

Marguerite	Mme. MIOLAN-CARVALHO.
Siebel	Mlle. FAIVRE.
Faust	M. BARBOT.
Valentin	M. REGNAL.
Mephistopheles	M. BALANQUÉ.
Martha	Mme. DUCLOS.

The opera was first produced in London as "Faust," June 11, 1863; in English, January 23, 1864; and in Germany as "Margarethe."

The story of the opera follows Goethe's tragedy very closely, and is confined to the first part. It may be briefly told: Faust, an aged German student, satiated with human knowledge and despairing of his ability to unravel the secrets of nature, summons the evil spirit Mephistopheles to his assistance, and contracts to give him his soul in exchange for a restoration to youth. Mephistopheles effects the transformation, and reveals to him the vision of Marguerite, a beautiful village maiden, with whom Faust at once falls in love. They set out upon their travels and encounter her at the Kermesse. She has been left by her brother Valentin, a soldier, in care of Dame Martha, who

Melba as *Marguerite*

Copyright, Aimé Dupont

proves herself a careless guardian. Their first meeting is a casual one; but subsequently he finds her in her garden, and with the help of the subtle Mephistopheles succeeds in engaging the young girl's affection. Her simple lover, Siebel, is discarded, and his nosegay is thrown away at sight of the jewels with which Faust tempts her. When Valentin returns from the wars he learns of her temptation and subsequent ruin. He challenges the seducer, and in the encounter is slain by the intervention of Mephistopheles. Overcome by the horror of her situation, Marguerite becomes insane, and in her frenzy kills her child. She is thrown into prison, where Faust and Mephistopheles find her. Faust urges her to fly with them, but she refuses, and places her reliance for salvation upon earnest prayer, and sorrow for the wrong she has done. Pleading for forgiveness, she expires; and as Mephistopheles exults at the catastrophe he has wrought, angels appear amid the music of the celestial choirs and bear the sufferer to heaven.

The first act is in the nature of a prelude, and opens with a long soliloquy ("Interrogo invano") by Faust, in which he laments the unsatisfactoriness of life. It is interwoven with delightful snatches of chorus heard behind the scenes, a duet with Mephistopheles ("Ma il ciel"), and the delicate music accompanying the vision of Marguerite.

The second act is contained in a single setting, the Kermesse, in which the chorus plays an important part. In the first scene the choruses of students, soldiers, old men, girls, and matrons are quaintly contrasted, and full of animation and characteristic color. In the second, Valentin sings a tender song ("O santa medaglia") to a medallion of his sister which he wears as a charm. It is followed by a grim and weird drinking-song ("Dio dell' or"), sung by Mephistopheles. The latter then strikes fire from the fountain into his cup, and proposes the health of Marguerite. Valentin springs forward to resent the insult, only to find his sword broken in his hands. The students and soldiers recognize the spirit of evil, and overcome him by presenting the hilts of their swords in the form of a cross, the scene being accompanied by one of the most effective choruses in the work ("Tu puvi la spada"). The tempter gone, the scene resumes its gayety, and the act closes with one of the most animated and delightful of waltz tempos ("Come la brezza").

The third act is the garden scene, full of fascinating detail, and breathes the very spirit of poetry and music combined in a picture of love which has never been excelled in tenderness and beauty on the operatic stage. Its principal numbers are a short and simple but very beautiful ballad for Siebel ("La parlate d' amor"); a passionate aria for tenor ("Salve dimora casta e pura"), in which Faust greets Marguerite's dwelling; a double number, which is superb in its contrasts, — the folk-song ("C'era un re di Thule"), a plaintive little ballad sung at the spinning-wheel by Marguerite, and the bravura jewel-song ("Ah! e' strano poter"), which is the very essence of delicacy and almost childish glee; the quartet commencing, "V'appogiato al bracchio mio," which is of striking interest by the independent manner in which the two pairs of voices are treated and combined in the close; and the closing duet ("Sempre amar") between Faust and Marguerite, which is replete with tenderness and passion, and closes in strains of almost ecstatic rapture, the fatal end of which is foreshadowed by the mocking laugh of Mephistopheles breaking in upon its lingering cadences.

The fourth act is known as the Cathedral act, and established Gounod's reputation as a writer of serious music. It opens with a scena for Marguerite, who has been taunted by the girls at the fountain ("Nascose eran là le crudeli"), in which she laments her sad fate. The scene abruptly changes to the square in front of the cathedral, where the

Saleza as *Faust*
Copyright, Aimé Dupont

Plançon as *Mephistopheles*
Copyright, Aimé Dupont

soldiers, Valentin among them, are returning, to the jubilant though somewhat commonplace strains of the march, "Deponiam il branda." As the soldiers retire and Valentin goes in quest of Marguerite, Faust and Mephistopheles appear before the house, and the latter sings a grotesque and literally infernal serenade ("Tu, che fai l' addormentata"). Valentin appears and a quarrel ensues, leading up to a spirited trio. Valentin is slain, and with his dying breath pronounces a malediction ("Margherita! maledetta") upon his sister. The scene changes to the church, and in wonderful combination we hear the appeals of Marguerite for mercy, the taunting voice of the tempter, and the monkish chanting of the "Dies Iræ," mingled with the solemn strains of the organ.

The last act is usually presented in a single scene, the prison, but it contains five changes. After a weird prelude, the Walpurgis revel begins, in which short, strange phrases are heard from unseen singers. The night scene changes to a hall of pagan enchantment, and again to the Brocken, where the apparition of Marguerite is seen. The orgy is resumed, when suddenly by another transformation we are taken to the prison where Marguerite is awaiting death. It is unnecessary to give its details. The scene takes the form of a terzetto, which is worked up with constantly increasing power to a climax of passionate energy, and at last dies away as Marguerite expires. It stands almost alone among effects of this kind in opera. The curtain falls upon a celestial chorus of apotheosis, the vision of the angels, and Mephistopheles cowering in terror before the heavenly messengers.

ROMÉO ET JULIETTE

"Roméo et Juliette," grand opera in five acts, words by Barbier and Carré, the subject taken from Shakespeare's tragedy of the same name, was first produced at the

Théâtre Lyrique, Paris, April 27, 1867, with Mme. Miolan-Carvalho in the role of Juliet. The story as told by the French dramatists in the main follows Shakespeare's tragedy very closely in its construction as well as in its dialogue. It is only necessary, therefore, to sketch its outlines. The first act opens with the festival at the house of Capulet. Juliet and Romeo meet there and fall in love, notwithstanding her betrothal to Paris. The hot-blooded Tybalt seeks to provoke a quarrel with Romeo, but is restrained by Capulet himself, and the act comes to a close with a resumption of the merry festivities. In the second act we have the balcony scene, quite literally taken from Shakespeare, with an episode, however, in the form of a temporary interruption by Gregory and retainers, whose appearance is rather absurd than otherwise. The third act is constructed in two scenes. The first is in the Friar's cell, where the secret marriage of the lovers takes place. In the second, we are introduced to a new character, invented by the librettist, — Stephano, Romeo's page, whose pranks while in search of his master provoke a general quarrel, in which Mercutio is slain by Tybalt, who in turn is killed by Romeo. When Capulet arrives upon the scene he condemns Romeo to banishment, who vows, however, that he will see Juliet again at all hazards. The fourth act is also made up of two scenes. The first is in Juliet's chamber, and is devoted to a duet between the two lovers. Romeo departs at dawn, and Capulet appears with Friar Laurence and announces his determination that the marriage with Paris shall be celebrated at once. Juliet implores the Friar's help, and he gives her the potion. The next scene is devoted to the wedding festivity, in the midst of which Juliet falls insensible from the effects of the sleeping-draught. The last act transpires in the tomb of the Capulets, where Romeo arrives, and believing his mistress dead takes poison.

Geraldine Farrar as *Juliet*

Juliet, reviving from the effects of the potion, and finding him dying, stabs herself with a dagger, and expires in his arms.

While many numbers are greatly admired, the opera as a whole has not been very successful. Had not "Faust," which it often recalls, preceded it, its fate might have been different. Still, it contains many strong passages and much beautiful writing. The favorite numbers are the waltz arietta, very much in the manner of the well-known "Il Bacio," at the Capulet festival, the Queen Mab song, by Mercutio ("Mab, regina di menzogne"), and the duet between Romeo and Juliet ("Di grazia, t' arrestaanc or!"), in the first act; the love music in the balcony scene of the second act, which inevitably recalls the garden music in "Faust"; an impressive solo for Friar Laurence ("Al vostro amor cocente"), followed by a vigorous trio and quartet, the music of which is massive and ecclesiastical in character, and the page's song ("Ah! col nibbio micidale"), in the third act; the duet of parting between Romeo and Juliet ("Tu dei partir ohime!"), the quartet ("Non temero mio ben") between Juliet, the nurse, Friar Laurence, and Capulet, and the dramatic solo for the Friar ("Bevi allor questo filtro"), as he gives the potion to Juliet, in the fourth act; and the elaborate orchestral prelude to the tomb scene in the last act.

Philémon and Baucis

"Philémon et Baucis," mythological idyl, in two acts, text by Barbier and Carré, was first produced at the Théâtre Lyrique, Paris, February 18, 1860.

This musical piece was originally composed for the Casino at Baden-Baden and in one act. Before it was produced there, Mme. Carvalho was so impressed with the score that she induced Gounod to make a three-act opera of it for her, and in that form she brought it out at the

Théâtre Lyrique, Paris, as stated above, the manager of the Casino in the meantime agreeing to exchange it for Gounod's "Colombe." It was not greatly appreciated at the Théâtre Lyrique, however, and it was next reset in two acts and transferred to the Opéra Comique where it has ever since remained in the repertory. It was first produced in England at Covent Garden in 1891.

The libretto of "Philémon et Baucis" is founded upon the well-known classical legend. Jupiter and Vulcan come down to earth to punish the Phrygians for their impiety, as reported by Mercury, and arriving in a storm which is one of the god's own creating they seek shelter in the cottage of the aged Philemon and Baucis. Finding that the old couple have lived happily together for many years and greatly pleased with his hospitable welcome, Jupiter transforms the milk at the simple supper into wine. Baucis recognizes Jupiter by this act and is greatly awed, but he calms her fears and promises to grant whatever she may wish. Her only wish is that she and Philemon may be young again. Jupiter thereupon puts them to sleep. An intermezzo follows in which the Phrygians are seen engaged in wild orgies. Vulcan remonstrates with them but they only mock at him. Jupiter then appears upon the scene and punishes them by precipitating an awful storm.

When the old couple awake they are in a palace instead of their cottage and their lost youth has been restored; but this brings on a sad condition of affairs, for Jupiter, with his usual susceptibility, falls in love with the charming rejuvenated Baucis, to which Philemon makes vigorous protest. A quarrel, their first one, ensues between Philemon and Baucis. The former curses Jupiter's gift and wishes back his peaceful old age. He even goes so far as to upset Jupiter's statue and at last leaves his wife to the god. Baucis is overcome with grief and finally persuades

Jupiter to grant her a second wish, which he consents to do upon condition that she will love him. She entreats him to make her old again. Philemon overhears her and joins in the request. Jupiter for once is honorable enough to promise to go back to Olympus and never interfere with their happiness again.

After an instrumental introduction in pastoral style, the principal motive of which is given by the oboe and repeated by full orchestra, the curtain rises upon a duet by Philemon and Baucis, characterized by grace and delicacy of sentiment ("Du répos voici l'heure"), which is followed by a bacchanalian chorus sung in the wings.

The next number is a dignified trio for Philemon and the two gods, Jupiter and Vulcan, who are incognito ("Étrangères sur ces bords"), which in turn is followed by Vulcan's couplets ("Au bruit des lourds marteaux"), the rhythm of which is abrupt and broken, significant of the god's physical misfortune. Jupiter next has an arietta ("Eh, quoi parceque Mercure"), which is followed by Baucis's tender and charming song ("Ah! si je redevenais belle"), and this by a short quartet, after which Jupiter closes the act with stanzas in which he bids sleep come to his generous hosts.

The second act opens with a symphonic prelude, full of rich color, in which the pastoral motive in the introduction to the first act recurs. Baucis upon awaking sings a graceful arietta which is followed by Jupiter's song ("Que m'importent de vaines scrupules?"). The next number is a brilliant aria written especially for Mme. Carvalho ("O riante nature"). A light, airy and exceeding graceful duet follows for Jupiter and Baucis ("Ne crains pas que j'oublie"). The motive of the first duet between the aged couple is heard and a delightful quartet closes the opera.

HALÉVY

JACQUES FRANÇOIS FROMENTHAL ELIAS HALÉVY was born at Paris, May 27, 1799, of Israelitish parents. His real name was Levy. He entered the Conservatory in 1809, and in 1819 obtained the Grand Prize for his cantata of "Hermione." After his arrival in Italy he wrote several minor pieces, but his music did not attract public attention until his return to Paris, when his three-act opera, "Clari," brought out December 9, 1828, with Malibran in the principal role, made a success. "Le Dilettante d'Avignon" (a satire on Italian librettos), "Manon Lescaut" (a ballet in three acts), "La Langue Musicale," "La Tentation," and "Les Souvenirs" rapidly followed "Clari," with alternating successes and failures. In 1835 his great work, "La Juive," appeared, and in the same year, "L'Eclair," one of his most charming operas, written without chorus for two tenors and two sopranos. It was considered at the time a marvellous feat that he should have produced two such opposite works in the same year, and great hopes were entertained that he would surpass them. These hopes failed, however. He subsequently wrote over twenty operas, among them "Guido et Ginevra" (1838); "Charles VI" (1842); "La Reine de Chypre" (1842); "Les Mousequetaires de la Reine" (1846); "Le Val d'Andorre" (1848); "La Tempête" (1853); "Le Juif Errant" (1855), and others; but "La Juive" and "L'Eclair" remained his masterpieces, and procured him admission into the Institute. He was also a professor in the Conservatory, and among his pupils were Gounod, Massé, Bazin, Duvernoy, Bizet, and others. He enjoyed many honors, and died March 17, 1862. A De Profundis was sung on the occasion of his funeral, written by four of his pupils, MM. Gounod, Massé, Bazin, and Cohen. As a composer he was influenced largely by Meyerbeer, and is remarkable rather for his large dramatic effects than for his melody.

The Jewess

"La Juive," grand opera in five acts, words by Scribe, the libretto originally written for Rossini and rejected in favor of "William Tell," was produced for the first time at the Académie, Paris, February 23, 1835, with the following cast of the principal parts:

Rachel	Mlle. CORNELIA FALCON.
Eudoxia	Mme. DORUS-GRAS.
Eleazar	M. NOURRIT.
Cardinal	M. LEVASSEUR.

It was first produced in England in French, July 29, 1846, and in Italian under the title of "La Ebrea," July 25, 1850. In this country it is most familiar in the German version. The scene of the opera is laid in Constance; time, 1414. Leopold, a prince of the empire, returning from the wars, is enamoured of Rachel, a beautiful Jewess, daughter of Eleazar, the goldsmith. The better to carry out his plans, he calls himself Samuel, and pretends to be a Jewish painter. Circumstances, however, dispel the illusion, and Rachel learns that he is no other than Leopold, husband of the princess Eudoxia. Overcome with indignation at the discovery of his perfidy, she publicly denounces his crime, and the Cardinal excommunicates Leopold, and pronounces his malediction on Rachel and her father. Rachel, Eleazar, and Leopold are thrown into prison to await the execution of the sentence of death. During their imprisonment Eudoxia intercedes with Rachel to save Leopold's life, and at last, moved by the grief of the rightful wife, she publicly recants her statement. Leopold is banished, but Rachel and her father are again condemned to death for conspiring against the life of a Christian. Eleazar determines to be revenged in the moment of death upon the Cardinal, who has sentenced them, and who is at the head of a church which he hates; and just before they are thrown into a caldron of boiling oil, reveals to the spectators that Rachel is not his own, but an adopted daughter, saved from the ruins of the Cardinal's burning palace, and that she is his child.

The opera of "The Jewess" is preëminently spectacular, and its music is dramatic and declamatory rather than melodious. The prominent numbers of the first act are the solemn declaration of the Cardinal ("Wenn ew'ger Hass"), in which he replies to Eleazar's hatred of the Christain; the romance sung by Leopold ("Fern vom Liebchen weilen"), which is in the nature of a serenade to Rachel; "Eilt herbei," the drinking-song of the people at the fountain, which is flowing wine; and the splendid chorus and march ("Leht, es nahet sich der Zug"), which preludes the imposing pageantry music of the Emperor's arrival, closing with the triumphant Te Deum to organ accompaniment and the greeting to the Emperor ("Hosanna, unser Kaiser hoch").

The second act opens with the celebration of the Passover in Eleazar's house, and introduces a very solemn and impressive prayer ("Allmächt'ger blicke gnädig"). In the next scene there is a passionate ensemble and duet for Eudoxia and Leopold ("Ich will ihn seh'n"), which is followed by a second spirited duet between Rachel and Leopold ("Als mein Herz"); an intensely dramatic aria ("Ach! Vater! Halt ein!"), in which she claims her share of Leopold's guilt; and the final grand trio in which anathema is pronounced by Eleazar.

Falcon as *Rachel*

The third act is principally devoted to the festivities of the royal pageants, and closes with the anathema of the Cardinal ("Ihr, die ihr Gottes Zorn"), which is a concerted number of magnificent power and spirited dramatic effect. The fourth act contains a grand duet between Eleazar and the Cardinal ("Hort ich recht?"), and closes with one of the most powerful scenas ever written for tenor ("Das Todesurtheil sprich"), in which Eleazar welcomes death and hurls defiance at the Christians. The last act is occupied with the tragic denouement, which affords splendid opportunities for action, and is accompanied by very dramatic music to the close, often rising to real sublimity. In stage pageantry, in the expression of high and passionate sentiment, in elaborateness of treatment, and in broad and powerful dramatic effect, "The Jewess" is one of the strongest operas in the modern repertory.

L'Eclair

"L'Eclair," comic opera in three acts, text by Planard and Saint George, was produced for the first time at the Opera Comique, Paris, December 16, 1835. The action takes place near Boston, Massachusetts, in the year 1790. "L'Eclair," composed for two tenors and two sopranos and without chorus, was written in the same year as "The Jewess," but so widely different are the two operas in style, treatment, and music that many at the time doubted whether they could be the work of the same composer.

The first act opens with a tuneful duet ("De la campagne et de la solitude") for Madame Darbel, a young widow living in Boston, and her sister Henriette, who is staying in the country, some miles away from the city, in which the respective charms of country and city are mutually and melodiously discussed. They are awaiting the appearance of George, a young English cousin, who has been sent for by their uncle with instructions to choose one of the sisters and marry her, whereupon he will arrange for a division of his property among them. George makes his appearance with a very amusing aria ("Je vous que dans trois semaine"), in which he shows himself an unusually conceited coxcomb. This is followed by a lively trio ("Eh, bien! decidez-vous"), in which the cousins entertain themselves at his expense. George finally is left alone to comfort himself at a repast, during which Lionel, a young American naval office, who has rowed ashore from his vessel in the harbor to hunt, enters and makes his acquaintance. Lionel joins him in a social glass and sings a stirring barcarole ("Parlons, la mer est belle"), in which he pictures the happiness of sea life and describes a sea fight, after which he takes his leave and returns to his boat. A sudden storm has come up, however, his boat is shattered by a thunderbolt, and he is hurled upon the beach blinded by the lightning. Henriette finds him and conducts him back to the house, and a trio in which Lionel mourns his fate and the others sympathize with him closes the act.

The second acts opens with a gay rondo for Mme. Darbel ("Ah! ma sœur jolie"). George in the meantime has decided he will marry Henriette, and assumes that it is already an accomplished fact without giving himself the trouble to consult her. Henriette, however, who has been tenderly caring for Lionel, has fallen in love with him, and he also tells her his love in the Provençal song of "Gentille Hélène." The duet is exquisitely melodious and very expressive, and is shortly followed by an amusing aria for George ("Après ce trait de perfidie") which is made all the more amusing by Mme. Darbel singing in the garden ("Pres d'une belle être fidele"), setting off much coquetry against George's philosophy and vanity. In the meantime, the uncle, who is a doctor, has Lionel for a patient, and he has progressed so well under his treatment that at last his bandages are removed. Lionel, who has never seen Henriette, mistakes her sister for her, falls upon his knees and protests undying love for Mme. Darbel, who had been vainly besieged by George when he learned that Henriette loved Lionel. As Henriette sees her lover protesting his undying affection to her sister, she believes him perfidious and faints. When she recovers she disappears. Days afterwards she writes to Lionel consenting to his marriage with Mme. Darbel and also to George, promising to be his wife. As a ruse to draw her back, word is sent out of the marriage of Lionel to her sister. She returns prepared to keep the promise made to George, when explanations are in order. She is undeceived and is united to Lionel while the coquettish widow takes up with her very conceited but amusing cousin who protests he has always loved her. The most effective number in the last act is Lionel's romance, which is familiar by its English title of "Call me thine own." The work is very melodious and sprightly throughout, and is in striking contrast with its tragic companion, "The Jewess."

HEROLD

LOUIS JOSEPH FERDINAND HEROLD was born in Paris, January 28, 1791, and died in the same city, January 19, 1833. He secured the Grand Prix de Rome at the Conservatory in 1812, and during the next two years in Italy wrote several minor pieces. Upon his return he began the composition of dramatic music in earnest. In 1816 he collaborated with Boieldieu in the opera "Charles de France," and in 1817 made a complete success with "Les Rosières." During the next ten years he wrote a large number of operas, many graceful ballets, variations for the piano, and several other instrumental pieces, besides doing regular work in assisting operatic artists and directing choruses. The great successes of his career were made, however, in 1831, when his "Zampa" appeared followed by "Le Pré aux Clercs" in 1832. Both operas created great sensations in Europe, and showed masterly musical ability as well as dramatic power. He died the next year at the very beginning of a great career, for he had now displayed evidences of musical and dramatic skill which promised to place him in the front rank if not at the head of all his contemporaries. He himself said to a friend, a few days before his death: "I am going too soon; I was just beginning to understand the stage."

Zampa

"Zampa," opera comique in three acts, text by Mélesville, was first performed in Paris, May 3, 1831. The libretto is based upon the old story of "The Statue Bride."

HEROLD

The curtain rises upon a group of Sicilian girls who are selecting gifts at the bidding of Alfonso, Camilla's lover, who assures them that Signor Lugano, Camilla's father, has authorized him to take this method of disposing of some of his wealth. Rita, Camilla's maid, makes the announcement that Lugano left that morning to meet one of his vessels coming from Smyrna. Camilla is alarmed for his safety, but Alfonso allays her anxiety by telling her that Zampa, the corsair, has been captured and condemned to death. Rita bitterly inveighs against Zampa as the cause of her early widowhood. Saying that she must forget her troubles and look after the wedding breakfast, she leaves Camilla and Alfonso alone together, bidding the latter offer prayers to their patron saint, and pointing to a statue upon which is inscribed "Albina de Manfredi, 1814." Struck by the name, Alfonso begs Camilla to tell its story, which deeply impresses Alfonso as it recalls his own brother, who abandoned a maid named Albina. Camilla is shortly startled by the arrival of Dandolo, the messenger who had been commissioned to bring the priest for the wedding. He announces that they had been stopped by ruffians who declared his errand useless, as Camilla's wedding would never take place. During the narration Zampa himself appears and tells her that her father is in his power, and that his safety depends upon her submission to his purpose, which is to marry her and secure the father's wealth. At a subsequent carousal, Zampa approaches the statue of Albina, and recognizing the features as those of the maid he betrayed, he places a ring upon its finger, whereupon the arm of the statue is raised menacingly.

The second act opens at Signor Lugano's chateau. Zampa is warned that he is tracked, but he declares the wedding shall be solemnized before he leaves. His identity with the corsair, however, is announced, but he escapes by producing a letter offering pardon to himself and his crew if he will accept service against the Turks, to which he has assented. To save her father's life Camilla promises to wed him in spite of the warning gesture of the statue.

The third act discloses Camilla lamenting over her promise to Zampa, but rejoicing because he has signed the release of her father. Alfonso enters and she gives him the document. Zampa declares she is not to be the bride of a common corsair, but of the Count de Monza, Alfonso's brother. Camilla implores him to leave her, as she has decided to seek refuge in a convent. Her prayer is rejected, and Camilla is only saved by her father and Alfonso, who, with drawn swords, force Zampa to the oratory. Disarmed and about to be struck down, the statue seizes him and carries him to his destruction.

The overture, one of the most attractive of concert numbers, even at this day, is very effective with its bacchanalian opening, the sweet and sacred character of the middle portion, and its lively finish. The most striking numbers of the first act are the attractive opening chorus of the girls ("Dans ces présents"); the charming aria ("A ce bonheur") sung by Camilla; the dignified and beautifully harmonized quartet ("Le voilà"); and the finale with its strongly contrasted couplets and choral effects. The principal numbers of the second act are the canticle with harp accompaniment ("Aux pieds de la Madone"); the dramatic duet, "Juste Ciel," and the finale with its brilliant choruses and melodious rondo, "Douci' jouvencelli." The third act is even more important from the musical point of view, its great numbers being the lovely gondola nocturne ("Où vas-tu, pauvre Gondolier?"); the serenade ("La nuit profonde"); and the cavatina ("Pourquoi trembler?"), which is one of the inspirations of the opera.

LE PRÉ AUX CLERCS

"Le Pré aux Clercs," opera comique in three acts, text by de Planard, was first produced in Paris, December 15, 1832. The story is founded upon one of Mérimée's novels, called "Une chronique du temps de Charles IX." The plot is concerned with the love adventures of Mergy, an ambassador sent to the French court by the King of Navarre to request the return of his wife, who is detained in Paris by the Queen Mother. Mergy is enamored of Isabella, a young countess, who returns his passion. The course of true love does not run smooth in this case, for Mergy has a rival, one Comminge, a noted duellist and a *protégé* of the French king. The outcome of the situation is a duel between the two suitors at the Pré aux Clercs, a famous rendezvous for duellists at that period, in which Comminge is killed. Mergy and Isabella, secretly married, are aided in their flight from Paris by the Queen of Navarre. The plot is quite simple, and there is an under-plot concerning the love affairs of Girot, an innkeeper at the Pré aux Clercs, and Nicette, which adds to the interest of the story.

The principal numbers in the first act are the duet for Girot and Nicette ("Les Rendezvous le noble Compagnie"), which has a charming refrain, the tenor aria ("O ma tendre Bien-aime"), and the romanza for soprano ("Souvenirs de jeune Âge"); in the second act, the well-known soprano aria, "Jours de mon Enfance," the melodious Masquerade Chorus ("Chansons, chansons, dansons, toujours"), and the very dramatic finale; and in the third act, Nicette's rondo ("Le Fleur du bel Âge"), the trio for Mergy, Isabella, and Marguerite ("C'est en fait le Ciel même"), and the chorus of archers ("Nargue de la

Folie"). It is somewhat singular that while "Zampa" has always been considered Herold's masterpiece by the rest of the world, the French have most esteemed "Le Pré aux Clercs," probably because of its peculiar French qualities of grace, elegance, and animation.

HUMPERDINCK

ENGELBERT HUMPERDINCK, the latest star in the German musical firmament, was born September 1, 1854, at Siegburg on the Rhine, and received his earliest musical training at the Cologne Conservatory. He made such rapid progress in his studies, showing special proficiency in composition, that he carried off in succession the three prizes of the Mozart, Mendelssohn, and Meyerbeer stipends. These enabled him to continue his lessons at Munich, and afterwards in Italy. While in Naples, in 1880, he attracted the attention of Richard Wagner as a rising genius, and two years later had the honor of an invitation to go to Venice as his guest, upon the occasion of the performance of Wagner's only symphony. In 1885 he went to Barcelona, Spain, where he taught composition, and was the director of a quartet at the Royal Conservatory for two years. In 1887 he returned to Cologne, and since 1890 has been identified with a Conservatory at Frankfort-on-the-Main. In addition to the opera "Hansel and Gretel," which has given him a world-wide fame, he produced, a few years ago, a chorus ballad, "Das Glück von Edenhall," and a cantata, "Die Wallfahrt nach Kevelaar," based upon Heine's poem, and scored for soloists, chorus, and orchestra. He has also written several songs and piano pieces, and a dramatic composition called "The Royal Children." He is regarded in Germany as the one composer who gives promise of continuing and developing the scheme of the music-drama as it was propounded by Wagner.

Hansel and Gretel

"Hansel and Gretel," fairy opera in three acts, words by Adelheid Wette, was first produced in Germany in 1894. In January, 1895, it was performed in London by the Royal Carl Rosa Opera Company, rendered into English by Constance Bache; and in the fall of the same year it had its first representation in New York, at Daly's Theatre, with the following cast:

Peter, a broom-maker	Mr. JACQUES BARS.
Gertrude, his wife	Miss ALICE GORDON.
The Witch	Miss LOUISE MEISSLINGER.
Hansel	Miss MARIE ELBA.
Gretel	Miss JEANNE DOUSTE.
Sandman, the Sleep Fairy	Miss CECILE BRANI.
Dewman, the Dawn Fairy	Miss EDITH JOHNSTON.

The story is taken from one of Grimm's well-known fairy tales, and the text was written by the composer's sister, Adelheid Wette. It was Frau Wette's intention to arrange the story in dramatic form for the amusement of her children, her brother lending his co-operation by writing a few little melodies, of a simple nature, to accompany the performance. When he had read it, however, the story took his fancy, and its dramatic possibilities so appealed to him that he determined to give it an operatic setting with full orchestral score. He thus placed it in the higher sphere of world performance by an art which not alone reveals the highest type of genial German sentimentality, but, curiously enough, he applied to this simple little story of angels, witches, and the two babes in the wood the same musical methods which Wagner has employed in telling the stories of gods and demigods. Perhaps its highest praise was sounded by Siegfried Wagner, son of Richard Wagner, who declared that "Hansel and Gretel" was the most

HUMPERDINCK

important German opera since "Parsifal," notwithstanding its childishness and simplicity.

After a beautifully instrumented prelude, which has already become a favorite concert piece, the curtain rises upon the home of Peter, the broom-maker. The parents are away seeking for food, and Hansel and Gretel have been left in the cottage with instructions to knit and make brooms. There is a charming dialogue between the two children, beginning with a doleful lament over their poverty, and ending with an outburst of childish hilarity in song and dancing, — a veritable romp in music, — which is suddenly interrupted by the return of Gertrude, the mother, empty-handed, who chides them for their behavior, and in her anger upsets a jug of milk which was the only hope of supper in the house. With an energetic outburst of recitative she sends them into the forest, telling them not to return until they have filled their basket with strawberries. After lamenting her loss, and mourning over her many troubles, she falls asleep, but is awakened by the return of Peter, who has been more fortunate, and has brought home some provisions. A rollicking scene ensues, but suddenly he misses the children, and breaks out in a fit of rage when he is informed that they have gone into the forest. To the accompaniment of most gruesome and characteristic music he tells his wife of the witch who haunts the wood, and who, living in a honey-cake house, entices little children to it, bakes them into gingerbread in her oven, and then devours them.

The second act, "In the Forest," is preluded by a characteristic instrumental number, "The Witches' Ride." The children are discovered near the Ilsenstein, among the fir-trees, making garlands, listening to the cuckoos, and mocking them in a beautiful duet with echo accompaniment. At last, however, they realize that they are lost; and in the midst of their fear, which is intensified by strange sights and sounds, the Sandman, or sleep fairy, approaches them, strews sand in their eyes, and sings them to sleep with a most delicious lullaby, after they have recited their prayer ("When at night I go to sleep, fourteen Angels watch do keep"). As they sleep the mist rolls away, the forest background disappears, and the fourteen angels come down a sort of Jacob's ladder and surround the children, while other angels perform a stately dance, grouping themselves in picturesque tableau as the curtain falls.

The third act is entitled "The Witch's House." The children are still sleeping, but the angels have vanished. The Dawn Fairy steps forward and shakes dewdrops from a bluebell over them, accompanying the action with a delightful song, "I'm up with early Dawning." Gretel is the first to wake, and rouses Hansel by tickling him with a leaf, at the same time singing a veritable tickling melody, and then telling him what she has seen in her dream. In place of the fir-trees they discover the witch's house at the Ilsenstein, with an oven on one side and on the other a cage, both joined to the house by a curious fence of gingerbread figures. The house itself is constructed of sweets and creams. Attracted by its delicious fragrance and toothsomeness, the hungry children break off a piece and are nibbling at it, when the old witch within surprises and captures them. After a series of incantations, and much riding upon her broomstick, which are vividly portrayed in the music, she prepares to cook Gretel in the oven; but while looking into it the children deftly tumble her into the fire. The witch waltz, danced by the children and full of joyous abandon, follows. To a most vivid accompaniment, Hansel rushes into the house and throws fruit, nuts, and sweetmeats into Gretel's apron. Meanwhile the oven falls into bits, and a crowd of children swarm around them, released from their gingerbread disguises, and sing a swelling chorus of gratitude as two of the boys drag the witch from the ruins of the oven in the form of a big gingerbread-cake. The father and mother appear. Their long quest is ended. The family join in singing a pious little hymn ("When past bearing is our grief, God the Lord will send relief"), and the children dance joyously around the reunited group. The story is only a little child's tale, but it is wedded to music of the highest order. The union has been made so deftly, the motives are so charming and take their places so skilfully, and the music is so scholarly and characteristic throughout, that no one has yet considered this union as incongruous.

JAKOBOWSKI

EDOUARD JAKOBOWSKI, a composer residing in London, is the writer of a very pleasant musical comedy, "Erminie." Though not an opera or even operetta in the strict sense, being rather a comedy with incidental music, its numbers are so tuneful, and the comedy has been and still remains so popular, that it is included in this volume. The composer has also produced an operetta, "Paolo," but it has not made the success of "Erminie," which has had since its first performance in 1885 nearly three thousand presentations.

Erminie

"Erminie," musical comedy in two acts, text by Bellamy and Paulton, was first produced at the Comedy Theatre, London, November 9, 1885, and in New York at the Casino, March 10, 1886. The story of "Erminie" is based upon the old melodrama "Robert Macaire," the two vagabonds, Ravannes and Cadeaux, taking the places of the two murderers, Macaire and Jacques Strop. Few melodramas were more popular in their day than "Robert Macaire," in which Lemaitre, the great French actor, made one of his most conspicuous successes. It is also true that few musical comedies have been more successful than "Erminie." At the opening of the opera, a gallant on the way to his betrothal with a young lady whom he has never seen is attacked by two thieves, Ravannes and Cadeaux, who carry off his wardrobe and tie him to a tree. Later, Ravannes arrives in the midst of the betrothal festivities, and passes himself off as the expected guest.

He introduces Cadeaux as a nobleman, and explains their lack of proper attire with the statement that they had been robbed while on their way there. Erminie has an affection for Eugene, her father's secretary, and none for the man who claims to be a suitor for her hand. Ernst, who was the real victim of the robbery, and who is in love with Cerise, escapes from the predicament in which the two thieves placed him, and arrives in time for the festivities, to find himself denounced by Ravannes as the highwayman who had attacked them earlier in the day. Ravannes, by assuming great magnanimity and a certain nobility of conduct, and by his proffers of help to Erminie in securing the man she loves in return for her assistance in his plans, of which she of course is ignorant, so ingratiates himself in her confidence that he nearly succeeds in robbing the house. In the end, however, the two vagabonds are unmasked. Eugene obtains the hand of Erminie, and Ernst and Cerise are equally fortunate.

The music of "Erminie" is light and graceful throughout. Its principal numbers are Erminie's song ("Ah! when Love is young"); the duet for Eugene and Erminie ("Past and Future"); the Marquis' stirring martial song ("Dull is the Life of the Soldier in Peace"); the thieves' rollicking duet ("We're a philanthropic Couple, be it known"); Erminie's pretty dream song ("At Midnight on my Pillow lying"), and the lullaby ("Dear Mother, in Dreams I see her"), which is the gem of the opera; the song and whistling chorus ("What the Dicky Birds say"); the vocal gavotte ("Join in Pleasures, dance a Measure"); and the concerted piece ("Good-night"), which leads up to the close of the last act.

LECOCQ

CHARLES LECOCQ was born in Paris, June 3, 1832. He entered the Conservatory in 1849, carried off many prizes, and proved himself a superior musical scholar and a good organist. Indeed, his attainments at that time were so excellent that he might have risen to a high position in the musical world, but almost from the first his ambition was to make a success with light works for the theatre, especially on the lines which Offenbach had followed. After a series of comic operas produced between 1864 and 1868 he became firmly established in public favor, and all his works met with a cordial reception. Among his most successful operas are the following: "Fleur de Thé" (1868); "Le Barbier de Trouville" (1871); "Les Cent Vierges" (1872); "La Fille de Mme. Angot" (1873); "Giroflé-Girofla" (1874); "La Petite Mariée" (1876); "La Marjolaine" (1877); and "Le Petit-Duc" and "Camargo" (1878). The list of his dramatic works includes over fifty numbers, besides which he wrote ballads, songs, and piano pieces. Lecocq was made Chevalier of the Legion of Honor in 1894.

GIROFLÉ-GIROFLA

"Giroflé-Girofla," opera bouffe in three acts, text by Vanloo and Aterrier, was first produced at the Théâtre des Fantasies Parisiennes, Brussels, March 21, 1874; in Paris, November 11, 1874; in New York at the Park Theatre in 1875. The scene is laid in Spain. The opening scene introduces Don Bolero d'Alcarazas, a Spanish grandee, and Aurore, his wife, also their twin daughters, Giroflé and Girofla, who, being of marriageable age, have been hastily betrothed, Giroflé to Marasquin, a banker, to whom Don Bolero is heavily indebted, and Girofla to Mourzook, a Moorish chief, who has made regular demands upon Don Bolero for money on penalty of death. By the double marriage he expects to get rid of his obligations on the one hand and avoid the payment of the enforced tribute on the other. Giroflé is married as arranged, but Girofla, who was to have been married the same day, is abducted by pirates before the ceremony can be performed. When Mourzook arrives and finds he has no bride, he is in a terrible rage, but is quieted down when, after a little manœuvring by Aurore, Giroflé is passed off on him as Girofla, and is thus to be married a second time.

In the second act the wedding festivities are going on and both bridegrooms are clamoring for their brides. No word is heard from Admiral Matamoras, who has been sent to capture the pirates. Don Bolero and Aurore resort to all kinds of expedients to settle matters and pacify the irate banker and the furious Moor, and besides have much trouble in restraining Giroflé from flying to her Marasquin. At last she is locked up. She manages to get out, however, and goes off with some of her cousins for a revel. Her absence is explained by a report that the pirates have carried her off also, which adds to the parents' perplexity as well as to the fury of Marasquin and Mourzook. At last Giroflé appears in a tipsy condition and is claimed by both. The act closes with the report that Matamoras has been defeated, and that the pirates have carried Girofla to Constantinople.

The third act opens on the following morning. The two would-be husbands have been locked into their apartments

Marasquin has passed a quiet night, but Mourzook has smashed the furniture and escaped from his chamber through the window. The parents assure Marasquin that even if Mourzook returns he will have to leave that afternoon, and suggest that there can be no harm in letting him have Giroflé for his wife until that time. Marasquin reluctantly consents, and when Mourzook returns and Giroflé is presented to him as Girofla, a ridiculous love scene occurs, which Marasquin contrives to interrupt by various devices. Finally the return of Girofla is announced, and Matamoras with his sailors appear, leading her by the hand. Explanations are made all round, the parents are forgiven, and Mourzook is satisfied.

The music is lively throughout and oftentimes brilliant, and of a higher standard than usually characterizes opera bouffe. The most taking numbers are the ballad with pizzicato accompaniment, sung by Paquita, "Lorsque la journée est fini" ("When the Day is finished"); the concerted ensemble, "À la chapelle" ("To the Church"); the grotesque pirates' chorus, "Parmi les choses délicates" ("Among the delicate Things to do"), and the sparkling duet for Giroflé and Marasquin, "C'est fini, le mariage" ("The Marriage has been solemnized"), in the first act; the bacchanalian chorus, "Écoutez cette musique" ("Listen to this Music"), leading up to a dance; a vivacious and well-written quintet, "Matamoras, grand capitaine" ("Matamoras, our great Captain"); a fascinating drinking song, "Le punch scintillé" ("See how it sparkles"), and the andante duet, "O Giroflé, O Girofla," a smooth, tender melody, which is in striking contrast with the drinking-music preceding it and that which immediately follows the chorus of the half-tipsy wedding-guests, "C'est le canon" ("It is the Cannon"), in the second act; and the rondo, "Beau père, une telle demand" ("Oh, my Father, now you ask"), sung by Marasquin, and the duet for Mourzook and Giroflé, "Ma belle Giroflé" ("My Lovely Giroflé"), in the third act.

LA FILLE DE MADAME ANGOT

"La Fille de Madame Angot," opera bouffe in three acts, text by Clairville, Sirandin, and Konig, was first produced at the Fantasies Parisiennes, Brussels, November, 1872; in Paris at the Folies Dramatiques, February 23, 1873. The first act opens in a market square in Paris, where the market women and others in holiday attire are making ready to celebrate the wedding of Pomponnet, the hairdresser, and Clairette, the daughter of the late Madame Angot. During the festive preparations, for which Clairette has little desire, as her affections are fixed upon Ange Pitou, a street singer, who is continually in trouble by reason of his political songs, the latter makes his appearance. He is informed of the forthcoming wedding, which has been arranged by the market people, who have adopted Clairette as the child of the market. At the same time Larivaudière and Louchard, the police officials who caused his arrest because of his knowledge of the relations of Larivaudière and Mademoiselle Lange, the comedienne and favorite of Barras, are surprised to find him at large. To prevent him from reciting his knowledge in a song which he is sure has been written, Larivaudière buys him off. Pitou subsequently regrets his bargain. When the crowd clamors for a song, he says he has none. The people are furious with him, but Clairette comes to his rescue. She has found the song denouncing Larivaudière, sings it, and is arrested, notwithstanding Pitou's declaration that he is the author of it.

The second act opens in Mademoiselle Lange's salon. She has persuaded Barras to release Clairette and have her brought to her apartments, so that she may discover why she sings this song denouncing the government and insulting her also. In the meantime she has also sent for Pomponnet, her hairdresser, and informs him what his future wife has done. He replies that Pitou wrote the song, and that he (Pomponnet) has it. She orders him to fetch it to her. When Clairette arrives they recognize each other as old school friends. Mademoiselle Lange assures her she shall not go back to prison and that she need not marry Pomponnet. She retires to Mademoiselle Lange's boudoir when a visitor is announced. It is Ange Pitou, and a love scene at once occurs. The jealous Larivaudière enters and accuses them of being lovers. To justify herself Mademoiselle Lange declares that Pitou and Clairette are lovers, and the latter confirms the statement. Pomponnet's voice is heard in the outer room. He is admitted, and promptly arrested for having the revolutionary song on his person. The act closes with a meeting of conspirators, and Mademoiselle Lange's clever foiling of the grenadiers who have come to arrest them, by turning the whole affair into a grand ball, to which they are invited.

The last act is occupied with plots and counter-plots which at last succeed in disentangling all the complications. Mademoiselle Lange's perfidy, as well as Pitou's, is shown up, Larivaudière has his revenge, and Clairette and Pomponnet are made happy.

The music of the opera is so bright, gay, and characteristic that it made Lecocq a dangerous rival of Offenbach. The most conspicuous numbers are Clairette's pretty romance, "L'enfant de la halle" ("The Child of the Market"); Amaranthe's jolly couplets, "Marchande de marée" ("A beautiful Fishwoman"); Ange Pitou's rondo, "Certainement j'aimais Clairette" ("'T is true I loved Clairette") and Clairette's spirited song, "Jadis les rois, race proscrite" ("Once Kings, a Race proscribed"),

Emily Soldene as *Mdlle. Lange*

in the first act; another equally spirited song, "Comme un Coursier" ("Like a Courser"); Pomponnet's pretty air, "Elle est tellement innocente" ("She is so innocent"); a charming sentimental duet for Mademoiselle Lange and Clairette, "Jours fortunés de notre enfance" ("Happy Days of Childhood"); a striking ensemble in the form of a quintet, "Oui, je vous le dis, c'est pour elle" ("Yes, 't is on her Account alone"); and the famous conspirators' chorus, "Quand on conspire" ("When one conspires"), in the second act; and Clairette's couplets with chorus, "Vous aviez fait de la dépense" ("You put yourselves to great Expense"); the humorous duet, "Larivaudière and Pomponnet," and Clairette's song, "Ah! c'est donc toi" ("Ah! 't is you, then"), in the last act.

LEONCAVALLO

RUGGIERO LEONCAVALLO, a promising representative of the young Italian school, was born in Naples, March 8, 1858. He first studied with Siri, and afterwards learned harmony and the piano from Simonetti. While a student at the Naples Conservatory he was advised by Rossi, one of his teachers, to devote himself to opera. In pursuance of this counsel, he went to Bologna, and there wrote his first opera, "Tommaso Chatterton," which still remains in manuscript and unperformed. Then followed a series of "wander years," during which he visited many European countries, giving lessons in singing and upon the piano, and meeting with varying fortunes. In all these years, however, he cherished the plan of producing a trilogy in the Wagnerian manner with a groundwork from Florentine history. In a letter he says: "I subdivided the historical periods in the following way: first part, 'I Medici,' from the accession of Sextus IV to the Pazzi conspiracy; second part, 'Savonarola,' from the investiture of Fra Benedetto to the death of Savonarola; third part, 'Cesare Borgia,' from the death of the Duke of Candia to that of Alexander VI." The first part was completed and performed in Milan in November, 1893, and was a failure, notwithstanding its effective instrumentation. It was not so, however, with the little two-act opera "I Pagliacci," which was produced May 21, 1892, at Milan, and met with an instantaneous and enthusiastic success. His next work was a chorus with orchestral accompaniment, the text based upon Balzac's rhapsodical and highly wrought "Seraphita," which was performed at Milan in

1894. Of his works, "I Pagliacci" is the only one known in the United States. It has met with great favor here, and has become standard in the Italian repertory.

I Pagliacci

"I Pagliacci," Italian opera in two acts, words by the composer, Ruggiero Leoncavallo, was first performed at Milan, May 21, 1892, and was introduced in this country in the spring of 1894, Mme. Arnoldson and Signors Ancona, Gromzeski, Guetary, and De Lucia taking the principal parts. The scene is laid in Calabria during the Feast of the Assumption. The Pagliacci are a troupe of itinerant mountebanks, the characters being Nedda, the Columbine, who is wife of Canio, or Punchinello, master of the troupe; Tonio, the Clown; Beppe, the Harlequin; and Silvio, a villager.

The first act opens with the picturesque arrival of the troupe in the village, and the preparations for a performance in the rustic theatre, with which the peasants are overjoyed. The tragic element of the composition is apparent at once, and the action moves swiftly on to the fearful denouement. Tonio, the clown, is in love with Nedda, and before the performance makes advances to her, which she resents by slashing him across the face with Beppe's riding-whip. He rushes off vowing revenge, and upon his return overhears Nedda declaring her passion for Silvio, a young peasant, and arranging to elope with him. Tonio thereupon seeks Canio, and tells him of his wife's infidelity. Canio hurries to the spot, encounters Nedda; but Silvio has fled, and she refuses to give his name. He attempts to stab her, but is prevented by Beppe, and the act closes with the final preparation for the show, the grief-stricken husband donning the motley in gloomy and foreboding silence.

The second act opens with Tonio beating the big drum,

and the people crowding to the show, among them Silvio, who manages to make an appointment with Nedda while she is collecting the money. The curtain of the little theatre rises, disclosing a small room barely furnished. The play to be performed is almost an identical picture of the real situation in the unfortunate little troupe. Columbine, who is to poison her husband, Punchinello, is entertaining her lover, Harlequin, while Taddeo, the clown, watches for Punchinello's return. When Canio finally appears the mimic tragedy becomes one in reality. Inflamed with passion, he rushes upon Nedda, and demands the name of her lover. She still refuses to tell. He draws his dagger. Nedda, conscious of her danger, calls upon Silvio in the audience to save her; but it is too late. Her husband kills her, and Silvio, who rushes upon the stage, is killed with the same dagger. With a wild cry full of hate, jealousy, and despair, the unfortunate Canio tells the audience "La commedia è finita" ("The comedy is finished"). The curtain falls upon the tragedy, and the excited audience disperses.

The story is peculiarly Italian in its motive, though the composer has been charged with taking it from "La Femme de Tabarin," by the French novelist, Catulle Mendès. Be this as it may, Leoncavallo's version has the merit of brevity, conciseness, ingenuity, and swift action, closing in a denouement of great tragic power and capable, in the hands of a good actor, of being made very effective. The composer has not alone been charged with borrowing the story, but also with plagiarizing the music. So far as the accusation of plagiarism is concerned, however, it hardly involves anything more serious than those curious resemblances which are so often found in musical compositions. As a whole, the opera is melodious, forceful, full of snap and go, and intensely dramatic, and is without a dull moment from the prologue ("Si puó?

Fritzi Scheff as *Nedda*
Copyright, Aimé Dupont

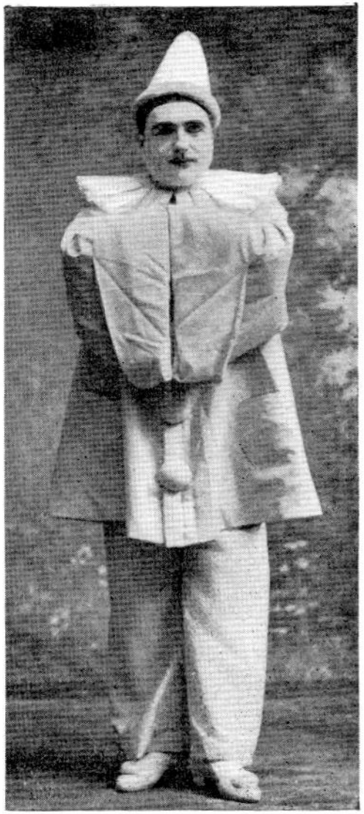

Alvarez as *Cano*
Copyright, Aimé Dupont

LEONCAVALLO

Signore "), sung before the curtain by Tonio, to that last despairing outcry of Canio (" La commedia è finita "), upon which the curtain falls. The prominent numbers are the prologue already referred to; Nedda's beautiful cavatina in the second scene (" O, che volo d'angello ") ; her duet with Silvio in the third scene (" E allor perchè ") ; the passionate declamation of Canio at the close of the first act (" Recitur ! mentre preso dal delirio ") ; the serenade of Beppe in the second act (" O Colombino, il tenero ") ; and the graceful dance music which plays so singular a part in this fierce struggle of the passions, that forms the motive of the closing scenes.

LÖRTZING

GUSTAV ALBERT LÖRTZING was born at Berlin, October 23, 1803, and died there January 21, 1851. His parents were actors and in 1823 he married an actress. As a musician he was almost self-taught, but his connections with the theatre were of great dramatic advantage to him. His first opera, "Ali Pascha von Janina," was performed at Cologne in 1824. Two years later, he became an actor and for eleven years was tenor singer at the Leipzig Theatre. While thus engaged he brought out "Die beiden Schützen (1837), and the "Czar und Zimmermann" (1839), both of which became very popular and still remain so. These were followed by several other operas, the most successful one being "Der Wildschütz" (1842). In 1844 he was conductor of the Leipzig opera for a short time. He then travelled through Germany and brought out more new operas, among them "Undine" (1845), "Der Waffenschmied" (1846), "Zum Grossadmiral" (1847), and "Die Roland's Knappen" (1848). In 1850, he became Capellmeister at the Friedrich-Wilhelmstädtisches Theatre in Berlin, where he spent the last year of his life. The characteristics of his works are melody, brightness, freshness, and humor.

Czar and Carpenter

"Czar and Carpenter," opera comique in three acts, text as well as music by Lörtzing, was first produced in Berlin in 1839. The opening of the first act of the "Czar and Carpenter" discloses Peter the Great and Peter Ivanoff, a deserter from the Russian army, at work in the great shipyard of Saardam. The British and French ambassadors, having been notified that the Czar is there in disguise, are searching for him with the object of negotiating a treaty with him, or, failing in that, to abduct him. The British ambassador employs the pompous burgomaster of Saardam to find him a Russian named Peter, without, however, disclosing his real character to him. The burgomaster happens upon Peter Ivanoff and brings him to the ambassador, who, supposing him to be the Czar, seeks to arrange a treaty with him, and finally gives him a passport so that he may visit England. Meanwhile the people of Saardam, being informed that the Czar is with them, prepare a reception for him.

The French ambassador, who has also been searching for the Czar, finds the real one by telling him the story of a Russian defeat which causes him to betray himself. The Czar, who is now anxious to go home and crush out the rebellion, seeks for some means to get away without the knowledge of the Dutch and the English. Finding out by chance that Ivanoff has an English passport, he secures it, and gives Ivanoff another paper which he is not to open until an hour has passed. During this time Ivanoff is enjoying the public reception, which suddenly is interrupted by the firing of cannon. The gateway of the port is opened, showing the Czar with the Russian and French ambassadors sailing away. Ivanoff opens his paper, and finds that his companion was the Czar, who has given him a good situation as well as his consent to his marriage with Marie, the burgomaster's niece.

The leading numbers of the first act are the carpenter's spirited song ("Grip your Axes"); Marie's jealousy song ("Ah! Jealousy is a bad Companion"); the humorous aria of Van Bett ("Oh! Sancta Justitia, I shall go raving"); the long duet for Van Bett and Ivanoff ("Shall I make a full Confession?"), and the effective quartets in the finale.

The second act contains the best music of the opera. It opens with a mixed chorus of a bacchanalian sort ("Long live Joy and Pleasure"), which after a long dialogue is followed by the tenor romanza ("Fare thee well, my Flandrish Maiden"), a quaint melody, running at the end of each stanza into a duet, closing with full chorus accompaniment. A sextet ("The Work that we're beginning") immediately follows, which, though brief, is the most effective number in the opera. The next number of any consequence in this act is a rollicking bridal song ("Charming Maiden, why do Blushes"), sung by Marie. The last act has a comic aria and chorus ("To greet our Hero with a stately Reception"), and an effective song for the Czar ("In Childhood, with Crown and with Sceptre I played").

MARSCHNER

HEINRICH MARSCHNER was born at Zittau, Saxony, August 16, 1796, and died at Hanover, December 14, 1861. In 1816 he went to Leipzig with the intention of studying law, but upon the advice of Rochlitz and other musicians he decided to study music instead. At a little later period he was confirmed in his decision by Beethoven, whom he met in Vienna. His first operatic works were "Der Kyffhäuser Berg" and "Heinrich IV." The latter was produced at Dresden by Weber, and led to Marschner's appointment as joint Capellmeister with Weber and Morlacchi. He resigned the position in 1826, and settled at Leipzig in 1827 as Capellmeister of the theatre. His first romantic opera, "Der Vampyr," was produced in that city in 1828, with extraordinary success. It also met with great favor in London and led to his composing "Der Templer und die Jüdin" for England. In 1831 he was appointed Capellmeister at Hanover, where he brought out his masterpiece, "Hans Heiling," the libretto originally written by Edouard Devrient, for Mendelssohn, but declined by him. After "Hans Heiling" he wrote several operas, operettas, overtures, songs, and incidental music, but he reached his highest success in the weird story of the "King of the Gnomes." As a composer he is ranked with Weber and Spohr. It was a curious characteristic of his nature that while he abounded in humor and was fond of nature his favorite subjects were of the supernatural and ghostly kind.

HANS HEILING

"Hans Heiling," romantic opera in three acts with a prologue, text by Edouard Devrient, was first produced in Berlin in 1833. Its theme is an old Erzgebirg legend. Hans Heiling, the king of the gnomes, has fallen in love with Anna, a beautiful girl of the upper earth. He announces to the gnomes in the prologue that he proposes to leave them and join Anna, and succeeds in his purpose notwithstanding the remonstrances of his mother. Finding him bent upon going, she gives him a magic book and set of jewels.

Arrived in the upper world Hans meets Anna, who accepts his suit and a golden chain. Her old mother, Gertrude, heartily approves of the match as well as of the chain. Anna, desirous of displaying her ornaments, as well as her lover, begs him to accompany her to a fair, but he declines to go. She is greatly disappointed, and her disappointment changes to fear when she finds the magic book in his room. She implores him to destroy it, and at last he consents, thus cutting off his only connection with the under world. Anna still remains so disappointed that he at last consents to go to the fair upon condition that she will not dance. She accepts the condition, but at the fair she meets another of her lovers, Conrad, the hunter, and at his urgent solicitation she violates the promise she has made.

The second act discovers Anna in the forest, thinking only of Conrad. To her suddenly appear the gnomes and their queen, who reveal to her the real identity of Hans and beg her to give him back to them. She soon meets Conrad and implores his help. He goes home with her, delighted to learn that she loves him, but immediately Hans appears with his bridal gift. He makes no impression upon Anna, who informs him that she has learned his origin. In a rage he hurls his dagger at Conrad and rushes out.

The third act reveals Hans alone in the mountains where he decides to go back to the gnomes. They appear, but have little comfort for him as they tell him that having destroyed the magic book he has no further power over them, and they add to his wretchedness by the announcement that Anna is going to marry Conrad. The gnomes, however, at last take pity upon him, and he returns with them to the queen. The act closes with the wedding. As Anna appears for the ceremony Hans is by her side. Conrad attacks him, but his sword breaks. Hans summons the gnomes, but the queen appears and persuades him to forgive Anna and Conrad and go back to the gnome realm with her.

The prologue consists of a chorus ("Rastlos geschäfft") and a duet for Heiling and the Queen ("Genug beendet"). The principal numbers in the first act are the aria for the Queen ("O bleib' bei mir"), with chorus of spirits; terzetto for Anna, Heiling, and Gertrude ("Ha! welche Zeichen"); a delightful aria for Heiling ("An jenem Tag"); a brisk unison chorus of peasants ("Juchheisen"); a song for Conrad with choral accompaniment ("Ein sprodes allerliebstes Kind"); and the stirring finale ("Wie hupft mir von Freude das Herz").

The second act opens with a scene and aria for Anna ("Einst war so tiefer Freude"), which inevitably suggests Marguerite's song in the garden in Gounod's "Faust." The principal numbers in the act are the ensemble and aria for the Queen with choral accompaniment ("Aus der Klufte"); the scena ("Wohl durch der grünen Wald"); the duet for Conrad and Anna (Ha! dieses Wort"); Gertrude's effective melodramatic scene and aria ("Des Nacht"); and the finale ("Ihr hört es schon").

The most important numbers in the last act are the opening melodramatic scena and air with chorus ("Herauf"); the charming peasants' wedding march; the stately choral song in the chapel ("Segne Allmächtiger"); the animated duet for Anna and Conrad ("Nun bist du mein"); and the finale ("So wollen wir auf kurze Zeit").

MASCAGNI

PIETRO MASCAGNI, who leaped into fame at a single bound, was born at Leghorn, December 7, 1863. His father was a baker, and had planned for his son a career in the legal profession; but, as often happens, fate ordered otherwise. His tastes were distinctly musical, and his determination to study music was encouraged by Signor Bianchi, a singing teacher, who recognized his talent. For a time he took lessons, unknown to his father, of Soffredini, but when it was discovered, he was ordered to abandon music and devote himself to the law. At this juncture his uncle Stefano came to his rescue, took him to his house, provided him with a piano, and also with the means to pursue his studies. Recognizing the uselessness of further objections, the father at last withdrew them, and left his son free to follow his own pleasure. He progressed so rapidly under Soffredini that he was soon engaged in composition, his first works being a symphony in C minor and a "Kyrie," which were performed in 1879. In 1881 he composed a cantata, "In Filanda," and a setting of Schiller's hymn, "An die Freude," both of which had successful public performances. The former attracted the attention of a rich nobleman who furnished young Mascagni with the means to attend the Milan Conservatory. After studying there a short time, he suddenly left Milan with an operatic troupe, and visited various Italian cities, a pilgrimage which was of great value to him, as it made him acquainted with the resources of an orchestra and the details of conducting. The troupe, however, met with hard fortunes, and was soon disbanded, throwing Mascagni upon the world. For a few years he made a precarious living in obscure towns by teaching, and had at last reached desperate extremities when one day he read in a newspaper that Sonzogno, the music publisher, had offered prizes for the three best one-act operas, to be performed in Rome. He at once entered into the competition, and produced "Cavalleria Rusticana." It took the first prize. It did more than this for the impecunious composer. When performed, it made an enthusiastic success. He was called twenty times before the curtain. Honors and decorations were showered upon him. He was everywhere greeted with serenades and ovations. Every opera house in Europe clamored for the new work. In a day he had risen from utter obscurity and become world-famous. His sudden popularity, however, had a pernicious effect, as it induced him to rush out more operas without giving sufficient time to their preparation. "L'Amico Fritz," based upon the well-known Erckmann-Chatrian story, and "I Rantzau" quickly followed "Cavalleria Rusticana," but did not meet with its success. However, he produced two operas at Milan, "Guglielmo Ratcliff" and "Silvano," which proved successful and his Japanese opera "Iris" has met with favor.

Cavalleria Rusticana

"Cavalleria Rusticana," opera in one act, words by Signori Targioni-Tozzetti and Menasci, was written in 1890, and was first performed at the Costanzi Theatre, in Rome, May 20, of that year, with Gemma Bellinconi and Roberto Stagno in the two principal roles. It had its first American production in Philadelphia, September 9, 1891, with Mme. Kronold as Santuzza, Miss Campbell as Lola, Guille as Turridu, Del Puente as Alfio, and Jeannie Teal as Lucia.

MASCAGNI

The story upon which the text of "Cavalleria Rusticana" is based is taken from a Sicilian tale by Giovanni Verga. It is peculiarly Italian in its motive, running a swift, sure gamut of love, flirtation, jealousy, and death, — a melodrama of a passionate and tragic sort, amid somewhat squalid environments, that particularly lends itself to music of Mascagni's forceful sort. The overture graphically presents the main themes of the opera, and these themes illustrate a very simple but strong story. Turridu, a young Sicilian peasant, arrived home from army service, finds that his old love, Lola, during his absence has married Alfio, a carter. To console himself he makes love to Santuzza, who returns his passion with ardor. The inconstant Turridu, however, soon tires of her and makes fresh advances to Lola, who, inspired by her jealousy of Santuzza, and her natural coquetry, smiles upon him again. The latter seeks to reclaim him, and, when she is rudely repulsed, tells the story of Lola's perfidy to Alfio, who challenges Turridu and kills him.

During the overture Turridu sings a charming Siciliana (" O Lola, c'hai di latti"), and the curtain rises, disclosing a Sicilian village with a church decorated for Easter service. As the sacristan opens its doors, the villagers appear and sing a hymn to the Madonna. A hurried duet follows, in which Santuzza reveals to mother Lucia her grief at the perfidy of Turridu. Her discourse is interrupted by the entrance of Alfio, singing a rollicking whip-song ("Il cavallo scalpita") with accompaniment of male chorus. The scene then develops into a trio, closing with a hymn ("Inneggiamo, il Signor"), sung by the people in the square, and led by Santuzza herself, and blending with the "Regina Coeli," performed by the choir inside the church with organ accompaniment, the number finally working up into a tremendous climax in genuine Italian style.

In the next scene Santuzza tells her sad story to Lucia, Turridu's mother, in a romanza of great power ("Voi lo sapete"), closing with an outburst of the highest significance as she appeals to Lucia to pray for her. In the next scene Turridu enters. Santuzza upbraids him, and a passionate duet follows in which Santuzza's suspicions are more than confirmed by his avowal of his passion for Lola. The duet is interrupted by a song of the latter, heard in the distance with harp accompaniment ("Fior di giaggolo"). As she approaches the pair the song grows livelier, and at its close she banters poor Santuzza with biting sarcasms, and assails Turridu with all the arts of coquetry. She passes into the church, confident that the infatuated Turridu will follow her. An impassioned duo of great power follows, in which Santuzza pleads with him to love her, but all in vain. He rushes into the church. She attempts to follow him, but falls upon the steps just as Alfio comes up. To him she relates the story of her troubles, and of Turridu's baseness. Alfio promises to revenge her, and another powerful duet follows.

As they leave the stage, there is a sudden and most unexpected change in the character of the music and the motive of the drama. In the place of struggle, contesting passions, and manifestations of rage, hate, and jealousy ensues an intermezzo for orchestra, with an accompaniment of harps and organ, of the utmost simplicity and sweetness, breathing something like a sacred calm, and turning the thoughts away from all this human turmoil into conditions of peace and rest. It has not only become one of the favorite numbers in the concert repertory, but is ground out from every barrel-organ the world over, and yet it has retained its hold upon popular admiration.

At its close the turmoil begins again and the action hastens to the tragic denouement. The people come out

Calvé as *Santuzza*

of the church singing a glad chorus which is followed by a drinking-song ("Viva il vino"), sung by Turridu, and joined in by Lola and chorus. In the midst of the hilarity Alfio appears. Turridu invites him to join them and drink; but he refuses, and the quarrel begins. Lola and the frightened women withdraw. Turridu bites Alfio's right ear, — a Sicilian form of challenge. The scene closes with the death of the former at Alfio's hands, and Santuzza is avenged; but the fickle Lola has gone her way bent upon other conquests.

Iris

"Iris," opera in three acts, text by Luigi Illica, was first produced at the Theatre Costanzi, Rome, in November, 1898, and in a revised form at Milan in 1899. The first act opens with a musical picture of dawn and reveals Iris, a beautiful Japanese girl, daughter of Cieco, a blind man, playing with her dolls and talking adoringly to the sun. Osaka, a young *roué*, plans to abduct her with the aid of his accomplice, Kyoto. They arrange a puppet show, and disguising themselves as players, seize Iris and carry her off as she is watching the play. Osaka has left money for the father, who, when he receives it, believes she has left him voluntarily. His rage is increased when he is told she has fled to the Yoshimara, a place of evil resort, and he begs to be taken there that he may curse her.

In the second act Iris wakens to find herself in a beautiful apartment in the Yoshimara, with Osaka and Kyoto standing near and admiring her. As she awakens, they leave, and she fancies herself dead and in paradise. Osaka however shortly returns and makes love to her, but is baffled by her ignorance of what he is doing. Thereupon he abandons her to Kyoto, and seeks to make money by placing her on exhibition to the street crowds. Osaka makes a second attempt to win her, but in vain. Soon the blind father appears and Iris flies to him, but he flings mud in her face and curses her. She rushes from the spot and throws herself into a sewer basin.

The third act opens with her discovery by rag-pickers who seek to despoil the body of its dress and ornament, but Iris moves and scares them away. She sinks back and dies, but hovering between life and death she beholds the rising sun, and they discourse together. Flowers spring up about her as she is lifted up and taken to the Infinite.

The opening scene is by far the strongest number in "Iris." The curtain rises upon a dark stage. Gloomy rumblings tell of the night. Successive ascents towards a climax paint the approach of dawn, the opening of the flowers, the increase of light, and finally the uprising of the sun in a powerful outburst of instrumentation with full chorus ("Il sole son ioson io la vita"). Other important numbers are the opening song of Iris with harp accompaniment ("Ho fatto un triste sogno pauroso"); the graceful orchestration accompanying the washerwomen's chorus; the characteristic puppet show music, in which one of the geishas hums an oriental melody; Iris's solo ("Un di al tempio vidi") in the second act; and the finale to the third act in which she sings to the sun as she sinks into death and the sun answers her as in the beginning of the opera.

L'AMICO FRITZ

"L'Amico Fritz," comic opera in three acts, had its first performance at the Theatre Costanzi, Rome, October 31, 1891. The text is by Suaratoni, after the well-known Erckmann-Chatrian story. The plot of the opera is very simple. Fritz, a wealthy bachelor, is a confirmed woman-hater and has determined never to marry. David, the rabbi, is an equally determined matchmaker and vainly seeks to induce Fritz to take a wife. Wearied with his efforts in his behalf, Fritz finally makes a wager with the rabbi, pledging his vineyard, that he will never marry. While visiting in the country he meets Suzel, the young and beautiful daughter of one of his tenants, and in spite of himself falls in love with her. The cunning rabbi confirms him in his passion by telling him how many admirers and what fine offers she has had. Provoked with himself because of his jealousy, he attempts to fly from the charmer, and she, who is already deeply in love with him, weeps bitterly. This so works upon Fritz's sympathies that he asks her to be his bride. The rabbi wins the wager and all ends with a dance and song.

The first act opens at Fritz's house in Alsace. It is his birthday and the congratulations of Hanezo, his friend, and the rabbi lead up to a delightful romanza for Suzel ("Son piochi fiori"), as she offers him a gift of violets. The romanza is one of the most melodious and characteristic numbers in the opera. During the pretty scene, Beppe, a gypsy, appears with his violin and sings a charming bit ("Luceri, miseri tanti bambini"). The act closes with an effective march, taken from an Alsatian popular song, "I bin lusti."

The second act reveals Suzel standing near a cherry tree. Gathering some flowers, she sings the ballad ("Bel cavalier, che vai per la foresta"). A long duet follows for the two lovers ("Suzel, buon di"), closing with Suzel's singing of a delightful bird song. The remaining numbers of importance in the act are a scherzo (instrumental) called "L'Arrivo del Biroccino," the music, of a religious nature, to the story of Rebecca and Isaac, which is mutually related to Fritz by Suzel and David; and a powerful scena for Fritz ("Una strano turbamento").

The third act is preluded with an instrumental number somewhat resembling the popular "Intermezzo" in "Cavalleria Rusticana" but which ought to have more staying qualities. The two great numbers of this act are Fritz's love aria ("O amore, o bella luce del core"), which culminates in a fine duet between Fritz and Suzel ("Io t'amo, t'amo"). Though "L'Amico Fritz" has not been as popular as "Cavalleria Rusticana," musically it is a more finished work.

MASSÉ

FELIX MARIE MASSÉ, usually called Victor, was born at Lorient, France, March 7, 1822, and died in Paris, July 5, 1884. For ten years (1834-1844) he was a piano pupil of Zimmerman and studied theory of Halévy at the Paris Conservatory, where he won the Grand Prix de Rome. His first opera, "La Chambre Gothique" (1849), was very successful. He was also chorusmaster at the opera and in 1872 was professor of counterpoint in the Conservatory. His most successful operas are "Galatée" (1852); "Les Noces de Jeannette" (1853); "Miss Fauvette" (1855); "La Reine Topaze" (1856); "Paul and Virginia" (1876); "Une Nuit de Cléopâtre" (1877).

Paul and Virginia

"Paul and Virginia," romantic opera in three acts and seven tableaux, text by Carré and Barbier, was first produced at the Opéra Nationale Lyrique, Paris, November 15, 1876; in London, June 1, 1878; in New York, March 28, 1883. The scene is laid upon an island on the African coast. The story follows the lines of Bernardin St. Pierre's beautiful romance of the same name. The first act opens with the recital of the history of Madame de la Tour, mother of Virginia, and Margaret, the mother of Paul, and reveals the love of the two children for each other. While they are discussing the advisability of sending Paul to India for a time, against which his slave Domingo piteously protests, islanders come rushing towards the cabin announcing the arrival of a vessel from France. In hopes that she will have a letter announcing that she has been forgiven by the relatives who have renounced her, Madame de la Tour goes to the port. A love scene between the children follows, which is interrupted by the hurried entrance of the slave Meala, who is flying from punishment by her master, St. Croix. The two offer to go back with her and to intercede for her forgiveness, in which they are successful. St. Croix, who has designs upon Virginia, begs them to remain until night; but Meala warns them of their danger in a song, and they leave while St. Croix wreaks his revenge upon Meala.

The second act opens in the home of Madame de la Tour. She has had a letter from her aunt forgiving her, making Virginia her heiress if she will come to France, and sending money for the journey. After a long struggle between duty to her mother and love for Paul, Virginia declines to go. Meala makes them another hurried call, again flying from St. Croix, who this time is pursuing her with a twofold purpose, first, of punishing Meala and, second, of carrying out his base designs against Virginia. He soon appears at the house and demands his slave, but Paul refuses to give her up. At last St. Croix offers to sell her to Paul, and Virginia furnishes the money. The faithful Meala that night informs them of St. Croix's plot to seize Virginia when she goes to the vessel; but he is foiled, as she does not leave. The act closes with a call from the governor of the island, who bears express orders from Virginia's relatives, signed by the King, that she must go to France.

The last act is brief, and relates the tragedy. It opens at a grotto on the seashore, where the melancholy Paul has waited and watched week by week for the vessel which will bring Virginia back to him. At last it is sighted, but a storm comes up and soon develops into a hurricane, and when it subsides the vessel is a wreck, and Virginia is found dead upon the beach.

The opera is replete with beautiful melodies. There are, in the first act, a characteristic minor song for Domingo ("Ah! do not send my dear young Master"), which the composer evidently intended to be in the Ethiopian manner; a chanson of the genuine French style ("Ah! hapless Black"), though sung by a negro boy; a lovely and expressive melody sung by Virginia, as she pleads with St. Croix ("What I would say, my Tongue forgetteth"); the weird Bamboula chorus, sung by the slaves; and a very dramatic aria for Meala ("'Neath the Vines entwining"), in which she warns the children of their danger. The principal numbers in the second act are Virginia's romance ("As last Night thro' the Woods"); a beautiful chanson for Domingo ("The Bird flies yonder"); Paul's couplets ("Ah! crush not my Courage"); the passionate duet for Paul and Virginia ("Ah! since thou wilt go"), closing in unison; and Virginia's florid aria ("Ah, what entrancing Calm"), the cadenza of which is exceedingly brilliant. The best numbers in the short last act are Meala's song ("In vain on this distant Shore"); Paul's letter song ("Dearest Mother"); and the vision and storm music at the close.

La Reine Topaze

"La Reine Topaze," opera comique, in three acts, text by Lockroy and Battu, was first produced at the Théâtre Lyrique, Paris, December 27, 1856. The scene is laid in France. "La Reine Topaze" is one of the few of Massé's earlier works which have held the boards, mainly on account of its charming melodiousness. The role of the Queen was a great favorite with Miolan-Carvalho and Parepa-Rosa, as it offers opportunities for brilliant vocal execution. Its story is of the slightest kind. In her infancy Topaze is stolen by a band of gypsies and eventually becomes their queen. She falls in love with Rafael, a captain whom she wins from his affianced, a rich noblewoman. He does not marry her, however, until she discloses to him the secret of her birth. Some byplay among the gypsies supplies the humor of the situations. As to the text, it is far from dramatic in character, and the dialogue is tedious and dragging.

The music, however, is excellent, and it was to this feature that Massé owed his election in the year of its production as Auber's successor in the French Academy. The gypsy music is particularly charming. There are also a clever sextet, "We are six Noblemen" — indeed, there is an unusual amount of six and seven part writing in the opera; the "Song of the Bee," a delightful melody for Queen Topaze with a particularly characteristic accompaniment, likewise a brilliant bolero; a lovely romance in the last act for Rafael, and a somewhat dramatic narrative song for him in the first act; and a skilfully constructed trio for Annibal and the two gypsies. The remaining number of importance is "The Carnival of Venice," with the Paganini variations, interpolated, which was first introduced by Miolan-Carvalho, the creator of the title role.

THE MARRIAGE OF JEANNETTE

"The Marriage of Jeannette" ("Les Noces de Jeannette"), opera comique in one act, text by Carré and Barbier, was first produced at the Opéra Comique, Paris, February 4, 1853; and in New York, in 1861. The scene is laid in a French village. Nothing could be simpler than the story of this little opera, which was first given in this country in 1861, with Clara Louise Kellogg and M. Dubreul in the two principal parts, and twenty-five years later was a favorite in the repertory of the American Opera Company, under the direction of Theodore Thomas, who produced it as an after-piece to Delibes's two-act ballet, "Sylvia." The story concerns only two persons. Jean, a boorish rustic, falls in love with Jeannette and proposes marriage. On the wedding day, however, he suddenly changes his mind, and just as the notary hands him the pen to sign the contract, takes to his heels and runs home. Jeannette follows him up to demand an explanation, and pretends that she will not force him to marry her. In lieu of that she asks him to sign another contract from which she will withhold her name just to show that he was willing to do so. She furthermore promises publicly to reject him. When he has signed the new contract, she suddenly changes her mind also, and declares they are man and wife. In his fury Jean breaks up nearly everything in the house before he goes to sleep. The next day in his absence Jeannette provides new furniture from her own store, places things to rights again, sets the dinner, and awaits Jean's return. When he comes back again, he is in more tractable mood, and seeing what Jeannette has done acknowledges her as his wife.

This simple story the composer has framed in a dainty musical setting, the principal numbers being the song, "Others may hastily marry," sung by Jean after his escapade; Jeannette's pretty, simple melody, "From out a Throng of Lovers"; Jean's vigorous and defiant "Ah! little do you fancy"; the graceful song by Jeannette, "Fly now, my Needle, glancing brightly"; her brilliant and exultant song, "Voice that's sweetest"; and the spirited unison male chorus, "Ring out, Village Bells," that closes this refined and beautiful little work.

MASSENET

JULES ÉMILE FRÉDÉRIC MASSENET, one of the most distinguished of modern French composers was born at Monteaux near Saint Etienne, France, May 12, 1842. He began his musical studies at an early age and at the age of twenty-one secured the Grand Prix de Rome through a cantata, "Rizzio," in 1863. He remained in Rome two years and in accordance with the conditions of the prize he produced a one-act comic opera, "La Grande Tante," in 1867 at the Opéra Comique. His next opera, "La Coupe du Roi de Thulé," was written for a competition in 1869, but he was unsuccessful. One of his most important works about this period was the incidental music to De Lisle's drama, "Les Erinnyes," which is still a great favorite as a concert number. The oratorio of "Marie Magdaleine" followed and produced a great musical sensation in 1873 when it was given at the Odéon. About this time he also composed a series of suites, "Scènes Dramatiques," after Shakespeare; the "Scènes Hongroises" and "Scènes Alsaciennes," as well as the overture to Racine's "Phèdre." His opera, "Le Roi de Lahore," produced in 1877, obtained a great success and this was followed by "La Vierge," a religious cantata, and the opera "Hérodiade." The opera best known, "Manon," founded upon the famous novel of the Abbé Prévost, was produced in 1884, and in rapid succession "Le Cid" (1885); "Esclarmonde" (1889); "Thaïs" (1894), and "Werther" (1894). Massenet has also written a large number of minor instrumental pieces and songs.

MASSENET

Le Roi de Lahore

"Le Roi de Lahore" ("The King of Lahore"), opera in five acts, text by Luigi Gallet, was first produced in Paris, April 27, 1877. The scene is laid at Lahore and in the Gardens of the Blessed in the Paradise of Indra. Nair, a priestess of Indra, is sworn to celibacy but is in love with King Alim and is also loved by his minister, Scindia. The latter declares his passion but is repulsed. Thereupon he informs Timour, the High Priest, that Nair entertains a lover in the Temple. A watch is kept and the King is discovered entering by a secret door. The High Priest demands that he shall atone for this profanation by going to the war against the Mussulmans, and he consents. Eventually he is betrayed by Scindia, deserted by his army and killed. He is then transported to the gardens of Indra and there begs the divinities to permit him to return to earth that he may find Nair. His prayer is granted but upon condition that he shall go back as an ordinary person, never resume his former position, and give up his life when Nair dies. When he reaches earth he finds that Scindia has usurped the throne and forced Nair to be his wife. Alim proclaims him a traitor and Scindia in turn denounces Alim as an impostor. Nair, however, recognizes her lover and improves the first opportunity to join him. They are pursued by Scindia, whereupon Nair, rather than submit to him, stabs herself, whereupon Alim also dies and the lovers are welcomed by Indra.

The first act opens with an impressive temple prayer to Indra, mostly in unison. A duet between Nair and Scindia follows with beautiful violin obbligato accompaninent to Nair's recitative. The finale is very dignified and the ensemble massive, especially as the King enters the temple and agrees to go to the wars, and the act closes with a spirited war chorus behind the scenes.

The striking numbers of the second act are the opening song for mezzo soprano, which is followed by a spectacular scene in the camp of Alim enlivened by the sports and dances of the slaves, and a most brilliant ballet, though the scene lies in the desert. No place is too remote, no time too incongruous, for a French composer's ballet. A duet for Nair and Kaled leads to a vigorous and most spirited chorus, dealing with the rebellion against Alim and this is followed by the delightful love-music of Nair and Alim, with a tenderly melodious 'cello accompaniment, leading up to a strong finale.

The third act might well be called the Apotheosis of the Dance. The act opens in the Gardens of the Blessed in the Paradise of Indra with a celestial march and chorus of happy spirits, followed by a ballet, the music based upon Hindu melodies and charming waltz movements. As a spectacle and as an example of refined, graceful, fascinating music, this ballet is hardly excelled in modern operas. Another effective number in this act is Alim's song of joy which is heard in the celestial chorus as consent is given to his return.

The fourth act opens with a repetition of the spirits' incantation music in the finale of the third act. The other important numbers are the pompous march attending the coronation of Scindia; Alim's aria, "Anima doler," followed by the baritone aria, "O casta fior"; the priestesses' chorus in the second act, repeated by the orchestra, followed by the animated chorus, "Re dei regi."

The fifth act from a musical point of view may be summed up in the passionate love-music for Nair and Alim, and the dramatic music illustrating Scindia's rage and Indra's welcome to the lovers. The opera is a spectacular one in every sense of the word and yet of much musical importance. Hervey, one of Massenet's biographers, says: "In the third act, Massenet has given full rein to his fancy, and has composed dance-music of a really superior kind, which he has enriched with a piquant and effective instrumentation."

Le Cid

"Le Cid," opera in four acts and ten tableaux, text by Dennery, Gallet, and Blau, was first produced at L'Académie-Nationale de Musique, Paris, November 30, 1885, Jean de Reszke creating the part of Rodrigue, Edouard de Reszke that of Don Diègue, Pol Plançon that of Comte de Gormas and Madame Fidès-Devriès that of Chimène. The first performance in the United States was in New Orleans. The first act opens in Burgos at the house of Count Gormas, Chimène's father, upon the occasion of the knighting of Rodrigue by Ferdinand IV. It appears also that Count Gormas is to have a share of the honors by appointment as governor to the King's son. It is further developed, by the announcement of Chimène, that she is in love with Rodrigue. The daughter of the King is also in love with him but as her high position forbids personal attachments she relinquishes her claim in favor of Chimène. In the next scene, Rodrigue receives his new sword in the cathedral and becomes a Knight of Saint Jacques. The unsuspecting King meanwhile makes Don Diègue, Rodrigue's father, the governor instead of Gormas. The Count thereupon in a fury insults and assaults Don Diègue and he is left disarmed and humiliated. He calls upon his son to revenge him, which the latter is ready to do until he learns that his opponent is Chimène's father, but in the end filial duty prevails.

The second act opens with a duel between Gormas and Rodrigue in which the former is killed. Chimène coming upon the scene recognizes his murderer and falls fainting into the arms of her attendants, monks chanting a dirge behind the scenes. The next tableau represents a Spanish fete. In the midst of the revelry Chimène appears and implores the King to punish Rodrigue. Her pleadings are interrupted by the sudden appearance of a Moorish cavalier, sent by Boabdil, King of Grenada, to declare war. Thereupon Ferdinand decides to offer the leadership of his forces to Rodrigue and bids Chimène cherish and delay her revenge until the end of the campaign.

The third act reveals Chimène weeping in her chamber and Rodrigue in her presence; notwithstanding recent events they declare their love for each other and Rodrigue, the Cid, goes away happy. In the next scene, the Spanish soldiers in the Cid's camp are seen revelling while the enemy is near. Rodrigue expostulates with them and finally retires, despairing of his fate, but the vision of Saint Jacques appears and proclaims him victor in the coming battle. The announcement is confirmed. In the last act a rumor of the Cid's death reaches court and Chimène is prostrated with grief and makes a passionate avowal of her love for him, but when the report is contradicted and Rodrigue is announced as approaching, the changeable Chimène demands his head. The sensible King apparently gives way and orders that she shall pronounce sentence. At this unexpected decision she once more changes and orders Rodrigue to live and love her. She is specially moved to this reconciliation when the Cid draws his dagger to kill himself because she refuses to accept the hand of the man who slew her father. Chimène was a changeable person.

The important numbers of the first act are the brief but graceful duet for Chimène and her father ("Que c'est beau"), and the duet for Chimène and the Infanta ("Ah! la chère promesse"), which intermingles with the chimes of bells, sonorous organ peals, and fanfares of the knightly ceremonial, followed up by Rodrigue's bold and soldierly sword song ("O, noble lame étincelant"), in

Breval as *Chimène*

Copyright, Aimé Dupont

which he sings his allegiance to Spain and dedicates his sword to Saint Jacques. The remaining numbers of striking importance in this act are the music to the quarrel scene and the soliloquy of the insulted Don Diègue ("O rage, O désespoir").

The second act opens with a fine declamatory scene for Rodrigue ("Percé jusques au fond du cœur"), followed by the duel music ("A moi, Comte, deux mots!"), and the dramatic music to Chimène's demand that the slayer of her father shall reveal himself, closing with the thrilling cry "Ah, lui! Ciel! Rodrigue! c'est lui!" which is heard through the solemn strains of the De Profundis. In the next scene occurs the fete music which is of the most attractive Spanish character, including the Castillane, Andalouse, Aragonaise, Catalane, Madrilène, and Navarraise. A distinctive feature in this scene is the Infanta's "Alleluia." The great ensemble ("Ah! je doute et je tremble") which follows Chimène's demand for justice closes the act.

The third act opens with Chimène's touching soliloquy ("De cet affreux combat"), followed by one of the most powerful numbers in the whole work, the duet between Chimène and Rodrigue ("Oh, jours de première tendresse"). Then follow the camp scene with its dance music of a Moorish rhapsody and the effective apparition of Saint Jacques, accompanied by harps and celestial voices promising victory. The sword song of the first act, transformed into a battle song, closes the act. The principal numbers of the last act are the duet of Diègue and Chimène mourning the supposed death of Rodrigue, the pageantry music ("Gloire à celui que les Rois maures"), in which Massenet always excels, and the climax at the close, in which Chimène accepts the hand of Rodrigue, closing with the spirited outburst, "Gloire au Cid, au vainqueur."

Manon

"Manon," opera in four acts, text by Meilhac and Gille, founded upon Abbé Prévost's famous novel, which was also the inspiration for Halévy's ballet and Balfe's and Auber's operas based on the same subject, was first produced in Paris, January 19, 1884, Mme. Heilbronn creating the part of Manon in London, May 7, 1885; and in the United States, at the New York Academy of Music, December 23, 1885. The first act opens in the courtyard of an inn where several travellers are arriving, among them Manon, who has been consigned to a convent against her will. There she meets the Chevalier des Grieux and they fall in love with each other, notwithstanding the remonstrances of her cousin Lescaut, who is travelling with her, and incontinently elope. Guillot Monfontaine, an old *roué* and gambler who has been captivated by her beauty, is much chagrined when he learns of the elopement.

In the second act the lovers are in Paris, where they have been followed by Lescaut and Bretigny, another of Manon's lovers. Lescaut's anger is appeased by Des Grieux's promise to marry her, but when she finds out that the latter has not wealth enough to suit her, and besides is informed by Bretigny that Des Grieux will be abducted that night, she consoles herself by becoming Bretigny's mistress.

The third act opens in the gardens of the Cours de la Reine during an open air fete. Manon is among the pleasure-lovers with Bretigny, but hearing that Des Grieux is about to take holy orders, she follows him to Saint Sulpice and prevails upon him to abandon his purpose and come back to her.

In the last act Des Grieux is found in a gambling room, where he has been winning large sums from Guillot, encouraged by Manon, who grows more and more affectionate as he increases his winnings. The playing is at last interrupted by the police, who have been privately called by Guillot in revenge against Manon, who had rejected his advances. She and Des Grieux are placed under arrest, but Des Grieux is saved by his father, who pays his debts. Manon is sentenced to transportation, but on the road to Havre she is overcome by exhaustion and sorrow and dies in Des Grieux's arms.

In an opera as musically compact as this, and in which the instrumentation plays so important a part, even to the accompaniment of spoken dialogue as well as in the characterization of the *dramatis personæ* by motifs, and in which the development of the story is perhaps given greater dramatic intensity by the orchestra than by the voice, it is difficult to follow the work by individual numbers. Manon, Des Grieux, and Lescaut are much more easily recognized by the melodies which introduce and accompany them than in any other manner. One critic has excellently said of the work in general:[1] "The subject is essentially French, or rather Parisian, and the music of Massenet fits it like a glove. The composer's mannerisms seem less out of place in the mouth of Manon than they do in that of Mary Magdalen. Massenet is essentially a colorist, and even as he had succeeded in imparting an Eastern *cachet* to his 'Roi de Lahore,' and giving a tinge of the antique to his music for 'Les Erinnyes,' so in 'Manon' he has felicitously caught the spirit of the last century. This delicately perfumed score is in many places suggestive of the boudoir of a *petite maîtresse*." While it is difficult to dissect "Manon," yet it may be said that some of the "suggestive places" are Manon's opening song; the charming romanza, just before the seizure of Des Grieux ("Piccolo casetta bianca"); the delightfully flowing dream song of Des Grieux with the muted violin accompaniment; the great impassioned duet

[1] See article "Jules Massenet" in Arthur Hervey's "Masters of French Music."

of Manon and Des Grieux in the Seminary with its even greater orchestral accompaniment, set off against the music of the church; the minuet in the fete which afterwards accompanies Manon so frequently, and which in this scene is heard through Manon's passionate pleading with Des Grieux; and the four effective finales which are all powerfully musical and dramatic in effect.

Esclarmonde

"Esclarmonde," designated by its composer "opera romanesque," in four acts and eight tableaux, besides prologue and epilogue, text by Blau and de Gramont, was produced for the first time at the Théâtre National de l'Opéra Comique, Paris, May 15, 1889, with the following cast of principal parts:

Esclarmonde	Miss Sybil Sanderson.
Parseis	Mlle. Nardi.
Roland	M. Gibert.
Phorcas	M. Taskin.
Bishop of Blois	M. Bouvet.

Phorcas, Emperor of Byzantium, tired of rule, resolves to delegate it to his daughter Esclarmonde, whom he has instructed in magic, but upon condition that she conceal her beauty from men until her twentieth year, when her hand shall be the prize at a tournament, the penalty for non-fulfilment, however, being the loss both of legal and magical powers. She falls in love with Roland, a French cavalier, who, of course, has never seen her face, and by her magic she discovers that he is affianced to a daughter of the King of France. She also sees him hunting in the forest of Ardennes. By her orders he is transported to an enchanted island where she joins him and enters into a mystical sort of alliance with him, still concealing her name and face. Meanwhile France is invaded by Saracens, so Esclarmonde gives him a magic sword with a blade that shines by night like the sun, is invincible in the hand of a true knight, but useless to a perjurer. Roland, with this weapon, delivers the city of Blois, and in reward the King of France offers him his daughter's hand, which Roland declines, subsequently telling the Bishop the secret cause of his action in his confession. The Bishop surprises the lovers, tears off Esclarmonde's veil, and drives her away by exorcism. She loses her power, but her father agrees to restore it to her if she will abandon Roland, otherwise he must die. Esclarmonde resigns herself to this sacrifice and Roland seeks for death in the tournament, but instead he is crowned with laurels and wins Esclarmonde.

The prologue contains a solo for Phorcas ("Dignitaires! Guerriers!") in which he announces his intention to abdicate, and the appearance of Esclarmonde, enveloped in her veil, who enters to the choral accompaniment ("O divine Esclarmonde"). The first acts opens with Esclarmonde's song ("Comme il tient ma pensée"), followed by a duet for her and Parseis ("O ma sœur"), this in turn followed by a trio for Esclarmonde, Parseis, and Eneas, the *fiancé* of Parseis ("Salut, Impératrice"). A very characteristic chorus of spirits ("O Lune! triple Hécate! O Tanit! Astarte!") leads up to a duet for Parseis and Esclarmonde ("Dans la forêt des Ardennes").

The second act opens with another of Massenet's always interesting ballets, after which comes a strong duet for Esclarmonde and Roland ("Sois bénie, O magie"), followed by another effective spirit chorus, reaching a fine climax on the words, "C'est l'heure de l'hyménée!"

The third act opens with a chorus of the people ("O Blois! misérable cité!), followed by the Bishop's prayer ("Dieu de miséricorde"), in which all join. The next number of striking merit is Roland's air ("La nuit sera bientôt venue"), followed by an expressive duet for Roland and the Bishop ("Mon fils, je te bénis"). At the close of this number, Esclarmonde's voice is heard calling Roland, followed by the bravura aria ("Roland! tu m'as trahie"), which is extremely brilliant and difficult, as it makes exacting demands upon the voice.

In the last act the principal numbers are a cantabile ("Regarde les yeux"); a melodious song for Esclarmonde ("Plus en profond sommeil"); and the duet with Roland ("Viens, viens"). The epilogue merely repeats the material of the prologue. The opera as a whole is quite spectacular but effective music also forms an important part of it. As in "Manon" the instrumental part is the strongest. It is built somewhat on the lines of the "music of the future" in its use of motifs. Indeed one of the French critics after the opening performance called Massenet "Mlle. Wagner."

MEYERBEER

GIACOMO MEYERBEER, the eldest son of Herz Beer, was born in Berlin, September 5, 1794. He was named Jacob Meyer Beer, but afterwards called himself Giacomo Meyerbeer. His early studies were pursued with the pianist Lauska and Bernard Anselm Weber, chief of the Berlin orchestra. At fifteen he became the pupil of Vogler in Darmstadt, with whom he displayed such talent in composition that he was named Composer to the Court by the Grand Duke. At eighteen, his first dramatic work, "The Daughter of Jephtha," was performed at Munich. He then began his career, and made his debut in Vienna as a pianist with great success. His first opera, "The Two Caliphs," met with complete failure, as it was not written in the Italian form. He at once transformed his style and brought out "Romilda e Costanza," a serio-comic opera, with great success, at Padua. In 1820 "Emma di Resburgo" appeared at Venice, and from this period his star was in the ascendant. "The Gate of Brandebourg," "Margherita d'Anjou," "Esule di Granata," and "Almanzar" followed in quick succession, and were well received, though with nothing like the furor which "Il Crociato in Egitto" created in Venice in 1824. His next great work, "Robert le Diable," was produced in Paris, November 21, 1831, the unparalleled success of which carried its fame to every part of the civilized world. In 1836 "The Huguenots," unquestionably his masterpiece, was brought out, and it still holds its place as one of the grandest dramatic works upon the lyric stage. In 1838 Scribe furnished him the libretto of "L'Africaine," but before the music was finished he had changed the text so much that Scribe withdrew it altogether. He was consoled, however, by Meyerbeer's taking from him the libretto of "Le Prophète," this opera being finished in 1843. During the following year he wrote several miscellaneous pieces besides the three-act German opera, "Ein Feldlager in Schlesien," in which Jenny Lind made her Berlin debut. In 1846 he composed the overture and incidental music to his brother's drama of "Struensee," and in 1847 he not only prepared the way for Wagner's "Flying Dutchman" in Paris, but personally produced "Rienzi," — services which Wagner poorly requited. In 1849 "Le Prophète" was given in Paris; in 1854, "L'Etoile du Nord"; and in 1859, "Dinorah"; but none of them reached the fame of "The Huguenots." In 1860 he wrote two cantatas and commenced a musical drama called "Goethe's Jugendzeit," which was never finished. In 1862 and 1863 he worked upon "L'Africaine," and at last brought it forward as far as a rehearsal, but it was not performed until two years after his death.

The Huguenots

"Les Huguenots," grand opera in five acts, words by Scribe and Deschamps, was first produced at the Académie, Paris, February 29, 1836, with the following cast of the principal parts:

Valentin	Mlle. FALÇON.
Marguerite de Valois	Mme. DORUS-GRAS.
Urbain	Mlle. FLÉCHEUX.
Count de St. Bris	M. LERDA.
Count de Nevers	M. DERIVIS.
Raoul de Nangis	M. NOURRIT.
Marcel	M. LEVASSEUR.

At its first production in London in Italian, as "Gli Ugonotti," July 20, 1848, the cast was even more

Nilsson as *Valentin*

remarkable than that above. Meyerbeer especially adapted the opera for the performance, transposed the part of the page, which was written for a soprano, and expressly composed a cavatina to be sung by Mme. Alboni, in the scene of the chateau and gardens of Chenonceaux, forming the second act of the original work, but now given as the second scene of the first act in the Italian version. The cast was as follows:

Valentin	Mme. PAULINE VIARDOT.
Marguerite de Valois	Mme. CASTELLAN.
Urbain	Mlle. ALBONI.
Count de St. Bris	Sig. TAMBURINI.
Count de Nevers	Sig. TAGLIAFICO.
Raoul de Nangis	Sig. MARIO.
Marcel	Sig. MARINI.

The action of the opera passes in 1572, the first and second acts in Touraine, and the remainder in Paris. The first act opens on a scene of revelry in the salon of Count de Nevers, where a number of noblemen, among them Raoul de Nangis, a Protestant, accompanied by his faithful old Huguenot servant, Marcel, are present, telling stories of their exploits in love. Marguerite de Valois, the betrothed of Henry IV, for the sake of reconciling the dispute between the two religious sects, sends her page to De Nevers's salon and invites Raoul to her chateau. When he arrives, Marguerite informs him of her purpose to give him in marriage to a Catholic lady, daughter of the Count de St. Bris. Raoul at first consents; but when Valentin is introduced to him and he discovers her to be a lady whom he had once rescued from insult and who had visited De Nevers in his salon, he rejects the proposition, believing that her affections have been bestowed upon another, and that his enemies are seeking to entrap him. St. Bris challenges Raoul for the affront, but the Queen disarms the angry combatants. Valentin is now urged to marry Count de Nevers, and begs that she may pass the day in prayer in the chapel

Meanwhile Count de St. Bris, who has been challenged by Raoul, forms a plot for his assassination, which is overheard by Valentin from within the chapel. She communicates the plot to Marcel, who lies in wait with a party of Huguenots in the vicinity of the duel, and comes to Raoul's rescue when danger threatens him. A general combat is about to ensue, but it is suppressed by Marguerite, who suddenly appears upon the scene. Raoul thus discovers that he owes his life to Valentin, and that her visit to De Nevers was to induce him to sever the relations between them, as she was in love with Raoul. The announcement comes too late, for the marriage festivities have already begun. Raoul visits her for the last time. Their interview is disturbed by the approach of De Nevers, St. Bris, and other Catholic noblemen, who meet to arrange the details of the plot conceived by Catherine de Médicis for the slaughter of the Huguenots on St. Bartholomew's Eve. Valentin hurriedly conceals Raoul behind the tapestries, where he overhears their plans and witnesses the conjuration and the blessing of the swords, as well as the refusal of the chivalrous De Nevers to engage in murder. After the conspirators have departed, Raoul and Valentin have a long and affecting interview, in which he hesitates between love and honor, Valentin striving to detain him lest he may be included in the general massacre. Honor at last prevails, and he joins his friends just before the work of slaughter begins. He rushes to the festivities which are about to be given in honor of the marriage of Marguerite with the King of Navarre, and warns the Huguenots of their danger. He then makes his way to a chapel where many of them are gathered for refuge. He finds Marcel, who has been wounded, and who brings him the tidings of the death of De Nevers. The faithful Valentin joins them to share their fate. Amid the horrors of the massacre Marcel blesses and unites them. They enter the church and all perish together.

The first act opens with the brilliant chorus of the revellers ("Piacer della mensa"), which is full of courtly grace. Raoul tells the story of the unknown fair one he has encountered, in the romanza, "Piu bianca del velo." When Marcel is called upon, he hurriedly chants the hymn, "O tu che ognor," set to the Martin Luther air, "Ein feste Burg," and heightened by a stirring accompaniment, and then bursts out into a graphic song ("Finita è pe' frati"), emphasized with the piff-paff of bullets and full of martial fervor. In delightful contrast with the fierce Huguenot song comes the lively and graceful romanza of Urbain ("Nobil donna e tanto onesta"), followed by a delightful septet. The scene now changes, and with it the music. We are in the Queen's gardens at Chenonceaux. Every number, the Queen's solo ("A questa voce sola"), the delicate "Bathers' Chorus," as it is called ("Andiam, regina, in questo amene sponde"), the brilliant and graceful allegretto sung by Urbain ("No, no, no, no"), the duet between the Queen and Raoul, based upon one of the most flowing of melodies, and the spirited and effective finale in which the nobles take the oath of allegiance ("Per la fè, per l' onore"), — each and every one of these is colored with masterly skill, while all are invested with chivalrous refinement and stately grace.

The second act opens with a beautiful choral embroidery in which different choruses, most striking in contrast, are skilfully interwoven. It is a picture, in music, of the old Paris. The citizens rejoice over their day's work done. The Huguenots shout their lusty rataplan, while the Papist maidens sing their solemn litany ("Ave Maria") on their way to chapel; and as they disappear, the quaint tones of the curfew chant are heard, and night and rest settle down upon the city. It is a striking introduction to what follows, — the exquisite duet between Marcel and Valentin, the great septet of the duel scene, beginning ("De dritti miei ho l' alma accesa") with the tremendous double chorus which follows as the two bands rush upon the scene. As if for relief from the storm of this scene, the act closes with brilliant pageantry music as De Nevers approaches to escort Valentin to her bridal.

The third act is the climax of the work, and stands almost unrivalled in the field of dramatic music, for the manner in which horror and passion are illustrated. After a dark and despairing aria by Valentin ("Eccomi sola ormai"), and a brief duet with Raoul, the conspirators enter. The great trio, closing with the conjuration, "Quel Dio," the awful and stately chant of the monks in the blessing of the unsheathed daggers ("Sia gloria eterna e onore"), and the thrilling unisons of the chorus ("D' un sacro zel l' ardore"), which fairly glow with energy, fierceness, and religious fury, — these numbers of themselves might have made an act; but Meyerbeer does not pause here. He closes with a duet between Raoul and Valentin which does not suffer in comparison with the tremendous combinations preceding it. It is filled with the alternations of despair and love, of grief and ecstasy. In its movement it is the very whirlwind of passion. In the Italian version the performance usually closes at this point; but there is still another striking and powerful scene, that in which Raoul and Valentin are united by the dying Marcel. Then the three join in a sublime trio, and for the last time chant together the old Lutheran hymn, and await their fate amid the triumphant harpings that sound from the orchestra and the hosanna they sing to its accompaniment.

THE STAR OF THE NORTH

"L'Étoile du Nord," opera in three acts, words by Scribe, was first performed at the Opera Comique, Paris, February 16, 1854, and in Italian as "La Stélla del Nord," at Covent Garden, London, July 19, 1855. In English it

Jean de Reszke as *Raoul*
Copyright, Aimé Dupont

Plançon as *St. Bris*
Copyright, Aimé Dupont

MEYERBEER

has been produced under the title of "The Star of the North." The opera contains several numbers from the composer's earlier work, "Feldlager in Schlesien," which was written for the opening of the Berlin opera house, in memory of Frederick the Great, and was subsequently (February 17, 1847) performed with great success in Vienna, Jenny Lind taking the role of Vielka. The "Feldlager," however, has never been given out of Germany.

The action of the opera transpires in Wyborg, on the Gulf of Finland, in the first act, at a camp of the Russians in the second, and at the palace of the Czar Peter in the third. In the first, Peter, who is working at Wyborg, disguised as a carpenter, makes the acquaintance of Danilowitz, a pastry cook, and Catharine, a *cantinière*, whose brother George is about to marry Prascovia. Catharine brings about this marriage; and not only that, but saves the little village from an invasion by a strolling horde of Tartars, upon whose superstition she practises successfully, and so conducts herself in general that Peter falls in love with her, and they are betrothed, though she is not aware of the true identity of her suitor. Meanwhile the conscription takes place, and to save her newly wedded brother she volunteers for fifteen days in his place, disguising herself as a soldier. In the next act we find Catharine going her rounds as a sentinel in the Russian camp on the Finnish frontier. Peter and Danilowitz are also there, and are having a roistering time in their tent, drinking and making love to a couple of girls. Hearing Peter's voice she recognizes it, and curiosity leads her to peep into the tent. She is shocked at what she beholds, neglects her duty, and is found by the corporal in this insubordinate condition. He remonstrates with her, and she answers with a slap on his ears, for which she incurs the penalties of disobedience to orders as well as insulting behavior to her superior officer. Peter at last is roused from his drunkenness by the news of an insurrection among his own soldiers and the approach of the enemy. He rushes out and promises to give the Czar into their hands if they will obey and follow *him*. At last, struck with his bearing and authority, they demand to know who he is, whereupon he declares himself the Czar. The mutiny is at once quelled. They submit, and offer their lives as warrant for their loyalty. The last act opens in the Czar's palace, where his old companion, Danilowitz, has been installed in high favor. Catharine, however, has disappeared. George and Prascovia arrive from Finland, but they know nothing of her. The faithful Danilowitz finds her, but she has lost her reason. Her friends try to restore it by surrounding her with recollections of home, and Peter at last succeeds by playing upon his flute the airs he used to play to her in Finland. Her senses come back, and thus all ends happily; for Catharine and Peter are at last united amid the acclamations of the people.

In the first act the character of Peter is well expressed in the surly, growling bass of his soliloquy ("Vedra, vedra"). It is followed by a characteristic drinking-chorus ("Alla Finlanda, beviam"), a wild, barbaric minor rhythm, which passes into a prayer as they invoke the protection of Heaven upon Charles XII. In the eighth scene occur the couplets of Gritzensko as he sings the wild song of the Kalmucks. In charming contrast, in the next scene, Catharine sings the gypsy rondo, which Jenny Lind made so famous ("Wlastla la santa"), which is characterized by graceful coquetry; and this in turn is followed by a striking duet between Catharine and Peter, in which the individual characteristics of the two are brought out in genuine Wagnerian style. In the thirteenth scene occurs the bridal song of Prascovia ("Al suono dell' ora"), with choral accompaniment, of a delicate and coquettish cast, leading up to the finale, beginning with the soldiers' chorus ("Onor che a gloria"), with an accompaniment of drums and fifes, again passing to a pathetic prayer ("Veglia dal ciel su lor") sung by Catharine amid the ringing of bells as the bridal wreath is placed upon Prascovia's head, and closing with a florid barcarole ("Vascel che lasci") as she sails away.

The second act opens with ballet music, full of Eastern color, and then ensues one of those choral combinations, like that in the second act of "The Huguenots," in which Meyerbeer so much delighted, — a cavalry chorus ("Bel cavalier del cuor d'acciar"), followed by the Grenadier's song, accompanied by chorus ("Granadier di Russia esperti"), the chorus taking up the "tr-r-r-um" refrain in imitation of the drum. In the eighth scene we have the orgy in the tent in the form of a very spirited dramatic trio, in which Peter sings a blithe drinking-song ("Vedi al par del rubino"); this in turn resolving into a quintet ("Vezzose vivandière"), and again into a sextet, as Ismailoff enters with a letter for the Czar. The finale is a superb military picture, made up of the imposing oath of death to the tyrant, the stirring Dessauer march, the cavalry fanfare, and the Grenadiers' march, interwoven with the chorus of women as they cheer on the marching soldiers.

The third act opens with a romanza ("Dal cor per iscacciare"), very tender and beautiful, in which the rugged Czar shows us the sentimental side of his character. In the third scene occurs a long buffo trio between Peter, Gritzensko, and Danilowitz, which is full of humor. In the finale we have Catharine in the mad scene, singing the scena, "L'aurora alfin succede," with bits of the old music running through the accompaniment; and in the final scene, as her reason returns, breaking out in the florid bravura, "Non s'ode alcun," accompanied by the first and second flutes, which is a triumph of virtuosity for the voice. This number was taken from "The Camp in Silesia," and was given by Jenny Lind with immense success, not only in the latter work, but upon the concert stage. The opera as a whole abounds in humor, its music is fresh and brilliant, and its military character makes it especially attractive.

ROBERT THE DEVIL

"Robert le Diable," grand opera in five acts, words by Scribe and Delavigne, was first produced at the Académie, Paris, November 21, 1831, with the following cast:

Alice	Mlle. DORUS.
Isabella	Mme. CINTI-DAMOREAU.
The Abbess	Signora TAGLIONI.
Robert	M. NOURRIT.
Bertram	M. LEVASSEUR.
Raimbaut	M. LAFONT.

In the following year two versions in English, both of them imperfect, were brought out by the rival theatres, Covent Garden and Drury Lane. On the 20th of February it appeared at Drury Lane under the title of "The Demon; or, the Mystic Branch," and at Covent Garden the next evening as "The Fiend Father, or Robert Normandy." Drury Lane had twenty-four hours the start of its rival, but in neither case were the representations anything but poor imitations of the original. On the 11th of the following June the French version was produced at the King's Theatre, London, with the same cast as in Paris, except that the part of Alice was taken by Mme. De Meric, and that of the Abbess by the danseuse Mlle. Heberlé. On the 4th of May, 1847, the first Italian version was produced at Her Majesty's Theatre, with Jenny Lind and Staudigl in the cast. Gruneisen, the author of a brief memoir of Meyerbeer, who was present, says: "The night was rendered memorable, not only by the massacre attending the general execution, but also by the debut of Mlle. Lind in this country, who appeared as *Alice*. With the exception of the debutante, such a disgraceful exhibition was never before witnessed on the operatic stage. Mendelssohn was sitting in the stalls, and at the end of the third act, unable to bear any longer the executive infliction, he left the theatre."

The libretto of "Robert the Devil" is absurd in its conceptions and sensational in its treatment of the story, notwithstanding that it came from such famous dramatists as Scribe and Delavigne; and it would have been still worse had it not been for Meyerbeer. Scribe, it is said, wished to introduce a bevy of sea-nymphs, carrying golden oars, as the tempters of Robert; but the composer would not have them, and insisted upon the famous scene of the nuns, as it now stands, though these were afterwards made the butt of almost endless ridicule. Mendelssohn himself, who was in Paris at this time, writes: "I cannot imagine how any music could be composed on such a cold, formal extravaganza as this." The story runs as follows: The scene is laid in Sicily, where Robert, Duke of Normandy, who by his daring and gallantries had earned the sobriquet of "the Devil," banished by his own subjects, has arrived to attend a tournament given by the Duke of Messina. In the opening scene, while he is carousing with his knights, the minstrel Raimbaut sings a song descriptive of the misdeeds of Robert. The latter is about to revenge himself on the minstrel, when Alice, his foster-sister and the betrothed of Raimbaut, appears and pleads with him to give up his wicked courses, and resist the spirit of evil which is striving to get the mastery of him. Robert then confides to Alice his hopeless passion for Isabella, daughter of the Duke. While they are conversing, Bertram, "the unknown," enters, and Alice shrinks back affrighted, fancying she sees in him the evil spirit who is luring Robert on to ruin. After she leaves, Bertram entices him to the gaming-table, from which he rises a beggar, — and worse than this, he still further prejudices his cause with Isabella by failing to attend the tournament, thus forfeiting his knightly honor.

The second act opens upon an orgy of the evil spirits in the cavern of St. Irene. Bertram is present, and makes a compact with them to loose Robert from his influence if he does not yield to his desires at once. Alice, who has an appointment with the minstrel in the cavern, overhears the compact, and determines to save him. Robert soon appears, mourning over his losses and dishonor; but Bertram promises to restore everything if he will visit the ruined Abbey of St. Rosalie, and carry away a mystic branch which has the power of conferring wealth, happiness, and immortality. He consents; and in the next scene Bertram pronounces the incantation which calls up the buried nuns. Dazed with their ghostly fascinations, Robert seizes the branch and flees. His first use of it is to enter the apartments of Isabella, unseen by her or her attendants, all of whom become immovable in the presence of the mystic talisman. He declares his intention of carrying her away; but moved by her entreaties he breaks the branch, which destroys the charm. In the last act Bertram is at his side again, trying to induce him to sign the fatal compact. The strains of sacred music which he hears, and the recollections of his mother, restrain him. In desperation Bertram announces himself as his fiend-father. He is about to yield, when Alice appears and reads to him his mother's warning against the fiend's temptation. As he still hesitates, the clock strikes, and the spell is over. Bertram disappears, and the scene changes to the cathedral, where Isabella in her wedding robes awaits the rescued Robert.

From the musical point of view "Robert le Diable" is

MEYERBEER

interesting, as it marks the beginning of a new school of grand opera. With this work, Meyerbeer abandoned the school of Rossini and took an independent course. He cut loose from the conventional classic forms and gave the world dramatic music, melodies of extraordinary dramatic force, brilliant orchestration, stately pageants, and theatrical effects. "Robert le Diable" was the first of the subsequent great works from his pen which still further emphasized his new and independent departure. It is only necessary to call attention to a few prominent numbers, for this opera has not as many instances of these characteristics as those which followed and which are elsewhere described. The first act contains the opening bacchanalian chorus ("Versiamo a tazza plena"), which is very brilliant in character; the minstrel's song in the same scene ("Regnava un tempo in Normandia"), with choral accompaniment; and a very tender aria for Alice ("Vanne, disse, al figlio mio"), in which she delivers his mother's message to Robert. The second act opens with a spirited duet between Bertram and Raimbaut, leading up to a powerful and characteristic chorus of the evil spirits ("Demoni fatali"). An aria for Alice ("Nel lasciar la Normandia"), a duet between Bertram and Alice ("Trionfo bramato"), and an intensely dramatic trio between Bertram, Alice, and Robert ("Lo sguardo immobile"), prepare the way for the great scena of the nuns, known as "La Temptation," in which Meyerbeer illustrates the fantastic and oftentimes ludicrous scene with music which is the very essence of diabolism, and in its way as unique as the incantation music in "Der Freischutz." The third act contains two great arias. The first ("Invano il fato"), sung at the opening of the act by Isabella, and the second the world-famous aria "Roberto, o tu che adoro," better known by the French words ("Robert! toi que j'aime"). The closing act is specially remarkable for the great terzetto in its finale, which is one of the most effective numbers Meyerbeer has written. The judgment of Hanslick, the well-known Viennese critic, upon this work is interesting in this connection. He compares it with "William Tell" and "Masaniello," and finds that in musical richness and blended effects it is superior to either, but that a single act of either of the works mentioned contains more artistic truth and ideal form than "Robert le Diable," — a judgment which is largely based upon the libretto itself, which he condemns without stint.

Dinorah

"Dinorah," opera in three acts, founded upon a Breton idyl, words by Barbier and Carré, was first produced at the Opera Comique, Paris, April 4, 1859, under the title of "Le Pardon de Ploermel." It contains but three principal characters, and these were cast as follows: Dinorah, Mme. Cabel; Corentin, M. Sainte-Foy; and Höel, M. Faure. On the 26th of July, 1859, Meyerbeer conducted the work himself at Covent Garden, London, with Mme. Miolan-Carvalho as Dinorah, and it was also produced the same year in English by the Pyne-Harrison troupe. The first representative of Dinorah in this country was Mlle. Cordier.

The scene of the opera is laid in Brittany, and when the first act opens, the following events are supposed to have transpired: On one of the days appointed by the villagers of Ploermel for a pilgrimage to the shrine of the Virgin, Höel, the goatherd, and Dinorah, his affianced, set out to receive a nuptial benediction. The festivity is interrupted by a thunder-storm, during which Les Herbiers, the dwelling-place of Dinorah, is destroyed by lightning. Dinorah is in despair. Höel determines to make good the loss, and upon the advice of Tonick, an old wizard, resolves to go in quest of a treasure which is

MEYERBEER

under the care of the Korigans, a supernatural folk belonging to Brittany. In order to wrest it from them, however, it is necessary for Höel to quit the country and spend a year in solitude in a desolate region. He bravely starts off, and Dinorah, thinking he has abandoned her, loses her wits, and constantly wanders about the woods with her goat, seeking him. Meanwhile the year expires and Höel returns, convinced that he has the secret for securing the treasure.

The overture to the work is unique among operatic overtures, as it has a chorus behind the curtain interwoven with it. It is a picture of the opera itself, and contains a will-o'-the-wisp passage, a rustic song with accompaniment of goat-bells, a storm, and in the midst of the storm a chant to the Virgin, sung by the unseen chorus, and then a Pilgrimage march, the whole being in the nature of a retrospect. The curtain rises upon a rustic chorus, after which Dinorah appears, seeking her goat, and sings a slumber-song ("Si, carina, caprettina") which is very graceful, and concludes with phrases in imitation of birds. In the next scene, Corentin, the bagpiper, who has been away three months, and is nearly dead with terror of goblins and fairies, returns to his cottage, and to reassure himself sings a very quaint and original song ("Sto in casa alfine"), to the accompaniment of his pipe. Dinorah suddenly appears and enters the cottage, and much to his alarm keeps him playing and singing, which leads to a very animated vocal contest between her and the bagpiper. It is abruptly terminated, however, by the arrival of Höel. Dinorah makes her escape by a window, and Höel relates to Corentin the story of the Korigans' treasure. As the first person who touches it will die, he determines that Corentin shall be his messenger, and to rouse his courage sends for wine. While Corentin is absent, Höel sings an aria ("Se per prender") which has always been a favorite with baritones. After Corentin returns, the tinkling of the goat's bell is heard. Dinorah appears in the distance, and a charming trio closes the act, to the accompaniment of the whistling wind and booming thunder on the contra basses and drums of the orchestra.

The second act opens with a drinking-song by woodcutters, and as they withdraw, Dinorah enters, seeking Höel. She sings a tender lament, which, as the moonlight falls about her, develops into the famous "Shadow Song," a polka mazurka, which she sings and dances to her shadow. The aria, "Ombra leggiere," is fairly lavish in its texture of vocal embroidery, and has always been a favorite number on the concert stage. The next scene changes to the Val Maudit (The Cursed Vale), a rocky, cavernous spot, through which rushes a raging torrent bridged by a fallen tree. Höel and Corentin appear in quest of the treasure, and the latter gives expression to his terror in a very characteristic manner, with the assistance of the orchestra. Dinorah is heard singing the legend of the treasure ("Chi primo al tesor"), from which Corentin learns that whoever touches it first will die. He refuses to go on, and a spirited duet ensues between them, which is interrupted by the entrance of Dinorah and her goat. Höel, fancying it is a spirit sent to keep him back, sings a very beautiful aria ("Le crede il padre"). The act closes with the fall of Dinorah, who attempts to cross the bridge, into the torrent, and her rescue by Höel, to the accompaniment of a storm set to music. The scene, though melodramatic, is very strong in its musical effects.

The last act opens with a scene in striking contrast, introduced with a quintet of horns, followed by a hunter's solo, a reaper's solo, a duet for shepherds, and a quartet in the finale. Höel arrives, bearing the rescued Dinorah, and sings to her an exquisite romance ("Sei vendicata assai"). The magic of his singing and her bath in the torrent restore her wandering senses. Höel persuades her that all which has transpired has been a dream. The old song of the Pardon of Ploermel comes to her, and as she tries to recall it the chorus takes it up ("Santa Maria! nostra donna") as it was heard in the overture. A procession is seen in the distance, and amid some striking pageant music Höel and Dinorah wend their way to the chapel, where the nuptial rites are supposed to be performed.

THE PROPHET

"Le Prophète," opera in five acts, words by Scribe, was first produced in Paris, April 16, 1849, with Mme. Viardot-Garcia as Fides, and M. Roger as John of Leyden. "The Prophet" was long and carefully elaborated by its composer. Thirteen years intervened between it and its predecessor, "The Huguenots"; but in spite of its elaboration it can only be said to excel the latter in pageantry and spectacular effect, while its musical text is more declamatory than melodious, as compared with "The Huguenots." In this sense it was disappointing when first produced.

The period of the opera is 1534. The first act transpires in Dordrecht and Leyden, in Holland, and the other three in Munster, Germany. The text closely follows the historical narrative of the period when Munster was occupied by John of Leyden and his fanatics, who, after he had been crowned by them as Emperor of Germany, was driven out by the bishop of the diocese. The first act opens in the suburbs of Dordrecht, near the Meuse, with the chateau of Count Oberthal, lord of the domain, in the distance. After a very fresh and vigorous chorus of peasants, Bertha, a vassal of the Count, betrothed to John of Leyden, enters and sings a cavatina ("Il cor nel sento"), in which she gives expression to emotions of delight at her approaching union. As she cannot go to Leyden, where the marriage is to take place, without the Count's consent, Fides, the mother of John, joins her to make the request. In the meantime the three Anabaptists, Zacarie, Gione, and Mathisen, leaders of the revolt in Westphalia, arrive on their mission of raising an insurrection in Holland, and in a sombre trio of a religious but stirring character ("O libertade") incite the peasants to rise against their rulers. They make an assault upon the castle of Count Oberthal, who speedily repels them, and turns the tide of popular feeling against the Anabaptists, by recognizing Gione as a former servant who had been discharged from his service for dishonesty. Fides and Bertha then join in a romanza ("Della mora un giorno"), imploring his permission for the marriage of Bertha and John. The Count, however, struck with her beauty, not only refuses, but claims her for himself, and seizes both her and Fides, and the act closes with a repetition of the warning chant of the Anabaptists.

The second act opens in the hostelry of John of Leyden, and is introduced with a waltz and drinking-chorus, in the midst of which the Anabaptists arrive and are struck with his resemblance to a portrait of David in the Munster Cathedral. From a very descriptive and highly wrought scena ("Sotto le vasti arcati") sung by him they also learn that he is given to visions and religious meditations. They assure him that he shall be a ruler; but in a beautiful romanza ("Un impero piu soave") he replies that his love for Bertha is his only sovereignty. Just as they depart, Bertha, who has escaped, rushes in and claims his protection. He conceals her; but has hardly done so when the Count enters with his soldiers, bringing Fides as a prisoner, and threatens to kill her unless Bertha is given up. He hesitates; but at last, to save his mother's life,

Schumann-Heink as *Fidès*
Copyright, Aimé Dupont

Alvarez as *The Prophet*
Copyright, Aimé Dupont

delivers Bertha to her pursuers. Mother and son are left alone, and she seeks to console him. In this scene occurs one of the most dramatic and intense of Meyerbeer's arias ("O figlio mio, che diro"), known more popularly by its French words, beginning, "Ah! mon fils." It has enjoyed a world-wide popularity, and still holds its place in all its original freshness and vigor. Fides hardly disappears before the ominous chant of the Anabaptists is heard again. He does not need much persuasion now. They make their compact in a quartet of great power, which closes the act; and some of John's garments are left behind stained with blood, that his mother may believe he has been killed.

The third act opens in the Anabaptists' camp in a Westphalian forest, a frozen lake near them, and Munster, which they are besieging, in the distance. In the second scene Zacarie sings a stirring pæan of victory ("In coppia son"), followed by the beautiful ballet music of the skaters as they come bringing provisions to the troops. Count Oberthal meanwhile has been taken prisoner and brought into camp. A buffo trio between himself and his captors follows, in which Gione penetrates his disguise and recognizes him. They are about to fall upon him; but John, learning from him that Bertha is still alive and in Munster, saves his life. He immediately resolves to take the place by assault, rouses his followers with religious chants of a martial character, and the act concludes with the march on the city.

The fourth act opens in the city itself after its capture. A mendicant appears in the public square begging for bread. It is Fides; and in a plaintively declamatory aria of striking power ("Pieta! pieta!") she implores alms. She meets with Bertha disguised as a pilgrim, and bent upon the destruction of the Prophet, who, she believes, has been the cause of John's death. The next scene opens in the cathedral, where the coronation of the Prophet is to take place; and among all Meyerbeer's pageants none are more imposing than this, with its accompaniment of pealing bells, religious chants, the strains of the organ, and the stately rhythms of the great Coronation March. It is a splendid prelude to the dramatic scene which follows. In the midst of the gorgeous spectacle, the voice of Fides is heard claiming the Prophet as her son. John boldly disavows her, and tells his followers to kill him if she does not confirm the disavowal. The feelings of the mother predominate, and she declares that she is mistaken. The multitude proclaim it a miracle, and Fides is removed as a prisoner. The dramatic situation in this finale is one of great strength, and its musical treatment has hardly been excelled.

The last act opens with a trio by the Anabaptist leaders, who, learning that the enemy is approaching in force, determine to save themselves by betraying John. In the third scene Fides in prison, learning that John is coming to see her, invokes the punishment of Heaven upon him in the passionate aria, "Spirto superno." A duet ("Tu che del cielo") of great power follows, in which Fides convinces him of the errors of his course. As they are about to leave, Bertha enters, bent upon the destruction of the palace, and in the trio which ensues learns that John and the Prophet are one. She stabs herself, and dying in the arms of Fides curses him. The last scene opens in a banqueting hall of the palace, where John is revelling, with the Anabaptists around him. He sings a bacchanalian song of a wild description ("Bevian e intorno"), and, as it closes, the Bishop of Munster, the Elector, Count Oberthal, and the three Anabaptists who have betrayed him, enter the apartment. The revenge which John has planned is now consummated. An explosion is heard. Flames break out on all sides. Fides rushes in and forgives her son, and the Prophet, his mother, and his enemies perish together.

Although "The Prophet" did not meet with the popularity of some of his other operas, it contains some of the most vigorous and dramatic music Meyerbeer has written, —notably the arias of Zacarie and Fides, the skating-ballet, the Coronation March, and the drinking-song. As a pageant, "The Prophet" has never been surpassed.

L'AFRICAINE

"L'Africaine," grand opera in five acts, words by Scribe, was first produced at the Académie, Paris, April 28, 1865, with the following cast:

Selika	Mme. MARIE SAXE.
Inez	Mlle. MARIE BATTEO.
Vasco di Gama	M. NAUDIN.
Nelusko	M. FAURE.
Don Pedro	M. BELVAL.
High Priest	M. OBIN.

The libretto of the opera was first given to Meyerbeer by Scribe in 1838; but such were the alterations demanded by the composer, that at last Scribe withdrew it altogether, although the music was already set. In 1852 he furnished a revised libretto, and the music was revised to suit it. The work was not finished until 1860, and owing to the difficulty of filling the cast satisfactorily, was not brought to rehearsal until the Fall of 1863. While still correcting and improving it, Meyerbeer died, and it was not produced until two years later. Shortly after the Paris performance it was brought out in London, with Mlle. Lucca in the part of Selika. Mme. Zucchi was one of the earliest representatives of the slave in this country.

The scene of the opera is laid in Portugal and Africa, and the first act opens in the council chamber of the king of the former country. Inez, his daughter, is mourning the long absence of her betrothed, Vasco di Gama, the explorer. Her father, wishing to marry her to Don Pedro, the President of the Council, tries to persuade her that Vasco has perished by shipwreck; but the refutation of the story comes in the sudden appearance of Vasco himself, who is summoned before the Council and narrates to them his discovery of a strange land, producing two of the natives, Selika and Nelusko, as confirmations of his announcement. Don Pedro incites the inquisitors to deny the truth of the story, at which Vasco breaks out in such a furious rage against them that he is arrested and thrown into a dungeon. The second act opens in the prison, where Selika is watching the slumbering Vasco. As he wakens she declares her love for him, and at the same time saves him from the dagger of the jealous Nelusko. She also indicates to him the course he should have taken to discover the island of which he is in quest. To save her lover, Inez consents to wed Don Pedro; and the latter, to cheat Vasco of his fame, takes command of the expedition under the pilotage of Nelusko, and sets sail for the new land. The Indian, thirsting for vengeance, directs the vessel out of her course towards a reef; but Vasco, who has followed in another vessel, arrives in time to warn Don Pedro of his danger. He disregards the warning, distrusts his motives, and orders him to be shot; but before the sentence can be carried out, the vessel strikes and is boarded by the savages, who slaughter the commander and most of his men. The fourth act opens on the island which Selika pointed out on the map, and of which she is queen. To save him from her subjects, she declares herself his spouse; but as the marriage rite is about to be celebrated, Vasco hears the voice of Inez in the distance, deserts Selika, and flies to her. In the last act, as the vessel sails away bearing Vasco and Inez back to Portugal, Selika throws herself down under the

Dippel as *Vasco di Gama*

Copyright, Aimé Dupont

poisonous manchineel tree and kills herself with its fatal flowers; expiring in the arms of Nelusko, who shares the same fate.

The first act opens with a very sweet but sombre ballad sung by Inez ("Del Tago sponde addio"), which recalls the English song, "Isle of Beauty, fare thee well," and is followed by a bold and flowing terzetto. The third scene opens with a noble and stately chorus ("Tu che la terra adora") sung by the basses in unison, opening the Council before which Vasco appears; and the act closes with an anathema hurled at him ("Ribelle, insolente"),— a splended ensemble, pronounced in its rhythm and majestic in the sweep of its passionate music.

The second act opens with the quaint slumber-song ("In grembo a me") which Selika sings to Vasco in prison. It is Oriental in color, and is broken here and there by a barcarole which Vasco murmurs in his sleep. In striking contrast with its dreamy, quiet flow, it leads up to a passionate aria ("Tranquillo e già") based upon a strong and fiery motive. In the next scene follows an aria of equal vigor sung by Nelusko ("Figlia dei Re"), in which his devotion to Selika changing to his hatred of Vasco is characterized by a grand crescendo. The act closes with a vigorous sextet, the motive of which is strangely similar to the old song, "The Minstrel Boy."

The third act contains a very impressive number, Nelusko's invocation of Adamastor ("Adamastor, re dell' onde profondo"), but is mainly devoted to the ship scene, which, though grotesque from the dramatic point of view, is accompanied by music of a powerful and realistic description, written with all the vividness and force Meyerbeer always displays in his melodramatic ensembles. The fourth act contains the most beautiful music of the opera, — Vasco's opening aria, "O Paradiso," an exquisite melody set to an equally exquisite accompaniment; the ensemble in the fourth scene, in which Selika protects Vasco and Nelusko swears vengeance ("Al mio penar de fine"); the grand duet between Vasco and Selika ("Dove son"), which has often been compared to the duet in the fourth act of "The Huguenots," though it has not the passionate intensity of the scene between Raoul and Valentin; and the graceful choruses of the Indian maidens and Inez's attendants which close the act.

The last act contains two scenes, — the first in Selika's gardens, where there is a long and spirited duet between Inez and Selika. The second, known as "La Scene du Mancenillier," has a symphonic prelude in the form of a funeral march, based upon a fascinating melody, which is beyond question the finest of Meyerbeer's instrumental numbers in any of his works. From this point the story hastens to its tragic denouement; and nearly the entire scene is occupied with Selika's dying song, which opens with a majestic apostrophe to the sea ("Da qui io vedo il mar"), then turns to sadness as she sings to the fatal tree ("O tempio sontuoso"), and at the close develops into a passionate outcry of joy ("O douce extase"). Though the plot of "L'Africaine" is often absurd, many of its incidents preposterous, and some of its characters unattractive, the opera is full of effective situations, and repeatedly illustrates Meyerbeer's powers of realization and his knowledge of musical and dramatic effects.

MILLÖCKER

CARL MILLÖCKER, a composer of operettas, was born in Vienna, May 29, 1842. He obtained his musical education at the conservatory in that city, and has been connected with several theatres, for which he has written operettas. He has also composed a large number of musical farces and a long list of light and sprightly piano pieces. His best known works are "Die Frauen-insel" (1867); "Der Regimentstambour" (1869); "Drei Paar Schuhe" (1870); "Ein Abenteuer in Wien" (1873); "The Beggar Student" (1881).

THE BEGGAR STUDENT

"The Beggar Student," opera comique in three acts, text by Zell and Genée, was first produced at Vienna in 1882. The scene is laid in Krakow, in the year 1704. General Ollendorf, the military governor of that city, is in a rage because he has been repulsed by Laura, daughter of the Countess Palmatica, to whom he has shown some unwelcome attentions. To punish what he considers an insult, he conceives the idea of dressing some poor and low-born young fellow in the finery of a prince, and passing him off as such upon the Countess and her daughter, trusting that their poverty will induce them to accept the impostor. After such a marriage his revenge would be complete. He finds his accomplice in the military prison. Symon Symonovicz, a vagabond Polish student, is ready to play the gentleman, and only insists on taking along with him Janitsky, a fellow-prisoner, to act as his secretary. The plot is successful.

The Countess and her daughter, who have been living for a long time in genteel poverty, are dazzled by the finery and prospects of the suitor, and the act closes with the betrothal of Symon and Laura.

In the second act the two find that they are really in love with each other. As the money furnished by the General is all spent, Symon decides to tell Laura of the deception practised upon her, though it may cost him the marriage, which was to have taken place that day. Afraid to tell her in person, he writes the disclosure, and intrusts the letter to the Countess with the request to have it given to Laura before the ceremony. The General, however, thwarts this scheme, and the pair are married, whereupon he exposes Symon to the assembled guests as an impostor and has him driven from the palace.

At the opening of the third act Symon appears in melancholy plight and contemplating suicide. His friend Janitsky, who is in love with Laura's sister, Bronislava, comes to his rescue. He comes forward as a Polish officer engaged in a plot for the capture of the citadel and the reinstatement of King Stanislaus upon the throne of Poland. The plot with Symon's help succeeds, and in return Symon is not only ennobled, but the Countess and his wife forgive him, and the governor-general is foiled at every point.

The principal numbers are Ollendorf's entrance song in waltz time ("And they say that towards Ladies"); the characteristic duet by Symon and Janitsky on leaving jail ("Confounded Cell, at last I leave thee"); the charming entrance trio for Laura, Bronislava, and the Countess ("Some little Shopping really we ought to do"); and Laura's brilliant song, "But when the Song is sweetly sounding," in the finale of the first act; Laura's humorous song, "If Joy in married Life you'd find"; the sentimental duet of Bronislava and Janitsky ("This Kiss, sweet Love"); Ollendorf's grotesque songs, "One Day I was perambulating" and "There in the Chamber Polish," which is usually adapted as a topical song; and the long and cleverly concerted finale of the second act; and Bronislava's song, "Prince a Beggar's said to be," and Symon's couplet, "I'm penniless and outlawed too," in the third act.

MOZART

JOHANN CHRYSOSTOMUS WOLFGANG AMADEUS MOZART was born at Salzburg, January 27, 1756. To this wonderful child music was a divine gift, for his first work, a minuet and trio for piano, was written in his fifth year. He began to study with his father when but three years of age, and at once gave signs of extraordinary promise. His sister was also very talented; and in 1762 the father determined to travel with his prodigies. They were absent a year, the most of that time being spent at Munich, Vienna, and Presburg, where they created a furor by their performances. A longer journey was then resolved upon. The principal German cities, Brussels, Paris, London, The Hague, Amsterdam, and the larger towns of Switzerland were visited in succession, and everywhere the children were greeted with enthusiasm, particularly when they played before the French and English courts. They returned to Salzburg in 1766, already famous all over Europe; and during the next two years Mozart composed many minor works. In 1768 he was again in Vienna, where he produced his little operetta, "Bastien und Bastienne," and in the same year the Archbishop of Salzburg made him his concertmeister. The next year he went to Italy, where he both studied and composed, and was received with extraordinary honors. In 1771 he brought out his opera, "Mitridate, Rè di Ponto," at Milan, with great success. The next year he produced "Lucio Silla," also in Milan, and during the next four years composed a great number of symphonies and other instrumental works. The mass of music which he composed up to his twenty-first year is simply bewildering. In 1781 he brought out "Idomeneo" at Munich, which left no doubt as to his position as a dramatic composer. In 1782 his "Die Entführung aus dem Serail" was produced at Vienna by the Emperor's command. His next great opera was "Le Nozze di Figaro," which was performed in 1786, and made all Vienna go wild. "Don Giovanni" followed it the next year, and was received with equal enthusiasm. In 1789 he composed the famous "Requiem"; and the same year "Die Zauberflöte," his last great opera, appeared, and made a success even greater than its two predecessors. Two years later, December 5, 1791, Mozart died in poverty, and amid the saddest of surroundings. One of the world's greatest geniuses was carried to his last resting-place unaccompanied by friends, and was buried in the pauper's grave. God endowed him with a wonderful genius, which the world of his time failed to recognize. It was only the great who recognized his real greatness.

THE MARRIAGE OF FIGARO

"Le Nozze di Figaro," in the German version, "Die Hochzeit des Figaro," opera buffa in four acts, the words by Lorenzo da Ponte, after Beaumarchais's comedy, "Le Mariage de Figaro," was first produced at the National Theatre, Vienna, May 1, 1786, with the following cast:

Countess Almaviva	Signora STORACE.
Susanna	Signora LASCHI.
Cherubino	Signora MANDINI.
Marcellina	Signora BUSSANI.
Barbarina	Frau GOTTLIEB.
Count Almaviva	Sig. MANDINI.
Figaro	Sig. BENUCCI.
Bartolo	Sig. OCCHELEY.
Basilio	Sig. BUSSANI.

It was first brought out in Paris in 1793, with Beaumarchais's spoken dialogue, in five acts, as "Le Mariage de Figaro," and in 1858 at the Théâtre Lyrique in the same city, in four acts, as "Les Noces de Figaro," with text by Barbier and Carré. The late Mme. Parepa-Rosa introduced it in this country in its English form with great success.

At the time the libretto was written, Beaumarchais's satirical comedy, "Le Mariage de Figaro," had been performed all over Europe, and had attracted great attention. It had been prohibited in Paris, and had caused great commotion in Vienna. Mozart's notice was thus drawn to it, and he suggested it to Da Ponte for a libretto, and the Emperor Joseph subsequently commissioned the composer to set it to music, though he had already composed a portion of it. The entire opera was written during the month of April, and the wonderful finale to the second act occupied him for two nights and a day. When it came to a performance, its success was remarkable. Kelly, who was present, says, in his "Reminiscences": "Never was there a greater triumph than Mozart enjoyed with his 'Figaro.' The house was crowded to overflowing, and almost everything encored, so that the opera lasted nearly double the usual time; and yet at its close the public were unwearied in clapping their hands and shouting for Mozart." Popular as it was, it was soon laid aside in Vienna through the influence of the Italian faction headed by Salieri, one of Mozart's rivals.

The story of the opera is laid in Spain. Count Almaviva, who had won his beautiful Countess with the aid of Figaro, the barber of Seville, becomes enamored of her maid Susanna, and at the same time, by the collusion of the two, in order to punish him, is made jealous by the attentions paid to the Countess by Cherubino, the

Sigrid Arnoldson as *Cherubino*

page. Meanwhile Figaro, to whom Susanna is betrothed, becomes jealous of the Count for his gallantry to her. Out of these cross-relations arise several humorous surprises. Besides these characters there are two others who have been disappointed in love, — Bartolo, who has been rejected by Susanna, and Marcellina, whose affection for Figaro has not been requited. The Count seeks to get rid of Cherubino by ordering him off to the wars, but he is saved by Susanna, who disguises him in female attire. The Countess, Susanna, Figaro, and Cherubino, then conspire to punish the Count for his infidelity. The latter suddenly appears at his wife's door, and finding it locked demands an entrance. Cherubino, alarmed, hides himself in a closet and bars the door. The Count is admitted, and finding the Countess in confusion insists upon searching the closet. He goes out to find some means of breaking in the door, and Cherubino improves the opportunity to jump out of the window, while Susanna takes his place and confronts the puzzled Count. Antonio, the gardener, comes in and complains that some one has jumped from the window and broken his flower-pots. Figaro at once asserts that he did it.

A ludicrous side plot unfolds at this point. Marcellina appears with a contract of marriage signed by Figaro, bringing Bartolo as a witness. The Count decides that Figaro must fulfil his contract, but the latter escapes by showing that he is the son of Marcellina, and that Bartolo is his father. Meanwhile the main plot is developed in another conspiracy to punish the Count. Susanna contrives a rendezvous with the Count at night in the garden, having previously arranged with the Countess that she shall disguise herself as the maid, the latter also assuming the part of the Countess, and arrive in time to surprise the two. The page also puts in an appearance, and gets his ears boxed for his attentions to the disguised Countess. Figaro, who has been informed that Susanna and the Count are to meet in the garden, comes on the scene, and in revenge makes a passionate declaration of love to the supposed Countess, upon which the Count, who is growing more and more bewildered, orders lights and makes his supposed wife unveil. The real wife does the same. Covered with confusion, he implores pardon of the Countess, which is readily given. The two are reconciled, and Figaro and Susanna are united.

The whole opera is such a combination of playfulness and grace that it is a somewhat ungracious task to refer to particular numbers. In these regards it is the most Mozartean of all the composer's operas. The first act opens with a sparkling duet between Figaro and Susanna, in which she informs him of the Count's gallantries. As she leaves, Figaro, to the accompaniment of his guitar, sings a rollicking song ("Se vuol ballare, Signor Contino"), in which he intimates that if the Count wishes to dance he will play for him in a style he little expects. In the second scene Bartolo enters, full of his plans for vengeance, which he narrates in a grim and grotesque song ("La Vendetta"). The fourth scene closes with an exquisite aria by Cherubino ("Non so più cosa son"). After an exceedingly humorous trio ("Cosa sento? tosto andate") for the Count, Basilio, and Susanna, and a bright, gleeful chorus ("Giovanni liete"), Figaro closes the act with the celebrated aria, "Non più andrai." Of the singing of this great song at the first rehearsal of the opera Kelly says in his "Reminiscences": "I remember Mozart well at the first general rehearsal, in a red furred coat and a gallooned hat, standing on the stage and giving the tempi. Benucci sang Figaro's aria, 'Non più andrai,' with the utmost vivacity and the full strength of his voice. I stood close beside Mozart, who exclaimed, *sotto voce*, 'Brava! brava! Benucci!' and when that fine passage came, 'Cherubino, alla vittoria, alla gloria militar,' which Benucci gave in a stentorian voice, the effect was quite electrical, both upon the singers on the stage and the musicians in the orchestra. Quite transported with delight, they all called out, 'Brava! brava, Maestro! viva! viva! viva il grande Mozart!' In the orchestra the applause seemed to have no end, while the violin players rapped their bows on their desks. The little Maestro expressed his gratitude for the enthusiasm, testified in so unusual a manner, by repeatedly bowing."

The second act is the masterpiece of the opera, and contains in itself music enough to have made any composer immortal. It opens with a serious aria by the Countess ("Porgi amor"), followed by Cherubino's well-known romanza ("Voi, che sapete"), one of the sweetest and most effective songs ever written for contralto, and this in turn by Susanna's coquettish song, "Venite, inginocchiatevi," as she disguises Cherubino. A spirited trio and duet lead up to the great finale, begun by the Count ("Esci omai, garzon malnato"). Upon this finale Mozart seems to have lavished the riches of his musical genius with the most elaborate detail and in bewildering profusion. It begins with a duet between the Count and Countess, then with the entrance of Susanna changes to a trio, and as Figaro and Antonio enter, develops into a quintet. In the close, an independent figure is added by the entrance of Marcellina, Barbarina, and Basilio, and as Antonio exits, this trio is set against the quartet with independent themes and tempi.

The third act opens with a duet ("Crudel! perchè finora") for the Count and Countess, followed by a very dramatic scena for the Count, beginning with the recitative, "Hai già vinto la causa!" which in turn leads up to a lively and spirited sextet ("Riconosci in questo amplesso"). The two numbers which follow the sextet are recognized universally as two of the sweetest and most melodious ever written, — the exquisite aria, "Dove sono," for the Countess, and the "Zephyr Duet," as it is popularly known ("Canzonetta sull' aria. Che soave zefiretto"), which stands unsurpassed for elegance, grace, and melodious beauty. The remaining numbers of prominent interest are a long and very versatile buffo aria for tenor ("In quegl' anni"), sung by Basilio, Figaro's stirring march number ("Ecco la marcia"), and a lovely song for Susanna ("Deh, vieni, non tardar"). The opera is full of life and human interest. Its wonderful cheerfulness and vital sympathy appeal to every listener, and its bright, free, joyous tone from beginning to end is no less fascinating than the exquisite melodies with which Mozart has so richly adorned it. Like "Don Giovanni" and the "Magic Flute," the best test of the work is, that in its second century it is as fresh and bright and popular as ever.

Don Giovanni

"Don Giovanni," opera buffa in two acts, words by Da Ponte, was first produced at Prague, October 29, 1787. The full title of the work is "Il dissoluto punito, ossia il Don Giovanni," and the subject was taken from a Spanish tale by Tirso de Molina, called "El combidado de piedra." The original cast of the opera was as follows:

Donna Anna	Signora TERESA SAPORITTI.
Donna Elvira	Signora MICELLI.
Zerlina	Signora BONDINI.
Don Ottavio	Sig. BAGLIONI.
Don Giovanni	Sig. LUIGI BASSI.
Leporello	Sig. FELICE PONZIANI.
Masetto and *Don Pedro*	Sig. LOLLI.

Sontag as *Donna Anna*

MOZART

The success of "The Marriage of Figaro" prepared the way for "Don Giovanni." Mozart wrote the opera in Prague, and completed it, except the overture, October 28, 1787, about six weeks after he arrived in the city. The first performance took place the next evening. The overture was written during the night, the copyist received the score at seven o'clock in the morning, and it was played at eight in the evening. He had only a week for stage rehearsals, and yet the opera created a furor. As an instance of his extraordinary memory, it is said that the drum and trumpet parts to the finale of the second act were written without the score, from memory. When he brought the parts into the orchestra, he remarked, "Pray, gentlemen, be particularly attentive at this place," pointing to one, "as I believe that there are four bars either too few or too many." His remark was found to be true. It is also said that in the original score the brass instruments frequently have no place, as he wrote the parts continually on separate bits of paper, trusting to his memory for the score. The next year (1788) the opera was brought out in Vienna, and for this production he wrote four new numbers, — a recitative and aria for Donna Elvira ("In quali eccessi, O Numi"); an aria for Masetto ("Ho capito, Signor, si"); a short aria for Don Ottavio ("Dalla sua pace"); and a duet for Zerlina and Leporello ("Per queste tue manine").

The scene of the opera is laid in Spain. Don Giovanni, a licentious nobleman, becomes enamored of Donna Anna, the daughter of the Commandant of Seville, who is betrothed to Don Ottavio. He gains admission to her apartments at night, and attempts to carry her away; but her cries bring her father to her rescue. He attacks Don Giovanni, and in the encounter is slain. The libertine, however, in company with his rascally servant, Leporello, makes good his escape. While the precious pair are consulting about some new amour, Donna Elvira, one of his victims, appears and taxes him with his cruelty; but he flies from her, leaving her with Leporello, who horrifies her with an appalling list of his master's conquests in various countries. Don Giovanni next attempts the ruin of Zerlina, a peasant girl, upon the very eve of her marriage with her lover, Masetto. Donna Elvira, however, appears and thwarts his purposes, and also exposes him to Donna Anna as the murderer of her father, whereupon she binds her lover, Don Ottavio, to avenge his death. Don Giovanni does not abandon his purpose, however. He gives a fete, and once more seeks to accomplish Zerlina's ruin, but is again thwarted by her three friends.

The second act opens in a public square of Seville at night. Don Giovanni and Leporello appear before the house of Donna Elvira, where Zerlina is concealed. Leporello, disguised in his master's cloak, and assuming his voice, lures Donna Elvira out, and feigning repentance for his conduct induces her to leave with him. Don Giovanni then proceeds to enter the house and seize Zerlina; but before he can accomplish his purpose, Masetto and his friends appear, and supposing it is Leporello before them, demand to know where his master is, as they are bent upon killing him. Don Giovanni easily disposes of Masetto, and then rejoins his servant near the equestrian statue, which has been erected to the memory of the murdered Don Pedro. To their astonishment the statue speaks, and warns the libertine he will die before the morrow. Don Giovanni laughs at the prophecy, and invites the statue to a banquet to be given the next day at his house. While the guests are assembled at the feast, an ominous knock is heard at the door and the statue unceremoniously enters. All except

Edouard de Reszke as *Leporello*

Copyright, Aimé Dupont

Scotti as *Don Giovanni*

Copyright, Aimé Dupont

MOZART

Leporello and Don Giovanni fly from the room in terror. The doomed man orders an extra plate, but the statue extends its hand and invites him to sup with it. He takes the marble hand, and its cold fingers clutch him in a firm grasp. Thrice the statue urges him to repent, and as many times he refuses; whereupon, as it disappears, demons rise, seize Don Giovanni, and carry him to the infernal regions.

Musically considered, "Don Giovanni" is regarded as Mozart's greatest opera, though it lacks the bright joyousness of "The Marriage of Figaro," and its human interest. Its melodies are more pronounced, and have entered more freely into general use, however, than those of the former. Repulsive as the story is, some of the melodies which illustrate it have been impressed into the service of the church. The first act is introduced with a humorous aria by Leporello ("Notte e giorno faticar"), in which he complains of his treatment by his master. After the murder of Don Pedro, in the second scene, occurs a trio between Donna Elvira, Don Giovanni, and Leporello, the leading motive of which is a beautiful aria sung by Donna Elvira ("Ah! chi mi dice mai"). The scene closes with the great buffo aria of Leporello ("Madamina! il catalogo") popularly known as the "Catalogue Song," which is full of broad humor, though its subject is far from possessing that quality. In the third scene occur the lovely duet for Don Giovanni and Zerlina ("Là, ci darem la mano"), two arias of great dramatic intensity for Donna Elvira ("Mi tradì") and Donna Anna ("Or sai, chi l' onore"), and Don Giovanni's dashing song ("Fin ch'han dal vino"), the music of which is in admirable keeping with the reckless nature of the libertine himself. The last scene is a treasure-house of music, containing the exquisitely coquettish aria, "Batti, batti," which Zerlina sings to the jealous

Masetto, and the beautiful trio of Donna Anna, Donna Elvira, and Don Ottavio, known as the Masked Trio, set off against the quaint minuet music of the fete and the hurly-burly which accompanies the discovery of Don Giovanni's black designs.

The second act opens with a humorous duet between master and servant ("Eh, via, buffone"), followed by the trio, "Ah! taci, ingiusto core!" as Elvira appears at her window. After she leaves with Leporello, Don Giovanni sings a serenade ("Deh vieni alla finestra?") to Zerlina, which is interrupted by the appearance of Masetto and his friends. Zerlina is summoned to the scene by the cries of Masetto after Don Giovanni has beaten him, and sings to him for his consolation the beautiful aria, "Vedrai, carino," which has more than once been set to sacred words, and has become familiar as a church tune, notwithstanding the unsanctity of its original setting. The second scene opens with a strong sextet ("Sola, sola, in bujo loco"), followed by the ludicrously solemn appeal of Leporello, "Ah! pietà, Signori miei," and that aria, beloved of all tenors, "Il mio tesoro." The finale is occupied with the scenes at the statue and at the banquet, a short scene between Donna Anna and Don Ottavio intervening, in which she sings the aria, "Non mi dir." The statue music throughout is of a sepulchral character, gradually developing into strains almost as cold and ominous as the marble of the Commandant himself, and yet not without an element of the grotesque as it portrays the terror of Leporello.

It is said that in revenge at his Italian rivals, Mozart introduced an aria from Martin's "La Cosa Rara," arranged for wind instruments, and also a favorite aria of Sarti's, to be played at the banquet when the hungry Leporello beholds his master at the table and watches for some of the choice morsels, and parodied them in an amusing manner. He never could retain an enmity very long, however, and so at the end of the banquet he parodied one of his own arias, the famous "Non più andrai," by giving it a comical turn to suit Leporello's situation. The criticism of one of the best biographers of Mozart upon this opera is worth repeating in this connection: "Whether we regard the mixture of passions in its concerted music, the profound expression of melancholy, the variety of its situations, the beauty of its accompaniment, or the grandeur of its heightening and protracted scene of terror, — the finale of the second act, — 'Don Giovanni' stands alone in dramatic eminence."

The Magic Flute

"Die Zauberflöte," opera in two acts, words by Emanuel Schickaneder, was first produced at Vienna, September 30, 1791, with the following cast:

Queen of Night	Frau HOFER.
Pamina	Frl. GOTLIEB.
Papagena	Frau GORL.
Tamino	Herr SCHACK.
Monostatos	Herr GORL.
Sarastro	Herr SCHICKANEDER, Sr.
Papageno	Herr SCHICKANEDER, Jr.

"The Magic Flute" was the last great work of the composer, and followed the "Cosi fan tutte," which was given in January, 1791. In 1780 Mozart had made the acquaintance of Schickaneder at Salzburg. He was a reckless, dissipated theatre manager, and at the time of the composition of "The Magic Flute" was running a small theatre in Vienna. The competition of the larger theatres had nearly beggared him, and in the midst of his perplexities he applied to Mozart to write him an opera, and intimated that he had discovered an admirable subject for a fairy composition. Mozart at first objected, but Schickaneder, like himself, was a Freemason, had been his companion in dissipation, and exercised a great influence over him. Mozart at last consented. A compact was made, and Schickaneder set to work on the libretto. As he was a popular buffoon, he invented the part of Papageno, the bird-catcher, for himself, and arranged that it should be dressed in a costume of feathers. It is a trivial part, but Schickaneder intended to tickle the fancy of the public, and succeeded. The first act was finished, when it was found that the same subject had been chosen by a rival theatre, the Leopoldstadt, which speedily announced the opera of "Kaspar der Fagottist, oder die Zauber-Zither," by a popular composer, Wenzel Müller. The piece had a successful run, and in order to prevent a duplication, Schickaneder reversed the point of his story, and changed the evil magician, who stole the daughter of the Queen of Night, into a great philosopher and friend of man. It is owing to this change that we have the magnificent character of Sarastro, with its impressive music.

The scene of the opera is laid in Egypt. Sarastro, the high priest of Isis, has induced Pamina to leave her mother, Astrifiamenti, the Queen of Night, who represents the spirit of evil, and come to his temple, where she may be trained in the ways of virtue and wisdom. At the opening of the opera the dark Queen is trying to discover some plan of recovering her daughter and punishing Sarastro. In the first act appears Tamino, an Egyptian prince, who has lost his way, and is attacked by a huge serpent, from which he is rescued by the three attendants of the Queen. The latter accosts him, tells him her daughter's story, and demands that, as the cost of his deliverance, he shall rescue her. He consents. She gives him a magic flute, and with his companion

Gadski as *Pamina*
Copyright, Aimé Dupont

Dippel as *Tamino*
Copyright, Aimé Dupont

Papageno, a rollicking bird-catcher, who is also presented with a magical chime of bells, they set out for Sarastro's temple. Papageno arrives there first, and in time to rescue Pamina from the persecutions of Monostatos, a slave, who flies when he beholds Papageno in his feather costume, fancying him the devil. They seek to make their escape, but are intercepted. Tamino also is caught, and all are brought before Sarastro. The prince consents to become a novitiate in the sacred rites, and to go through the various stages of probation and purification, and Pamina again returns to her duties. They remain faithful to their vows, and the last ordeal, that of passing through a burning lake up to the altar of the temple, is triumphantly accomplished. The Queen of Night, however, does not abandon her scheme of revenge. She appears to Pamina in her sleep, gives her a dagger, and swears that unless she murders Sarastro she will cast her off forever. Pamina pays no heed to her oath, but goes on with her sacred duties, trusting to Sarastro's promise that if she endures all the ordeals she will be forever happy. In the closing scene, Monostatos, who has been inflamed against Sarastro by the Queen, seeks to kill him, but is vanquished by the might of the priest's presence alone. The night of the ordeals is over. At a sign from Sarastro, the full sunlight pours in upon them. The evil spirits all vanish, and Tamino and Pamina are united amid the triumphant choruses of the priests and attendants, as the reward of their fidelity.

In the opening scene, after the encounter of Tamino with the serpent, Papageno has a light and catching song ("Der Vogelfänger bin ich ja"), which, like all of Papageno's music, was specially written for Schickaneder, and has been classed under the head of the "Viennese ditties." Melodious as Mozart always is, these songs must be regarded as concessions to the buffoon who sang them. Papageno's song is followed by another in a serious strain ("Dies Bildniss ist bezaubernd schön") sung by Tamino. In the sixth scene occurs the first aria for the Queen of Night ("O zittre nicht, mein lieber Sohn"), which, like its companion to be mentioned later, is a remarkable exercise in vocal power, range, and gymnastics, written for an exceptional voice. The next scene, known as the Padlock Quintet, is very simple and flowing in style, and will always be popular for its humorous and melodious character. In the eleventh scene occurs the familiar duet between Pamina and Papageno ("Bei Männern, welche Liebe fühlen"), which has done good service for the church, and will be recognized in the English hymn version, "Serene I laid me down." It leads up to the finale, beginning, "Zum Ziele führt dich diese Bahn," and containing a graceful melody for Tamino ("O dass ich doch im Stande wäre"), and another of the Viennese tunes ("Könnte jeder brave Mann") — a duet for Papageno and Pamina, with chorus.

The second act opens with a stately march and chorus by the priests, leading up to Sarastro's first great aria ("O Isis und Osiris"), a superb invocation in broad, flowing harmony, and the scene closes with a strong duet by two priests ("Bewahret euch vor Weibertücken"). The third scene is a quintet for Papageno, Tamino, and the Queen's three attendants ("Wie ihr an diesem Schreckensort?"), and is followed by a sentimental aria by Monostatos ("Alles fühlt der Liebe Freuden"). In the next scene occurs the second and greatest aria of the Queen of Night ("Der Hölle Rache kocht"), which was specially written to show off the bravura ability of the creator of the part, and has been the despair of nearly all sopranos since her time. In striking contrast with it comes the majestic aria for Sarastro in the next scene ("In diesen heil'gen Hallen"), familiarly known on the concert stage by its English title, "In these sacred Halls," the successful performance of which may well be the height of any basso's ambition. In the twelfth scene there is a terzetto by the three boys ("Seid uns zum zweitenmal"), and in the next scene a long and florid aria for Pamina ("Ach! ich fühl's es ist verschwunden"), full of plaintive chords and very sombre in color. The sixteenth scene contains another stately chorus of priests ("O Isis und Osiris"), based upon a broad and massive harmony, which is followed by a terzetto between Sarastro, Pamina, and Tamino ("Soll ich dich, Theurer, nicht mehr sehen?"). Once more a concession to the buffoon occurs in a melody "Ein Mädchen oder Weibchen," which would be commonplace but for Mozart's treatment of the simple air. The finale begins with another terzetto for the three boys ("Bald prangt, den Morgen zu verkünden"). It may be termed a finale of surprises, as it contains two numbers which are as far apart in character as the poles, — the first, an old choral melody ("Der, welcher wandelt diese Strasse"), the original being, "Christ, our Lord, to Jordan came," set to an accompaniment, strengthened by the trombones and other wind instruments; and the second, a nonsense duet ("Pa-pa-Papageno") for Papageno and Papagena, which would close the opera in a burst of childish hilarity but for the solemn concluding chorus of the priests ("Heil sei euch Geweihten").

The great charm of the opera is its originality, and the wonderful freshness and fruitfulness of the composer in giving independent and characteristic melodies to every character, as well as the marvellous combination of technicality with absolute melody. Beethoven said of it that this was Mozart's one German opera in right of the style and solidity of its music. Jahn, in his criticism, says: "'The Zauberflöte' has a special and most important position among Mozart's operas. The whole musical conception is pure German, and here for the first time German opera makes free and skilful use of all the elements of finished art."

NESSLER

VICTOR E. NESSLER was born at Baldenheim, Alsatia, January 28, 1841, and died at Strasburg, May 28, 1890. At the outset he was a student, both of theology and music, but eventually chose the latter for his profession — a choice which was justified by his production of one of the most popular of modern operas in Germany, a description of which follows. His first successful opera was "Fleurette," performed in 1864. After further studies, and considerable experience as a chorus master and conductor, he produced during the next thirty years several operas, besides ballads, choruses, songs, and song cycles. Nearly all his compositions outside of operas are for male voices. His most successful operas are "Dornröschens Brautfahrt" (1867); "Der Rattenfänger von Hameln" (1879); "Der wilde Jäger" (1881); and "Der Trompeter von Säkkingen" (1884).

THE TRUMPETER OF SÄKKINGEN

"Der Trompeter von Säkkingen" ("The Trumpeter of Säkkingen"), opera comique in a prelude and three acts, text by Rudolph Bunge, was first produced at the Stadt Theatre, Leipzig, May 4, 1884. The scene is laid in Säkkingen, on the Rhine, in 1650, near the close of the Thirty Years' War. Few operas have had the advantage of such an excellent book as Nessler's "Trumpeter of Säkkingen," and few light operas have had their stories so legitimately and skilfully illustrated with music. The text is based upon the metrical romance of Victor von Scheffel's "Trompeter von Säkkingen," known and admired all over Germany, which tells the story of the young Werner and the fair Margaretha, their romantic wooing and final union. The time is near the close of the Thirty Years' War, and the hero is Werner Kirchoff, a handsome, dashing young student, who, with others of his comrades, is expelled from the University of Heidelberg because of their frequent carousals. They join a body of troopers, Werner in the capacity of a trumpeter, and go with them to Säkkingen. While there he has the good fortune to protect Margaretha, on a saint's fete day, from the rudeness of some Hauenstein peasants who are ready for a revolt against the Baron von Schoenau, her father. Margaretha, who is in company with the Countess Wildenstein, a cousin of the Baron, who has separated from her husband, gratefully gives Werner a forget-me-not. The Countess inquires his name of his trooper comrade, Conradin, and is struck with his resemblance to her son who had been carried off by gypsies in his childhood. In the next scene the Baron has received a letter from Count Wildenstein, in which he states that his second wife has died, that he wishes to settle the misunderstanding with his first wife, the Countess, and proposes Damian, his son by the second marriage, as a husband for Margaretha, — a proposal which the Baron promptly accepts. When Margaretha enters and tells of her adventures with Werner, the Baron regrets that his old trumpeter, Rassmann, is not alive to summon assistance from the city in case of attack by the peasants. Margaretha tells him of Werner, and notwithstanding the Countess' objections, he gives the position to him.

The second act opens with a love scene between Werner and Margaretha, which is discovered by the Countess, who at once informs the Baron. When Werner asks him for the hand of Margaretha, he not only refuses it, but orders him to leave the castle. Werner takes his farewell of Margaretha, and leaves for his old position with the troopers in the city. Meanwhile the Count of Wildenstein arrives with Damian, but he makes no impression upon Margaretha notwithstanding the Baron's favor.

In the last act the denouement comes quickly. The peasants attack the castle, and the Baron calls upon Damian to head his retainers and go out to meet the mob. He proves himself, however, an arrant coward, and in the midst of his irresolution Werner rides up at the head of his troopers, performs prodigies of valor, and saves the inmates of the castle. A birthmark upon his arm reveals him as the long-lost son of the Countess, and nothing now stands in the way of Margaretha's and Werner's felicity.

In the prelude and first act the most noticeable numbers are the students' and troopers' choruses, written in the best German style — the prelude indeed is almost entirely choral; the peasants' choruses and lively dances on St. Fridolin's Day; the characteristic growl of the Baron over his gout and the unreasonable peasants; and the charming lyric sung by Margaretha, "How proud and grand his Bearing." The most conspicuous numbers in the second act are a lyric, sung by Werner, "On Shore I played me a merry Tune"; the love scene between Margaretha and Werner, "Sun, has thy Light not grown in Splendor?"; the dramatic quintet, "Must so soon the Sunshine vanish?"; and Werner's sentimental and beautiful farewell, "Oh, it is sad that in this Life below." The principal numbers of the third act are Margaretha's song, "My Love rode out to the wide, wide World"; the May song, "There comes a Youth of sweet Renown"; the pantomime and dance composing a May idyl; the duet for Margaretha and Werner, "True Love, I give thee Greeting"; and the ringing mass chorus, "Faithful Love and Trumpet blowing," which closes the opera.

NICOLAI

OTTO NICOLAI, a favorite opera composer in Germany, was born at Königsberg, June 9, 1810, and died at Berlin, May 11, 1849. After studying with his father for a time, he left home, owing to domestic trouble, and was sent by a patron to Berlin, where he studied with Zelter and Klein. Shortly after this he was appointed organist at the embassy chapel at Rome where he made a special study of Italian music. From 1841 to 1847 he was Court Capellmeister at Vienna, succeeding Kreutzer. In 1842 he founded the Philharmonic Society in that city. In 1847 he was called to Berlin as Capellmeister of the opera as well as of the Domchor. He died in that city. His most important operas are "Der Templer" (1840); "Die Heimkehr des Verbannten" (1842); "The Merry Wives of Windsor" (1849). The last opera, his masterpiece, was begun in Vienna and finished in Berlin and its first performance was given only two months before his death. Besides his operas, Nicolai wrote a festival overture upon the theme "Ein' feste Burg," which is a great concert favorite, a Te Deum and Requiem, a few piano compositions, and many songs.

THE MERRY WIVES OF WINDSOR

"The Merry Wives of Windsor," opera comique, in three acts, text by Mosenthal, was first produced in Berlin, March 9, 1849; in London, May 3, 1864; in New York, April 27, 1863. The story of the opera follows closely that of the Shakespearean comedy, though the action is principally concerned with Falstaff's adventures with the merry wives, the attachment between Fenton and Anne furnishing the romantic incident. Though the work of a German, the music is largely in the Italian style, and the dramatic finish is French. It is unnecessary to indicate the plot in further detail than to say it includes the receipt of Sir John's amatory epistles by Mrs. Ford and Mrs. Page, his concealment among the foul linen in the hamper and subsequent sousing in the Thames, his sad experiences with Ford's cudgels, and his painful encounter with the mock fairies, elves, and other sprites in Windsor Park.

The leading numbers in the opera are a duet for the two merry wives, opening the opera, in which they read Falstaff's letters ("No, no, this really is too bad"), closing with an exquisitely humorous phrase as they pronounce the name of the writer in unison; a beautiful little aria ("Joking and Laughter"), in the Italian style, sung by Mrs. Ford; and the finale to the first act, beginning with a serio-comic aria in which Mrs. Ford bewails her husband's jealousy, followed by a sextet and chorus, and closing with a highly dramatic aria in which Mrs. Ford changes from grief to rage and violently denounces Ford.

The second act opens with a drinking-song for Falstaff ("Whilst yet a Child on my Mother's Breast"), which, as well as the accessories of the song, is full of rollicking, bacchanalian humor. Falstaff sings one verse, and his followers drain their huge mugs to the bottom. One of them falls senselessly drunk, and is immediately borne out upon the shoulders of his comrades with funereal honors, led off by Falstaff, all chanting a sort of mock dirge. A descriptive and spirited buffo duet between Falstaff and Ford follows, in which the former relates his adventures in the hamper. The only remaining number of consequence in this act is the romanza, "Hark, the Lark in yonder

Grove," sung by Fenton. The last act is very short, and made up of a beautiful trio for Mrs. Ford, Mrs. Page, and Falstaff ("The Bell has pealed the Midnight Chime"); the romantic ballad ("Of Herne, the Hunter, a Legend old"), and the fairy dance and chorus ("About, about, ye Elves, about"), which close the opera.

OFFENBACH

NO name is more familiar in the records of musical pleasantry and burlesque than that of Jacques Offenbach, who may be designated the founder of modern opera bouffe. And no composer in this school has had such a vogue. He was born in Cologne, June 21, 1819, and died in Paris, October 5, 1880. Though of German birth, he was a Parisian of the Parisians. He went to Paris when very young, studied in the Conservatory and was soon playing the 'cello in the Opéra Comique orchestra. In 1849 he became conductor at the Théâtre Français and in 1855 opened a theatre of his own, the Bouffes-Parisiens, where many of his works were produced. From 1872 to 1876 he was manager of the Théâtre de la Gaîté and in 1877 made a most successful tour of this country. The few remaining years of his life were devoted to composition. He produced one hundred and two works for the stage, nearly all of which met with tremendous success on the French boards and many of them were great favorites in Germany, England, and the United States. The furor which they created can only be compared with that aroused by the Sullivan operettas. From the long catalogue, the following may be selected as the most important: "Le Mariage aux Lanternes" (1857); "Orphée aux Enfers" (1858); "Genevieve de Brabant" (1859); "Les Bavards" (1863); "Lischen et Fritzchen" and "La Belle Hélène" (1864); "Barbe Bleue" and "La Vie Parisienne" (1866); "La Grande Duchesse de Gérolstein" (1867); "La Perichole" (1868); "La Princesse de Trebizonde" and "Les Brigands" (1869); "La Jolie Parfumeuse" (1873); "La Marocaine" and "Mme.

Favart" (1879); and "Les Contes d' Hoffmann" (1881). In making a selection from these for description, three have been chosen which combine the most characteristic music with the least objectionable text.

THE GRAND DUCHESS OF GEROLSTEIN

"The Grand Duchess of Gerolstein," opera bouffe in three acts, text by Meilhac and Halévy, was first produced at the Variétés, Paris, April 12, 1867. The scene is laid in the imaginary duchy of Gerolstein, in the year 1720. "The Grand Duchess of Gerolstein," though in some respects inferior musically to "Orpheus," by the same composer, is altogether the most perfect type of the opera bouffe. For the drollness of its story, the originality of its characters as well as of its music, its obstreperous gayety, dash, and geniality mixed with occasional seriousness and grace, this work when it first appeared was unique, though Offenbach rose to his highest achievement when dealing with the gods and goddesses of Olympus in his "Orpheus," which revealed his powers of musical burlesque at their best.

The first act opens with a grand review of the army of the duchy, commanded by the pompous General Boum, at which the Duchess is present. In its ranks there is a recruit, known by the name of Fritz, who has already aroused the General's jealousy by his attentions to Wanda, a peasant girl. He continues still further to add to this jealousy when the Duchess, attracted by his good looks, singles him out for her regard and promotes him to the post of corporal. When she learns of his relations to Wanda, she raises him to the rank of lieutenant, evidently to separate him from Wanda by the new elevation. The review over, the Duchess studies the plan of a pending campaign against a neighboring enemy. She summons General Boum in the presence of Baron Puck, her court chamberlain, Prince Paul, a feeble and neglected suitor of the Duchess, and Lieutenant Fritz, who is now her special bodyguard, and asks him for his plan of campaign, which he states, much to the disgust of Fritz, who declares it to be sheer nonsense. The Duchess then asks the latter for his plan, and is so much pleased with it that she appoints him general and raises him to the rank of baron, much to the discomfort and indignation of the others.

The second act opens with the return of Fritz. He has been victorious, and at the public reception given him he tells the story of his adventures. Subsequently, at a *tête-à-tête* with the Duchess, she makes open love to him; but he is so occupied with thoughts of Wanda that he is insensible to all her advances, which puts her in a rage. Overhearing a conspiracy between Puck, Paul, and the deposed General Boum against his life, she joins with them, and the act closes with a wild, hilarious dance.

In the third act Baron Grog, emissary of Prince Paul's father, appears upon the scene to expedite the marriage of the Prince to the Duchess. He joins the conspiracy against Fritz, and so ingratiates himself with the Duchess that she finally consents to marry the Prince. In the meantime she countermands the order for Fritz's assassination, and gives him permission to marry Wanda. The conspirators, however, play a practical joke upon Fritz by a false message summoning him to the battlefield. He leaves at once on the wedding-night, but through the connivance of General Boum is waylaid and badly beaten. While the betrothal of the Duchess is being celebrated, Fritz returns in sad plight, with the sabre which the Duchess had given him in a battered condition. She adds to his misfortunes by depriving him of his command and bestowing it upon Baron Grog, but learning that he has a family, she reinstates General Boum. In the denouement Fritz is restored to his Wanda and the Duchess marries Prince Paul.

Mme. Schneider as *La Grande Duchesse*

The music is in keeping with the drollery of the situations, and abounds in vivacity and odd descriptiveness, defying all accepted laws and adapting itself to the grotesquerie and extravagance of the action. The principal numbers in the first act are the pompous " Pif, paf, pouf" song of General Boum; the Grand Duchess's air ("Ah! que j'aime les militaires"); the regiment song for her and Fritz ("Ah! c'est un fameux régiment"); the couplets of Prince Paul ("Pour épouser une Princesse"); and the famous sabre song ("Voici, le sabre de mon père"). The best numbers of the second act are Fritz's spirited rondo ("En très bon ordre nous partîmes"), in which he tells the story of his victory; the romanza ("Dites lui"), a delightful little song, and so refined that it hardly seems to belong to the opera; and the conspirators' trio ("Max était soldat de fortune"), which is irresistible in its broad humor and queer rhythms. The musical interest really reaches its climax in the second act. Outside of the chorus work in the third act there is little of interest except the Duchess's ballad ("Il était un de mes aïeux"), and Fritz's song to the Duchess ("Eh bien, Altesse, me voilà!").

La Belle Hélène

"La Belle Hélène," opera bouffe in three acts, text by De Meilhac and Halévy, was first produced at the Théâtre des Variétés, December 17, 1864. In "La Belle Hélène" Offenbach goes back to the mythical period, and presents the heroes of the time of Helen and Paris in modern burlesque. The first act opens at the temple of Jupiter in Sparta, where, among others who have placed their offerings at his shrine, is Helen. When alone with Calchas, the augur, they discuss some means of avoiding the decree of the oracle which has declared she is to leave Menelaus, her husband, and flee with Paris, son of Priam, to Troy. Before a decision is reached, Paris, disguised as a shepherd, arrives, and soon he and Helen are lovers. They meet again in a grand tournament in which the two Ajaxes, Achilles, Agamemnon, and others announce themselves in the most comic fashion and guess at conundrums for a prize. Paris wins, and proclaims his name and lineage, to the joy of Helen, whose delight is still further enhanced when the oracle orders Menelaus to set off at once for Crete.

In the second act Helen struggles against the decrees of Venus. Paris has an interview with her, but she will not yield, and he retires. By the aid of Calchas he secures admission to the chamber of the slumbering Queen, when Menelaus suddenly returns and an altercation ensues, during which Paris defies all the Grecian heroes, and Helen philosophically informs Menelaus he should have announced his coming beforehand. Paris again retreats, and Helen is now in despair.

In the third act Helen and Menelaus have a family quarrel, and he charges her with being false. She denies it, and declares he has been dreaming. Calchas now appears, and announces that a new augur has been appointed and is on his way there. A golden galley is seen approaching, and the augur is found to be Paris himself. He brings word that Venus is angry at what has been going on, but will relent if Helen will return with him to her shrine and sacrifice white heifers. She is reluctant to go, but finally decides to obey the voice of destiny, and sails away with him, leaving all behind in grief and Menelaus in rage.

The dialogue of "La Belle Hélène" is very witty, though coarse at times, and many of the situations are full of a humorous incongruity and drollness growing out of the attempt to modernize these mythological heroes. The music admirably fits the text, and though not so gay as that of "The Grand Duchess," yet is fresh, original, and interesting throughout. The chief numbers of the work are Helen's passionate song of mourning for Adonis ("Amours divins");

Paris's fable ("Au Mont Ida, trois déesses"), in which he tells the well-known apple story; the march and chorus ("Voici les rois de la Grèce"), in which, one after the other, they come forward and announce themselves in an irresistibly funny manner; Helen's mock sentimental song ("Nous naissons toutes soucieuses"); the droll goose march of the kings; a fascinating chorus ("En couronnes tressons roses"); Helen's song ("Un mari sage"), one of the most characteristic numbers in the opera; and in the last act Orestes's song ("Malgré cette ardente flamme"); the spirited trio ("Lorsque la Grèce est un camp de carnage"); and the final chorus ("Que notre colère"), which preludes the Trojan war.

Orphée aux Enfers

"Orphée aux Enfers," opera bouffe, in three acts, text by Cremieux, was first produced at the Bouffes Parisiens, Paris, October 21, 1858. The best musical work of Offenbach undoubtedly is to be found in his "Orphée aux Enfers," and the text which his librettist furnished him is in keeping with the music. It was a bold as well as droll conception to invest the Olympian gods and goddesses with human attributes and make them symbols of worldly departments of action and official life, to parade them in processions like the ordinary street pageant, to present them in banquets, to dress them in the most fantastically individual manner, and to make nineteenth-century caricatures of the whole Olympian coterie.

The first scene of the opera discloses Eurydice in the Theban meadows plucking flowers with which to decorate the cabin of Aristeus, the shepherd, who is really Pluto in disguise. Suddenly Orpheus appears, not with his tortoise-shell lyre, but playing the violin and serenading, as he supposes, a shepherdess with whom he is in love. His mistake reveals the fact that each of them is false to the other, and a violent quarrel of the most ludicrous description ensues, ending in their separation. He goes to his shepherdess, she to her shepherd. Shortly afterwards, Aristeus meets Eurydice in the fields and reveals his real self. By supernatural power he turns day into night and brings on a tempest, in the midst of which he bears her away to the infernal regions, but not before she has written upon Orpheus's hut the fate that has overtaken her. When Orpheus returns he is overjoyed at his loss, but in the midst of his exultation, Public Opinion appears and commands him to go to Olympus and demand from Jupiter the restoration of his wife. Orpheus reluctantly obeys the order.

The second act opens in Olympus, where the gods and goddesses are enjoying a nap, from which they are awakened by the blasts of Diana's horn. Thereupon much slanderous gossip is circulated amongst them, the latest news discussed being Pluto's abduction of Eurydice. Pluto himself shortly comes in, and is at once taxed by Jupiter with his unseemly behavior, whereupon Pluto retaliates by reference to Jupiter's numerous amours with mortals. This arouses the jealousy of Juno. Venus, with Cupid's assistance, starts a veritable riot, which is suddenly interrupted by the arrival of Orpheus and his guide, Public Opinion. He demands that his wife shall be restored to him, and Jupiter not only consents, but agrees to attend to the matter personally.

The third act finds Eurydice in Hades, carefully guarded by John Styx. Jupiter is faithful to his promise, and soon arrives there, but not in his proper person. He appears in the disguise of a fly, and allows Eurydice to catch him, after which he reveals himself. When Pluto comes in, he finds her transformed into a bacchante of the most convivial sort. Other deities make their appearance, and finally Orpheus comes sailing up the Styx, playing his violin, and demanding of Jupiter the fulfilment of his contract.

Jeanne Granier as *Eurydice*

Jupiter consents, but makes the condition that he shall return to his boat, Eurydice following him, and that he must not look back. Orpheus sets out, but just before he reaches the boat, the cunning Jupiter launches a thunderbolt after him, which causes him to turn and lose Eurydice, much to the disgust of Public Opinion, but greatly to the edification of Orpheus, who is now at liberty to return to his shepherdess on the Theban plain.

The most striking numbers in this curious travesty are the opening aria of Eurydice, as she gathers the flowers ("La femme dont la cœur rêve"); the pastoral sung to her by Aristeus ("Voir, voltiger sous les treilles") the fascinating hunting-song of Diana ("Quand Diane descend dans la plaine"); the characteristic and taking song of John Styx ("Quand j'étais roi de Beotie"), which in its way is as striking as the sabre song in "The Grand Duchess"; Eurydice's delicate fly-song ("Bel insecte, à l'aile dorée"); the drinking-song in the infernal regions ("Vive le vin"); and Eurydice's vivacious bacchanalian song which immediately follows it ("J'ai vu le dieu Bacchus").

PADEREWSKI

IGNACE JAN PADEREWSKI, the piano virtuoso, was born in Podolia, Russian Poland, November 6, 1859. He began the study of the piano at the age of seven with a local teacher, Sowinski, with whom he remained four years. After this he studied with Roguski in Warsaw; Urban, Wuerst, and Kiel in Berlin; and then made a tour in eastern Europe playing his own compositions. At eighteen he was nominated professor in the Warsaw Conservatory and in 1884 held a professorship at the Conservatory at Strasburg. During that year, however, he abandoned teaching and decided to become a virtuoso. He accordingly placed himself under Leschetizky in Vienna and after hard study with that famous teacher for three years made a brilliantly successful debut before a critical Viennese audience. Since that time he has devoted himself to concert tours, making his first appearance in France in 1889, in England in 1890, and in this country in 1891. "Manru" is his only opera and only vocal composition of great importance, but his piano compositions are numerous, including ballads, nocturnes, legends, minuets, polonaises, sonatas, fugues, and fantasies on original themes. He has also written several graceful songs. As a virtuoso his success has been extraordinary and continuous.

Manru

"Manru," opera in three acts, text by Alfred Nossig, was first produced at the Court Theatre, Dresden, May 29, 1901, with the following cast:

Manru	Herr ANTHES.
Ulana	Frl. KRULL.
Hedwig	Frl. VON CHAVANNE.
Urok	Herr SCHEIDEMANTEL.
Asa	Frl. KAMMER.

The first performance in this country was given in New York, February 14, 1902, with the following cast of the above characters:

Manru	Mr. von BANDROWSKI.
Ulana	Mme. SEMBRICH.
Hedwig	Mme. HOMER.
Urok	Mr. BISPHAM.
Asa	Miss FRITZI SCHEFF.

The other parts were cast as follows: *Landmädchen*, Mme. Van Cauteren; *Oros*, Mr. Muhlmann; and *Jagu*, Mr. Blass.

The libretto of "Manru" is based upon a Polish novel by Kraszewski, called "Chata za wsia," or "The Cabin behind the Wood." The scene is laid in the Tatra Mountains on the border of Hungary. In a hut in these mountains lives Manru, a gypsy, who has abandoned his own people and Asa, his gypsy love, for the sake of Ulana, daughter of Hedwig and belle of the village, whom he has married and taken to this lonely spot. She also has been disowned by her people and their only associate is Urok, an ugly dwarf, who is in love with Ulana. Her mother promises to forgive her if she will leave Manru, but she refuses. She confesses to Urok that Manru is growing restless and she fears the Wanderlust has seized him. At her bidding the dwarf mixes an herb potion which is to revive Manru's love.

The second act discloses Ulana rocking her child in the cabin. Manru is at work in his smithy and Urok is taunting the two. While bitterly lamenting that he ever left his people and longing to return to his old wandering ways, he hears Jagu, one of the band, approaching and playing on his violin to bring him back to his band and to Asa, his old love. Manru rushes to meet him; Urok appears bringing the potion which he gives to Ulana; Jagu labors with Manru and begs him to return, but Manru is not yet ready, however, to leave her, and Jagu departs; subsequently he drinks the potion and his love is restored for the time at least.

In the last act the old desire returns stronger than ever. The potion is no longer powerful, and Manru wanders off into the mountains to find his people. There he meets Asa, who urges him to return and make her his wife, offering him as an inducement the leadership of the tribe which has been assumed by Oros, his rival. Ulana, searching for him, finds him going away with Asa, and throws herself into the lake. As Oros appears, seeking to punish his rival, who, in the meantime, is seeking for Ulana, Urok comes up behind Manru and pushes him into the lake, where, it is to be assumed, his troubles are ended.

The opera is without overture. The opening scene is introduced by a brief, plaintive oboe melody preceding a very tender chorus of peasants ("Windet den Kranz"). Indeed the peasants' choruses, the motive of which is contained in the recurring phrase, "Ist der Mond am Himmel voll, dann wird der Zigeuner toll" ("When the Moon is full the Gypsy runs wild"), constitute the principal material of the act, which closes with a wild gypsy dance, full of fascinating melody and haunting rhythms.

The second act is also without prelude. Its opening scene is a powerful one, especially in the duet between Manru, working in his smithy ("Da sitzt sie d'rin und wiegt das Kind") and Ulana, during which the latter sings a charming lullaby ("Schlaf wohl, theures Kind"). The next point of interest is the strange, appealing gypsy

Bandrowski as *Manru*

Sembrich as *Ulana*

Bispham as *Urok*

Photos. Copyright, Aimé Dupont

strain played by Jagu upon his violin which is fascinating in its rhythmic effect. Then follow some long musical declamations leading up to the love duet closing the act ("Wie im Sonnenscheine") which is full of passionate energy.

There is a strong symphonic prelude to the last act descriptive of the tempest raging in Manru's soul which has much musical as well as poetical significance. The remaining numbers of the highest importance in this act are the gypsy march and choruses; what might be called Asa's Temptation scene or scenes which abound in Tzigane music with its marked rhythm and weird effects, in which the gypsy dulcimer plays its part; and the furious hurly-burly of the double tragedy at the close, which ends this wild gypsy orgy of jealousy, hate, and passion.

PLANQUETTE

ROBERT JEAN PLANQUETTE was born in Paris, July 31, 1850. He studied music in the Conservatory, Duprato being his teacher in composition. His first work was in chansons and other styles of popular lyrics for the cafes and vaudevilles; and his first regular stage work the operetta, "Paille d'Avoine" (1874). His first great success was "Les Cloches de Corneville" ("The Chimes of Normandy"), which was produced in 1877 and had the extraordinary run of 400 nights. His later works are "Surcouf" (1887); "Le Talisman" (1892); "Pamurge" (1895), and "Mam'zelle Quat'-sous" (1897). Besides these he has written "The Old Guard" (1887) and "Paul Jones" (1889), for London, but "The Chimes of Normandy" is the opera by which he is best known.

The Chimes of Normandy

"The Chimes of Normandy," opera comique in three acts, text by Clairville and Gabet, was first produced at the Folies Dramatiques, Paris, April 19, 1877. The scene is laid in Normandy in the time of Louis XV. The first act of this charming opera, one of the most popular of its class, opens in an old Norman village during the progress of a fair. Henri, the Marquis of Villeroi, who has been an exile since childhood, has just returned. The first scene discloses a number of village gossips who are retailing scandals about Serpolette, the good-for-nothing, who arrives in time to vindicate herself and retaliate upon the gossips. Gaspard, the miser, has arranged to give his niece Germaine in marriage to the sheriff, who is the chief dignitary in the village. Germaine, however, objects to the proposition, since if she marries at all she claims she must marry Jean Grenicheux, a young fisherman, in gratitude for saving her life. To escape the marriage she and Jean become the servants of the Marquis, and are joined by Serpolette, which is one of the privileges of fair-time.

The second act is occupied with the exposure of the ghosts in the castle of Villeroi. The Marquis is confident that there is nothing supernatural about the apparition which has been seen or the sounds which have been heard in the various apartments. He therefore introduces his servants into the castle, and after careful searching discovers that the ghost of Villeroi is old Gaspard, the miser, who, when he is found out, becomes crazy through fear of losing treasures which are concealed there.

In the last act the castle is restored to its old splendor, and the Marquis takes possession as master. He gives a fete and the villagers are invited, the crazy Gaspard being among them. Serpolette appears as a grand lady with Jean as her factotum, some papers found in the castle indicating she is the lost heiress. After a love scene between Henri and Germaine, however, Gaspard, who has recovered his reason, discloses that Germaine, and not Serpolette, is the rightful heiress and the true claimant to the title of marchioness. All the complications are now unravelled. Gaspard's treasure is restored to its rightful owner. Germaine comes to her rights, and Serpolette remains with her as her friend.

The music of the opera is delightful throughout, and has scarcely a dull moment. Its most conspicuous numbers are Serpolette's rondo ("In my mysterious History"); a delightful little fantasie ("Go, little Sailor"); the legend of the chimes ("Alas! we have lost excellent Masters"); Henri's grand aria ("I have thrice made the

Tour of the World"); and his couplets ("Under the Armor from Top to Toe"); Serpolette's sprightly aria ("Viscountess and Marchioness"); the chorus with the chimes, a most graceful and interesting number closing the second act; and in the last act Gaspard's quaint old Norman song ("We were full Five Hundred Rogues"); Serpolette's rondo ("The Apple's a Fruit full of Vigor"); and Henri's romance ("A Servant, what Matter to me?").

PONCHIELLI

AMILCARE PONCHIELLI was born in Cremona, August 31, 1834, and died in Milan, January 16, 1886. His early studies were at the Milan Conservatory (1843-1854). After leaving the Conservatory, he was organist at one of the Cremona churches and later bandmaster. After that time, however (1856), he devoted himself to composition, the only other position held by him being that of leader in the cathedral at Piacenza, for which he wrote sacred music. His first stage work was the opera "I Promessi Sposi," brought out at Cremona in 1856, which was followed by "La Savojarda" (1861); "Roderico, rè de' Goti" (1864); and "La Stella del Monte" (1867). A revision of his "I Promessi Sposi" in 1872 met with such success that he secured a commission for a ballet from La Scala which he filled with "Le Due Gemelle," produced in the following year. Several operas followed, all of which proved successful, among them, "I Lituani" (1874); "La Gioconda" (1876); "Il Figliuol Prodigo" (1880), and "Marion Delorme" (1885). Ponchielli also wrote several other light operettas, farces, and ballets, a cantata dedicated to the memory of Donizetti, a funeral march for Manzoni, and a hymn for Garibaldi.

LA GIOCONDA

"La Gioconda," opera in four acts, text by Tobia Garrio, anagram for Arrigo Boito, was first produced at La Scala, Milan, April 8, 1876, with the following cast:

Gioconda	Sig. MARIANI.
Laura	Sig. BIANCOLINI.
La Cieca	Sig. BARLANDINI.
Enzo	Sig. GAYARRO.
Barnaba	Sig. ALDIGHIERI.

The first performance in this country was in New York, December 20, 1883, under the direction of Signor Vianesi. The libretto is partly based upon Victor Hugo's drama, "Angelo, the Tyrant of Syracuse."

The scene is laid in Venice in the seventeenth century. The first act, called "The Lion's Mouth," opens in the courtyard of the Ducal Palace, upon a great festivity. After the lively regatta chorus ("Feste e pane"), and the departure of the crowd to see the sports, Barnaba, the Inquisition's spy, is left alone. He sings a monologue ("E danzan su lor tombe"), which contains a motive that follows him throughout. From this monologue it appears that he loves Gioconda, who appears at that instant leading her blind mother, La Cieca, to the neighboring church. Barnaba conceals himself and a very dramatic trio ("Figlia, che reggi il tremulo") follows, as Gioconda goes in quest of Enzo, a noble whom she loves. Barnaba seizes her and forces his protestation of love upon her so violently that the mother is alarmed and makes an outcry. The crowd returns bearing the winner of the regatta in triumph and making sport of Tuane, the loser, who is persuaded by Barnaba that his defeat was the result of La Cieca's spells. This raises another disturbance in the midst of which Enzo appears with La Gioconda. He goes to the rescue of La Cieca and denounces the crowd as cowards. As they turn against him he calls his comrades to his assistance, just as Aloise, one of the chiefs of the Inquisition, appears

Louise Homer in "La Gioconda"
Copyright, Aimé Dupont

Caruso as *Enzo*
Copyright, Aimé Dupont

with his wife Laura, who is masked. He restores order and releases La Cieca from the crowd, who gives Laura her rosary as a mark of her gratitude. During this scene Laura recognizes Enzo as the proscribed Prince of Santafior to whom she was once affianced and whom she still loves. Barnaba informs him that he is known, that his love for Laura is no secret, and that she will be on his ship at nightfall — it being Barnaba's purpose to get Enzo out of the way so that he may have Gioconda to himself. After an expressive air for La Cieca ("Voce di donna"), a very powerful duet for Enzo and Barnaba follows ("Pertutti ma non per me"). The crafty spy warns Aloise that Enzo is about to elope with Laura and the act closes with Gioconda's lament over Enzo's perfidy ("Tradita? Ahime!"), with the Angelus of the monks and people for a background. The finale is also greatly enlivened by the ballet ("La Furlana") danced by the revellers.

The second act is called "The Roses," and passes on board Enzo's vessel and on the banks of the Fusina lagoon. It opens with a vigorous marinaresca or sea chorus ("Ha! he! ha! he!"). Barnaba appears in his boat approaching the vessel and singing a graceful but significant barcarole ("Ah! pescator"), which is followed by the appearance of Enzo on the deck of his vessel where he sings a passionate romance of his love for Laura ("Cielo e mar"). Another boat approaches and Laura, escorted by Barnaba, steps on deck. Left alone, Laura sings a prayer for protection ("Stella del marinar"). The jealous Gioconda meanwhile has stolen on board. An intensely passionate duet ("E un anatema") follows, during which Gioconda attempts to stab Laura. She refrains, however, when Laura lifts the rosary which La Cieca had given her. Barnaba and Aloise are seen approaching, but Gioconda gets Laura away before their arrival. An intensely dramatic scene ensues between Enzo and Gioconda at the close of which he sets his vessel afire when he finds that the Venetian galleys are surrounding him.

The third act, "The House of Gold," opens with a sombre monologue by Aloise ("Si! moris-ella de!"), in which he determines upon the poisoning of Laura during a fete. Laura enters and a long duet follows in which she is notified she must drink the poison which he places before her, before some passing gondoliers sing the last notes of their serenade. He leaves and Gioconda enters bringing with her a narcotic, which she gives to Laura, at the same time transferring the poison to her own phial. Aloise returns and observing the empty bottle thinks his revenge is complete. The scene changes to a fete and the brilliant, graceful ballet of "The Hours" is introduced. Enzo appears, believing Barnaba's story that Laura is dead, and in a finale of great power discloses his love for her and at the same time is threatened with Aloise's vengeance.

The fourth act, called "The Orfano Canal," opens in the vestibule of a ruined palace, Gioconda's home. By her side are lighted lanterns, poison, and daggers. Two street singers enter bearing the sleeping Laura, whom they place upon a bed. Gioconda is tempted to take Laura's life but resists. Enzo comes in and supposing Laura to be dead he is about to wreak his vengeance upon Gioconda when she wakes and reveals to him who has saved her. The trio of parting between them ("Sulle tue mani") is intensely dramatic, and the intensity increases to the close, making a climax of extraordinary power. Gioconda, pretending to keep her word to Barnaba, arrays herself in her gayest attire and then stabs herself, with the words, "I have sworn to be thine. Take me, I am thine." The furious wretch, balked of his prey, exclaims: "Ah! stay thee! 'Tis a jest! Well then, thou

PONCHIELLI

shalt hear this, and die ever damned! Last night thy mother did offend me. I have strangled her. She hears me not!"

In "La Gioconda" the composer has departed from all the conventional Italian methods and his music clearly shows Wagner's influence It is a sombre theme that dominates the chapters of horrors and the music shares the nature of the libretto, though the score contains many attractive scenes and there are passages for the voice of much brilliancy as well as power.

PUCCINI

GIACOMO PUCCINI, descended from a long line of musicians, and one of a family of six, all devoted to music, was born at Lucca, Italy, in 1858. He began his musical studies at an exceedingly early age and after a time his talent manifested itself so conspicuously that the Queen of Italy granted him a pension sufficient to pay for his tuition at the Milan Conservatory, from which he was graduated with high honors — his graduation offering being a Sinfonia Capriccio for orchestra, which proved a great success. Puccini was a pupil of Ponchielli in the Conservatory and at his suggestion composed the one act opera, "Le Villi" (1884). It was written for a prize offered by a Milan publisher but failed to obtain it because of its almost unreadable caligraphy, but with Boito's assistance it was produced and made a great success. "Le Villi" was followed by "Edgar," produced at La Scala, April 21, 1889, but it did not add to his popularity. "Manon Lescaut" was his next opera, and showed stronger work. This in turn was followed by "La Bohème" (1896) and "La Tosca" (1900). Both these operas have proved very successful. "La Bohème" is unquestionably his masterpiece and deserves to be heard more frequently than it has been, as it is one of the most musical works in the modern Italian repertoire.

La Bohème

"La Bohème," opera in four acts, text by Giacosa and Illica, was first produced at the Teatro Regio, Turin, February 1, 1896, and in English, as "The Bohemians,"

Saleza as *Rodolfo*

Copyright, Aimé Dupont

Group from "La Bohème"

PUCCINI

by the Carl Rosa English opera troupe, at Manchester, England, April 22, 1897. As it would be next to impossible to make a connected libretto from Murger's famous realistic "La Vie de Bohème," the librettists have selected four scenes, which introduce the romantic poet Rodolphe, struggling with love and poverty; Marcel, the optimistic artist; Schaunard, the eccentric musician; Colline, the cheerful philosopher; the coquettish Musette, and Mimi, the pathetic little grisette. It is only a few chapters in their Bohemian life that have been used, but rarely has music been more closely adapted to characters than that which Puccini has furnished.

In the first act the four Bohemians are seen in their garret plunged in despair over their empty pockets. Rodolphe contributes his manuscripts to keep the fire alive, and Marcel holds off the landlord until Schaunard, who has had an unexpected streak of good fortune, arrives. Three of them at once go off to a cafe to enjoy Christmas Eve while Rodolphe remains behind to write. All this is but a prelude to the entrance of Mimi, the embroiderer, upon the pretext of getting a light. A love scene follows between her and Rodolphe and the two go to join their friends in the Latin Quarter, the little grisette happy as a bird, and Rodolphe in high spirits as they stroll arm in arm through the crowds, though Mimi is aware that a fatal malady has already touched her. The next scene really develops the character of Musette, and passes in the street before the Café Momus where Musette appears, escorted by a wealthy banker. She has little difficulty in getting rid of the banker and flying to the arms of Marcel, her old lover. The third act is full of quarrels and reconciliations between the two pairs of lovers, mingled with a vein of comedy, and the fourth act is dominated by the pathetic death of little Mimi.

There are few set pieces in "La Bohème" to be

described. The music is adapted to the characters and illustrates all the varying shades of gayety, tenderness, and pathos with a rich flow of melody, unique concerted effects, and most effective orchestration. It is Italian music throughout, but Italian music was never more deftly employed than in this remarkable picture of human emotions. The striking numbers in the first act are the colloquies between the four Bohemians which are preliminary to the fascinating love duet between Mimi and Rodolfo ("Mi chiamano Mimi"), closing with his rapturous outburst of passion ("O soave fanciulla"). The second act is a carnival of gayety and the street scene before the cafe furnishes opportunity for gay choruses of the most typical description — for soldiers, students, servants, working girls, grisettes, pedlers, and venders of cakes, candies, fruits, and delicacies mingle in a crowd of the motliest sort, each having characteristic bits of chorus, and all handled with consummate skill in concerted effect. The gem of the gay scene, however, is Musette's lively waltz and the rhythms of music sung by the four students. The principal numbers in the third act are the music to the separation of Mimi and Rodolfo at the barriers ("Addio, senza rancore"), which is set off in strong contrast with the quarrel scene of Musette and Marcel, in which they hurl epithets at each other ("Chè mi gridi? Chè mi canti?"). The music of the fourth act is tragic throughout and culminates in the pathetic duet between Mimi and Rodolfo ("Sono audati? Fingeos di dormire") after she has been brought back to the students' attic to die. Musically as well as dramatically it is a scene of absorbing interest and comes nearer to inspiration than most of the music of the modern Italian school. The whole score is so melodic that it is an ungrateful task to single out particular numbers.

Adelaide Norwood as *Tosca*

LA TOSCA

"La Tosca," opera in three acts, text by Giacosa and Illica, after Sardou's melodrama of the same name, was first produced at the Costanzi Theatre, Rome, in January, 1900. It was brought out in London during the same year, with Ternina, Scotti, and De Lucia in the principal roles, and was first heard in this country in New York, February 4, 1901, with the following cast:

Floria Tosca	Mme. MILKA TERNINA.
Mario Cavaradossi	Sig. CREMONINI.
Cesar Angelotti	Sig. DUFRICHE.
Il Sagrestano	Sig. GILIBERT.
Spoletta	Sig BARS.
Scianone	Sig. VIVIANI.
Scarpia	Sig. SCOTTI.

The story is repulsive but intensely dramatic. The first act opens in the Church of Saint Andrea alla Valle. Cavaradossi, a painter, working in the church, is visited by his mistress, Floria Tosca. Meanwhile, Cesar Angelotti, a political prisoner, seeks refuge in the church and conceals himself in the chapel. A love scene follows between the painter and Tosca. Angelotti, warned that his escape has been discovered, hurries away with the painter's help to the latter's villa. A crowd pours into the church to celebrate a victory over Napoleon, among them Scarpia, the chief of police, who has tracked Angelotti there and finds evidences of the prisoner's recent presence. Angelotti's sister had left a woman's dress as a disguise for him and in the hurry of the escape a fan was dropped which makes Tosca suspect that her lover had left with some woman as his companion.

In the second act Cavaradossi is found at Tosca's villa and is arrested by Scarpia's orders in the hope of finding Angelotti's hiding place. Scarpia conspires to secure Tosca by torturing Cavaradossi, but he reveals nothing. In desperation, Tosca secretly informs him of Angelotti's hiding place, and her lover is imprisoned. Angelotti is found but escapes by suicide. Scarpia thereupon presents the hideous alternative to Tosca of her lover's instant death or her own dishonor. Tosca agrees to yield if he will first sign a permit for herself and Cavaradossi to leave the city the next morning. Scarpia thereupon orders his deputy to have a mock execution by firing blank cartridges, and while signing the permit is stabbed by Tosca.

In the last act Tosca visits her lover in the prison and tells him of the feigned execution and a long love scene follows. Then comes the execution, but it is a real one, for the soldiers have unwittingly killed him. At the same time, Scarpia's guards appear upon the scene in quest of Tosca, for they have heard of their master's death and know that she killed him. As Tosca sees them and becomes aware of their purpose she leaps to death from the prison ramparts.

There is no overture to "La Tosca." Three gloomy chords, the motive of Scarpia, are sounded and the curtain rises upon the church interior. Nearly all the first act is occupied by the dialogue music between Cavaradossi, Angelotti, the Sacristan and Tosca, which is smoothly and melodiously written, followed by Cavaradossi's charming aria ("Recondita Armonia") leading up to his duet with Tosca, in which occurs a very beautiful passage for the latter ("Non la sospire"). The interruption of the number by the entrance of choristers, seminarians, and the people to celebrate the victory prepares the way for a finale of much power and brilliancy of effect in which Scarpia's furious soliloquy ("Va, Tosca, nel tuo cuor s'annida Scarpia") is sung against the ringing of bells, booming of cannon, pealing of the organ and the Te Deum of the choristers.

The second act is not rich in set numbers. Its music

Scotti as *Scarpia*

Copyright, Burr McIntosh

mainly accompanies and sets forth the spirit of the action in quick but graphic musical dialogue. The most striking effect is the gavotte music at the Queen's entertainment in honor of the victory and the singing of the cantata by Tosca and chorus behind the scenes, while Cavaradossi is undergoing examination and horrible torture at Scarpia's hands, and the tragedy music in the finale, with Tosca's imploring appeal to Scarpia ("Vissi d'arte e d'amour, no feci").

The third act opens more quietly and upon a gentler scene, made attractive by the shepherds' snatches of song, blending with delightful bits of orchestral music and the distant sound of bells. The rural quiet, however, is soon disturbed by the approaching tragedy. Cavaradossi bids his farewell to Tosca, to the accompaniment of a delightful 'cello obbligato, followed by his mournful soliloquy ("E lucevan le stelle"), and the duet with Tosca, ending "O dolci mani." As the duet closes, action and music rush swiftly to the tragic denouement and the ghastly story ends in melodramatic music of the most intense kind.

REYER

LOUIS ÉTIENNE ERNEST REY, usually known as Ernest Reyer, was born at Marseilles, December 1, 1823. He first studied in the free municipal school of music in that city, and then took a position in the office of his uncle, who was a paymaster in Algiers. Even there he continued the study of music, and when in 1848 he went to Paris he entered actively upon the pursuit of the art. He wrote many transcriptions and melodies, and at last produced his first public work, "Le Sélam," a symphonic ode with chorus, in which he recorded his impressions of Oriental life. His first stage work was "Maître Wolfram" (1854), a one-act comedy opera, and this was followed by "Sakonntala" (1858), "La Statue" (1861), "Erostrate" (1862), "Sigurd" (1884), and "Salammbô" (1890). Reyer has also written many cantatas, songs, and dramatic scenas. He succeeded Berlioz as librarian at the Opéra, was elected to the Academy in 1876, and was an officer of the Legion of Honor in 1886.

SIGURD

"Sigurd," opera in four acts, text by Du Locle and Blau, was first produced at the Theatre Monnaie, Brussels, January 7, 1884, with Mme. Rose Caron, Mme. Bosman, Mme. Deschamps, and Mm. Jourdain, Devries, Gresse, Renaud, Boussa, Goeffoel, Mansuède and Stalport in the principal parts. The subject of the opera is taken from the Eddas, and closely resembles in certain scenes Wagner's "Götterdämmerung" and "Siegfried," though it was written a long time before either of these music-dramas were performed. In fact "Sigurd" was not brought out in Paris until eighteen years after it was written. There is no ground for the accusation sometimes made that Reyer is an imitator. He has simply used some of the same materials employed by Wagner, but musically has treated them in an entirely different manner.

A long overture gives out several of the leading melodies of the opera. The first act opens in Gunther's palace, and discloses women embroidering battle standards and singing the martial chorus ("Brodons des étendards et préparons des armes"). Hilda, Gunther's sister, and her nurse, Uta, are in the group, and Hilda relates a dream which troubles her, and which is interpreted by Uta in a long and very dramatic aria ("Je sais des secrets merveilleux") to mean that her coming husband will be killed by a jealous rival. Hilda, whose hand is sought by Attila, king of the Huns, reveals the secret of her love for Sigurd (Siegfried). Uta assures her that she will bring Sigurd to her and give him a love potion. Attila's messengers arrive and are welcomed by Gunther, and the story is told of Brunehild sleeping amid the fire-guarded rocks in a scena of great power, accompanied by festive music ("C'était Brunehild, la plus belle"). Gunther resolves to win her. Then follows an interview between Hilda and Gunther, in which the latter presses Attila's suit, but before she can make reply a trumpet peal is heard, announcing Sigurd, whose entrance aria is one of great vigor ("Prince de Rhin, au pays de mon père"). Gunther and Sigurd declare their friendship for each other in the duet, "Nous nous promettons devant vous." Hilda advances with Uta's magic draught, which Sigurd drinks. He at once falls in love with her, and her hand is promised to him in consideration of his helping Gunther to win Brunehild.

The second act opens in Brunehild's land with a chorus of priests ("Dieux terribles qui vous plaisez") engaged in the worship of Odin and Freja. The rites are interrupted by the appearance of Sigurd, Gunther, and Hagen, who, in a strong scena ("O Brunehild, O vierge armée"), announce their errand. The priests and worshippers warn them that no one can succeed except one who has never known love. As Sigurd alone is fitted for the task, in the next scene we find him in the forest, where he sings an aria of great power and melodic beauty ("Le bruit des chants s'eteint dans la forêt immense"). He has been instructed to sound the horn given him by the priests three times. After an invocation to Hilda he blows a blast and is shown three Norns washing a shroud at a spring, which they intimate is for him. Sigurd prepares to sound another blast and is assailed by supernatural beings, but he overcomes them, and then they tempt him in a voluptuous scene, but in vain. At last the lake near by turns to a lake of fire, with a palace of fire rising from it. Nothing daunted he plunges in. The scene changes. Led by the Norns, he calls to Brunehild. She awakes, and at once offers her love to Sigurd in the brilliant aria, "Salut, splendeur du jour." Sigurd, faithful to Gunther, however, bids her follow him, and he leads her away with a drawn sword between them.

The third act opens in Gunther's gardens. Spirit voices are heard invoking the king's presence ("A la voix des esprits de l'air"), and a dramatic scene ensues in which Hilda and Uta overhear Sigurd's announcement of his success. Brunehild, who has been taken to the garden while sleeping by the spirits, wakes to find Gunther protesting his love for her, which she accepts, thinking him Sigurd, in a brilliant aria ("Vêtu de fer, la visière baissée"), followed by a powerful duet. The scene changes, and Hagen announces to the people the forthcoming nuptials of Gunther and Brunehild, accompanied by pageantry music and triumphal march ("Semons ces bords de joncs et de rameaux fleuris "), and followed by a brilliant ballet, after which the king prepares to go to the sacred grove. At this instant Sigurd appears and claims Hilda ("Roi Gunther, digne fils des héros"). Gunther consents and bids Brunehild join their hands. As she does so, both Brunehild and Sigurd exclaim that their hands burn. The act closes with the brilliant wedding march to the grove ("Frappons les airs joyeux").

In the last act the people are told that Brunehild is suffering from a mysterious malady, and they shrink away from her whenever she appears. In a long and powerful scena ("O palais radieux de la voûte étoilée") she confesses her love for Sigurd and implores Odin to destroy her. Hilda seeks to comfort her but Brunehild observes she is wearing a girdle which Sigurd took from her on the night of her deliverance. She realizes the trick played upon her and an excited scena of jealousy follows ("Sigurd m'aime! Si, brisant ma chaîne"). Brunehild dispels the influence of Uta's potion with a charm, and Sigurd's love changes. After a powerful and most passionate duet with Brunehild ("Avec ces fleurs que l'eau traîne en courant"), Sigurd goes hunting with Gunther. Hilda offers to save Sigurd from death at the hands of his rival if Brunehild will reject his love, but while she hesitates, Gunther slays him, and his body is brought in. Brunehild mounts the funeral pyre and a powerful apotheosis closes the opera ("Oublions les maux soufferts"), as their spirits are borne upward to paradise to the accompaniment of the celestial choir ("Pour vous les cieux ouvert").

RICCI

LUIGI RICCI was born at Naples, July 8, 1805, and died at Prague, December 31, 1859. His first work was an opera buffa, "L'Impresario in angustié" (1823). In 1836 he was appointed capellmeister of the Trieste cathedral, and was also choral director in the theatre at the same city. He wrote in all thirty operas, besides several masses, requiems, choruses, and songs. The best known of his operas is "Crispino e la Comare," which was written in collaboration with his brother Federico, and was brought out at Venice in 1850. The two brothers wrote four operas together. Luigi Ricci died in an asylum at Prague shortly after producing his opera, " Il diavolo a quattro." Federico, who was four years younger than Luigi, died at Conegliano in 1877.

CRISPINO

"Crispino," opera buffa, in three acts, text by Piave, was first produced in Venice in 1850. The first act of this charming little fairy opera opens with a unison chorus of apothecary's apprentices ("Batti, batti"). Crispino, a poor cobbler, over head and ears in debt, whose wife Annetta tries to help him out by ballad singing, is seated at his bench at work in front of his house. In the intervals of the chorus the Count, who figures in a side plot, sings a beautiful romanza ("Bella siccome un angelo"). Then Crispino bewails his hard fortune in a quaint melody ("Una volta un ciabattino"), after which Annetta introduces herself with a canzonetta ("Istorie belle a leggere"), leading up to a minor duet between them. In the sixth scene a buffo aria ("Io sono un po' filosofo ") is sung by Dr. Fabrizio. At last Crispino gets into such desperate straits that he resolves to make away with himself. He is about to jump into a well when a fairy appears and dissuades him, at the same time giving him a purse of gold and offering to set him up in business as a doctor, telling him he must look about him whenever he has a patient, and if she is not present he will be successful. The act closes with a duet for Crispino and Annetta (" Troppo so, basta per ora ").

The second act discloses Crispino in the midst of a flourishing business, and the delighted Annetta sings a joyous little melody (" Io non sono più l'Annetta "). A workman who has met with an accident is brought to Crispino for treatment, and as the fairy is not present he is successful. The musical handling of the healing scene is worked up with great skill. It begins with a baritone solo, leading up to a duet with soprano and chorus accompaniment. A sextet then takes up the theme, and in the close all on the stage give it with impressive effect. A broadly humorous but very melodious trio of the doctors follows (" Ma, signori, perchè tantes questione? "). In the next scene Annetta sings the pretty Fritola song (" Piero mio, go qua una fritola ") in which she boasts the merits of a cake she has made for the Carnival. Meanwhile Crispino grows so puffed up with his wealth that when Annetta invites some old friends to the house he drives them out, and is about to strike Annetta when the fairy suddenly appears.

In the last act the fairy has taken Crispino to a cavern, where she shows him crystal vases in which more or less brilliant lights are burning. She tells him that each represents a human life. The one burning brightly is Annetta's, the one dimly is his own. When he asks her to take some oil out of Annetta's lamp and put it into his, she upbraids him, reveals herself as Death, and tells him to make his last request, for he is about to die. In a doleful ballad (" Poco cerco, O mia Comare "), he asks for only a half hour more, so that he may see Annetta and the children. A sudden change of scene shows him in his own house, awaking from sleep in his chair. As he realizes that it has been only a nightmare, occasioned by a sudden fit of illness, he manifests his delight and Annetta expresses her joy in a brilliant waltz movement ("Non ha gioia in tal momento"), which closes the opera.

ROSSINI

GIOACCHINI ANTONIO ROSSINI was born at Pesaro, Italy, February 29, 1792. He first studied with Tesei, and as a lad also appeared upon the stage as a singer. In 1807 he was admitted to the class of Padre Mattei at the Bologna Conservatory, where he took a prize for a cantata at the end of his first year. At the beginning of his career in Italy he was commissioned to write an opera for Venice. It was "La Cambiale di Matrimonio," an opera buffa in one act, and was produced in 1810. During the next three years he wrote several works for Venice and Milan, which were successful, but none of them created such a furor as "Tancredi." This was followed by "L' Italiana in Algeri," "Aureliano in Palmira," and "Il Turco in Italia." In 1815 "The Barber of Seville" appeared. Strange as it may seem, it was at first condemned, not on its merits, but because the composer had trenched, as it was supposed, upon the ground already occupied by the favorite Paisiello, though he applied to the latter before writing it, and received his assurances that he had no objection to his use of the same subject. "Otello" followed the "Barber" at Naples in 1816, and "Cenerentola" in 1817, and both were extraordinarily successful. "Gazza Ladra" was produced at Milan in 1817, and was followed by "Armida" at Naples in the same year. His next great work was the oratorio, "Moses in Egypt," which is also given as opera. "Donna del Lago," based upon Sir Walter Scott's "Lady of the Lake," was produced at Naples in 1819. The same year he opened the Carnival in Milan with "Bianca e

Faliero," and before its close he produced "Maometto Secondo" at Naples. During the next two or three years his muse was very prolific, and in 1823 "Semiramide," another of his great works, appeared and made an enthusiastic success at Venice. That year he went to London and gave concerts, in which he sang, and thence to Paris, which was ever afterwards his home. His greatest work for Paris was "William Tell," which was produced in 1829, and it was also his last, though by an arrangement with the Government of Charles X it was to be the first of a series of five. The revolution of 1830 destroyed his plans. In 1836 he heard Meyerbeer's "Les Huguenots," and resolved to write no more. Four years before this he had written the "Stabat Mater," but it was not produced complete until 1842. From this time on he lived at his villa at Passy the life of a voluptuary, and died there November 13, 1868. The catalogue of his works is immense, including fifty operas alone.

THE BARBER OF SEVILLE

"Il Barbiere di Siviglia," opera buffa in two acts, words by Sterbini, founded on Beaumarchais's comedy, was first produced at the Argentina Theatre, Rome, February 5, 1816, with the following cast:

Rosina . . . . Mme. GIORGI RIGHETTI.
Berta . . . . Mlle. ROSSI.
Figaro . . . . Sig. LUIGI ZAMBONI.
Count Almaviva . . . . Sig. GARCIA.
Bartolo . . . . Sig. BOTTICELLI.
Basilio . . . . SIG. VITTARELLI.

The story of the writing of "The Barber of Seville" is of more than ordinary interest. Rossini had engaged to write two operas for the Roman Carnival of 1816. The first was brought out December 26, 1815, and the same day he bound himself to furnish the second by January 20, 1816, with no knowledge of what the libretto

Campanari as *Figaro*
Copyright, Aimé Dupont

Sembrich as *Rosina*
Copyright, Aimé Dupont

would be. Sterbini furnished him with the story of the "Barber" by piecemeal, and as fast as the verses were given him he wrote the music. The whole work was finished in less than three weeks. Its original title was "Almaviva, ossia l' inutile precauzione," to distinguish it from Paisiello's "Barber of Seville." The original overture was lost in some manner, and that of "Aureliano" substituted. In the scene beneath Rosina's balcony, Garcia introduced a Spanish air of his own which failed, and before the second performance Rossini wrote the beautiful cavatina, "Ecco ridente il cielo" in its place, the melody borrowed from the opening chorus of his "Aureliano," and that in turn from his "Ciro in Babilonia." The subject of the effective trio ("Zitti, zitti") was taken from Haydn's "Seasons," and the aria sung by the duenna Berta ("Il vecchietto cerca moglie"), from a Russian melody he had heard a lady sing in Rome and introduced for her sake. For the music-lesson scene Rossini wrote a trio which has been lost; and thus an opportunity has been given Rosinas to interpolate what they please.

The scene of the opera is laid at Seville, Spain. Count Almaviva has fallen in love with Rosina, the ward of Dr. Bartolo, with whom she resides, and who wishes to marry her himself. After serenading his mistress, who knows him only by the name of Count Lindoro, he prevails upon Figaro, the factotum of the place, to bring about an interview with her. In spite of her guardian's watchfulness, as well as that of Don Basilio, her music teacher, who is helping Bartolo in his schemes, she informs the Count by letter that she returns his passion. With Figaro's help he succeeds in gaining admission to the house disguised as a drunken dragoon, but this stratagem is foiled by the entrance of the guard, who arrest him. A second time he secures admission, disguised as a music teacher, and pretending that he has been sent by Don Basilio, who is ill, to take his place. To get into Bartolo's confidence he produces Rosina's letter to himself, and promises to persuade her that the letter has been given him by a mistress of the Count, and thus break off the connection between the two. By this means he secures the desired interview, and an elopement and private marriage are planned. In the midst of the arrangements, however, Don Basilio puts in an appearance, and the disconcerted lover makes good his escape. Meanwhile Bartolo, who has Rosina's letter, succeeds in arousing the jealousy of his ward with it, who thereupon discloses the proposed elopement and promises to marry her guardian. At the time set for the elopement the Count and Figaro appear. A reconciliation is easily effected, a notary is at hand, and they are married just as Bartolo makes his appearance with officers to arrest the Count. Mutual explanations occur, however, and all ends happily.

The first act opens after a short chorus, with the serenade ("Ecco ridente in cielo"), the most beautiful song in the opera. It begins with a sweet and expressive largo and concludes with a florid allegro, and is followed by a chorus in which the serenaders are dismissed. In the second scene Figaro enters, and after some brief recitatives sings the celebrated buffo aria ("Largo al factotum"), in which he gives an account of his numerous avocations. The aria is full of life and gayety, and wonderfully adapted to the style of the mercurial Figaro. A light and lively duet between Figaro and the Count, closing with the sprightly melody, "Ah! che d'amore," leads up to the chamber aria of Rosina, so well known on the concert stage ("Una voce poco fa"), which is not only very expressive and of great compass, but is remarkably rich in ornamentation. A short dialogue in recitative then occurs between Bartolo and Basilio, in which they plot to circumvent Rosina by calumny, which gives occasion for the Calumny aria, as it is generally known ("La Calunnia"), a very sonorous bass solo, sung by Basilio. Another dialogue follows between Figaro and Rosina, leading to the florid duet ("E il maestro io faccio"). A third dialogue follows between Rosina and Bartolo, ending in a bass aria ("Non piu tacete"), very similar in its general style to the Calumny song, but usually omitted in performances. In the tenth scene the Count arrives disguised as the drunken soldier, and the finale begins. It is composed of three scenes very ingeniously arranged, and full of glittering dialogue and very melodious passages.

The second act opens with a soliloquy by Bartolo ("Ma vedi il mio destino"), in which he gives vent to his suspicions. It is interrupted at last by a duet with the Count, in which the two characters are strikingly set off by the music. The music-lesson scene follows, in which the artist personating Rosina is given an opportunity for interpolation. In the next scene occurs a dialogue quintet, which is followed by a long aria ("Sempre gridi") by the duenna Berta, called by the Italians the "Aria di Sorbetto," because the people used to eat ices while it was sung; reminding one of the great aria from "Tancredi," "Di tanti palpiti," which they called the "aria dei rizzi," because Rossini composed it while cooking his rice. In the eighth scene, after a long recitative, an instrumental prelude occurs, representing a stormy night, followed by a recitative in which the Count reveals himself, leading up to a florid trio, and this in turn to the elegant terzetto, "Zitti, zitti." A bravura and finale of light and graceful melody close the opera.

SEMIRAMIDE

"Semiramide," lyric tragedy in two acts, words by Gaetano Rossi, the subject taken from Voltaire's "Semiramis," was first produced at the Fenice Theatre, Venice, February 3, 1823, with the following cast:

Semiramide	Mme. ROSSINI-COLBRAN
Arsaces	Mme. MARIANI.
Idreno	Mr. SINCLAIR.
Assur	Sig. GALLI.
Oroe	Sig. MARIANI.

On the 9th of July it was produced in French at the Académie, Paris, as "Semiramis," with Carlotta Marchisio as Semiramide, Barbara, her sister, as Arsaces, and M. Obin as Assur. At Rossini's request M. Carafa arranged the recitatives and wrote the ballet music. "Semiramide" was the last opera Rossini wrote for Italy; and so far did he depart from the conventional Italian style, that he was charged with imitating the German. It was probably for this reason that the opera when first performed did not meet with a kindly reception from the Venetians. Although he was occupied six months in negotiating for his stipulated price (one thousand dollars), he wrote the opera in three weeks. Of its first performance, a correspondent of the "Harmonicon," who was present, writes: "The first act, which lasted two hours and fifteen minutes, was received very coldly, with the exception of one passage in the overture, which overture, however, was unconscionably long. The second act, which lasted two hours and a half, began to please in an air of Mariani, but the applause was rather directed to this favorite singer. After this a duet between her and Colbran, together with an air of Galli, and particularly a terzetto between him and the two ladies, were well received. Rossini was also called for at the end of the second act."

The scene of the opera is laid in Babylon, and the story briefly told is as follows: Ninus, the King of Babylon, has been murdered by his Queen, Semiramis, aided by

Assur, a prince enamored of her and aspiring to the throne. One of the Queen's warriors, Arsaces, supposed to be of Scythian origin, but in reality her own son, returns from a foreign expedition and is loaded with honors for the victory he has won. Semiramis, ignorant of his parentage, has a secret passion for him, he in the meantime being devoted to Azema, one of the princesses royal. As all gather together in the temple to swear allegiance to the Queen, the gates of Ninus's tomb suddenly open, and his ghost appears and announces that Arsaces will be the successor to the Crown. At midnight Semiramis, Assur, and Arsaces meet at the tomb, and by mistake Assur stabs her instead of Arsaces, who in turn kills Assur, and, all obstacles being removed, is united to Azema and ascends the throne.

An introductory chorus of Babylonians and a terzetto by Idreno, Assur, and Oroe open the opera and lead up to the first appearance of Semiramis, which is followed by a very dramatic quartet ("Di tanti Regi"). In the fourth scene Arsaces has a brilliant aria ("O! come da quel di"), which also did service in one or two of Rossini's other operas, and is followed by an animated duet ("Bella imago degli dei") between himself and Assur. The eighth scene is introduced by a graceful female chorus which leads to Semiramis's brilliant and well-known aria, "Bel raggio." In the tenth scene occurs an elegant duet ("Serbami ognor si fido"), followed in the next scene by a stately priests' march and chorus ("Ergi omai la fronte altera!"), set to ecclesiastical harmony and accompanied by full military band as well as orchestra, this being the first instance where a military band was used in Italian opera. It leads to the finale, where Semiramis on her throne announces to her people her choice for their future king. The oath of allegiance follows in an impressive quartet with chorus ("Giuro al numi"), and a defiant aria by the Queen leads to the sudden appearance of the ghost of Ninus, accompanied by characteristic music repeated in quintet with chorus. As the ghost speaks, the statue scene in "Don Giovanni" is inevitably recalled, especially in some phrases which are literally copied.

The second act opens with a vindictively passionate duet ("Assur, i cenni miei") between Assur and Semiramis, closing with a fierce outburst of hatred ("La forza primiera"). The scene is a very long and spirited one, and is followed by a second chorus of priests, leading to a great aria with chorus ("Ah! tu gelar mi fai") for Arsaces. In the fifth scene occurs a long duet between Arsaces and Semiramis, the second part of which ("Giorno d' orrore") is the strongest number in the opera. Though intensely passionate in its tone, the music is smooth and flowing and very florid for both voices. The seventh scene is composed of a scena, aria, and chorus, followed by still another chorus in the mausoleum. Semiramis sings a prayer of great pathos and beauty ("Al mio pregar"). A terzetto ("L'usato ardir"), which like the mausoleum chorus is based upon an aria from Mozart's "Cosi fan tutti," closes the opera. "The Harmonicon," to which reference has already been made, in an analysis of the work, has the following apt criticism: "It has been said, and truly, that 'Semiramide' is composed in the German style, but it is the German style exaggerated. Rossini is become a convert to this school, and his conversion does his judgment credit, though like all proselytes he passes into extremes. Not satisfied with discarding the meagre accompaniments of the Italian composers, he even goes far beyond the tramontane masters in the multitude and use of instruments, and frequently smothers his concerted pieces and choruses by the overwhelming weight of his orchestra." But what would the "Harmonicon" have said, could it have had Wagner's or Richard Strauss's instrumentation before it?

Alboni as *Arsace*   Grisi as *Semiramide*   Tamburini as *Assur*

From an old illustration in "Harper's Weekly"

WILLIAM TELL

"William Tell," opera in three acts, words by Étienne Jouy and Hippolyte Bis, the subject taken from Schiller's drama of the same name, was first produced at the Académie, Paris, August 3, 1829, with the following cast:

Mathilde	Mme. DAMOREAU-CINTI.
Jemmy	Mme. DABODIE.
Hedwig	Mlle. MORI.
Arnold	M. NOURRIT.
Walter	M. LEVASSEUR.
Tell	M. DABODIE.
Ruodi	M. DUPONT.
Rodolphe	M. MASSOL.
Gessler	M. PRÉVOST.
Leutold	M. PRÉVOT.

Rossini wrote for Paris only two operas, "Le Comte Ory" and "William Tell," — the latter his masterpiece in the serious style. The libretto was first prepared by M. Jouy, but it was so bad that M. Bis was called in, and to him is due the whole of the second act. Even after the two authors had changed and revised it, Rossini had to alter it in many places. When it was first performed the weakness of the drama was at once recognized, though its music was warmly welcomed, especially by the critical. It was presented fifty-six times in its original form, and was then cut down to three acts, the original third act being omitted and the fourth and fifth condensed into one. For three years after this time the second act was alone performed in Paris; but when M. Duprez made his debut in the part of *Arnold*, a fresh enthusiasm was aroused, and there was a genuine Tell revival.

The scene of the opera is laid in Switzerland, period, the thirteenth century, and the action closely follows the historical narrative. The disaffection which has arisen among the Swiss, owing to the tyranny of Gessler, suddenly comes to a climax when one of Gessler's followers attempts an outrage upon the only daughter of the herdsman Leutold, and meets his death at the hands of the indignant father. Leutold seeks protection at the hands of Tell, who, in the face of the herdsman's pursuers, succeeds in placing him beyond the reach of danger, and this circumstance arouses the wrath of Gessler. Melchtal, the village patriarch, is accused by him of inciting the people to insubordination, and is put to death. Meanwhile Arnold, his son, is enamored of Mathilde, Gessler's daughter, and hesitates between love and duty when he is called upon to avenge his father's death. At last duty prevails, and he joins his comrades when the men of the three cantons, who are loyal to Tell, meet and swear death to the tyrant. In the last act occurs the famous archery scene. To discover the leading offenders Gessler erects a pole in the square of Altorf, upon which he places his hat and commands the people to do homage to it. Tell refuses, and as a punishment is ordered to shoot an apple from his son's head. He successfully accomplishes the feat, but as he is about to retire Gessler observes a second arrow concealed in his garments, and inquires the reason for it, when Tell boldly replies it was intended for him in case the first had killed his son. Gessler throws him into prison, whereupon Mathilde abandons her father and determines to help in the rescue of Tell and his son. Her lover, Arnold, meanwhile, raises a band of brave followers and accomplishes the rescue himself. After slaying the tyrant and freeing his country Tell returns to his family, and Arnold and Mathilde are united.

The overture to "William Tell," with its Alpine repose, its great storm-picture, the stirring "Ranz des Vaches," and the trumpet-call to freedom, is one of the most perfect and beautiful ever written, and is so familiar that it does not need analysis. The first act opens with a delightfully fresh Alpine chorus ("E il ciel sereno"), which is followed by a pastoral quartet between a fisherman, Tell, Hedwig, and Jemmy. Arnold enters, and a long duet, one of Rossini's finest inspirations, follows between Arnold and Tell. The duet is interrupted by the entrance of several of the peasants escorting two brides and bridegrooms, which is the signal for a most graceful chorus and dance ("Cinto il crine"). Leutold then appears, seeking Tell's protection, and a very dramatic finale begins, closing with the arrest of Melchtal, which leads to an ensemble of great power.

The second act opens with a double chorus of huntsmen and shepherds ("Qual silvestre metro intorne"), which is followed by a scena preluding a charming romanza ("Selva opaco") sung by Mathilde. Its mild, quiet beauty is in strange contrast with the remainder of this great act. It is followed by a passionate duet with Arnold, a second and still more passionate duet between Tell and Walter, which leads to the magnificent trio of the oath ("La gloria inflammi"), and this in turn is followed by the splendid scene of the gathering of the cantons. For melodic and harmonic beauty combined, the spirited treatment of masses, and charm and variety of color, this great scene stands almost alone.

The last act opens with a duet between Mathilde and Arnold, which is followed in the next scene by a march and chorus as the multitude gathers in the square of Altorf, closing with a lovely Tyrolean chorus sung by the sopranos and accompanied with the dance. The dramatic scene of the archery follows, and then Arnold has a very passionate aria ("O muto asil"). Some vivid storm-music, preluding the last scene, and the final hymn of freedom ("I boschi, i monti") close an opera which is unquestionably Rossini's masterpiece, and in which his musical ability reached its highest expression. "Manly, earnest, and mighty," Hanslick calls it; and the same authority claims that the first and second acts belong to the most beautiful achievements of the modern opera.

RUBINSTEIN

ANTON GREGOR RUBINSTEIN was born November 30, 1829, at Weghwotynez in Russia. His mother gave him lessons at the age of four, with the result that by the time he was six she was unable to teach him anything more. He then studied the piano with Alexander Villoing, a pupil of John Field. In 1840 he entered the Paris Conservatory, where he attracted the attention of Liszt, Chopin, and Thalberg. He remained in that city eighteen months, and then made some professional tours, in which he met with extraordinary success. In 1844 his parents removed to Berlin, and he was placed under Dehn, the famous contrapuntist, to study composition. From 1846 to 1848 he taught music in Pressburg and Vienna, and then went back to Russia. For eight years he studied and wrote in St. Petersburg, and at the end of that time had accumulated a mass of manuscripts destined to make his name famous all over Europe, while his reputation as a skilful pianist was already world-wide. He visited England again in 1857, and the next year returned home and settled in St. Petersburg, about which time he was made Imperial Concert Director, with a life pension. At this period in his career he devoted himself to the cause of music in Russia. His first great work was the foundation of the Conservatory in that city in 1862, of which he remained principal until 1867. He also founded the Russian Musical Society in 1861, and in 1869 was decorated by the Czar. In 1870 he directed the Philharmonic and Choral Societies of Vienna, and shortly afterwards made another tour, during which, in 1872, he came to this country with the eminent violinist, Wieniawski, as will be well remembered. His greatest works are the "Ocean Symphony," "Dramatic Symphony," and a character sketch for grand orchestra called "Ivan the Terrible"; his operas, "Children of the Heath," "Feramors," "Nero," "The Maccabees," "Dimitri Donskoi," and "The Demon"; the oratorios "Paradise Lost," and "Tower of Babel," and a long and splendid catalogue of chamber, salon, and concert music, besides some beautiful songs, which are great favorites in the concert room.

NERO

"Nero," opera in four acts, text by Jules Barbier, was first produced in Hamburg in 1879 — though it was originally intended for the French stage — and in this country, in New York, March 14, 1887, by the American Opera Company, under the direction of Theodore Thomas, with the following cast:

Nero	Mr. CANDIDUS.
Julius Vindex	Mr. LUDWIG.
Tigellinus	Mr. STODDARD.
Balbillus	Mr. WHITNEY.
Saccus	Mr. FESSENDEN.
Sevirus	Mr. HAMILTON.
Terpander	Mr. LEE.
Poppœa Sabina	Miss BERTHA PIERSON.
Epicharis	Miss CORNELIA VAN ZANTEN.
Chrysa	Miss EMMA JUCH.
Agrippina	Miss AGNES STERLING.
Lupus	Miss PAULINE L'ALLEMAND.

The first act opens in the house of Epicharis, a courtesan, a rendezvous for the dissolute Roman nobles. The guests assembled sing a chorus in praise of the establishment, followed by a scene in which Vindex, the prince of Aquitania, Saccus the poet, Terpander the citharist, and others conspire against Nero. Suddenly Chrysa, daughter of Epicharis, who is ignorant of her mother's real character and dwells apart from her, rushes in and implores the protection of Vindex from a crowd of revellers who have pursued her. A very spirited duet follows in which the prince promises her his assistance. Upon hearing the shouts of her pursuers he conceals her just in time to escape the masked band, headed by Nero himself, which bursts into the apartment. The tyrant demands the girl; and as he throws off his mask the guests stand amazed. Saccus at last breaks the spell by the suggestion that Nero shall marry the girl. When she is led out, and Vindex discovers that Epicharis is her mother, he no longer espouses her cause. Then follows the music of the mock marriage, interspersed with dance strains and sardonic choruses by the courtesans and their associates, at last rising to a wild bacchanalian frenzy, in the midst of which Vindex breaks out in a spirited song, with harp accompaniment, and finally hurls invectives at Nero, as Chrysa, who has drunk a narcotic at her mother's order, falls senseless. The latter declares she has been poisoned, and the act closes with a scene of great power in which Vindex is hurried away as Nero's prisoner.

The second act opens in the dwelling of Poppœa, Nero's mistress, whose attendants are trying to console her. She has heard of Nero's new infatuation; but her apprehensions are relieved when Balbillus, the astrologer, enters and not only announces that Chrysa is dead, but the equally grateful news that Octavia, Nero's wife, has been condemned to die. Nero himself now appears upon the scene, and a duet follows in which Poppœa reproaches him for his fickleness and he seeks to console her with flattery. At its close the death of Octavia is announced, and Poppœa is appeased by the prospect of sharing the throne. Meanwhile Chrysa has fallen into the custody of Agrippina, Nero's mother, who keeps close charge of her to further her own ambitions. During the interview between the tyrant and his mistress, Epicharis rushes in and implores Nero to give up Chrysa, which leads to a powerful ensemble. Learning that Chrysa is still alive he leaves the apartment to find her. The second scene is brilliantly spectacular. Nero and his mother appear in front of the temple, followed by a long procession to the music of a brilliant march. They enter the temple. After a short episode, in which Poppœa informs Epicharis of the refuge Chrysa has found, the ballet is given in the open square, with its fascinating dances of warriors, bacchantes, jugglers, and buffoons, and their mimic combats, the music of which is very familiar from its frequent performance in the concert room. Nero then appears and announces his divinity in a finale, which is rich with scenic, spectacular, and choral effects, accompanied by full military band and orchestra.

The third act opens in Chrysa's new asylum of refuge. The persecuted girl sings a beautiful prayer, at the close of which Vindex joins her in a love-duet, which will always remain as one of the most refined and noble products of Rubinstein's skill in harmony. The next number is one of almost equal beauty, — a duet for Chrysa and Epicharis, the motive of which is a cradle song. Its soothing tones are interrupted by the appearance of Nero, followed by Poppœa and Saccus, the last-named announcing to the tyrant that Rome is in flames, which leads up to a vigorous trio. The concluding scene is full of characteristic music. It shows us Nero watching the fire from his tower, while he sings a hymn ("O Ilion") to the accompaniment of his lyre; the death of Chrysa, who proclaims herself a Christian and is killed by the infuriated populace; and the fate of Epicharis, who is crushed beneath a falling house as she mourns for her daughter.

The fourth act furnishes a dramatic denouement to the mournful story. The tyrant, wild with rage and frenzy, appears in the tomb of Augustus, where the shades of his murdered victims terrify him. Saccus enters and tells him of the revolt of his army and the danger which threatens him. He rushes out again and kills himself on the highway of the Campagna, just as Vindex at the head of his legions comes up with him. As he expires a cross appears in the sky and a chant is heard, herald of the coming Christianity.

THE DEMON

"The Demon," fantastic opera in three acts, text by Wiskowatoff, the libretto based upon Lermontoff's poetic tale with the same name, was first produced at St. Petersburg, January 25, 1875; in German, at Hamburg, in 1880; and in Italian, at London, as "Il Demonio," in 1881. In the prologue the Demon is seen in the midst of the evil spirits defying the Creator and the Angel of Light and bent upon destroying all existing things. When, however, he beholds Tamara, daughter of Prince Gudal, enjoying herself with her maidens by the brookside, and awaiting the arrival of her lover, the Prince of Sinodu, he is enamored of her and his fury disappears. He decides upon the death of the latter and accomplishes it by a horde of marauding Tartars who murder him as he lies in magic slumber. The Demon next is seen comforting Tamara as she weeps over the body of her lover. He visits her in the convent whither she has retired, reveals his real self to her, and invites her to share earthly dominion with him. She agrees to do this if he will forsake his evil ways and renew his allegiance to the offended deity. He takes the vow, apparently in good faith, but while in the act of doing so the Angel of Light appears, accompanied by the ghost of the Prince, and the Demon is forced to abandon Tamara, who is carried to heaven by angels after the manner of Marguerite in the "Faust" apotheosis.

The first act is introduced with fantastic choruses of

evil spirits, winds, waters, rocks, and flames, mingled with those of the good spirits and spirits of nature. The Demon appears at the call of the evil spirits ("He, Dämon! wir warten"), and hurls his curses against the world in a powerful aria ("Verhasste, verfluchte Welt!"). The next scene is introduced by some charming choruses of maidens ("Täglich eilen wir im Fluge"), leading up to Tamara's brilliant entrance aria ("Ach! liebe Mädchen"), which is shortly followed by her attendant's ballad ("Ach, Tamara"). Alternate dialogues between Tamara and her maidens and the Prince and his attendants lead up to the surprise of the Prince's caravan by the Tartars, who appear in a characteristic refrain ("Stille, stille! schleichet näher!"), and the murder of the Prince.

The second act opens with a wedding feast introduced by the lively chorus of guests ("Rufet Heil unserm Fürsten"). After phrases of greeting, as Tamara enters, the guests grow hilarious and indulge in a genuine old-fashioned Italian brindisi ("Der Wein, der Wein"). A lively, charming ballet, full of Eastern color and abandon, follows. Its gay sounds have hardly died away before a short funeral march announces the approach of attendants bearing the body of the Prince, who are greeted with the mournful chorus, "Weh uns! ein Trauerzug." A pathetic quintet with chorus is followed by one of the most beautiful numbers in the opera, the romanza, "Süsses Kind, Du weinst vergebens," in which the Demon consoles Tamara for the loss of her lover. The act closes with a strong declamatory war chorus ("Auf zum Kampfe! Räche nus, beseele uns") appended to the ensemble, sung by Prince Gudal and repeated by a male chorus. The last act is occupied entirely with the long and very dramatic duet between the Demon and Tamara and the apotheosis, with its beautiful chorus of the invisible angels.

SAINT-SAËNS

CAMILLE SAINT-SAËNS, foremost of modern French composers, was born at Paris, October 9, 1835. He learned the rudiments of music from a great-aunt, and later on studied with Stamaty and Maleden. He entered the Conservatory in a class presided over by Halévy and competed without success for the Prix de Rome in 1852. His first prize was obtained in 1867, when his cantata, "Les Noces de Prométhée," was accepted for the opening of the International Exhibition. In 1852 he was organist at the church of Saint-Méry and in 1858 succeeded Lefébune-Wély in a similar position at the Madeleine, but resigned the place in 1877, as his time was much occupied with piano concert tours. He first appeared as a pianist in London in 1871 and during the next twenty years made many visits there, and in 1893 was honored with a degree by Cambridge University. Meanwhile his chamber music, piano concertos, and his symphonic poems, "Le Rouet d'Omphale," "Danse Macabre," "Phaéton," and "La Jeunesse d'Hercule" had spread his fame far and wide. His first opera, "La Princesse Jaune," was heard in 1872, "Le Timbre d'Argent" was brought out in 1877, "Samson et Delila" in the same year, "Étienne Marcel" in 1879, "Henri VIII" in 1883, "Proserpine" in 1887, "Ascanio" in 1890, "Phryne" in 1893, and "Fredegonde" in 1895. The last-named opera was begun by Guiraud and finished by Saint-Saëns. Besides the works enumerated above, Saint-Saëns has written five symphonies and numerous pieces for piano, violin, and other instruments as well as songs and cantatas.

SAMSON AND DELILA

"Samson et Delila," opera biblique, in three acts, text by Ferdinand Lemaire, was first produced in its entirety at Weimar, December 2, 1877, with Ferenczy as Samson, Mlle. Von Müller as Delila and Mitle as the High Priest. The score of this opera was finished in 1872. Two years later, Mme. Viardot-Garcia gave a private performance of the second act, and the first act was given at one of the Colonne concerts in Paris in 1875. It was not until 1877 that the whole opera was performed, under the direction of Edouard Lassen, at Weimar. It was done at Brussels, April 6, 1878, under the direction of the composer, and in Hamburg in 1883 with Frau Sucher as Delila. It was not given entire in France until 1890, when it was heard at Rouen and again in the same year at Paris, with Mme. Bloch and M. Talazac in the principal roles. It was next heard in various French cities during 1892 and at last, after twenty years, was produced upon a grand scale at the Paris Opera House. It was first performed in this country as an oratorio at New York, March 25, 1892, under the direction of Mr. Walter Damrosch.

The first act opens in the public square of the city of Gaza, and the curtain rises upon a crowd of Hebrews, Samson among them, who give expression to their dejection in choruses constructed after the conventional oratorio methods. Samson comforts them, however, assures them of help, and urges them to pray for deliverance. In the second scene, Abimelech, satrap of Gaza, enters, and mocks at their prayers. Samson denounces him as a blasphemer and calls upon his people to take up arms and free themselves. Abimelech attacks him but Samson wrests his sword from him and slays him as he is calling for help. The Philistines make an attack but Samson worsts them. The third scene is at the gates of the temple of

Tamagno as *Samson*

Copyright, Aimé Dupont

Dagon. The High Priest ascends to the temple, and, pausing by Abimelech's body, urges the Philistines to avenge his death. While they are hesitating, a messenger arrives with the tidings that the Israelites are on the march with Samson at their head, whereupon the High Priest curses both them and their leader. As Abimelech's body is carried away the old Hebrew men and women enter, followed by Samson and his victorious band, singing choruses of rejoicing. In the next scene Delila enters, followed by Philistine women wearing garlands of flowers. At this point the temptation begins with fascinating dances by the priestesses of Dagon in which Delila takes part, the act closing with a beautiful aria ("Printemps qui commence") sung by her, in which she seeks to cast her spells over Samson.

The second act discloses Delila richly clad, in front of his dwelling. She sings a passionate invocation to Love to aid her in her spells, and in the next scene occurs a vigorous dramatic duet in which the High Priest tells her of the disaster to the Philistines and strengthens her in her purpose. In the next scene Samson enters, disturbed and troubled. An exceedingly passionate duet follows with a peculiarly beautiful motive for Delila, which is several times repeated in the progress of the work. In the midst of an approaching storm Samson declares his love, and, as it breaks in all its fury, he follows her into her dwelling, which, at the same time, is stealthily approached by Philistine soldiers.

The third act reveals Samson blinded, in chains, and with shorn locks, grinding at a mill as a captive, as the Hebrews sing their mournful plaints behind the scenes. Then follows a pathetic prayer in which Samson bewails his loss of sight. The Philistines enter and remove Samson and the scene changes to the interior of Dagon's temple, where the High Priest is seen surrounded by the Philistine leaders. Escorted by young Philistine women with wine cups in their hands Delila enters, and a fascinating ballet, full of rich Oriental color, occupies the stage. Samson is led in and is taunted by the High Priest, who tells him that if Jehovah will restore his sight they will all adore His name. In the finale Samson is ordered to offer oblation to Dagon. A lad leads him to a position between two pillars. With an invocation to the Lord he exerts all his strength and the temple falls amid the shrieks of the Philistines.

It will be observed from this sketch that the opera story differs from the biblical narrative and that it has more of the love motive in it. It thus gives larger opportunity for dramatic music and the opportunities have been enlarged by the use of motives in the Wagner manner. This makes it all the more difficult to select individual numbers for description. The instrumentation is highly colored and very descriptive. Hervey, in his biographical sketch of Saint-Saëns, notes the following composition of the orchestra for this opera: " In addition to the strings and usual woodwinds he employs a third flute, a cor anglais, a bass clarinet, a double bassoon, four horns, two trumpets, two cornets, three trombones, a bass tuba, two ophicleides, two harps, three kettledrums, a grossccaisse, cymbals, a triangle, a glockenspiel, crotales, castagnettes made of wood and iron, a tambour de basque, and a tamtam." With such an orchestral force in the hands of a master, all things are possible.

Henry VIII

"Henry VIII," opera in four acts, text by Détroyat and Silvestre, was first produced in Paris, March 5, 1883, with Lasalle as the King, Dereim as Don Gomez, Mlle. Krauss as Catherine, and Mlle. Richard as Anne. The first act opens in a hall of the palace. The Duke of Norfolk is in conversation with Don Gomez, the Spanish ambassador, who is explaining to the Duke that his presence there is due to Queen Catherine, and his object is to be near to

Anne Boleyn, with whom he is in love. It develops also that Catherine is aware of this attachment and holds a letter from Anne Boleyn to him containing assurances of love. The Duke, however, warns him to be on his guard against the King, who is suspected of desiring Anne Boleyn for himself. At the close of the somewhat long dialogue-duet, which is very skilfully constructed, several persons enter bringing the news that Buckingham has been condemned to death, which leads to an effective quartet and ensemble. As the King enters all withdraw except Surrey, Norfolk, and Don Gomez. The King greets the latter and engages to advance his suit, informing him at the same time that he is about to give Catherine a new maid of honor. The announcement disturbs Don Gomez, as he surmises Anne Boleyn may be the maid. In the next scene the King discusses with Surrey the hostility of the Pope to his divorce from Catherine and sings a most graceful romanza ("Qui donc commande"), in which he boasts his slavery to love. The Queen enters and in a light, simple melody asks the King why she is summoned. He replies that he is about to present her with a new maid of honor. She accepts the gift and then pleads for the life of Buckingham, which the King refuses. A very dramatic duet follows, the Queen charging him with the loss of his love for her, the King replying that their marriage is in violation of the divine law. At the close of the duet they watch the entrance of the courtiers, among them Anne Boleyn, accompanied by graceful procession music. With an expression of surprise that she and Don Gomez are acquainted, the King presents her to the Queen, at the same time creating her Marchioness of Pembroke. The funeral march of Buckingham is heard outside, during which the King presses his suit upon Anne Boleyn and the Queen mourns the tragedy. As the former hears the march she is greatly alarmed, and in the final ensemble

— a seven-part chorus with quintet — the themes of the march are repeated with a gloomy motif, significant of the approaching fate of the new favorite.

The second act opens in Richmond Park, with a graceful chorus of pages disporting themselves. Don Gomez enters and sings a very dramatic aria, ending in a great climax of power. Anne appears with court ladies to the accompaniment of a graceful chorus. A duet between Don Gomez and Anne follows, in which she answers his reproaches with assertions of love. The King enters and Don Gomez retires and another duet follows, at the close of which Anne consents to become his wife upon condition of being made Queen. A joyous duet ensues, but before it closes the sombre motif of her tragic fate is heard again. A dramatic trio follows as the Queen enters and reproaches Anne, who appeals to the King. In the midst of the scene, the papal legate enters with unfavorable news from Rome, but the King will not hear it until the morrow. A fete begins, accompanied by most elaborate and graceful Scotch and English dance music, thus designated: 1. Introduction et Entrée des Clans; 2. Idylle Ecossaise; 3. La Fête des Houblon; 4. Danse de la Gipsy; 5. Pas des Highlander; 6. Scherzetto; 7. Sarabande, Gigue and finale.

The third act opens with the interview between the legate and the King, during which the latter defies the wrath of Rome in a long and passionate scene. Then follows an interview between the King and Anne Boleyn, in which his jealousy is revealed. After another interview with the legate, which closes with the King's announcement that he will appeal from Rome to his people, the scene changes to the Hall of Judgment, the musical setting of which is very stately. The act closes with an imposing ensemble, in which the people support the King, and the King proclaims himself head of the English Church, and Anne Boleyn, Queen.

The fourth act discloses Queen Anne in her apartments watching a charming minuet dance in the gardens. Surrey and Norfolk are conversing aside about the King and his doubts of the Queen. Don Gomez enters upon a special errand from Catherine to the King, and asks to be left alone with the Queen. In the dialogue which follows, he informs her that Catherine still has that compromising letter in her possession. The King enters in a furious mood, dismisses Anne and orders Don Gomez to leave the country. The latter gives the King Catherine's dying words of affection, and they go to the castle where she lies. In a long soliloquy Catherine reveals her longing for Spain, then distributes keepsakes, among them her Book of Hours, in which she places Anne's fatal letter from Don Gomez. At this point Anne enters with the intention of securing the letter. She begs for it, but Catherine refuses. An intensely dramatic scene follows. The King enters and makes every effort to incite Catherine's anger against Anne but fails. With a last supreme effort she throws the letter into the fire and dies, as the measures of the Death March are heard, and among them the decapitation motif, significant of Anne Boleyn's fate.

In "Henry VIII," even more frequently than in "Samson and Delila," Saint-Saëns has used the Wagner device of the leit-motif, and built up his work upon the basis of continuous melody, as best adapted for dramatic effect. This effect is particularly apparent in the many duets as well as in the ensembles of the work. It is intensely dramatic throughout, and is in nearly every respect the composer's operatic masterpiece.

PROSERPINE

"Proserpine," drama lyrique in four acts, text by Louis Gallet, based upon a dramatic poem entitled "Proserpine," by M. Auguste Vacquerie, was first produced at the Opéra Comique, Paris, March 14, 1887. "Proserpine" is not a classical or mythological opera, as its name would seem to indicate, but a lyric drama of a clearly melodramatic type. The scene passes in Italy in the sixteenth century. Proserpine is a courtesan, in love with one Sabatino, but the latter is in love with Angiola, sister of his friend, Renzo, who advises him to pay court to Proserpine, so that having been exposed to temptation he may be faithful to Angiola. When Sabatino discovers that Proserpine really loves him, he treats her in such a manner that she becomes furious with him and her fury increases when she learns that Sabatino loves another. In order to avenge herself she seeks the aid of a ruffian, named Squarocca, who is bound to her by a debt of gratitude, for she has released him when he was caught stealing in her palace. Squarocca contrives to seize Angiola as she is coming from a convent to be married and to arrange so that Proserpine shall meet her. At this interview, the latter tries to persuade her not to marry Sabatino. Angiola resists all persuasion and as Proserpine is about to stab her she is rescued by her brother, Renzo. Proserpine subsequently gains admission to Sabatino's house and declares her passion for him, but he spurns her. She waits for her revenge until Sabatino and Angiola are married, when she turns upon the bride and stabs her. Seizing her dagger, Sabatino thereupon kills Proserpine. In the original poem Angiola dies but in the operatic version she recovers.

The first act is introduced with a few bars of prelude. Proserpine's opening measures ("En verité, messieurs"), taken up by her lovers, in chorus, introduce the *pavane*, heard behind the scenes, just previous to which Sabatino sings a fascinating aria ("Ne crains plus que mon âme change"). The pavane is followed by a pensive soliloquy for Proserpine ("Amour vrai"), and this in turn by long declamatory duets between Proserpine and Sabatino and Proserpine and Squarocca, the act closing with a powerful finale ("Allons, a nous la grande orgie!").

The second act opens in a convent with a simple but beautifully harmonized Ave Maria, followed by a chorus of the nuns and novices ("Un cavalier à la moustache noire") in which they chatter with Angiola about her coming marriage. The next number of importance is Sabatino's impassioned love song to Angiola ("Comment dire bien ce que je veux dire?"), which is followed by a brief unison trio. The finale is extremely effective, being composed of choruses by beggars, nuns, pilgrims, and others, interwoven with trios, and dominated by the strong, high soprano phrases by Angiola.

The second act is the most beautiful and effective of the work. The third and fourth are melodramatic and the music loses something of its grace and delicate finish. The principal numbers of the third act are Proserpine's invocation ("Ah! je n'avais que de l'amour"); Squarocca's characteristic drinking-song ("Vin qui rougis ma trogne"), and the melodramatic finale; and of the fourth act, the tenor solo for Sabatino ("Puis-je croire que c'est bien vrai"), and the long duet between Sabatino and Proserpine, leading up to the tragic denouement. There are delightful passages all through the work, but much of the musical effect of the last two acts is sacrificed to the demands of the absurd and sensational melodrama.

STRAUSS (JOHANN)

JOHANN STRAUSS, familiarly known as "The Waltz King," was a member of a waltz family. His father, Johann, was known all over Europe as "The Father of the Waltz," and his brothers, Joseph and Edouard, were also waltz writers. Johann, junior, was born at Vienna, October 25, 1825, and died in that city, June 3, 1899. He made his debut in public life as a conductor in 1844, and in 1849, after his father's death, united his orchestra with the latter's and made many tours on the Continent, meeting with enthusiastic success everywhere. In 1855 he was engaged for a season of ten years to conduct summer concerts in St. Petersburg. From 1863 to 1870 he was court ball conductor,—a position which he resigned in favor of his brother Edouard, in order that he might have more time for composition. His list of waltzes includes over four hundred, all of which have become favorites the world over—among them such well known ones as the "Wine, Woman, and Song," "Geschichten aus dem Wiener Wald," "Blue Danube," "Thousand and One Nights," "Künstler Leben," and "Vienna Temper." In 1870 he gave up dance music, in which he was without a rival, for operettas. The most famous of these are "Indigo" (1871); "Die Fledermaus" (1874); "Prinz Methusalem" (1877); "Das Spitzentuch der Königin" (1880); "Der Lustige Krieg" (1881); "Eine Nacht in Venedig" (1883); "Der Zigeunerbaron" (1885); "Simplicius" (1887); "Furstin Ninetta" (1893); "Jabuka" (1894); "Waldmeister" (1895); and "Die Göttin der Vernunft" (1896).

THE MERRY WAR

"The Merry War," opera comique, in three acts, text by Zell and Genée, was first produced in Vienna, November 25, 1881. The scene is laid in Genoa in the eighteenth century. In analyzing this, as well as the other Strauss operettas contained in this volume, it is hardly needful to go into very close detail. They may be termed merry stories set to merry and fascinating dance rhythms. "The Merry War" is not a very serious one, as may be inferred from its title. It is a quarrel between two petty states, Genoa and Massa Carrara, growing out of the fact that a popular dancer has made simultaneous engagements at the theatres of each. Both claim her, and the question at issue is at which theatre the dancer shall appear. One harmless hand grenade is thrown from either side with monotonous regularity each day, and the "Merry War" is without interesting incident until the pretty Countess Violetta appears in one of the camps. She is seeking to make her way in disguise into the city of the other camp, to take command of the citadel. Umberto, the colonel commanding, is deceived by her, and allows her to pass through the lines. When informed of the deception he determines to take his revenge by marrying her. Understanding that she is to marry the Duke de Limburg by proxy, he impersonates the Duke and is married to Violetta without arousing her suspicions. He is assisted in his scheme by Balthasar Groats, a Dutch speculator in tulip bulbs, whom the soldiers have arrested, thinking him a spy, and who is naturally willing to do anything for the Colonel to get him out of his predicament. Complications arise, however, when Groats's wife appears and becomes jealous, also because of Violetta's antipathy towards her supposed husband and her affection for Umberto. All these matters are arranged satisfactorily, however, when there is an opportunity for explanation, and a treaty of peace is signed between the two states, when it is found that the cause of the "Merry War" will not keep her engagement with either theatre.

The music of "The Merry War" is light and gay throughout. Like all the rest of the Strauss operas, it might be said that it is a collection of marches and waltzes, and a repetition of dance music which has done good service in ballrooms, strung upon the slight thread of a story. Its most taking numbers are Umberto's couplets ("Till now no Drop of Blood"); Balthasar's comical song ("General, ho!") and his tulip song ("From Holland to Florence in Peace we were going"); Violetta's arietta ("In vain, I cannot fly"); the dainty duet for Violetta and Umberto ("Please do"); Else's romantic song ("I wandered on"); the ensemble and Dutch song by Artemisia ("The much admired One"); Umberto's love song ("The Night begins to Creep"); Violetta's song ("I am yet Commander for To-day"), leading to a terzetto and spirited final chorus ("Of their warlike Renown").

The Bat (Die Fledermaus)

"The Bat," opera comique in three acts, text by Haffner and Genée, was first produced in Vienna in July, 1874. It is founded upon Meilhac and Halévy's "Le Revillon." The scene opens with Adele, maid of the Baroness Rosalind, seeking permission to visit her sister Ida, a ballet-dancer, who is to be at a masked ball given by Prince Orlofsky, a Russian millionaire. She receives permission, and after she is gone, Dr. Falke, a notary, who has arranged the ball, calls at the house of the Baron Eisenstein, and induces him to go to it before going to jail, to which he has been sentenced for contempt of court. The purpose of the doctor is to seek revenge for his shabby treatment by the Baron sometime before at a masquerade which they had attended, — Eisenstein dressed as a butterfly, and Falke as a bat. The doctor then notifies the Baroness that her

Sembrich as *Rosalind*

Copyright, Aimé Dupont

STRAUSS (JOHANN)

husband will be at the ball. She thereupon decides that she will also be present. An amusing scene occurs when the Baron seeks to pass himself off as a French marquis, and pays his devotions to the ladies, but is quite astonished to find his wife there, flirting with an old lover. There are further complications caused by Falke, who manages to have Alfred, the singing-master, in the Baroness' apartments when the sheriff comes to arrest the Baron, and arrests Alfred, supposing him to be Eisenstein. In the last act, however, all the complications are disentangled, and everything ends happily.

It would be impossible to name the conspicuous numbers in this animated and sprightly work without making a catalogue of them all. The opera is a grand potpourri of waltz and polka motifs and fresh, bright melodies. The composer does not linger long with the dialogue, but goes from one waltz melody to another in a most bewildering manner, interspersing them with romanzas, drinking-songs, czardas, an almost endless variety of dance rhythms and choruses of a brilliant sort. It is a charming mixture of Viennese gayety and French drollery, and, like all his operettas, is the very essence of the dance.

The Queen's Lace Handkerchief

"The Queen's Lace Handkerchief," opera comique, in three acts, text by Genée and Bohrmann-Riegen, was first produced in Vienna, October 2, 1880. The romance of its story has helped to make this opera one of the most popular of Strauss's works. The action begins at a time when Portugal is ruled by a ministry whose premier is in league with Philip II of Spain, and who, to keep possession of power, has fomented trouble between the young Queen and King, and encouraged the latter in all kinds of dissipations. At this time Cervantes, the poet, who has been banished from Spain, is a captain in the Royal Guards, and in love with

Irene, a lady-in-waiting. These two are good friends of both the King and Queen, and are eager to depose the ministry. Cervantes is reader to the Queen, and the latter, having a sentimental attachment for him, writes upon her handkerchief, "A queen doth love thee, yet art thou no king," and placing it in a volume of "Don Quixote," hands it to him. The book is seized, and as "Don Quixote" is Minister of War and "Sancho Panza" Minister of Instruction, Cervantes is arrested for libel and treason. Irene and the King, however, save him by proving him insane, and the King and Queen ascend the throne. In desperation the Premier hands the King the handkerchief with the inscription on it, which leads to the rearrest of Cervantes and the banishment of the Queen to a convent. Cervantes escapes, however, and joins some brigands. They capture the Queen on her way to the convent, and in the disguise of the host and waiting-maid of an inn, they serve the King, who happens there on a hunting trip. Everything is satisfactorily accounted for, and the inscription on the handkerchief is explained as a message which the Queen sent to the King by Cervantes.

The music is light and brilliant. Much of it is in the waltz tempo, and the choral work is a strong feature. Its best numbers are the Queen's humorous romanza ("It was a wondrous fair and starry Night"); another humorous number, the King's truffle song ("Such Dish by Man not oft is seen"); the epicurean duet for the King and Premier, ("These Oysters"); Cervantes's recitative ("Once sat a Youth"), in the finale of the first act; a dainty little romanza for Cervantes ("Where the wild Rose sweetly doth blow"); the trio and chorus ("Great Professors, learned Doctors"); the fine duet for the King and Cervantes ("Brighter Glance on him shall repose"); Sancho's vivacious couplet ("In the Night his Zither holding"); the Queen's showy song ("Seventeen Years had just passed o'er me "); and the two closing choruses (" Now the King all hail ") in march time, and the bull-fight, which is full of dash and spirit.

The Gypsy Baron

"The Gypsy Baron," opera comique in three acts, text by Schnitzer, and based upon a romance of the same name by M. Jokai, was first produced October 24, 1885, in Vienna. The story is a simple one. The so-called " Gypsy Baron," Sandov Barinkay, who left his home when a lad, returns to find it desolate and in possession of gypsies. His nearest neighbor is Zsupan, with whose daughter Arsena he falls in love. She orders him never to call upon her again as a suitor until he can come as a baron. Barinkay goes off in a rage to the gypsies, who adopt him and make him their Waywolde, or gypsy baron. Forgetful or unmindful of Arsena, he falls in love with Saffi, a gypsy girl, and marries her. In the second act he finds a hidden treasure, but is arrested for keeping it a secret. He manages to escape by turning over his treasure to the government and joining the Austrian army with his whole band. In the last act he returns with the victorious troops to Vienna, is made a real baron for his bravery, and Saffi turns out to be the daughter of a real pasha.

The opera abounds in brilliant melodies, dance rhythms, and gypsy music. The most conspicuous numbers in the first act are the entrance couplets ("Als flotter Geist"), closing in waltz time, the melodrama and ensemble ("So tauschte mich die Ahnung nicht "), the ensemble (" Dem Freier naht die Braut "), and Saffi's delightful gypsy song (" So elend und so treu ") ; in the second act, the terzetto for Saffi, Czipsa, and Barinkay (" Mein Aug bewacht ") and (" Ein Greis ist mir in Traum erschienen "), the duet for Saffi and Barinkay (" Wer uns getraut "), the Werberlied with chorus (" Her die Hand "), and the finale

("Nach Wien"); and in the third act, the chorus ("Freut euch"), the couplets for Arsena, Mirabella, and Carnero ("Hat es gar nicht gut"), the march couplet and chorus ("Von der Tajos Strand"), the brilliant military march ("Huora der Schlacht gemacht"), and the finale ("Heirathen Vivat"). "The Gypsy Baron" is one of the few light operas in which the interest steadily progresses and reaches its brilliant climax in the last act.

STRAUSS (RICHARD)

RICHARD STRAUSS was born at Munich, June 11, 1864. He began the study of music at a very early age, and even before his school studies commenced he had produced compositions of a promising character. In 1875 he began a five years' course in theory and composition and even at that time had mastered the technics of the violin and piano. His first important composition performed in public was a string quartet, his first symphony in D minor was next given a hearing, and in 1883 his overture in C minor appeared. Van Bülow shortly afterward placed his serenade for wind instruments in the repertory of the Meiningen orchestra. Several songs, concertos, and sonatas, as well as a second symphony, were soon produced and added to his reputation. He held several important positions during the next few years, among them that of music director at Meiningen in 1885, director of the Munich court theatre in 1886, music director at Weimar in 1890, and court Capellmeister at the Berlin Opera in 1900. He also has conducted at all the great European festivals and made trips to Italy, England, and the United States. His opera " Guntram " was produced in 1894; " Feuersnot " in 1902; and " Salome " in 1906. Of these three, " Feuersnot " has been the most popular. This composer, who seems to have taken Wagner's place as the representative of " music of the future," is best known in this country by his tone-poems, " Macbeth," " Tod und Verklärung," " Till Eulenspiegel," " Also sprach Zarathustra," " Ein Heldenleben," " Don Quixote," and " Symphonia Domestica."

Feuersnot

"Feuersnot," song-poem in one act, text by Ernest von Wolzogen, and dramatized from an episode in an old Dutch saga, was first produced at Weimar, October 28, 1902. Both story and music are illustrative of German burgher life in mediæval times. The plot is connected with the celebration of the "Sonnenwende" (the turning of the sun) on the longest night of the year and the lighting of the Johannis fire, emblematical of the glorification of the senses. The scene is laid in Munich in the fabled "Notime" or "Bad Time." As the curtain rises Kunrad der Ebner is roused from his meditations by the children of the city who are marching through the streets gathering sticks for their fires from the people. Kunrad is occupying a dismal house whose former occupant was driven away for alleged witchcraft. He realizes how foolish he has been to devote himself to books and to neglect the practical things of life, and bids the children take his books and put them in their fire. Meanwhile, the burgomaster's daughter Diemut, as well as others, manifest more than ordinary interest, which so emboldens him that he kisses her. In revenge she pretends to be in love with him, and plans a meeting at midnight if he will ascend to her in a basket which she will hang out and draw up to her room. Kunrad consents, and comes at night and gets into the basket. Diemut, however, only draws him part way up and leaves him hanging there, whereupon she summons the neighbors to jeer at him. Kunrad now revenges himself in turn by magically extinguishing all the fires in town and announcing that they cannot be lit again until Diemut has consented to be his. He then manages to climb to the balcony above him and there awaits events. Diemut appears at her window, and, moved by the piteous appeals of the burghers, relents and admits him to her chamber. As she at last consents to be his, light gradually appears in her room and suddenly they break out all over the city and the "song poem" closes with a grand pæan of love.

The opening number is a children's chorus ("Gebts uns a Holz zum Subendfeuer"), which is charmingly bright, graceful, and even catchy, especially in the theme of the accompaniment which follows the children whenever they appear. It is the lightest theme in the score, and the prattle of the youngsters ("Memma's verbrenna hamma nix Majà, Majà, unà mö, lober, lober lujà") is charmingly illustrated. Diemut's opening song, as she appears among the children ("Süsse Amarellen"), is very melodious, and is followed by another of their choruses ("Zu Minka, steht a neu' baut's Haus"). After the choruses follow characteristic bits for Iörg Pöschel, Kunz Gilgenstock, and Hamerlein full of humor and spirit, and these minor characters are admirably pictured in the instrumentation. Tulbeck's legend of Duke Heinrich and the Lion ("Als Herzog Heinrich mit dem Löwen kam") is sufficiently described by its designation in the score, "to be delivered with disagreeable and excessive monotony." The next conspicuous number is Kunrad's declamation ("Sonnenwend! Sonnenwend! Klingst mir in Ohr") which is rather declamation, as already designated, than melody, and set to a very complicated and descriptive accompaniment. The boys' and girls' choruses, "Heissa! hellerlichten," and "Majà, majà, mia, mö," which follow it, are enormously difficult, especially as they are sung against dramatic and descriptive accompaniments, and the harmonies and intervals are unusual. The next long scene for Kunrad ("Dass ich den Zauber lerne"), is a relief by reason of its melodious and romantic character. A little later on there is further relief as the choruses are graceful and set to lively waltz tempo, though they are too complicated and difficult to be easily caught. The burgomaster's solo which follows ("Miau, miau! Oh jèh! — Was formmts?") is also full of humor and spirit, and would be quite comprehensible even without words. Kunrad's next aria ("Feuersnot! Minnegebot") is impressive and beautiful, and is set to a very dramatic and involved accompaniment. The aria is Wagnerian in style throughout. It is immediately followed by Diemut's great song, "Mitsommernacht-wehvolle Wacht," which is not only romantic and delightfully melodious but beautiful in harmonic effect. The duet for Diemut and Kunrad which follows ("Mitsommernacht! Wonnige Wacht") is up to the same standard, and though full of complications and difficulties, chromatics, accidentals, and unusual intervals, is tender, melodious, and spirited by turns and fairly dazzling in its effect. Kunrad's magical appeal ("Hilf mir, Meister!") is strong and distinctly ghostly in effect. His next number ("Im Hause, das ich heut zerbann"), mostly in waltz tempo, is not only remarkable as a spirited and attractive declamation with an accompaniment full of color, but it has an added interest as a bit of satire upon the people of Munich. It is Kunrad's address from the balcony to the crowd. Kunrad, who is typical of the new spirit, says that the house in which he lives was once that of Master Reichardt, the ruler of spirits (Wagner), and that although he did much for them they cast out "the bold man" (der Wagner). But, he adds, they could not drive out the new spirit (Strauss). As he designates Wagner "the ruler of spirits," the Walhalla motif is heard and the words describing his banishment are sung by Kunrad to "The Flying Dutchman's" motif, while the allusion to "the new spirit" is accompanied by a motif from Strauss's own opera, "Guntram." From this point to the close of the opera the music is marked by a great dignity and impressiveness of declamation, and closes with a symphonic movement of remarkable beauty and power, which has already found its way to the concert stage, and became a favorite.

"Guntram," the first of Strauss's operas, is so difficult that its performance is practically impossible so far as effect is concerned. "Salome," his last opera, is even more difficult, and requires such a colossal orchestra that it probably will not be given many times, but there is no reason why "Feuersnot," after a few hearings, should not make a favorable impression. Its subject is partly humorous. The treatment is masterful and dignified, and feeling is also developed. The accompaniments are complicated, but very dramatic and descriptive, and the songs take their own way without any apparent relation to the accompaniment. But the combination of humor, sentiment, and feeling in the work is remarkable. The accompaniment is Strauss's masterwork. It is so complete that the work might be given with spoken dialogue and text throughout and lose but little in effect, as the song parts with but few exceptions are but declamations, the dramatic expression being in the orchestra.

SULLIVAN

ARTHUR SEYMOUR SULLIVAN, whose operettas, written in collaboration with W. S. Gilbert, have made him world-famous, was born in London, May 14, 1842, and died in that city in 1900. He began his musical career as a choir boy in the Chapel Royal, and published his first song in 1855. He entered the Royal Musical Academy in 1857, and from 1858 to 1861 studied at Leipzig. He conducted numerous concerts and festivals in England, and from 1876 to 1881 was at the head of the National Training School for Music. He received many honors at home and abroad during his career, and was knighted in 1883. He wrote, among other works, incidental music to many of Shakespeare's plays, the well-known oratorios, "Prodigal Son" (1869), "The Light of the World" (1873), "The Martyr of Antioch" (1880), a festival Te Deum (1872), a symphony in E (1866), and the beautiful overtures, "In Memoriam," "Marmion," "De Ballo," and "Sapphire Necklace." Had he continued composing the higher music, undoubtedly he would have achieved still greater works, but the temptations of the immense popularity which attended the performances of his operettas evidently were too much for him. As works of their class, however, they have never been excelled for melodiousness, humor, and delicacy. The list of these is as follows: "Cox and Box" (1867); "The Contrabandista" (1867); "Thespis" (1871); "Trial by Jury" (1875); "The Zoo" (1875); "The Sorcerer" (1877); "H. M. S. Pinafore" (1878); "The Pirates of Penzance" (1880); "Patience" (1881); "Iolanthe" (1882); "Princess

Ida" (1884); "The Mikado" (1885); "Ruddygore" (1877); "The Yeomen of the Guard" (1888); and "The Gondoliers" (1889). Besides these, he wrote the grand opera "Ivanhoe" (1891), and "Haddan Hall" (1892), but the fame of the operettas overshadowed his last works and they were neglected.

THE SORCERER

"The Sorcerer," comic opera in two acts, text by Gilbert, was first produced at the Opéra Comique, London, November 18, 1877, and in New York, February 21, 1879. The success of the two earlier operettas, "Cox and Box" and "Trial by Jury," led to the organization of a company under the management of Mr. D Oyly Carte for the production of the Sullivan-Gilbert collaborations, and the first of its performances was "The Sorcerer." Incidentally it may be stated that this opera introduced Mr. George Grossmith to the stage, and its success led to a proposition from "Lewis Carroll" to Sullivan to set his "Alice in Wonderland" as an opera, though the scheme was never realized. The libretto of "The Sorcerer" is replete with humor, the music is original and characteristic, and particularly noticeable for its admirable parodies of the Italian operas, and yet it is always scholarly. The original cast was as follows:

Sorcerer	GEORGE GROSSMITH.
Lady Sangazure	Mrs. HOWARD PAUL.
Aline	Miss ALICE MAY.
Alexis	Mr. BENTHAM.
Baronet	Mr. TEMPLE.
Constance	Mrs. G. WARWICK.

The first act opens upon the grounds of Sir Marmaduke Pointdextre's estate, where the villagers are gathered to celebrate the betrothal of his son Alexis, and Aline, daughter of Lady Sangazure, with whom, fifty years before,

Sir Marmaduke had been in love. Mrs. Partlet, the pew-opener, enters with her daughter Constance, who is hopelessly in love with Dr. Daly, the vicar, — for he cannot be made to understand, either by her demonstrations or by the mother's hints, that he is the object of her devotion. Alexis and Aline are congratulated by all and sign the marriage contract. When alone together Alexis discourses upon his favorite theory that all artificial barriers should be broken down and that marriage should be contracted without regard to rank. To put this theory into practice he procures from the firm of J. W. Wells & Co., the old established family sorcerers of the place, a large quantity of their love potion, which has no effect upon married persons but will cause unmarried ones to couple without regard to rank or condition, mixes it with the tea and serves it to all who are in attendance at the betrothal banquet. Gradually all fall insensible, and the act closes.

The second act opens upon Sir Marmaduke's grounds at midnight. The guests, one after the other, are waking. Alexis tells Aline she must take some of the potion so that he may be sure of her love, which she does after much protesting. As they regain their senses, each guest makes offer of marriage to the first one seen. Constance declares her love for the old notary. Sir Marmaduke enters with Mrs. Partlet, the venerable pew-opener, on his arm and announces his intention of marrying her. Wells appears on the grounds in a remorseful condition as he beholds the mischief he has caused, and Lady Sangazure proposes to him, and leaves in great anguish when he declares he is already engaged to "a maiden fair on a South Pacific Isle." Aline beholds Dr. Daly and begins to fall violently in love with him and he with her. Alexis, in alarm at the trouble he is making, seeks out Wells and demands that he shall remove the spell. Wells explains that in order to do this, one or the other of them must offer his life to Ahrimanes. Alexis is not willing to give up Aline, and Wells is averse to losing his profitable business. They agree to leave the decision to the guests, and the latter agree that Wells shall make the sacrifice. He consents, and all go back to their old lovers as he sinks through a trap amid red fire.

The most conspicuous numbers in the first act are Dr. Daly's ballad ("Time was when Love and I were well acquainted"); the duet between Sir Marmaduke and Lady Sangazure ("Welcome Joy, adieu to Sadness"); Alexis's ballad ("Love feeds on many Kinds of Food I know"); Wells's long and rollicking song ("Oh! my Name is John Wellington Wells"); and the incantation music ("Sprites of Earth and Air"). The second act opens with a charming little country dance. The principal numbers which follow it are Constance's aria ("Dear Friends, take Pity on my Lot"); the ensemble for Aline, Alexis, Constance, and the Notary ("O, Joy! O, Joy!"); Alexis's ballad ("Thou hast the Power thy vaunted Love"); the quintet ("I rejoice that it's decided"); Dr. Daly's humorous song ("Oh! my Voice is sad and low"); and the finale ensemble ("Now to the Banquet we press").

H. M. S. PINAFORE

"H. M. S. Pinafore; or, The Lass that Loved a Sailor," comic opera in two acts, text by Gilbert, was first produced at the Opéra Comique, London, May 28, 1878, and in New York, January 15, 1879, with the following cast:

Captain Corcoran	RUTLAND BARRINGTON
Josephine	Miss E. HOWSON.
Ralph Rackstraw	Mr. POWER.
Rt. Hon. Sir Joseph Porter	GEO. GROSSMITH, Jr.
Little Buttercup	Miss EVERARD.
Dick Deadeye	Mr. R. TEMPLE.
Hebe	Miss J. BOND.
Bill Bobstay	Mr. CLIFFORD.

Although "Pinafore," when it was first produced in London, was received so coolly that it was decided to take it off the boards, yet eventually, with the exception of "The Beggar's Opera," it proved to be the most popular opera ever produced in England; while in the United States it was for years the rage, and is still a great favorite. The first scene introduces the leading characters on the deck of "H. M. S. Pinafore" in the harbor of Portsmouth. Little Buttercup, a bumboat woman, "the rosiest, the roundest, and the reddest beauty in all Spithead," comes on board and has an interview with Dick Deadeye, the villain of the story, and Ralph Rackstraw, "the smartest lad in all the fleet," who is in love with Josephine, Captain Corcoran's daughter. The Captain appears on deck in a melancholy mood because Josephine has shown herself indifferent to Sir Joseph Porter, K.C.B., who is to ask for her hand that afternoon. She confesses to her father that she loves a common sailor, but will carry her love to the grave without letting him know of it. Sir Joseph comes on board with a long retinue of sisters, cousins, and aunts, who chant his praises. After attending to some minor details, he has a fruitless interview with the Captain and Josephine. She protests she cannot love him. Shortly afterwards she meets Ralph, who declares his love for her, but she haughtily rejects him. When he draws his pistol and declares he will shoot himself, she acknowledges her love, and they plan to steal ashore at night and be married. Dick Deadeye overhears the plot and threatens to thwart it.

The second act opens at night. Captain Corcoran is discovered sadly complaining to the moon, and wondering why everything is at "sixes and sevens." Little Buttercup sympathizes with him, and is about to become affectionate, when he informs her he can only be her friend. She grows enraged, and warns him there is a change in store for him. Sir Joseph enters, and informs the Captain he is much disappointed at the way Josephine has acted. The Captain replies that she is probably dazzled by his rank, and that if he will reason with her and convince her that "love levels all ranks," everything will be right. Sir Joseph does so, but only pleads his rival's cause. She tells him she has hesitated, but now she hesitates no longer. Sir Joseph and the Captain are rejoicing over her apparent change of heart, when Dick Deadeye reveals the plot to elope that night. The Captain confronts them as they are stealthily leaving the vessel, and insists upon knowing what Josephine is about to do. Ralph steps forward and declares his love, whereupon the Captain grows furious and lets slip an oath. He is overheard by Sir Joseph, who orders him to his cabin "with celerity." He then inquires of Ralph what he has done to make the Captain profane. He replies it was his acknowledgment of love for Josephine, whereupon, in a towering rage, Sir Joseph orders his imprisonment in the ship's dungeon. He then remonstrates with Josephine, whereupon Little Buttercup reveals her secret. Years before, when she was practising baby-farming, she nursed two babies, one of "low condition," the other "a regular patrician," and she "mixed those children up and not a creature knew it." "The well-born babe was Ralph, your Captain was the other." Sir Joseph orders the two before him, gives Ralph the command of " H. M. S. Pinafore," and Corcoran Ralph's place. As his marriage with Josephine is now impossible, he gives her to Ralph, and Captain Corcoran, now a common seaman, unites his fortunes with those of Little Buttercup.

It is one of the principal charms of this delightful work that it is entirely free from coarseness and vulgarity. The wit is always delicate, though the satire is keen. Words and music rarely go so well together as in this opera. As a prominent English critic said of "Trial by Jury," "it seems, as in the great Wagnerian operas, as though poem and music had proceeded simultaneously from one and the same brain." The chorus plays a very important part in it, and in the most solemnly ludicrous manner repeats the assertions of the principals in the third person. All its numbers might be styled the leading ones, but those which have become most popular are the song "I'm called Little Buttercup"; Josephine's sentimental song ("Sorry her Lot who loves too well"), one of the few serious numbers in the opera; Sir Joseph Porter's song ("I am the Monarch of the Sea"), with its irresistible choral refrain ("And so are his Sisters and his Cousins and his Aunts, his Sisters and his Cousins, whom he reckons by the Dozens"), leading up to the satirical song "When I was a Lad, I served a Term"; the stirring trio ("A British Tar is a soaring Soul"); Captain Corcoran's sentimental ditty ("Fair Moon, to thee I sing"); Josephine's scena ("The Hours creep on apace"), with its mock heroic recitative; Dick Deadeye's delightful song ("The merry Maiden and the Tar"); the pretty octet and chorus ("Farewell, my own"); Little Buttercup's legend ("A many Years ago, when I was young and charming"); and the choral finale ("Then give three Cheers and one Cheer more").

The Pirates of Penzance

"The Pirates of Penzance; or, the Slave of Duty," comic opera, text by Gilbert, was first produced in New York, December 31, 1879, and in England at the Opéra Comique, London, April 3, 1880. "The Pirates of Penzance" has a local interest from the fact that it was first produced under the immediate supervision of both Mr. Sullivan and Mr. Gilbert. When the composer left England he had only finished the second act, and that was without orchestration.

After his arrival here he wrote the first act and scored the entire opera. By this performance the profits of the representations in this country were secured. The work was not published until after their return to England.

At the opening of the opera it is disclosed that Frederic, when a boy, in pursuance of his father's orders, was to have been apprenticed to a pilot until his twenty-first year, but by the mistake of his nurse-maid, Ruth, he was bound out to one of the pirates of Penzance, who were celebrated for their gentleness and never molested orphans because they were orphans themselves. In the first scene the pirates are making merry, as Frederic has reached his majority and is about to leave them and seek some other occupation. Upon the eve of departure Ruth requests him to marry her, and he consents, as he has never seen any other woman, but shortly afterwards he encounters the daughters of General Stanley, falls in love with Mabel, the youngest, and denounces Ruth as a deceiver. The pirates encounter the girls about the same time, and propose to marry them, but when the General arrives and announces that he also is an orphan, they relent and allow the girls to go.

The second act opens in the General's ancient baronial hall, and reveals him surrounded by his daughters, lamenting that he has deceived the pirates by calling himself an orphan. Frederic appears, and bids Mabel farewell, as he is about to lead an expedition for the extermination of the pirates. While he is alone, the Pirate King and Ruth visit him and show him the papers which bound him to them. It is stated in them that he is bound " until his twenty-first birthday," but as his birthday is the 29th of February, he has had but five. Led by his strong sense of duty, he decides that he will go back to his old associates. Then he tells them of the General's orphan story, which so enrages them that they swear vengeance. They come by night to carry off the General, but are overpowered by the police and sent to prison, where they confess they are English noblemen. Upon promising to give up their piratical career, they are pardoned, and this releases Frederic.

The principal numbers in the first act are Ruth's song ("When Frederic was a little Lad"); the Pirate King's song ("Oh! better far to live and die"); Frederic's sentimental song ("Oh! is there not one Maiden Breast"); Mabel's reply ("Poor wandering One"); and the descriptive song of the General ("I am the very Pattern of a modern Major-General"), which reminds one of Sir Joseph's song "When I was a Lad, I served a Term," in "Pinafore," and Wells's song, "Oh! my Name is John Wellington Wells," in "The Sorcerer." The second act opens with a chorus of the daughters and solo by Mabel ("Dear Father, why leave your Bed?"). The remaining most popular numbers are the "Tarantara" of the Sergeant; the Pirate King's humorous chant ("For some ridiculous Reason"); Mabel's ballad ("Oh, leave me not to pine"), and the Sergeant's irresistible song ("When a Fellow's not engaged in his Employment"), which has become familiar as a household word by frequent quotation.

PATIENCE

"Patience; or, Bunthorne's Bride." comic opera in two acts, text by Gilbert, was first produced at the Opéra Comique, London, April 23, 1881, with the following cast:

Patience	LEONORA BRAHAM.
Bunthorne	Mr. GROSSMITH.
Jane	ALICE BARNETT.
Archibald	R. BARRINGTON.

The opera of "Patience" is a pungent satire upon the fleshly school of poetry as represented by Oscar Wilde and his imitators, as well as upon the fad for æsthetic culture which raged so violently a quarter of a century ago.

SULLIVAN

Bunthorne, in one of his soliloquies, aptly expresses the hollowness of the sham, —

> "I am *not* fond of uttering platitudes
> In stained-glass attitudes;
> In short, my mediævalism 's affectation
> Born of a morbid love of admiration."

In these four lines Gilbert pricked the æsthetic bubble, and nothing did so much to end the fad of lank, languorous maidens, and long-haired, sunflowered male æsthetes, as his well-directed shafts of ridicule in this opera.

The story of the opera tells of the struggle for supremacy over female hearts between an æsthetic (Bunthorne) and an idyllic poet (Grosvenor). In the opening scene lovesick maidens in clinging gowns, playing mandolins, sing plaintively of their love for Bunthorne. Patience, a healthy milkmaid, comes upon the scene, and makes fun of them, and asks them why they sit and sob and sigh. She announces to them that the Dragoon Guards will soon arrive, but although they doted upon Dragoons the year before they spurn them now and go to Bunthorne's door to carol to him. The Guards duly arrive, and are hardly settled down when Bunthorne passes by in the act of composing a poem, followed by the twenty lovesick maidens. After finishing his poem he reads it to them, and they go off together, without paying any attention to the Dragoons, who declare they have been insulted and leave in a rage. Bunthorne, when alone, confesses to himself he is a sham, and at the close of his confession Patience comes in. He at once makes love to her, but only frightens her. She then confers with Lady Angela, who explains love to her, and tells her it is her duty to love some one. Patience declares she will not go to bed until she has fallen in love with some one, when Grosvenor, the idyllic poet and "apostle of simplicity," enters. He and Patience had been playmates in early childhood, and she promptly falls in love with him, though he is indifferent. In the closing scene Bunthorne, twined with garlands, is led in by the maidens, and puts himself up as a prize in a lottery; but the drawing is interrupted by Patience, who snatches away the papers and offers herself as a bride to Bunthorne, who promptly accepts her. The maidens then make advances to the Dragoons, but when Grosvenor appears they all declare their love for him. Bunthorne recognizes him as a dangerous rival, and threatens " he shall meet a hideous doom."

The opening of the second act reveals Jane, an antique charmer, sitting by a sheet of water mourning because the fickle maidens have deserted Bunthorne, and because he has taken up with " a puling milkmaid," while she alone is faithful to him. In the next scene Grosvenor enters with the maidens, of whom he is tired. They soon leave him in low spirits, when Patience appears and tells him she loves him, but can never be his, for it is her duty to love Bunthorne. The latter next appears, followed by the antique Jane, who clings to him in spite of his efforts to get rid of her. He accuses Patience of loving Grosvenor, and goes off with Jane in a wildly jealous mood. In the next scene the Dragoons, to win favor with the maidens, transform themselves into a group of æsthetes. Bunthorne and Grosvenor finally meet, and Bunthorne taxes his rival with monopolizing the attentions of the young ladies. Grosvenor replies that he cannot help it, and would be glad of any suggestion that would lead to his being less attractive. Bunthorne tells him he must change his conversation, cut his hair, have a back parting, and wear a commonplace costume. Grosvenor at first protests, but yields when threatened with Bunthorne's curse. In the finale, when it is discovered that Grosvenor has become a commonplace young man, the maidens decide that if " Archibald the All-Right " has discarded æstheticism, it is right for them to do so. Patience takes the same view of the case, and leaves Bunthorne for Grosvenor. The maidens find suitors among the Dragoons, and even the antique Jane takes up with the Duke, and Bunthorne is left alone with his lily, nobody's bride.

The most popular musical numbers in the opera are the Colonel's song ("If you want a Recipe for that popular Mystery"); Bunthorne's ", wild, weird, fleshly" song, ("What Time the Poet hath hymned"), also his song ("If you're anxious for to shine"); the romantic duet of Patience and Grosvenor ("Prithee, pretty Maiden"); the sextet ("I hear the soft Note of the echoing Voice"); Jane's song ("Silvered is the raven Hair"); Patience's ballad ("Love is a plaintive Song"); Grosvenor's fable of the magnet and the churn; the rollicking duet of Bunthorne and Grosvenor ("When I go out of Door"), and the "prettily pattering, cheerily chattering" chorus in the finale of the last act.

IOLANTHE

"Iolanthe; or, the Peer and the Peri," comic opera in two acts, text by Gilbert, was first produced at the Savoy Theatre, London, November 25, 1882, with the following cast:

Iolanthe	JESSIE BOND.
Queen of Fairies	ALICE BARNETT.
Phyllis	LEONORE BRAHAM.
Lord Chancellor	GEORGE GROSSMITH.
Strephon	RICHARD TEMPLE.
Earl of Montararat	RUTLAND BARRINGTON.
Earl of Tololler	DURWAR LELY.
Private Willis	CHARLES MANNERS.

The first act of "Iolanthe" opens in Arcady. Iolanthe, a fairy, having offended her Queen by marrying a mortal, has been banished for life; but in the opening scene, after twenty years of exile, she is pardoned. She tells the

Queen of her marriage, and her son Strephon, half a fairy and half a shepherd, who is engaged to Phyllis, a shepherdess, and ward in chancery. At this point Strephon enters and informs his mother that the Lord Chancellor will not permit him to marry Phyllis, but that he will do so in spite of him. He curses his fairyhood, but the Queen says she has a borough at her disposal, and will return him to Parliament as a Liberal-Conservative. In the next scene Strephon meets Phyllis and pleads against delay in marriage, since the Lord Chancellor himself may marry her, and many of the lords are attentive to her. Meanwhile the lords meet to decide which one of them shall have Phyllis, the Lord Chancellor waiving his claim, as it might lay his decision open to misconstruction. Phyllis is summoned before them, but is deaf to all entreaties, and declares she is in love with Strephon, who has just entered. The peers march out in a dignified manner, while the Lord Chancellor separates Phyllis and Strephon and orders her away. He then refuses Strephon his suit, whereupon the latter invokes the aid of his fairy mother, who promises to lay the case before her Queen. In the finale the peers are seen leading Phyllis. She overhears something said by Strephon and Iolanthe which induces her to believe he is faithless, and she denounces him. He replies that Iolanthe is his mother, but cannot convince her. She charges him with deceit, and offers her hand to any one of the peers. He then appeals to the Queen, who threatens vengeance upon the peers and declares that Strephon shall go into Parliament. The peers beg her for mercy, and Phyllis implores Strephon to relent, but he casts her from him.

The second act opens at Westminster. Strephon is in Parliament and carrying things with a high hand. Phyllis is engaged to two of the lords and cannot decide between them, nor can they settle the matter satisfactorily, whereupon the Lord Chancellor decides to press his own suit for her hand. Strephon finally proves his birth to Phyllis and explains away all her fears. Iolanthe then acknowledges that the Lord Chancellor is her husband and pleads with him in Strephon's behalf. When she makes this confession, she is condemned to death for breaking her fairy vow. Thereupon all the fairies confess that they have married peers. As it is impracticable to kill them all, the Queen hunts up a husband, and finds one in Private Willis, the sentry in the palace yard. All the husbands join the fairies, and thus matters are straightened out.

The music of " Iolanthe " is peculiarly refined and fanciful, and abounds in taking numbers. The best of these are Strephon's song ("Good Morrow"); the delightful duet between Strephon and Phyllis ("None shall part us from each other"), one of the most felicitous of the composer's lighter compositions; the Lord Chancellor's song ("When I went to the Bar"); Strephon's charming ballad ("In Babyhood upon her Lap I lay"); Private Willis's song ("When all Night long a Chap remains"); the patter song of the Lord Chancellor ("When you're lying awake with a dismal Headache"); the duet of Strephon and Phyllis ("If we're weak enough to tarry"); and Iolanthe's pretty ballad ("He loves! if in the by-gone Years").

Princess Ida

"Princess Ida; or, Castle Adamant," comic opera in three acts, text by Gilbert, was first produced at the Savoy Theatre, London, January 5, 1884, and in New York, February 11, 1884. It is the least effective of the Sullivan operas. Its libretto is also the least effective of the Gilbert stories set to the former's music. At the time it was written the composer was depressed by a severe family affliction, and at the same time had met the misfortune of losing all his savings through the failure of those to whom he had intrusted them. It may have been also that the labored and heavy style of the story had something to do with the dry and somewhat forced style of the music, as well as its lack of the brightness and fancy which are so apparent in "Pinafore" and "Patience." It was wittily called by the authors "a respectful operatic perversion of Tennyson's 'Princess.'"

The first act opens at King Hildebrand's palace, where the courtiers are watching for the arrival of King Gama and his daughter, the Princess Ida, who has been promised in marriage to Hilarion, Hildebrand's son. When Gama finally comes, Ida is not with him, and he explains to the enraged Hildebrand that she is at Castle Adamant, one of his country houses, where she is president of a woman's university. Gama and his three sons, Avac, Guron, and Scynthius, are seized and held as hostages for her appearance, and in the meantime Hilarion, and his two friends, Cyril and Florian, determine to go to Castle Adamant and see if they cannot make some impression upon the Princess.

The second act opens at Castle Adamant, and discloses the pupils of the university in discourse with Lady Psyche, the Professor of Humanities, and Lady Blanche, Professor of Abstract Science, who is ambitious to get control of the institution. Hilarion and his two friends scale the wall and get into the grounds, and finding some academic robes they disguise themselves as girls. They first meet the Princess and explain to her that they wish to enter the university, to which she gives her consent upon their subscription to the rules. They sign with enthusiasm, especially when they discover that there is one which requires them to give the fullness of their love to the hundred maidens of the university. Shortly afterwards they encounter Lady Psyche, who recognizes Florian as her brother. They tell their secret to her. Melissa, the daughter of Lady Blanche, overhears them, and is in raptures at her first sight of men. She discloses to her mother what she has discovered, but urges her not to speak of it, for if Hilarion is successful in his suit she (the Lady Blanche) may succeed to the presidency. At the luncheon, however, the Princess discovers she is entertaining three men and flees from the spot. In crossing a bridge she falls into the river, but is rescued by Hilarion. Her anger is not appeased by his gallantry, and she orders the arrest of the three. As they are marched off, there is a tumult outside. Hildebrand, with an armed force and with his four hostages, has arrived, and gives the Princess until the morrow afternoon to release Hilarion and become his bride.

The last act opens with the preparations of the Princess and her pupils to defend themselves, but one after the other their courage deserts them. Gama proposes that his three sons shall be pitted against Hilarion and his two friends, and if the latter are defeated the Princess shall be free. In the contest Gama's sons are defeated, whereupon the Princess at once resigns and accepts Hilarion. The Lady Psyche falls to Cyril, and the delighted Melissa to Florian, and it is to be presumed the presidency of the woman's college falls to Lady Blanche.

As has already been intimated, the music as a whole is labored, but there are some numbers that are fully up to the Sullivan standard; among them Hilarion's ballad ("Ida was a twelvemonth old"); Gama's characteristic song ("If you give me your Attention"), and the trio of Gama's sons ("For a Month to dwell") in the first act; the Princess's long aria ("At this my Call"); Lady Blanche's song ("Come, mighty Must"); Lady Psyche's sarcastic evolution song ("A Lady fair of Lineage high"); Cyril's song ("Would you know the Kind of Maid"); and Hilarion's song ("Whom thou hast chained must wear his Chain"), in the second act; and the Princess's song ("I built upon a Rock"); Gama's song ("Whene'er I spoke sarcastic Joke"); the soldiers' chorus ("When Anger spreads his

Wings"); and the finale ("With Joy abiding"), in the third act.

THE MIKADO

"The Mikado; or, the Town of Titipu," comic opera in two acts, text by Gilbert, was first produced at the Savoy Theatre, London, March 14, 1885, and in New York, August 19, 1885. That the "Princess Ida," ineffective as it is in some respects, did not indicate that the resources of Gilbert and Sullivan were exhausted, is shown by the great success of both in "The Mikado," which immediately followed it. This charming travesty of Japan, with the exception perhaps of "Pinafore," has proved to be the most popular of the Sullivan operas, and has even made an impression in Germany. It has been an equal success for both the musician and the librettist, and still retains its freshness and vivacity after more than twenty years of performance.

The story of "The Mikado" is so well known that it need not be given with much fulness of detail. Nanki-Poo, the Mikado's son, is in love with Yum-Yum, the ward of the tailor Ko-Ko, who is also Lord High Executioner, and to whom she is betrothed, as Nanki-Poo is informed by Pooh-Bah, when he comes to Titipu in quest of her. Pooh-Bah, who accepted all the offices of the Ministers of State after their resignations when Ko-Ko was made Lord High Executioner, is also "the retailer of state secrets at a low figure," and furnishes much of the delightful comedy of the opera. Nanki-Poo nevertheless manages to secure an interview with Yum-Yum, confesses to her he is the Mikado's son, and that he is in disguise to escape punishment for not marrying the elderly Katisha. Ko-Ko's matrimonial arrangements are interfered with by a message from the Mikado, that unless some one is beheaded in Titipu within a month he will be degraded. Nanki-Poo consents to be beheaded if he is allowed to marry Yum-Yum and live with her for the month. This being satisfactory, the arrangements for the nuptials are made.

The second act opens with Yum-Yum's preparations for her marriage. A *tête-à-tête* with Nanki-Poo is interrupted by Ko-Ko, who announces that by the law when a married man is beheaded his wife must be buried alive. This cools Yum-Yum's passion, and to save her Nanki-Poo threatens to perform the "happy despatch" that day. As this would endanger Ko-Ko, he arranges to swear to a false statement of Nanki-Poo's execution. Suddenly the Mikado arrives. Ko-Ko gives him the statement, but a great danger is imminent when the Mikado informs him he has killed the heir apparent and must suffer some horrible punishment. In the denouement Nanki-Poo reappears, and Ko-Ko gets out of trouble by marrying the ancient Katisha, leaving Yum-Yum to Nanki-Poo.

The opera abounds in charming lyrics, though with a single exception, a march chorus in the second act ("Miya sama, miya sama"), there is no local color to the music, as might have been expected in an opera entirely Japanese in its subject and dramatic treatment. Its lyrics are none the less delightful on that account. The most popular numbers in the first act are Ko-Ko's song, with its choral response, ("You may put 'em on the List and they never will be missed"); the fascinating trio for Yum-Yum, Peep-Bo, and Pitti-Sing ("Three little Maids from School are we"); Nanki-Poo's song ("A wandering Minstrel"); and the trio for Ko-Ko, Pooh-Bah, and Pish-Tush ("My Brain, it teems"). The leading numbers of the second act are Yum-Yum's song ("The Sun, whose Rays"); the quartet ("Brightly dawns our Wedding-Day"); the Mikado's song ("A more humane Mikado never"); Ko-Ko's romantic ballad ("On a Tree by a River a little Tomtit"), which is in the genuine old English manner, and the well-known duet for Nanki-Poo and Ko-Ko ("The Flowers that bloom in the Spring, tra la ").

RUDDYGORE

"Ruddygore; or, the Witch's Curse," comic opera in two acts, text by Gilbert, was first produced at the Savoy Theatre, London, January 22, 1887, and in New York, February 21, 1887. Although "Ruddygore," a satire upon the old English melodramas, has not been as successful as some of the other Sullivan operas, it is as entertaining as any in the series, while the story, with its grotesque, dramatic features, is peculiarly Gilbertian in its humor. The first act opens in Cornwall. Sir Rupert Murgatroyd, the first of the baronets, employed his leisure in persecuting witches and committing other crimes. The chorus of "the legend," sung by Hannah, an old spinster, prophesies that each Murgatroyd will die "with sinning cloyed." To avoid this fate, the last inheritor of the title, Sir Ruthven, secludes himself under the name of Robin Oakapple, in the Cornish village of Rederring, and his younger brother, Despard, believing him to be dead, succeeds to the title. Robin, who is shy and modest, is in love with Rose, a foundling, who is very discreet. The love-making lags, and meanwhile Richard, his foster-brother, a man-o'-war's man, returns from sea, and so commiserates Robin that he offers to plead his case with Rose. Instead of that he pleads his own case, and is accepted by her, much to the disappointment of Robin, who supports Richard's claim, however. Robin's younger brother, Sir Despard, next appears, and hears from Richard of the existence of the brother whom he had thought dead. He thereupon claims Robin as his elder brother, and Rose shows her preference for Sir Despard, who is also claimed by Mad Margaret, a village maiden, whom he had mistreated when he was under the influence of the Murgatroyd curse.

The second act opens in the picture gallery of Ruddygore Castle. Robin and Adam, his faithful servant, are in the gallery, the former as Sir Ruthven, and Adam as Gideon Crawle, a new name he has taken. The new Sir Ruthven is under the curse, and asks his servant to suggest some daily crime for him to commit. The strong scene of the act is the coming to life of the various baronets whose portraits hang upon the walls, and their announcement that Robin will die in fearful agony unless he abducts some lady, it matters not whom. In the denouement it is revealed that a Ruddygore baron can only die through refusing to commit the daily crime, but that such a refusal is tantamount to suicide. Hence none of the ancestors ought to have died at all, and they come back to life greatly to the delight of the professional bridesmaids, and Rose and Robin are at last united.

The principal numbers in the first act are the weird legend ("Sir Rupert Murgatroyd, his Leisure and his Riches"), sung by Hannah; Richard's breezy sea song ("I shipped, d'ye see, in a Revenue Sloop"); the very tuneful chorus of the bridesmaids ("Hail the Bridegroom, hail the Bride"); Mad Margaret's whimsical song ("Cheerily carols the Lark"); the melodious chorus of the bucks and blades ("When thoroughly tired of being admired"); Sir Despard's song, with its alternating choral refrains ("Oh, why am I moody and sad"); the madrigal ("Where the Buds are blossoming"), written in the early English style, and supported by the chorus; and the charming gavotte leading to the finale, which contains some admirable duet and trio numbers. The leading numbers of the second act are the opening duet for Robin and Adam ("I once was as meek as a new-born Lamb"), with a most melodramatic "Ha ha," followed by another charming duet for Richard and Rose, with choral refrain ("Happily coupled are we"); the weird song of Sir Roderic ("When the night Wind howls in the Chimney

Cowls"), which is finely artistic in construction; the patter trio for Robin, Despard, and Margaret ("My Eyes are fully open to my awful Situation"); Hannah's pretty ballad ("There grew a little Flower"); and the brilliant finale, beginning with Robin's number ("Having been a wicked Baronet a Week").

THE YEOMEN OF THE GUARD

"The Yeomen of the Guard; or, the Merry Man and his Maid," comic opera in two acts, text by Gilbert, was first produced at the Savoy Theatre, London, October 3, 1888, and in New York, October 3, 1889. Although "The Yeomen of the Guard" has not enjoyed the popularity of some others of Sullivan's works, the composer himself believed it to be the best of his operas. The music is in some numbers a parody of the old English; the story is melodramatic. Colonel Fairfax had been sentenced to death for sorcery. As he has twice saved the life of Sergeant Meryll in battle, the latter and his daughter, Phœbe, are anxious to save him also. The chance comes when the brother of Phœbe, who has been appointed a yeoman of the Guard, is induced to let Fairfax take his place in the ranks. The latter is brought to the lieutenant of the Tower and declares his readiness to die, but asks, as he has been condemned for sorcery through the machinations of one of his kinsmen who will succeed to the estate in case he dies unmarried, that he will find him some one whom he can marry at once. Elsie Maynard, a strolling singer, happens along with Jack Point, a jester, and she agrees for a money consideration to be married blindfolded to Fairfax, provided she can leave immediately after the ceremony. She marries him, and then the question arises how to get the yeoman suit to Fairfax in his cell and let him escape, as the keys are in the possession of Wilfred, the head jailer, who is in love with Phœbe.

SULLIVAN

The problem is solved by Phœbe, who steals the keys, releases Fairfax, and returns them before Wilfred discovers their absence. The executioner comes forward, and the first act closes as he is waiting for his victim.

The second act discloses the civilians and Dame Carruthers denouncing the warders for permitting their prisoner to escape. Point arranges with Wilfred that if he will discharge his arquebus and state that he has killed Fairfax he shall be a jester. When the shot is heard, Wilfred and Point notify the governor that Fairfax is dead. Dame Carruthers enters and informs Meryll that from what she has heard Elsie mutter in her sleep she is sure Fairfax is the man she married. Fairfax, in order to test her, makes love to Elsie in Point's interest, but ends by falling in love with her himself. In the denouement, Leonard, son of Sergeant Meryll, arrives with a pardon which had been kept back by Fairfax's kinsmen. Now that he is free, Fairfax claims Elsie, Phœbe consents to marry Wilfred, and the Sergeant surrenders to Dame Carruthers.

The music is in humorous imitation of the antique, in which kind of work Sullivan is always happy. The choruses are interesting, especially the opening double one ("Tower Warders under Orders"), which is swinging and tuneful. The principal numbers in the first act are Dame Carruthers's song with chorus ("When our gallant Norman Foes"); Fairfax's sentimental song ("Is Life a Boon"); the irresistibly funny chorus both in music and words ("Here's a Man of Jollity, Jibe, Joke, jollify; gives us of your Quality, come, Fool, follify"); the extremely melodramatic duet for Elsie and Point ("I have a Song to sing"); Point's recitative and song ("I've Jest and Joke"); Elsie's pretty ballad ("'Tis done! I am a Bride"); Phœbe's graceful song ("Were I thy Bride"); and the trio in the finale ("To thy fraternal

Care "). The leading numbers of the second act are Point's rollicking song ("Oh! a private Buffoon is a light-hearted Loon"); Fairfax's ballad ("Free from his Fetters grim"); the quartet ("Strange Adventure! Maiden wedded"); the trio ("If he's made the best Use of his Time"), and the quartet ("When a Wooer goes a-wooing"), which leads through a melodramatic ensemble to the finale,

> "Heighdy! heighdy!
> Misery me, lackadaydee!
> He sipped no sup and he craved no crumb,
> As he sighed for the love of a ladyee."

THE GONDOLIERS

"The Gondoliers; or, the King of Barataria," comic opera, in two acts, text by Gilbert, was first produced at the Savoy Theatre, London, December 7, 1889. "The Gondoliers" will always bring a feeling of regret to the admirers of the Gilbert and Sullivan operas, as it was their last joint production. It was during its run at the London theatre that their partnership was dissolved after the extraordinary collaboration of twenty-three years. Both were at their best in their Swan Song. "The Gondoliers" is not so much melodrama or pleasant satire as it is genuine comedy. Among all the books which Gilbert furnished the composer, none is more delightful or more full of his rollicking humor than this. The story opens in Venice. The contadine are weaving garlands for the two favorite gondoliers, Marco and Giuseppe, who, as they have no preference, make their choice blindfolded, and secure Tessa and Gianetta for their brides. As all gayly dance off, a gondola arrives with the Spanish Duke of Plaza-Toro, the Duchess, their daughter Casilda, and Luiz, their attendant. While waiting for an audience with the Grand Inquisitor, the Duke tells Casilda the object of their visit. When she was an infant she was married by proxy to the infant son of the King of Barataria. When the latter abandoned the creed of his fathers and became a Methodist, the Inquisitor had the young husband stolen and taken to Venice. Now that the King is dead, they have come to find the husband, and proclaim Casilda queen. During the audience the Inquisitor announces that the husband is a gondolier, and that the person who brought him up had "such a terrible taste for tippling" that he was never certain which child had been intrusted to him, his own or the other. The nurse, however, who is Luiz's mother, would know, and he could induce her to tell in the torture chamber. Shortly afterwards the Inquisitor meets the newly wedded gondoliers, Marco and Giuseppe, and decides that one or the other of them is the new king, but as he cannot tell which, he arranges that both of them shall rule until the nurse can be found and made to settle the matter. Thereupon they bid their wives good-bye, and sail away for Barataria.

The second act discloses the two kings upon the thrones. While they are cleaning the crown and sceptre, and their friends, the gondoliers, are playing cards, contadine arrive with Tessa and Gianetta. The delighted kings give them a grand banquet and ball, but the dance is interrupted by the Inquisitor, who informs them that the ducal party will shortly arrive, and that Casilda will claim one of them for her husband. When Tessa and Gianetta realize that neither of them can be queen, they begin to weep, but are somewhat comforted when the Inquisitor assures them they will not be kept long in suspense as the foster-mother is in the torture chamber. In the denouement she confesses that the late king intrusted the Prince to her, and when traitors came to steal him she substituted her own son and kept the Prince in hiding, and that Luiz is the real prince. Thereupon Luiz ascends the throne with Casilda as his queen, and Marco and Guiseppe sail joyfully back to Venice with Tessa and Gianetta.

The music is of Sullivan's best. He has reproduced in the score the old Italian forms, employs the legitimate modern ballad and song styles, and introduces also the "patter" songs and the "chant" songs which are so common in his other operas. Besides this, he has given strong local color with fandangoes, boleros, cachucas, and other dance rhythms. The best numbers are the ensemble for Marco and Giuseppe ("We're called Gondolieri"); the pompous song of the Duke ("In Enterprise of martial Kind"); the serious duet for Casilda and Luiz ("There was a Time"); the Inquisitor's song ("I stab the Prince"); Tessa's beautiful song ("When a merry Maiden marries"); the frolicsome quartet ("Then one of us will be a Queen"); the song of Marco with chorus ("For every one who feels inclined"); the characteristic song of Giuseppe ("Rising early in the Morning"); the gay and fascinating ensemble ("We will dance a Cachuca"), with the brilliant dance music that follows it; the song of the Inquisitor ("There lived a King"); the ensemble ("In a contemplative Fashion"), a quiet movement with alternating comments by chorus, reaching a crescendo and then returning to the original movement, one of the most effective numbers in the opera; the Duchess's song ("On the Day when I was wedded"); and the quintet in the finale ("I am a Courtier grave and serious").

SUPPÉ

FRANZ VON SUPPÉ, one of the most popular of the German light opera composers, has been called the German Offenbach, though the styles of the two composers differ widely. His operas are more purely comic operas or operettas than burlesques. He was born in Dalmatia, April 18, 1820, and died in Vienna, May 22, 1893. He made his first success with an operetta "Das Mädchen vom Lande," which was produced in Vienna in 1847, and his next work, a musical comedy called "Paragraph 3," made him known all over Germany. He was conductor at several theatres, and most of his stage works were written for these theatres and brought out by him. His entire list of light operas, musical farces, and vaudevilles, includes over one hundred and sixty titles. The most popular among them are "Paragraph 3" (1858); "Flotte Bursche" (1863); "Pique Dame" (1864); "Franz Schubert" (1864); "Die schöne Galatea" (1865); "Leichte Cavallerie" (1866); "Fatinitza" (1876); "Boccaccio" (1879); "Die Afrikareise" (1883); and "Bellmann" (1887). He also wrote several overtures, one of which, "Poet and Peasant," is a favorite everywhere.

FATINITZA

"Fatinitza," opera comique in three acts, text by Zell and Genée, was first produced in Vienna, January 5, 1876. The story is an interesting one. Vladimir Samoiloff, a young lieutenant in the Russian army, while masquerading in girl's costume under the name of Fatinitza, encounters a Russian general, Count Timofey Kantschakoff, who falls desperately in love with him. He manages to escape from him, and subsequently meets the General's niece, the Princess Lydia, whom he knows only as Lydia, and the two fall in love. Hearing of the attachment, the General transfers the young officer to the Russian outposts. The first act opens in camp at Rustchuk. Julian, a war correspondent, has just been brought in as a spy, but is recognized by Vladimir as an old friend. They plan private theatricals, in which Vladimir takes a female part. The General unexpectedly appears at the play, and recognizes Vladimir as his Fatinitza. When the opportunity presents itself, he resumes his love making, but it is interrupted by the arrival of Lydia, whose noble rank Vladimir learns for the first time. Any danger of recognition, however, is averted by the correspondent, who tells Lydia that Fatinitza is Vladimir's sister. The doting old General commends Fatinitza to the Princess, and goes off to inspect his troops. In his absence some Bashi-Bazouks surprise the camp and capture Lydia, Vladimir, and Julian, leaving the latter behind to arrange a ransom.

The second act opens in the harem of Izzet Pasha, governor of the Turkish fortress. Vladimir, in his female attire, and Lydia are brought in as captives, and the Pasha announces to his four wives that Lydia will be the fifth. Julian then arrives with the Russian sergeant, Steipann, to arrange for the release of his friends. The Pasha offers to give up Fatinitza, but declares he will retain Lydia. Steipann returns to the General with the Pasha's terms, carrying also a secret message from Julian, who has discovered how the Russians may capture the Turks. Julian remains with the Pasha, who gives him many entertainments, among them a shadow pantomime, during which the General and his soldiers rush in and rescue their friends.

The third act opens in the General's summer palace at Odessa. He has promised his niece to an old and crippled friend of his, but Julian once more straightens out matters by convincing the General that the real Fatinitza has died of grief because she was separated from him. Thereupon he consents to his niece's union with Fatinitza's brother, Vladimir.

The principal numbers of the first act are Vladimir's romance, in the sentimental vein ("Lost is the Dream that bound me"); the reporter's (Julian) jolly descriptive song ("With my Note-book in my Hand"); the pompously martial entrance song of General Kantschakoff ("Thunder, Lightning! who goes there?") which forcibly recalls General Boum's "Pif, paf, pouf" song in Offenbach's "Grand Duchess"; Lydia's sleighing-song ("When the Snow a Veil is flinging"); and the quartet in the next scene ("Not a Look shall tell"), in the mock Italian style. The second act opens with the characteristic toilet chorus in the harem ("Washing, dressing, brushing, combing"). The remaining most striking numbers are Izzet's song and dance ("I pine but for Progress"); the pretty duet for Vladimir and Lydia ("New Doubts, new Fears"); the effective sextet ("'T is well; then learn that this young Russian"); the brilliant kismet duet for Izzet and Julian ("We are simply what Fortune pleases"); the sextet in the finale ("Silver Tinkling, ringing brightly"), known as the Bell Sextet; and the characteristic music to the Karagois, or Turkish shadow pantomime, which forms a second finale. The leading numbers of the last act are Lydia's bell song ("Chime, ye Bells"), accompanied by the ringing of bells on the stage, and distant shots; the trio for Lydia, Vladimir, and Julian ("Again, Love, we meet"), which is one of the most effective bits in the opera; and the brilliant closing chorus ("Joy, Joy, Joy, to the Bride").

BOCCACCIO

"Boccaccio," opera comique in three acts, text by Zell and Genée, was first produced at the Carl Theatre, Vienna, February 1, 1879. Suppé is fond of introducing real characters among the personages of his operas, and in this one, which has become such a favorite, sharing equally in popularity with "Fatinitza," we find Boccaccio of the "Decameron," and the Fiametta whom he has immortalized in it (the Princess Maria of Naples, with whom he fell violently in love) masquerading as the adopted daughter of Lambertuccio, the grocer. In the opera he is rewarded with her hand in the finale. In reality, Maria, the Fiametta of the "Decameron," was already the wife of another when Boccaccio was enamored of her. She died long before her lover, but her memory was cherished by him, as in the case of Beatrice and Dante, and to her we owe undoubtedly the collection of tales in the "Decameron" which furnished such abundant material to subsequent poets, story-tellers, and dramatists.

The story of the opera is a simple one. Pietro, the Prince of Palermo, is to be married to Fiametta in accordance with the wishes of his father, and goes to Florence for that purpose. The Duke, her father, for reasons of his own, has had her reared as the adopted daughter of Lambertuccio, a grocer, who was not aware of her royal birth and intends that she shall marry Pietro, to whom she was betrothed in infancy. On his way to Florence Pietro falls in with a madcap lot of students, whose leader is Boccaccio, and he joins them in many of their pranks. Boccaccio himself has incurred the anger of the Florentine men for having ridiculed them in his stories, and he too is in love with Fiametta. Pietro among his other adventures has made love to a married woman whom the students induced him to believe was the niece instead of the wife of Lutteringhi,

SUPPÉ

the cooper. He has the misfortune before presenting himself to the Duke and Fiametta to be mistaken for Boccaccio and to receive a sound beating. In the denouement, when he is about to be united to Fiametta for reasons of state, Boccaccio, knowing that he is loved by her, arranges a play in which the misdeeds of Pietro are set forth in such strong light that she refuses the latter and gives her hand to the poet.

The most popular numbers in the opera are the serenade to Beatrice ("Lovely Charmer, hear these Sounds"); Boccaccio's song with chorus ("I see a gay young Fellow standing nigh"); the charming duet for Fiametta and Peronetta ("Listen to the Bells' sweet Chime"); Fiametta's romanza ("If I have but Affection"); the duet for Boccaccio and Fiametta ("A poor blind Man implores your Aid"); Leonetto's song, opening the second act ("The Girl of my Heart's a Treasure"); the cooper's rollicking song ("My Wife has a scolding Tongue"); the coquette song by Isabella ("Young Maidens must beware"); the "cretin" song by Boccaccio ("When they ask me for the News"); the graceful waltz song by Fiametta ("Blissful Tidings, reassuring"); the spirited drinking-song of Pietro ("See the Goblet flash and sparkle"); the duet for Boccaccio and Fiametta ("Mia bella Fiorentina"), in the Italian style; and the sextet ("Ye foolish Men") which leads up to the finale of the last act.

THE BEAUTIFUL GALATEA

"The Beautiful Galatea," opera comique in two acts, text by Zell and Genée, was first produced in Vienna in 1865. Though of slight construction it is one of Suppé's most melodious works, while the story is a clever setting of the familiar mythological romance in a somewhat modern frame, in which respect it resembles the stories of Helen of Troy and Orpheus and Eurydice, which Offenbach so cleverly travestied. The first act opens with a graceful chorus of Grecians on their way to worship at the temple of Venus, at dawn ("Aurora is awaking in Heaven above"). Ganymede, Pygmalion's servant, declines to go with them, preferring to sleep, and bids them good-bye with a lullaby ("With Violets, with Roses, let the Temple be decked"). His master, Pygmalion, who has finished a statue of Galatea, his ideal, also goes to the temple, and Ganymede decides to take a nap. His slumbers are interrupted, however, by Midas, a professional art patron, who has heard of the statue and informs Ganymede that he is ready to buy it, but first wishes to see it. The servant declares it is impossible, as his master is in love with it. Midas makes a further appeal to him in a long descriptive arietta ("My dear Father Gordias") in which he boasts of his abilities, his patronage, and his conquests. He finally bribes Ganymede to show it to him, and as he stands gazing at it and praising its loveliness, Pygmalion, who has suddenly returned, enters and upbraids them. After a spirited trio ("Boiling Rage I feel within me") Ganymede takes to his heels and Midas is driven out. When Pygmalion is alone with the statue, a sudden impulse moves him to destroy it because it has been polluted by Midas's glances, but his hand is stayed as he hears the chorus of the returning worshippers, and he makes an impassioned appeal to Venus ("Venus, oh, see, I fly to thee") to give life to the marble. Venus answers his prayer. The statue comes to life, and Galatea falls in love with Pygmalion, the first man she has seen, which gives an opportunity for a charming number, the Awakening Duet ("I feel so warm, so sweet"), and for a solo closing the act ("Lightly sways and gently sweeps").

The second act opens with the couplets of Ganymede ("We Grecians"), at the close of which he espies Galatea gathering flowers. As soon as the fickle Galatea sees Ganymede, she falls in love with him because he is younger and handsomer than Pygmalion. As they are

SUPPÉ

discoursing admiringly, Midas appears and recognizes Galatea, and proceeds to woo her with offers of jewels. A pretty trio follows ("See the Trinkets I have brought you"). She accepts his trinkets and his money, but declines to accept him. As they are negotiating, Pygmalion returns. Ganymede once more takes to his heels, and Galatea conceals Midas by putting him on the pedestal behind the screen where she had stood. She then hides her jewels, and tells Pygmalion she is hungry. Ganymede is summoned and arranges the table, and they sit down, the servant with them at Galatea's request. She sings a brilliant drinking-song ("Bright in Glass the foaming Fluid pass"), in which Pygmalion and Ganymede join. During the banquet Midas is discovered behind the screen, and Pygmalion also learns of Galatea's fickle conduct later, when he surprises her and Ganymede in a pretty love scene ("Ah, I'm drawn to thee"). By this time Pygmalion is so enraged that he prays Venus to let her become a statue again. The goddess graciously consents, and the sculptor promptly gets rid of Galatea by selling her to Midas.

THOMAS

CHARLES AMBROISE THOMAS was born at Metz, August 5, 1811, and died in Paris, February 12, 1896. He entered the Paris Conservatory in 1828, where he carried off the Grand Prize in 1832, which entitled him to go to Italy. During his Italian residence he wrote a cantata, "Hermann and Ketty," and several instrumental works. His first work at the Opéra Comique was the one-act opera, "La Double Échelle," produced in 1837 with success. He then brought out several ballets at the Académie, but returned to the Opéra Comique again, where, between 1840 and 1866, he composed thirteen operas, the most successful of which were "Le Songe d'une nuit d'été" (1850), "Raymond" (1851), "Psyche" (1857), and "Mignon" (1866). During this period he also wrote a large number of cantatas, choruses, part-songs, and instrumental works. His next great work was "Hamlet," first produced March 9, 1868, the success of which gained him the position of director of the Conservatory in 1871. After that time he wrote the operas "Gille et Gillotin" (1874); "Françoise de Rimini," performed April 14, 1882, and the ballet, "La Tempête." In 1880 he was made a member of the Legion of Honor. He has also written several pieces of chamber music, masses, motets, and many charming four-part male choruses.

MIGNON

"Mignon," opera comique in three acts, text by Barbier and Carré, the subject taken from Goethe's "Wilhelm

Calvé as *Ophelia* in "Hamlet"
Copyright, Aimé Dupont

Mlle. Ambré as *Mignon* in "Mignon"

Meister," was first produced at the Opéra Comique, Paris, November 17, 1866, with the following cast:

Mignon	Mme. GALLI-MARIÉ.
Wilhelm Meister	M. ACHARD.
Laertes	M. CONDERS.
Lotario	M. BATAILLE.
Filina	Mme. CABEL.

The scene of the first two acts is laid in Germany, and of the third in Italy. Mignon, the heroine, in her childhood was stolen by gypsies. She is of noble birth. The mother died shortly after her bereavement, and the father, disguised as the harper Lotario, has wandered for years in quest of his daughter. The opera opens in the yard of a German inn, where a troupe of actors, among them Filina and Laertes, are resting, on their way to the castle of a neighboring prince, where they are to give a performance. A strolling gypsy band arrives about the same time, and stops to give an entertainment to the guests. Mignon, who is with the band, is ordered to perform the egg dance, but, worn out with fatigue and abusive treatment, refuses. Giarno, the leader, rushes at her, but the old harper interposes in her behalf. Giarno then turns upon Lotario, when the wandering student, Wilhelm Meister, suddenly appears and rescues both Mignon and the harper. To save her from any further persecution he engages her as his page, and follows on in the suite of Filina, for whom he conceives a violent and sudden passion. Touched by his kind attentions to her, Mignon falls in love with Wilhelm, who, ignorant of his page's affection, becomes more and more a prey to the fascinations of Filina. At last the troupe arrives at the castle, Wilhelm and Mignon with them. Wilhelm enters with the others, leaving Mignon to await him outside. Maddened with jealousy, she attempts to throw herself into a lake near by, but is restrained by the notes of

Lotario's harp. She rushes to him for counsel and protection, and in her despair invokes vengeance upon all in the castle. As the entertainment closes, Filina and her troupe emerge, joyful over their great success. She sends Mignon back for some flowers she has left, when suddenly flames appear in the windows. Maddened by his own grief and Mignon's troubles Lotario has fired the castle. Wilhelm rushes into the burning building and brings out the unconscious Mignon in his arms.

The last act opens in Lotario's home in Italy, whither Mignon has been taken, followed by Wilhelm, who has discovered her devoted attachment to him, and has freed himself from the fascinations of Filina. Through the medium of a long-concealed casket containing a girdle which Mignon had worn in her childhood, also by a prayer which she repeats, and the picture of her mother, Lotario is at last convinced that she is his daughter, and gives his blessing to her union with Wilhelm.

The overture recites the leading motifs of the work. The first act opens with a fresh and melodious chorus of the townspeople over their beer in the inn yard ("Su borghesi e magnati"). During their singing a characteristic march is heard, and the gypsy band enters. The scene is a charming one, the little ballet being made still more picturesque by the fresh chorus and a song of Filina's in waltz time. The scene of the encounter with Giarno and Mignon's rescue follows, and leads up to a very spirited quintet, which is followed by a graceful trio between Wilhelm, Filina, and Laertes, the actor. In the next scene Wilhelm questions Mignon as to her history, and at the end of their pathetic duet, when he says, "Were I to break thy chains and set thee free, to what beloved spot wouldst thou take thy way?" she replies in the beautiful romanza, "Non conosci il bel suol," more familiarly known in Goethe's own words, "Kennst du das Land," — a song full of tender beauty and rare expression, and one of the most delightful inspirations of any composer. It is said that much of its charm comes from the composer's study of Ary Scheffer's picture of Mignon. Be this as it may, he has caught the inner sense of the poem, and expressed it in exquisite tones. It is followed almost immediately by a duet between Mignon and Lotario ("Leggiadre rondinelle") of almost equal beauty, known as the Swallow Duet. After a somewhat uninteresting scene between Laertes, Filina, and Frederick, who is also in love with Filina, the finale begins with the departure of the actors to fulfil their engagement, in which Filina, in a graceful aria ("Grazie al gentil signor"), invites Wilhelm to be of the number.

The second act opens in Filina's boudoir, where she is at her toilet, arraying herself for her part as Titania in the forthcoming performance of the "Midsummer Night's Dream" at the castle. As Wilhelm and Mignon enter the apartment, a very dramatic conversation ensues between them in the form of a terzetto ("Ohimé quell' acre riso"). Mignon is in despair at the attention Wilhelm pays Filina, and the latter adds to her pangs by singing with him a gay coquettish aria ("Gai complimenti"). As they leave the room Mignon goes to the mirror and begins adorning herself as Filina had done, hoping thereby to attract Wilhelm, singing meanwhile a characteristic song ("Conosco un zingarello") with a peculiar refrain, which the composer himself calls the "Styrienne." It is one of the most popular numbers in the opera, and when first sung in Paris made a furor. At the end of the scene Mignon goes into a cabinet to procure one of Filina's dresses, and the lovelorn Frederick enters and sings his only number in the opera, a bewitching rondo gavotte ("Filina nelle sale"). Wilhelm enters, and a quarrel between the jealous pair is prevented by the sudden appearance of Mignon in Filina's finery. She rushes between them, Frederick makes his exit in a fume, and Wilhelm announces to Mignon his intention to leave her, in the aria "Addio, Mignon, fa core," one of the most pathetic songs in the modern opera. In the next scene she tears off her finery and rushes out expressing her hatred of Filina. The scene now changes to the park surrounding the castle where the entertainment is going on. Mignon hears the laughter and clapping of hands, and overcome with despair attempts to throw herself into the lake, but is restrained by Lotario, and a beautiful duet ensues between them ("Sofferto hai tu?"). In the next scene Filina, the actors, and their train of followers emerge from the castle, and in the midst of their joy she sings the polacca ("Ah! per stassera"), which is a perfect *feu de joie* of sparkling music, closing with a brilliant cadenza. The finale, which is very dramatic, describes the burning of the castle and the rescue of Mignon.

The last act is more dramatic than musical, though it contains a few delightful numbers, among them the chorus barcarole in the first scene ("Orsu, sciogliam le vela"), a song by Wilhelm ("Ah! non credea"), and the love duet ("Ah! son felice") between Wilhelm and Mignon, in which is heard again the cadenza of Filina's polacca. "Mignon" has always been a success, and will unquestionably always keep its place on the stage, — longer even than the composer's more ambitious works, "Hamlet" and "Françoise de Rimini," by virtue of its picturesqueness and poetic grace, as well as by the freshness, warmth, and richness of its melodies. In this country opera-goers will long remember "Mignon" by the great successes made by Miss Kellogg as Filina, and by Mme. Lucca and Mme. Nilsson in the title role.

THOMAS

Hamlet

"Hamlet," grand opera in five acts, text by Carré and Barbier, after Shakespeare, was first produced at the Opéra, Paris, March 9, 1868, and in London, in Italian, as "Amleto," June 19, 1869. The cast of the three principal roles at the first performance included Christine Nilsson as Ophelia, M. Faure as Hamlet, and Mme. Guaymat as the Queen. The composer has divided his work into five acts, but a more natural division would be into seven parts. The first includes the celebration of the marriage of the Queen to the late king's brother, Hamlet's soliloquy thereupon, Ophelia's declaration of love, her farewell to Laertes, and Marcellus and Horatio's announcement of the appearance of the ghost; second, of the ghostly apparition upon the ramparts, and Hamlet's decision to execute his plan; third, Hamlet's struggle between duty and love, the interview with Ophelia and the scheme of the play; fourth, the paraphrase of the play scene and denunciation of the King before the court; fifth, Hamlet in the Queen's apartments, his famous soliloquy and the awakening of the Queen's guilty conscience; sixth, the death of Ophelia and the gravedigger's scene; seventh, the funeral and the appointment of Hamlet as king. The librettists have taken many liberties with the original text and story and sometimes in a manner that verges upon the ludicrous. Not the least of these liberties are the introduction of a ballet in a tragedy and the manner in which Ophelia's mad scene is treated. In the denouement, also, the King is killed, Hamlet is proclaimed his successor, the Queen lives to repent, and Laertes and also Polonius live. The graceful and at times very dramatic character of the music atones for any inconsistencies in the libretto. The most conspicuous numbers in the opera are the fanfare and march behind the scenes leading up to the first scene, a chorus of the courtiers ("Iuini lieti"), to the march accompaniment. This is immediately followed by a graceful aria for Ophelia ("Angli eterni"), followed by a lively duet for Hamlet and Ophelia, which in turn is followed by a song for Laertes ("Per patrio"), the scene ending with the sprightly chorus ("Banda allo via mestizia"). In the second and third acts, the striking numbers are Ophelia's brilliant scena, Hamlet's impressive address to the ghost, a simple but beautifully written drinking-song ("O liquore"), the play scene, Hamlet's soliloquy ("Essere o no"), accompanied by trombones in unison, Ophelia's tender solo ("A questa pie"), and the dramatic trio for the Queen, Ophelia, and Hamlet ("Deh! vanne a un chiostro"). The dance music for peasantry in the fourth act, incongruous as it appears, is charming, and few more beautiful numbers have been written than Ophelia's song in the mad scena, bound together by a waltz rhythm, and her apostrophe to the sirens, a native Swedish melody, as she is enticed by them to the waters upon which the song gradually dies away as she disappears. The best music in the fifth act is to be found in Hamlet's aria, the funeral music, and the closing chorus ("Povero fior").

TSCHAIKOWSKY

PETER ILYITCH TSCHAIKOWSKY was born at Votkinsk in the government of Viätka, Russia, May 7, 1840, and died in St. Petersburg, November 6, 1893. He first contemplated the study of the law, but abandoned it in 1862, and entered the St. Petersburg Conservatory as a student. Four years later he was instructor in harmony in the same institution, and remained as such until 1877. After that year he devoted himself to composition, and has been recognized as the foremost of Russian and one of the most distinguished of modern composers. His symphonies, the symphonic poems, "The Tempest," "Francesca da Rimini," "Manfred," and "Hamlet," his numerous overtures and marches, as well as his chamber music and songs, have made his name familiar on concert programmes the world over. His operas are not so well known outside of Russia as his other works, though one or two of them have met with success in Germany. The list of his principal dramatic works is as follows: "Voyevoda" (1869); "Opritchnik" (1874); "Vakoula, the Smith" (1875); "Jevgenjie," or "Eugen Onégin" (1877); "The Maid of Orleans" (1881); "Mazeppa" (1882); "Tcharavitchki" (1886); "Tcharodjeika" (1887); "Pique Dame" (1890); and "Iolanthe" (1893).

EUGEN ONÉGIN

"Eugen Onégin," grand opera in three acts, text by M. Kashkin, after M. Poushkin's novel in verse by the same title, was first produced in St. Petersburg in May, 1877. An introduction founded upon themes in the opera gives the substance of the musical material of the work. The first act opens in the gardens of the Levins's country house and discloses Madame Levin engaged in domestic duties, and her two daughters, Olga and Tatiana, seated by a window. The opening number is a charming duet for the sisters, based upon an old folk song ("Hearest thou the Nightingale?") through which is heard the chatter of the servants. After a quartet, the peasants enter with birthday congratulations, following which comes a pretty ballad for Olga ("I have no Mind for Languor or for Sadness"). The scene develops that Olga has a lover, Lenski, who now makes his appearance, bringing with him his friend, Eugen Onégin. The latter entertains Tatiana with some expressive recitative and they wander away into the garden. After they are gone, Lenski sings an impassioned love song ("I love you, Olga"). The next scene discloses Tatiana in her chamber, visited by the old nurse. The latter easily discovers that Tatiana has lost her heart to the young stranger. A very emotional scene occurs, especially the nurse's tale of love, which is in the style of the folk song, followed by Tatiana's confession of love for Eugen in the song, "Nay, though I be undone." The rest of the scene is an orchestral description of her emotions, as she writes a letter which she entrusts to the nurse to deliver to Onégin. The closing scene, opening with a chorus of peasant girls, is in the garden where Tatiana meets Eugen. He thanks her for the letter, but in a most nonchalant manner informs her he has only a brotherly regard for her, and then leaves her overcome with shame.

The second act opens with a ball-scene at the house in honor of Tatiana's birthday, in which a very effective waltz is heard. Onégin is there and rouses Lenski's jealousy by flirting with Olga and taking her away for a dance. In the same scene, Triquet, a Frenchman, sings couplets, based upon an old French chanson, to Tatiana, after which a mazurka takes the place of the waltz, and Olga is again seen dancing with Eugen. Lenski, losing his temper, challenges his friend, which makes a powerful concerted close to the scene. The last scene is a winter landscape in the early morning. Lenski, while awaiting Eugen's arrival, sings a sentimental song ("My Days of Youth, where have they fled?"). Then ensues the duel, and Lenski is killed.

The third act, after a supposed lapse of five years, opens in a handsome house in St. Petersburg, and guests are moving about to the music of a polonaise. Eugen is seen in a melancholy mood, the victim of remorse, which he describes in long and gloomy recitative. While thus engaged, he observes a familiar face and inquiring of a friend, Prince Gremin, who she is, finds she is the wife of the latter. He now falls hopelessly in love with Tatiana. The closing scene is in Princess Gremin's apartments. Eugen bursts in upon her with a declaration of love and tries to induce her to fly with him. A very dramatic duet follows between them, but even while acknowledging she still loves him, she breaks away from him, leaving him alone. His last words are, "Despised, rejected, O what Misery is mine!"

VERDI

GIUSEPPE VERDI was born at Roncole, Italy, October 9, 1813, and died at Busseto, January 27, 1902. He displayed his musical talent at a very early age; indeed, in his tenth year he was appointed organist in his native town. He then studied for a time at Busseto, and afterwards, by the help of a patron, M. Barezzi, went to Milan. Curiously enough he was refused a scholarship on the ground that he displayed no aptitude for music. Nothing daunted, he studied privately with the composer Lavigne, and five years afterwards commenced his career as an operatic writer. His first opera, "Oberto," was given at La Scala, Milan, with indifferent success. He was not fairly recognized until his opera "I Lombardi" was performed. In 1844 "Ernani" was received with great enthusiasm. "Attila" (1846) was his next great triumph; and then followed in rapid succession a large number of operas, among them: "I Masnadieri" (1847), written for the English stage, with Jenny Lind, Lablache, and Gardoni in the cast; "Luisa Miller" (1849); "Stiffelio" (1851); "Rigoletto" (1851); "Il Trovatore," Rome (1853); "La Traviata," Venice (1853); "I Vespri Siciliani," Paris (1855); "Simon Boccanegra," Venice (1857); "Un Ballo in Maschera," Rome (1859); "La Forza del Destino," St. Petersburg (1862); "Don Carlos," Paris (1867); "Aïda," (1871); "Othello" (1887); and "Falstaff" (1893). Verdi has also written several pieces of chamber music, songs, and cantatas, a Pater Noster and an Ave Maria (1880), and the "Requiem," composed in memory of the patriot Manzoni, and produced at Milan in 1874, on the occasion of the anniversary of his death.

ERNANI

"Ernani," opera in four acts, text by F. M. Piave, the subject taken from Victor Hugo's tragedy of "Hernani," was first produced at the Teatro Fenice, Venice, March 9, 1844. The earlier performances of the opera gave the composer much trouble. Before the first production the police interfered, refusing to allow the representation of a conspiracy on the stage, so that many parts of the libretto, as well as much of the music, had to be changed. The blowing of Don Silva's horn in the last act was also objected to by one Count Mocenigo, upon the singular ground that it was disgraceful. The Count, however, was silenced more easily than the police. The chorus "Si ridesti il Leon di Castiglia" also aroused a political manifestation by the Venetians. The opera was given in Paris, January 6, 1846, and there it encountered the hostility of Victor Hugo, who demanded that the libretto should be changed. To accommodate the irate poet, the words were altered, the characters were changed to Italians, and the new title of "Il Proscritto" was given to the work.

The action of the opera takes place in Aragon, Spain, and the period is 1519. Elvira, a noble Spanish lady, betrothed to the grandee Don Gomez de Silva, is in love with the bandit Ernani, who forms a plan to carry her off. While receiving the congratulations of her friends upon her approaching marriage with Silva, Don Carlos, the King of Spain, enters her apartment, declares his passion for her, and tries to force her from the castle. She cries for help, and Ernani comes to her rescue and defies the King. The situation is still further complicated by the sudden arrival of Silva, who declares he will avenge the insult. Finding, however, that it is the King whom he has challenged, he sues for pardon. In the second act, as the nuptials are about to be solemnized, Ernani enters, disguised as a pilgrim, and believing

Elvira false to him, throws off his disguise and demands to be given up to the King, which Silva refuses, as he cannot betray a guest. Discovering, however, that Elvira and Ernani are attached to each other, he determines on vengeance. The King eventually carries off Elvira as a hostage of the faith of Silva, whereupon the latter challenges Ernani. The bandit refuses to fight with him, informs him that the King is also his rival, and asks to share in his vengeance, promising in turn to give up his life when Silva calls for it, and presenting him with a horn which he is to sound whenever he wishes to have the promise kept. In the third act, the King, aware that the conspirators are to meet in the catacombs of Aquisgrana, conceals himself there, and when the assassins meet to decide who shall kill him, he suddenly appears among them and condemns the nobles to be sent to the block. Ernani, who is a duke, under the ban of the King of Castile, demands the right to join them, but the King magnanimously pardons the conspirators and consents to the union of Ernani and Elvira. Upon the very eve of their happiness, and in the midst of their festivities, the fatal horn is heard, and true to his promise Ernani parts from Elvira and kills himself.

The first act opens with a spirited chorus of banditti and mountaineers ("Allegri, beviami") as they are drinking and gambling in their mountain retreat. Ernani appears upon a neighboring height and announces himself in a despondent aria ("Come rugiada al cespite"). A brief snatch of chorus intervenes, when he breaks out in a second and more passionate strain ("Dell' esilio nel dolore"), in which he sings of his love for Elvira. The third scene opens in Elvira's apartments, and is introduced with one of the most beautiful of Verdi's arias, "Ernani, involami," with which all concert-goers have become acquainted by its frequent repetition. A graceful chorus of her ladies bearing gifts leads to a second and more florid number ("Tutto

Sembrich as *Elvira*

Copyright, Aimé Dupont

sprezzo che d' Ernani "). Don Carlos enters, and in the seventh scene has an aria ("Bella come un primo amore ") in which he declares his passion for Elvira, leading up to a very dramatic duet between them (" Fiero sangue d' Aragona "). This is followed in turn by a trio between the two and Ernani. The finale commences with an impressive and sonorous bass solo ("Infelice! e tuo credevi ") by Silva, and closes with a septet and chorus of great power.

The second act, like the first, opens with a chorus, this time, however, of mixed voices, the power of which is amplified by a military band on the stage. After three scenes of dramatic dialogue, an impassioned duet (" Ah! morir potessi adesso!") occurs between Ernani and Elvira, followed by a second, of great dramatic intensity, in the seventh scene (" La vendetta piu tremenda "). The finale begins with a spirited appeal by Silva and Ernani for vengeance against the King (" In arcione, cavalieri ") which is met by a stirring response from their followers (" Pronti vedi li tuoi cavalieri "), sung by full male chorus and closing the act.

The third act is devoted to the conspiracy, and in the second scene Don Carlos has a very impressive and at times thrilling soliloquy ("Gran Dio! costo sui sepolcrali marmi "). The conspiracy then begins with very characteristic accompaniments, closing with the chorus in full harmony ("Si ridesti il Leon di Castiglia "), which at the performance of the work in Venice roused such a fury among the Venetians. The finale commences with the appearance of Don Carlos among the conspirators, and closes with the great sextet and chorus, " O Sommo Carlo." Opening with a barytone solo it is gradually worked up in a crescendo of great power and thrilling effect. The number is very familiar from its English setting under the title, "Crowned with the Tempest."

The fourth act rapidly hurries to the tragic close, and is

less interesting from a musical point of view, as the climax was reached in the finale of the third. The principal numbers are the chorus of masks in the first scene ("O come felici"), accompanied by military band, and the great duet between Elvira and Ernani ("Cessaro i suoni") which passes from rapturous ecstasy to the despair of fate ("Per noi d' amore il talamo") as the horn of Silva is heard, reminding Ernani of his promise. Though one of the earliest of Verdi's works, "Ernani" is one of his strongest in dramatic intensity, in the brilliancy and power of its concerted finales, and in the beauty of its chorus effects.

RIGOLETTO

"Rigoletto," opera in three acts, text by Piave, the subject taken from Victor Hugo's tragedy, "Le Roi s'amuse," was first produced at Venice, March 11, 1851, with the following cast of the leading parts:

Rigoletto	Sig. COLETTI.
Duke	Sig. BEAUCARDE.
Gilda	Signora EVERS.

The part of Gilda has always been a favorite one with great artists, among whom Nantier-Didiée, Bosio, and Miolan-Carvalho played the role with extraordinary success. In the London season of 1860 Mario and Ronconi in the respective parts of the Duke and Rigoletto, it is said, gave dramatic portraitures which were among the most consummate achievements of the lyric stage. The records of its first production, like those of "Ernani," are of unusual interest. Verdi himself suggested Victor Hugo's tragedy to Piave for a libretto, and he soon prepared one, changing the original title, however, to "La Maledizione." Warned by the political events of 1848, the police flatly refused to allow the representation of a king on the stage in such situations as those given to Francis I. in the original

Louise Homer as *Gilda*
Copyright, Aimé Dupont

Caruso as *The Duke*
Copyright, Aimé Dupont

tragedy. The composer and the manager of the theatre begged in vain that the libretto should be accepted, but the authorities were obstinate. At last a way was found out of the difficulty by the chief of police himself, who was a great lover of art. He suggested to the librettist that the King should be changed to a duke of Mantua, and the title of the work to " Rigoletto," the name of the buffoon who figures in the place of the original Triboulet. Verdi accepted the alterations, and had an opera ready in forty days which by nearly all critics is considered his musical masterpiece, notwithstanding the revolting character of the story.

The scene of the opera is laid in Mantua. Rigoletto, the privileged buffoon of the Duke, who also plays the part of pander in all his licentious schemes, among numerous other misdeeds has assisted his master in the seduction of the wife of Count Ceprano and the daughter of Count Monterone. The latter appears before the Duke and Rigoletto, and demands reparation for the dishonor put upon his house, only to find himself arrested by order of the Duke, and taunted in the most insolent manner by the buffoon, upon whom he invokes the vengeance of Heaven. Even the courtiers themselves are enraged at Rigoletto's taunts, and determine to assist in Monterone's revenge by stealing Gilda, the jester's daughter, whom they suppose to be his mistress. Closely as she had been concealed, she had not escaped the observation of the Duke, who in the guise of a poor student wins her affections and discovers her dwelling-place. Pretending that it is Count Ceprano's wife whom they are about to abduct, they even make Rigoletto assist in the plot and help convey his own daughter to the Duke's apartments. In his blind fury when he discovers the trick that has been played upon him, he hires Sparafucile, a professional assassin, to kill the Duke. The bravo allures the Duke to his house, intending to carry out his agreement; but his sister, Magdalena, is so fascinated with the handsome stranger, that she determines to save him. Sparafucile at first will not listen to her, but finally promises if any one else comes to the house before the time agreed upon for the murder he shall be the victim. Rigoletto meanwhile disguises his daughter in male attire in order that she may escape to Verona; but before she sets out he takes her to the vicinity of Sparafucile's house, that she may witness the perfidy of the Duke. While outside, she overhears the quarrel between Sparafucile and Magdalena, and learns his intention to murder the Duke, who is even then sleeping in the house. With a woman's devotion she springs forward to save the Duke's life, knocks at the door, and demands admittance. Sparafucile opens it, and as she enters stabs her. He then thrusts her body into a sack, and delivers it to her father as the body of the man whom he had agreed to slay. Rigoletto, gloating over his revenge, is about to throw the sack into the river near by, when he suddenly hears the voice of the Duke. He tears open the sack to see whose body it contains, and by the glare of the lightning is horrified to find that it is his own daughter, and realizes that the malediction of Monterone has been accomplished. She expires in his arms, blessing her lover and father, while he sinks to the ground overwhelmed with the fulfilment of the terrible curse.

The first act opens in the ballroom of the ducal palace. After a brief dialogue between the Duke and one of his courtiers, the former vaunts his own fickleness in one of the most graceful and charming arias in the whole opera ("Questa o quella"). Some spirited dramatic scenes follow, which introduce the malediction of Monterone and the compact between Rigoletto and Sparafucile, and lead up to a scena of great power ("Io la lingua, egli ha il pugnali"), in which the buffoon vents his furious rage against the courtiers. A tender duet between Rigoletto and Gilda follows, and a second duet in the next scene between

Gilda and the Duke ("Addio, speranza ed anima"), which for natural grace, passionate intensity, and fervid expression is one of Verdi's finest numbers. As the Duke leaves, Gilda, following him with her eyes, breaks out in the passionate love-song, "Caro nome," which is not alone remarkable for its delicacy and richness of melody, but also for the brilliancy of its bravura, calling for rare range and flexibility of voice. The act closes with the abduction, and gives an opportunity for a delightful male chorus ("Zitti, zitti") sung pianissimo.

The second act also opens in the palace, with an aria by the Duke ("Parmi veder le lagrime"), in which he laments the loss of Gilda. Another fine chorus ("Scorrendo uniti remota via") follows, from which he learns that Gilda is already in the palace. In the fourth scene Rigoletto has another grand scena ("Cortigiani vil razza dannata"), which is intensely dramatic, expressing in its musical alternations the whole gamut of emotions, from the fury of despair to the most exquisite tenderness of appeal as he pleads with the courtiers to tell him where his daughter is. In the next scene he discovers her, and the act closes with a duet between them ("Tutte le feste al tempio"), which, after a strain of most impassioned tenderness, is interrupted by the passage of the guards conveying Monterone to prison, and then closes with a furious outburst of passion from Rigoletto. With the exception of two numbers, the last act depends for its effect upon the dramatic situations and the great power of the terrible denouement; but these two numbers are among the finest Verdi has ever given to the world. The first is the tenor solo sung in Sparafucile's house in the second scene by the Duke ("La donna e mobile"), an aria of extreme elegance and graceful abandon, which is heard again in the last scene, its lightly tripping measures contrasting strangely with the savage glee of Rigoletto, so soon to change to wails of despair as he realizes the full force of the malediction. The second is the great quartet in the third scene between the Duke, Gilda, Magdalena, and Rigoletto ("Bella figlia dell' amore") which stands out as an inspiration in comparison with the rest of the opera, fine as its music is. The story itself is almost too repulsive for stage representation; but in beauty, freshness, originality, and dramatic expression the music of "Rigoletto" is Verdi's best; and in all this music the quartet is the masterpiece.

La Traviata

"La Traviata," opera in three acts, text by Piave, is founded upon Dumas's "Dame aux Camelias," familiar to the English stage as "Camille," and was first produced at Venice, March 6, 1853, with the following cast of the principal parts:

Violetta . . . . Mme. DONATELLI.
Alfredo . . . . M. GRAZIANI.
Germont . . . . M. VARESI.

The original play is supposed to represent phases of modern French life; but the Italian libretto changes the period to the year 1700, in the days of Louis XIV.; and there are also some material changes of characters, — Marguerite Gauthier of the original appearing as Violetta Valery, and Olympia as Flora Belvoix, at whose house the ball scene takes place.

The opera at its first production was a complete failure, though this was due more to the singers than to the music. It is said that when the doctor announced in the third act that Mme. Donatelli, who impersonated the consumptive heroine, and who was one of the stoutest ladies ever seen on the stage, had but a few days to live, the whole audience broke out into roars of laughter. Time has brought its consolations to the composer, however, for "Traviata"

Geraldine Farrar as *Violetta*

is now one of the most popular operas in the Italian repertory. When it was first produced in Paris, October 27, 1864, Christine Nilsson made her debut in it. In London, the charming little singer Mme. Piccolomini made her debut in the same opera, May 24, 1856. Adelina Patti, subsequently, not only made Violetta the strongest character in her repertory, but has been without question the most finished representative of the fragile heroine the stage has seen.

The story as told by the librettist simply resolves itself into three principal scenes, — the supper at Violetta's house, where she makes the acquaintance of Alfred, and the rupture between them occasioned by the arrival of Alfred's father; the ball at the house of Flora; and the death scene and reconciliation, linked together by recitative, so that the dramatic unity of the original is lost to a certain extent. The first act opens with a gay party in Violetta's house. Among the crowd about her is Alfred Germont, a young man from Provence, who is passionately in love with her. The sincerity of his passion finally influences her to turn aside from her life of voluptuous pleasure and to cherish a similar sentiment for him. In the next act we find her living in seclusion with her lover in a country-house in the environs of Paris, to support which she has sold her property in the city. When Alfred discovers this he refuses to be the recipient of her bounty, and sets out for Paris to recover the property. During his absence his father, who has discovered his retreat, visits Violetta, and pleads with her to forsake Alfred, not only on his own account, but to save his family from disgrace. Touched by the father's grief, she consents, and secretly returns to Paris, where she once more resumes her old life. At a ball given by Flora Belvoix, one of Violetta's associates, Alfred meets her again, overwhelms her with reproaches, and insults her by flinging her miniature at her feet in presence of the whole company. Stung by her degradation, Violetta goes home to die, and too late Alfred learns the real sacrifice she has made. He hastens to comfort her, but she dies forgiving and blessing him.

After a short prelude the first act opens with a vivacious chorus of the guests at Violetta's supper, leading to a drinking song ("Libiamo, libiamo") in waltz time, sung first by Alfred and then by Violetta, the chorus echoing each couplet with very pretty effect. After a long dialogue between the two, closing with chorus, Violetta has a grand scena which is always a favorite show-piece with concert artists. It begins with an andante movement ("Ah! fors e lui"), expressive of the suddenly awakened love which she feels for Alfred, with a refrain of half a dozen measures in the finale which might be called the Violetta motive, and then suddenly develops into a brisk and sparkling allegro ("Sempre libera") full of the most florid and brilliant ornamentation, in which she again resolves to shut out every feeling of love and plunge into the whirl of dissipation. This number, unlike most of Verdi's finales which are concerted, closes the act.

The second act opens in the country-house with an effective tenor aria ("De' miei bollenti") sung by Alfred. In the next scene Germont enters, and after a brief dialogue with Violetta sings a short cantabile ("Pura siccome un angelo"), leading to a duet ("Dite alla giovine") with Violetta which is full of tenderness. In the interview which immediately follows between Germont and Alfred, the father appeals to his son with memories of home in an andante ("Di Provenza il mar") which in form and simplicity and simple pathos of expression might almost be called a ballad. It is always a favorite, and is usually considered the best number in the opera, notwithstanding its simple melody. The next scene changes to the ballroom of Flora, and is introduced with a peculiar chorus effect. A masked chorus of gypsies, accompanying their measures with tambourines, is followed by a second chorus of matadors, also in mask, who accent the time with the pikes they carry, the double number ending with a gay bolero. The act closes with a long duet between Violetta and Alfred, developing in the finale, by the entrance of Germont, into a very strong and dramatic trio.

The third act opens in Violetta's chamber with a reminiscence of the introduction. As she contemplates her changed appearance in the mirror, she bids a sad farewell to her dreams of happiness in the aria ("Addio! del passato") in harsh contrast with which is heard a bacchanalian chorus behind the scenes ("Largo al quadrupede"). In the next scene occurs the passionate duet with Alfred ("Parigi, o cara"), which is a close copy of the final duet in "Trovatore," between Manrico and Azucena. It is followed by the aria ("Ah! gran Dio") for Violetta, which leads to the concluding quintet and death scene.

Il Trovatore

"Il Trovatore," opera in four acts, words by Cammarano, was first produced in Rome, January 19, 1853, with Mme. Penco, Mme. Goggi, MM. Baucardé, Guicciardi, and Balderi in the cast. In 1857 it was brought out in Paris as "Le Trouvere," with Mario as the Count, Mme. Frezzolini as Leonora, and Mme. Borghi-Mamo as Azucena, and in London, 1856, in English, as "The Gypsy's Vengeance." It was first produced in New York with Signora Steffernone, Signorina Vestvali, Signori Brignoli, and Amodio in the cast May 2, 1855. It was produced in Rome in the same year with "La Traviata," but unlike the latter, it was greeted at once with an enthusiastic welcome. It has held the stage ever since and shares with "Martha" and "Faust" a high place in popular admiration.

The opera opens with a midnight scene at the palace of

Aliaferia, where the old servitor, Ferrando, relates to his associates the story of the fate of Garzia, brother of the Count di Luna, in whose service they are employed. While in their cradles, Garzia was bewitched by an old gypsy, and day by day pined away. The gypsy was burned at the stake for sorcery; and in revenge Azucena, her daughter, stole the sickly child. At the opening of the opera his fate has not been discovered. As the servitor closes his narrative and he and his companions depart, the Count di Luna enters and lingers by the apartment of the Duchess Leonora, with whom he is in love. Hearing his voice, Leonora comes into the garden, supposing it is Manrico, the troubadour, whom she had crowned victor at a recent tournament, and of whom she had become violently enamored. As she greets the Count, Manrico appears upon the scene and charges her with infidelity. Recognizing her error, she flies to Manrico for protection. The Count challenges him to combat, and as they prepare to fight she falls to the ground insensible.

In the second act we are introduced to a gypsy camp, where Azucena relates to Manrico, who has been wounded in the duel with the Count, the same story which Ferrando had told his friends, with the addition that when she saw her mother burning she caught up the Count's child, intending to throw it into the flames, but by a mistake sacrificed her own infant. As the story concludes, a messenger arrives, summoning Manrico to the defence of the castle of Castellar, and at the same time informing him that Leonora, supposing him dead, has gone to a convent. He arrives at the convent in time to rescue her before she takes her vows, and bears her to Castellar, which is at once besieged by the Count's forces.

The third act opens in the camp of the Count, where Azucena, arrested as a spy, is dragged in. She calls upon Manrico for help. The mention of his rival's name only

Campanini as *Manrico*

adds fuel to the Count's wrath, and he orders the gypsy to be burned in sight of the castle. Ferrando has already recognized her as the supposed murderer of the Count's brother, and her filial call to Manrico also reveals to him that she is his mother. He makes a desperate effort to rescue her, but is defeated, taken prisoner, and thrown into a dungeon with Azucena. Leonora vainly appeals to the Count to spare Manrico, and at last offers him her hand if he will save his life. He consents, and Leonora hastens to the prison to convey the tidings, having previously taken poison, preferring to die rather than fulfil her hateful compact. Manrico refuses his liberty, and as Leonora falls in a dying condition the Count enters and orders Manrico to be put to death at once. He is dragged away to execution, but as the Count triumphantly forces Azucena to a window and shows her the tragic scene, she reveals her secret, and informing the horror-stricken Count that he has murdered his own brother, falls lifeless to the ground.

The first act opens with a ballad in mazurka time ("Abbietta Zingara"), in which Ferrando relates the story of the gypsy, leading up to a scena for Leonora, which is treated in Verdi's favorite style. It begins with an andante ("Tacea la notte placida"), a brief dialogue with her attendant Inez intervening, and then develops into an allegro ("Di tale amor") which is a brilliant bit of bravura. A brief snatch of fascinating melody behind the scenes ("Deserto sulla terra") introduces Manrico, and the act closes with a trio ("Di geloso amor sprezzato"), which as an expression of combined grief, fear, and hate, is one of the most dramatic and intense of all Verdi's finales.

The second act opens with the Anvil Chorus in the camp of the gypsies ("La Zingarella"), the measures accented with hammers upon the anvils. This number is so familiar that it does not need further reference. As its strains die away in the distance, Azucena breaks out into an aria of intense energy, with very expressive accompaniment ("Stride la vampa"), in which she tells the fearful story of the burning of her mother. A very dramatic dialogue with Manrico ensues, closing with a spirited aria for tenor ("Mal reggendo") and duet ("Sino all' elsa"). The scene is interrupted by the notes of a horn announcing the arrival of a messenger. The second scene is introduced by a flowing, broad, and beautifully sustained aria for the Count ("Il balen del suo"), and, like Leonora's numbers in the garden scene, again develops from a slow movement to a rapid and spirited march tempo ("Per me ora fatale"), the act closing with a powerful concerted effect of quartet and chorus.

The third act is introduced with a very free and animated soldiers' chorus. Azucena is dragged in and sings a plaintive lament for Manrico ("Giorni poveri"). Two duets follow, between Azucena and the Count, and Manrico and Leonora, — the second worked up with beautiful effect by the blending of the organ in the convent chapel. The act closes with the spirited aria, "Di quella pirra," for Manrico, — a number which has always been the delight of great dramatic tenors, not alone for its fine melody, but for its opportunity of showing the voice and using the exceptional high C in the finale of the aria.

The last act is replete with beautiful melodies following each other in quick succession. It opens with a very florid aria for Leonora ("D' amor sull' ali rose"), leading to the exquisite scene of the Miserere ("Ah, che la morte") — a number which has never yet failed to charm and arouse audiences with the beauty and richness of its musical effect. As the Count enters, Leonora has another powerful aria ("Mira, di acerbe"), which in the next scene is followed by the familiar duet between Azucena and Manrico ("Si la stanchezza"), upon which Verdi lavished his musical skill with charming effect. The last scene closes with the tragedy. The whole opera is liberally enriched with melodies, and is dramatic throughout; but the last act is the crown of the work, and may successfully challenge comparison, for beauty, variety, and dramatic effect, with any other opera in the purely Italian school.

THE MASKED BALL

"Il Ballo in Maschera," opera in three acts, text by M. Somma, was first produced in Rome, February 17, 1859, with Fraschini as Ricardo and Mlle. Lagrua as Amelie. In preparing his work for the stage, Verdi encountered numerous obstacles. The librettist used the same subject which M. Scribe had adapted for Auber's opera ("Gustavus III."), and the opera was at first called by the same name, — "Gustavo III." It was intended for production at the San Carlo, Naples, during the Carnival of 1858; but while the rehearsals were proceeding, Orsini made his memorable attempt to kill Napoleon III., and the authorities at once forbade a performance of the work, as it contained a conspiracy scene. The composer was ordered to set different words to his music, but he peremptorily refused; whereupon the manager brought suit against him, claiming forty thousand dollars' damages. The disappointment nearly incited a revolution in Naples. Crowds gathered in the streets shouting, "Viva Verdi," implying at the same time, by the use of the letters in Verdi's name, the sentiment, "Viva Vittorio Emmanuele Re Di Italia." A way out of his difficulties, however, was finally suggested by the impresario at Rome, who arranged with the censorship to have the work brought out at the Teatro Apollo as "Un Ballo in Maschera." The scene was changed to Boston, Massachusetts, and the time laid in the colonial period, notwithstanding the anachronism that masked balls were unknown at that time in New England history. The Swedish king appeared as Ricardo, Count of Warwick and Governor of Boston, and his attendants as Royalists and Puritans, among them two negroes, Sam and Tom, who are very prominent among the conspirators. In this form, the Romans having no objection to the assassination of an English governor, the opera was produced with great success.

The first act opens in the house of the Governor, where a large party, among them a group of conspirators, is assembled. During the meeting a petition is presented for the banishment of Ulrico, a negro sorcerer. Urged by curiosity, the Governor, disguised as a sailor and accompanied by some of his friends, pays the old witch a visit. Meanwhile another visit has been planned. Amelie, the wife of the Governor's secretary, meets the witch at night in quest of a remedy for her passion for Richard, who of course has also been fascinated by her. They arrive about the same time, and he overhears the witch telling her to go to a lonely spot, where she will find an herb potent enough to cure her of her evil desires. The Governor follows her, and during their interview the Secretary hurriedly rushes upon the scene to notify him that conspirators are on his track. He throws a veil over Amelie's face and orders Reinhart, the Secretary, to conduct her to a place of safety without seeking to know who she is. He consents, and the Governor conceals himself in the forest. The conspirators meanwhile meet the pair, and in the confusion Amelie drops her veil, thus revealing herself to Reinhart. Furious at the Governor's perfidy, he joins the conspirators. In the denouement the Secretary stabs his master at a masquerade, and the latter while dying attests the purity of Amelie, and magnanimously gives his secretary a commission appointing him to a high position in England.

After a brief prelude, the first act opens with a double chorus, in which the attitude of the friends of the Governor and the conspirators against him is strongly contrasted. In the next scene Richard and his page, Oscar, enter; and

Emma Eames as *Amelia*

Copyright, Aimé Dupont

VERDI

after a short dialogue Richard sings a very graceful romanza ("La rivedra nell' estasi"), which in the next scene is followed by a spirited aria for Reinhart ("Di speranze e glorie piena"). In the fourth scene Oscar has a very pretty song ("Volta la terrea"), in which he defends Ulrico against the accusations of the judge, leading up to a very effective quintet and chorus which has a flavor of the opera bouffe style. In grim contrast with it comes the witch music in the next scene ("Re del abisso"), set to a weird accompaniment. As the various parties arrive, a somewhat talky trio ensues between Amelie, Ulrico, and Richard, followed in the next scene by a lovely barcarole ("Di' tu se fedele"), sung by Richard, leading to a concerted finale full of sharp dramatic contrasts.

The second act opens upon a moonlight scene on the spot where murderers are punished; and Amelie, searching for the magic herb, sings a long dramatic aria ("Ma dall arido") consisting of abrupt and broken measures, the orchestra filling the gaps with characteristic accompaniment. Richard appears upon the scene, and the passionate love-duet follows ("M' ami, m' ami"). The interview is ended by the sudden appearance of Reinhart, who warns the Governor of his danger, the scene taking the form of a spirited trio ("Odi tu come"). A buffo trio closes the act, Sam and Tom supplying the humorous element with their laughing refrain.

The last act opens in Reinhart's house with a passionate scene between the Secretary and his wife, containing two strong numbers, a minor andante ("Morro, ma prima in grazia") for Amelie, and an aria for Reinhart ("O dolcezzo perdute"), which for originality and true artistic power is worthy of being classed as an inspiration. The conspiracy music then begins, and leads to the ball scene, which is most brilliantly worked up with orchestra, military band, and stringed quartet behind the scenes supplying the dance music, and the accompaniment to the tragical conspiracy, in the midst of which, like a bright sunbeam, comes the page's bewitching song, "Saper vorreste." The opera closes with the death of Richard, set to a very dramatic accompaniment. "The Masked Ball" was the last work Verdi wrote for the Italian stage, and though uneven in its general effect, it contains some of his most original and striking numbers, — particularly those allotted to the page and Reinhart. In the intensity of the music and the strength of the situations it is superior even to "Trovatore," as the composer makes his effects more legitimately.

AÏDA

"Aïda," opera in four acts, was first produced for the inauguration of the new opera house at Cairo, Egypt, December 24, 1871, and was written upon a commission from the Khedive of that country, with the following cast:

Aïda	Signora POZZONI.
Amneris	Signora GROSSI.
Rhadames	Signor MONGINI.
Amonasro	Signor COSTA.
Ramfis	Signor MEDINI.
King	Signor STELLER.

The subject of the opera was taken from a sketch, originally written in prose, by the director of the Museum at Boulak, which was afterwards rendered into French verse by M. Camille de Locle, and translated thence into Italian for Verdi by Sig. A. Ghizlandoni. It is notable for Verdi's departure from the conventional Italian forms and the partial surrender he made to the constantly increasing influence of the so-called "music of the future." The subject is entirely Egyptian, and the music is full of Oriental color.

The action of the opera passes in Memphis and Thebes,

Gadski as *Aïda*

and the period is in the time of the Pharaohs. Aïda, the heroine, is a slave, daughter of Amonasro, the King of Ethiopia, and at the opening of the opera is in captivity among the Egyptians. A secret attachment exists between herself and Rhadames, a young Egyptian warrior, who is also loved by Amneris, daughter of the sovereign of Egypt. The latter suspects that she has a rival, but does not discover her until Rhadames returns victorious from an expedition against the rebellious Amonasro, who is brought back a prisoner. The second act opens with a scene between Amneris and Aïda, in which the Princess wrests the secret from the slave by pretending that Rhadames has been killed; and the truth is still further revealed when Rhadames pleads with the King to spare the lives of the captives. The latter agrees to release all but Aïda and Amonasro, bestows the hand of Amneris upon the unwilling conqueror, and the act closes amid general jubilation. Acting upon Amonasro's admonitions, Aïda influences Rhadames to fly from Egypt and espouse the cause of her father. The lovers are overheard by Amneris and Ramfis, the high priest. The Princess, with all the fury of a woman scorned, denounces Rhadames as a traitor. He is tried for treason and condemned to be buried alive in the vaults under the temple of the god Phtah. Pardon is offered him if he will accept the hand of Amneris, but he refuses and descends to the tomb, where he finds Aïda awaiting him. The stones are sealed above them and the lovers are united in death, while Amneris, heart-broken over the tragedy her jealousy has caused, kneels in prayer before their sepulchre.

After a short prelude, consisting of a beautiful pianissimo movement, mainly for the violins, and very Wagnerian in its general style, the first act opens in the hall of the King's palace at Memphis. A short dialogue between Rhadames and the priest Ramfis leads to a delicious romanza ("Céleste

Aïda") which is entirely fresh and original, recalling nothing that appears in any of Verdi's previous works. It is followed by a strong declamatory duet between Rhadames and Amneris, which upon the appearance of Aïda develops into a trio ("Vieni, o diletta"). In the next scene the King and his retinue of ministers, priests, and warriors enter, and a majestic ensemble occurs, beginning with a martial chorus ("Su! del Nilo") in response to the appeal of the priests. As the war chorus dies away and the retinue disappears, Aïda has a scena of great power. It begins with a lament for her country ("Ritorna vincitor"), in passionate declamatory phrases, clearly showing the influence of Wagner; but in its smooth, flowing cantabile in the finale ("Numi, pietà"), Verdi returns to the Italian style again. The final scene is full of Oriental color and barbaric richness of display. The consecrated arms are delivered to Rhadames. The priestesses behind the scene to the accompaniment of harps, and the priests in front with sonorous chant, invoke the aid of the god Phtah, while other priestesses execute the sacred dance. An impressive duet between Ramfis and Rhadames closes the act. In this finale, Verdi has utilized two native Egyptian themes, — the melody sung by the priestesses with the harps, and the dance-melody given out by the flutes.

The second act opens with a female chorus by the slave girls, the rhythm of which is in keeping with the Oriental scene, followed by an impassioned duet between Amneris and Aïda ("Alla pompa che si appresta"), through which are heard the martial strains of the returning conqueror. The second scene opens the way for another ensemble, which with its massive choruses, and its stirring march and ballet, heralding the victory of Rhadames, is one of the most picturesque stage scenes the opera has ever furnished. A solemn, plaintive strain runs through the general jubilation

Marie Brema as *Amneris*

VERDI

in the appeal of Amonasro ("Questa assisa ch' io vesto") to the King for mercy to the captives. The finale begins with the remonstrances of the priests and people against the appeals of Amonasro and Rhadames, and closes with an intensely dramatic concerted number, — a quintet set off against the successive choruses of the priests, prisoners, and people ("Gloria all' Egitto").

The third act, like the first, after a brief dialogue, opens with a lovely romanza ("O cieli azzurri"), sung by Aïda, and the remainder of the act is devoted to two duets, — the first between Amonasro and Aïda, and the second between Rhadames and Aïda. Each is very dramatic in style and passionate declamation, while they are revelations in the direction of combining the poetic and musical elements, when compared with any of the duets in Verdi's previous operas. In the last act the first scene contains another impressive duet between Rhadames and Amneris ("Chi ti salva, o sciagurato"), ending with the despairing song of Amneris ("Ohimè! morir mi sento"). In the last scene the stage is divided into two parts. The upper represents the temple of Vulcan, or Phtah, crowded with priests and priestesses, chanting as the stone is closed over the subterranean entrance, while below, in the tomb, Aïda and Rhadames sing their dying duet ("O terra, addio"), its strains blending with the jubilation of the priests and the measures of the priestesses' sacred dance. "Aïda" is unquestionably the greatest, if not the most popular, of Verdi's works. It marks a long step from the style of his other operas towards the production of dramatic effect by legitimate musical means, and shows the strong influence Wagner had upon him.

OTHELLO

"Othello," opera in four acts, text by Boito, after the Shakesperean tragedy, first produced at La Scala Theatre, Milan, February 5, 1887, with the following cast:

Othello	Sig. TAMAGNO.
Iago	Sig. MAUREL.
Cassio	Sig. PAROLI.
Roderigo	Sig. FORNARI.
Ludovico	Sig. NAVARRINI.
Desdemona	Signora PANTALEONI

The curtain rises upon a scene in Cyprus. A storm is raging, and a crowd, among them Iago, Cassio, and Roderigo, watch the angry sea, speculating upon the fate of Othello's vessel, which finally arrives safely in port amid much rejoicing. After returning the welcomes of his friends he enters the castle with Cassio and Montano. The conspiracy at once begins by the disclosure by Iago to Roderigo of the means by which Cassio's ruin may be compassed. Then follows the quarrel, which is interrupted by the appearance of Othello, who deprives Cassio of his office. A love scene ensues between Desdemona and the Moor; but in the next act the malignity of Iago has already begun to take effect, and the seeds of jealousy are sown in Othello's breast. His suspicions are freshly aroused when Desdemona intercedes in Cassio's behalf, and are changed to conviction by the handkerchief episode and Iago's artful insinuation that Cassio mutters the name of Desdemona in his sleep; at which the enraged Moor clutches him by the throat and hurls him to the ground. In the third act Iago continues his diabolical purpose, at last so inflaming Othello's mind that he denounces Desdemona for her perfidy. The act concludes with the audience to the Venetian embassy, during which he becomes enraged, strikes Desdemona, and falls in convulsions. The last act transpires in her chamber, and follows Shakespeare in all the details of the smothering of Desdemona and the death of Othello.

There is no overture proper to the opera. After a few vigorous bars of prelude, the scene opens with a tempestuous and very striking description of a sea-storm by the orchestra, with the choruses of sailors and Cypriots rising above it and expressing alternate hope and terror. After a short recitative the storm dies away, and the choral phrases of rejoicing end in a pianissimo effect. A hurried recitative passage between Iago and Roderigo introduces a drinking scene in which Iago sings a very original and expressive brindisi with rollicking responses by the chorus ("Inaffia l'ugola-trinca tra canna"). The quarrel follows, with a vigorous and agitated accompaniment, and the act comes to a close with a beautiful love-duet between Othello and Desdemona ("Già nella notte deusa").

The second act opens with recitative which reveals all of Iago's malignity, and is followed by his monologue, in which he sings a mock Credo ("Credo in un Dio crudel") which is Satanic in utterance. It is accompanied with tremendous outbursts of trumpets, and leads up to a furious declamatory duet with Othello ("Miseria mia"). The next number brings a grateful change. It is a graceful mandolinata ("Dove guardi splendono") sung by children's voices and accompanied by mandolins and guitars, followed by a charming chorus of mariners, who bring shells and corals to Desdemona. The intercession episode ensues, leading to a grand dramatic quartet for Desdemona, Emilia, Iago, and Othello. The latter then sings a pathetic but stirring melody with trumpet accompaniment, the farewell to war ("Addio sublimi incanti"), and the act closes with a tumultuous duet between himself and Iago.

The third act opens with a very expressive duet for Othello and Desdemona ("Dio ti giocondi"), in which the growing wrath of the former and the sweet and touching unconsciousness of the other are happily contrasted. A sad monologue by Othello ("Dio! mi potevi scagliar") prepares the way for the coming outbreak. The handkerchief trio follows, in which the malignity of Iago, the indignation of Othello, and the inability of Cassio to understand the fell purpose of Iago are brought out with great force. At its close a fanfare of trumpets announces the Venetian embassy, and the finale begins with much brilliancy. Then follows the scene in which Othello smites down Desdemona. She supplicates for mercy in an aria of tender beauty ("A terra! si, nel livido"), which leads up to a strong sextet. All the guests depart but Iago; and as Othello, overcome with his emotions, swoons away, the curtain falls upon Iago's contemptuous utterance, "There lies the lion of Venice."

The fourth act is full of musical beauty. After an orchestral introduction in which the horn has a very effective solo, the curtain rises and the action transpires in Desdemona's chamber. The scene opens with a touching recitative between Desdemona and Emilia. While the former prepares herself for slumber she sings the 'Willow Song" ("Piangea cantando"), an unaffected melody as simple and characteristic as a folk-song. Emilia retires, and by a natural transition Desdemona sings an "Ave Maria" ("Ave Maria plena de' grazia"), which is as simple and beautiful in its way as the "Willow Song." She retires to her couch, and in the silence Othello steals in, dagger in hand, the contra-basses giving out a sombre and deep-toned accompaniment which is startling in its effect. He kisses her, the motive from the love-duet appearing in the orchestra; then, after a hurried dialogue, stifles her. He then kills himself, his last words being a

Tamagno as *Othello*

Copyright, Falk

repetition of those in the duet, while the strings tenderly give out the melody again.

FALSTAFF

"Falstaff," opera in three acts, text by Arrigo Boito, was first performed March 12, 1893, at the Teatro alla Scala, Milan, with the following cast of characters:

Mistress Ford	Signora ZILLI.
Nannetta	Madame STEHLE.
Fenton	M. GARBIN.
Dr. Caius	Sig. PAROLI.
Pistola	Sig. ARIMONDI.
Mistress Page	Signora GUERRINI.
Mistress Quickly	Signora PASQUA.
Ford	Sig. PINI-CORSI.
Bardolfo	Sig. PELAGALLI-ROSSETTI.
Falstaff	M. MAUREL.

The libretto, though mainly based upon "The Merry Wives of Windsor," also levies some contributions upon "Henry IV," particularly in the introduction of the monologue upon honor, and illustrates Boito's skill in adaptation as well as his remarkable powers in condensation. In the arrangement of the comedy the five acts are reduced to three. The characters Shallow, Slender, William, Page, Sir Hugh Evans, Simple, and Rugby are eliminated, leaving Falstaff, Fenton, Ford, Dr. Caius, Bardolph, Pistol, Mistress Ford, Mistress Page, Anne, Dame Quickly, and three minor characters as the *dramatis personæ*, though Anne appears as Nannetta and is the daughter of Ford instead of Page.

The first act opens with a scene at the Garter Inn, disclosing an interview between Falstaff and Dr. Caius, who is complaining of the ill treatment he has received from the fat Knight and his followers, but without obtaining any satisfaction. After his departure, Falstaff seeks to induce Bardolph and Pistol to carry his love letters to

Mistresses Ford and Page; but they refuse, upon the ground that their honor would be assailed, which gives occasion for the introduction of the monologue from "Henry IV." The letters are finally intrusted to a page, and the remainder of the act is devoted to the plots of the women to circumvent him, with an incidental revelation of the loves of Fenton and Nannetta, or Anne Page. In the second act, we have Falstaff's visit to Mistress Ford, as planned by the merry wives, the comical episode of his concealment in the buck-basket, and his dumping into the Thames. In the last act, undaunted by his watery experiences, Falstaff accepts a fresh invitation to meet Mistress Ford in Windsor Park. In this episode occurs the fairy masquerade at Herne's Oak, in the midst of which he is set upon and beaten, ending in his complete discomfiture. Then all is explained to him; Nannetta is betrothed to Fenton; and all ends, merry as a marriage bell.

There is no overture. After four bars of prelude the curtain rises, and the composer introduces Dr. Caius with the single exclamation, "Falstaff," and the latter's reply, "Ho! there," which are emblematic of the declamatory character of the whole opera; for although many delightful bits of melody are scattered through it, the instrumentation really tells the story, as in the Wagner music-drama, though in this latest work of the veteran composer there is less of the Wagnerian idea than in his "Aïda." The first scene is mainly humorous dialogue, but there are two notable exceptions, — the genuine lyrical music of Falstaff's song ("'T is she with Eyes like Stars"), and the Honor monologue, a superb piece of recitative with a characteristic accompaniment in which the clarinets and bassoons fairly talk, as they give the negative to the Knight's sarcastic questions. The most attractive numbers of the second scene are Mistress Ford's reading of

Falstaff's letter, which is exquisitely lyrical, a quartet, a capella, for the four women ("He'll surely come courting"), followed by a contrasting male quartet ("He's a foul, a ribald Thief"), the act closing with the two quartets offsetting each other, and enclosing an admirable solo for Fenton.

The second act opens with the interview between Dame Quickly and Falstaff, in which the instrumentation runs the whole gamut of ironical humor. Then follows the scene between Ford and Falstaff, in which the very clink of the money, and Falstaff's huge chuckles, are deliberately set forth in the orchestra with a realism which is the very height of the ridiculous, the scene closing with an expressive declamation by Ford ("Do I dream? Or, is it reality?"). The second scene of the act is mainly devoted to the ludicrous incident of the buck-basket, which is accompanied by most remarkable instrumentation; but there are one or more captivating episodes; such as Dame Quickly's description of her visit ("'T was at the Garter Inn") and Falstaff's charming song ("Once I was Page to the Duke of Norfolk").

The third act opens in the Inn of the Garter, and discloses Falstaff soliloquizing upon his late disagreeable experiences:

> "Ho! landlord!
> Ungrateful world, wicked world,
> Guilty world!
> Landlord! a glass of hot sherry.
> Go, go thy way, John Falstaff,
> With thee will cease the type
> Of honesty, virtue, and might."

As the fat Knight soliloquizes and drinks his sack the orchestra joins in a trill given out by piccolo, and gradually taken by one instrument after the other, until the whole orchestra is in a hearty laugh and shaking with string, brass, and wood-wind glee. Then enters Dame Quickly, mischief-maker, and sets the trap at Herne's Oak in Windsor Forest, into which Falstaff readily falls. The closing scene is rich with humor. It opens with a delightful love song by Fenton ("From those sweet Lips a Song of Love arises"). The conspirators enter one after the other, and at last Falstaff, disguised as the sable hunter. The elves are summoned, and glide about to the delicious fairy music accompanying Nannetta's beautiful song ("While we dance in the Moonlight"). From this point the action hastens to the happy denouement, and the work concludes with a fugue which is imbued with the very spirit of humor and yet is strictly constructed. While the vocal parts are extraordinary in their declamatory significance, the strength of the opera lies in the instrumentation, and its charm in the delicious fun and merriment which pervade it all and are aptly expressed in the closing lines:

> "All in this world is jesting.
> Man is born to be jolly,
> E'en from grief some happiness wresting
> Sure proof against melancholy."

WAGNER

RICHARD WAGNER, who has been somewhat ironically called "the musician of the future," and whose music has been relegated to posterity by a considerable number of his contemporaries, was born at Leipsic, May 22, 1813. After his preliminary studies in Dresden and Leipsic, he took his first lessons in music from Cantor Weinlig. In 1836 he was appointed musical director in the theatre at Magdeburg, and later occupied the same position at Königsberg. Thence he went to Riga, where he began his opera "Rienzi." He then went to Paris by sea, was nearly shipwrecked on his way thither, and landed without money or friends. After two years of hard struggles he returned to Germany. His shipwreck and forlorn condition inspired the theme of "The Flying Dutchman," and while on his way to Dresden he passed near the castle of Wartburg, in the valley of Thuringia, whose legends inspired his well-known opera of "Tannhäuser." He next removed to Zurich, and about this time appeared "Lohengrin," one of his most popular operas. "Tristan and Isolde" was produced in 1856, and his comic opera, "Die Meistersinger von Nürnberg," three years later. In 1864 he received the patronage of King Louis of Bavaria, which enabled him to complete and perform his great work, "Der Ring der Nibelungen." He laid the foundation of the new theatre at Baireuth in 1872, and in 1875 the Ring was produced, and created a profound sensation all over the musical world. "Parsifal," his last opera, was first performed in 1882. His works have aroused great opposition, especially among conservative musicians, for the reason that he has set at defiance the conventional operatic forms, and in carrying out his theory of making the musical and dramatic elements of equal importance, and employing the former as the language of the latter in natural ways, has made musical declamation take the place of set melody, and swept away the customary arias, duets, quartets, and concerted numbers of the Italian school, to suit the dramatic exigencies of the situations. Besides his musical compositions, he enjoys almost equal fame as a *littérateur*, having written not only his own librettos, but four important works, — "Art and the Revolution," "The Art Work of the Future," "Opera and Drama," and "Judaism in Music." His music has made steady progress to success through the efforts of such advocates as Liszt, Von Bülow, and Richter in Germany, PasdeLoup in France, Hueffer in England, with Theodore Thomas and Anton Seidl in the United States. In 1870 he married Frau Cosima von Bülow, the daughter of Liszt, — an event which provoked almost as much comment in social circles as his operas have in musical. He died during a visit to Venice, February 13, 1883.

Rienzi

"Rienzi, der letzte der Tribunen," tragic opera in five acts, text by the composer, the subject taken from Bulwer's novel, "The Last of the Tribunes," was first produced at Dresden, October 20, 1842, with the following cast of leading parts:

Rienzi	Herr TICHATSCHEK.
Irene	Frl. WÜST.
Colonna	Herr DETMER.
Adriano	Mme. SCHRÖDER-DEVRIENT.
Orsini	Herr WACHTER.

The opera was first produced in the United States February 5, 1886. "Rienzi" was designed and partly completed during Wagner's stay in Riga as orchestra leader. In his Autobiography the composer says that he first read the story at Dresden in 1837, and was greatly impressed with its adaptability for opera. He began it in the Fall of the same year at Riga, and says: "I had composed two numbers of it, when I found, to my annoyance, that I was again fairly on the way to the composition of music *à la* Adam. I put the work aside in disgust." Later he projected the scheme of a great tragic opera in five acts, and began working upon it with fresh enthusiasm in the Fall of 1838. By the Spring of 1839 the first two acts were completed. At that time his engagement at Riga terminated, and he set out for Paris. He soon found that it would be hopeless for him to bring out the opera in that city, notwithstanding Meyerbeer had promised to assist him. He offered it to the Grand Opera and to the Renaissance, but neither would accept it. Nothing daunted, he resumed work upon it, intending it for Dresden. In October, 1842, it was at last produced in that city, and met with such success that it secured him the position of capellmeister at the Dresden opera house.

The action of the opera passes at Rome, towards the middle of the fourteenth century. The first act opens at night, in a street near the Church of St. John Lateran, and discovers Orsini, a Roman patrician, accompanied by a crowd of nobles, attempting to abduct Irene, the sister of Rienzi, a papal notary. The plot is interrupted by the entrance of Colonna, the patrician leader of another faction, who demands the girl. A quarrel ensues. Adriano, the son of Colonna, who is in love with Irene, suddenly appears and rushes to her defence. Gradually other patricians and plebeians are attracted by the tumult, among the latter, Rienzi. When he becomes aware of the insult offered his sister, he takes counsel with the Cardinal Raimondo, and they agree to rouse the people in resistance to the outrages of the nobles. Adriano is placed in an embarrassing position, — his relationship to the Colonnas urging him to join the nobles, while his love for Irene impels him with still stronger force to make common cause with the people. He finally decides to follow Rienzi, just as the trumpets are heard calling the people to arms and Rienzi clad in full armor makes his appearance to lead them.

The struggle is a short one. The nobles are overcome, and in the second act they appear at the Capitol to acknowledge their submission to Rienzi: but Adriano, who has been among them, warns Rienzi that they have plotted to kill him. Festal dances, processions, and gladiatorial combats follow, in the midst of which Orsini rushes at Rienzi and strikes at him with his dagger. Rienzi is saved by a steel breastplate under his robes. The nobles are at once seized and condemned to death. Adriano pleads with Rienzi to spare his father, and moved by his eloquence he renews the offer of pardon if they will swear submission. They take the oath only to violate it. The people rise and demand their extermination. Rienzi once more draws the sword, and Adriano in vain appeals to him to avert the slaughter. He is again successful, and on his return announces to Adriano that the Colonnas and Orsinis are no more. The latter warns him of coming revenge, and the act closes with the coronation of Rienzi.

The fourth act opens at night near the church. The popular tide has now turned against Rienzi, because of a report that he is in league with the German Emperor to restore the pontiff. A festive cortege approaches, escorting him to the church. The nobles bar his way, but disperse at his command; whereupon Adriano rushes at him with drawn dagger, but the blow is averted as he hears the chant of malediction in the church, and sees its dignitaries placing the ban of excommunication against Rienzi upon its doors. He hurries to Irene, warns her that her brother's life is no longer safe, and urges her to fly with him. She repulses him, and seeks her brother, to share his dangers or die with him. She finds him at prayer in the Capitol. He advises her to accept the offer of Adriano and save herself, but she repeats her determination to die with him. The tumult of the approaching crowd is heard outside. Rienzi makes a last appeal to them from the balcony, but the infuriated people will not listen. They set fire to the Capitol with their torches, and stone Rienzi and Irene through the windows. As the flames spread from room to room and Adriano beholds them enveloping the devoted pair, he throws away his sword, rushes into the burning building, and perishes with them.

The overture of "Rienzi" is in the accepted form, for the opera was written before Wagner had made his new departure in music, and takes its principal themes, notably Rienzi's prayer for the people and the finale to the first act, from the body of the work. The general style of the whole work is vigorous and tumultuous. The first act opens with a hurly-burly of tumult between the contending factions and the people. The first scene contains a vigorous aria for the hero ("Wohl an so mög es sein"), which leads up to a fiery terzetto ("Adriano du? Wie ein Colonna!") between Rienzi, Irene, and Adriano, followed by an intensely passionate scene ("Er geht und lässt dicht meinem Schutz") between the last two. The finale is a tumultuous mass of sound, through which are heard the tones of trumpets and cries of the people. It opens with a massive double chorus ("Gegrüsst, gegrüsst"), shouted by the people on the one side and the monks in the Lateran on the other, accompanied by an andante movement on the organ. It is interrupted for a brief space by the ringing appeal of Rienzi ("Erstehe, hohe Roma, neu"), and then closes with an energetic andante, a quartet joining the choruses. This finale is clearly Italian in form, and much to Wagner's subsequent disgust was described by Hanslick as a mixture of Donizetti and Meyerbeer, and a clear presage of the coming Verdi.

The second act opens with a stately march, introducing the messengers of peace, who join in a chorus of greeting, followed by a second chorus of senators and the tender of submission made by the nobles. A terzetto between Adriano, Orsini, and Colonna, set off against a chorus of the nobles, leads up to the finale. It opens with a joyful chorus (" Erschallet feier Klänge "), followed by rapid dialogue between Orsini and Colonna on the one hand and Adriano and Rienzi on the other. A long and elaborate ballet intervenes, divided into several numbers, — an Introduction, Pyrrhic Dance, Combat of Roman Gladiators and Cavaliers, and the Dance of the Apotheosis, in which the Goddess of Peace is transformed into the Goddess Protector of Rome. The scene abruptly changes, and the act closes with a great ensemble in which the defiance of the conspirators, the tolling of bells, the chants of the monks, and the ferocious outcries of the people shouting for revenge are mingled in strong contrasts.

The third act is full of tumult. After a brief prelude, amid the ringing of bells and cries of alarm, the people gather and denounce the treachery of the nobles, leading up to a spirited call to arms by Rienzi (" Ihr Römer, auf "). The people respond in furious chorus, and as the sound of the bells and battle-cries dies away Adriano enters. His scene opens with a prayer (" Gerechter Gott ") for the aversion of carnage, which changes to an agitated allegro (" Wo war ich? ") as he hears the great bell of the Capitol tolling the signal for slaughter. The finale begins with a massive march, as the bells and sounds of alarm are heard approaching again, and bands of citizens, priests and monks, the high clergy, senators and nobles, pass and repass in quick succession, followed at last by Rienzi, which is the signal for the great battle hymn, which is "to be sung with great fire and energy, accompanied by great and small bells ringing behind the scenes, the clash of swords upon shields, and full power of chorus and orchestra." A dialogue follows between Adriano and Rienzi, and then the various bands disappear singing the ritornelle of the hymn. A great duet ("Lebwohl, Irene") ensues between Adriano and Irene, which in its general outlines reminds one of the duet between Raoul and Valentin in "The Huguenots." At its conclusion, after a prayer by the chorus of women, the battle hymn is heard again in the distance, gradually approaching, and the act closes with a jubilee chorus ("Auf! im Triumpf zum Capitol"), welcoming the return of the conquerors.

The fourth act is short, its principal numbers being the introduction, terzetto and chorus ("Wer war's der euch hierher beschied?"), and the finale, beginning with a somewhat sombre march of the cortege accompanying Rienzi to the church, leading to the details of the conspiracy scene, and closing with the malediction of the monks ("Vae, vae tibi maledicto"). The last act opens with an impressive prayer by Rienzi ("Allmacht'ger Vater"), which leads to a tender duet ("Verlässt die Kirche mich") as Irene enters, closing with a passionate aria by Rienzi ("Ich liebte glühend"). The duet is then resumed, and leads to a second and intensely passionate duet ("Du hier Irene!") between Adriano and Irene. The finale is brief, but full of energy, and is principally choral. The denouement hurries, and the tragedy is reached amid a tumultuous outburst of voices and instruments. Unlike Wagner's other operas, set melody dominates in "Rienzi," and the orchestra, as in the Italian school, furnishes the accompaniments. We have the regular overture, aria, duet, trio, and concerted finale; but after "Rienzi" we shall observe a change, at last becoming so radical that the composer himself threw aside his first opera as unworthy of performance.

THE FLYING DUTCHMAN

"Der Fliegende Holländer," romantic opera in three acts, text by the composer, the subject taken from Heinrich Heine's version of the legend, was first produced at Dresden, January 2, 1843, with Mme. Schröder-Devrient and Herr Wachter in the two principal roles. It was also produced in London in 1870 at Drury Lane as "L' Ollandose dannato," by Signor Arditi, with Mlle. Di Murska, Signori Foli, Perotti, and Rinaldini, and Mr. Santley in the leading parts; in 1876, by Carl Rosa as "The Flying Dutchman," an English version; and again in 1877 as "Il Vascello Fantasma." In this country the opera was introduced in its English form by Miss Clara Louise Kellogg in 1886. Wagner conceived the idea of writing "The Flying Dutchman" during the storm which overtook him on his voyage from Riga to Paris. He says in his Autobiography: "'The Flying Dutchman,' whose intimate acquaintance I had made at sea, continually enchained my fancy. I had become acquainted, too, with Heinrich Heine's peculiar treatment of the legend in one portion of his 'Salon.' Especially the treatment of the delivery of this Ahasuerus of the ocean (taken by Heine from a Dutch drama of the same title) gave me everything ready to use the legend as the libretto of an opera. I came to an understanding about it with Heine himself, drew up the scheme, and gave it to M. Léon Pillet [manager of the Grand Opera], with the proposition that he should have a French libretto made from it for me." Subsequently M. Pillet purchased the libretto direct from Wagner, who consented to the transaction, as he saw no opportunity of producing the opera in Paris. It was then set by Dietsch as "Le Vaisseau

Frl. Hiedler as *Senta*

Muhlmann as *The Dutchman*

Copyright, Aimé Dupont

Fantôme," and brought out in Paris in 1842. In the meantime, not discouraged by his bad fortune, Wagner set to work, wrote the German verse, and completed the opera in seven weeks for Dresden, where it was finally performed, as already stated. Unlike "Rienzi," it met with failure both in Dresden and Berlin; but its merits were recognized by Spohr, who encouraged him to persevere in the course he had marked out.

The plot of the opera is very simple. A Norwegian vessel, commanded by Daland, compelled by stress of weather, enters a port not far from her destination. At the same time a mysterious vessel, with red sails and black hull, commanded by the wandering Flying Dutchman, who is destined to sail the seas without rest until he finds a maiden who will be faithful unto death, puts into the same port. The two captains meet, and Daland invites the stranger to his home. The two at last progress so rapidly in mutual favor that a marriage is agreed upon between the stranger and Senta, Daland's daughter. The latter is a dreamy, imaginative girl, who, though she has an accepted lover, Eric, is so fascinated with the legend of the stranger that she becomes convinced she is destined to save him from perdition. When he arrives with her father she recognizes him at once, and vows eternal constancy to him. In the last act, however, Eric appears and reproaches Senta with her faithlessness. The stranger overhears them, and concludes that as she has been recreant to her former lover, so too she will be untrue to him. He decides to leave her; for if he should remain, her penalty would be eternal death. As his mysterious vessel sails away Senta rushes to a cliff, and crying out that her life will be the price of his release, hurls herself into the sea, vowing to be constant to him even in death. The phantom vessel sinks, the sea grows calm, and in the distance the two figures are seen rising in the sunlight never to be parted.

The overture characterizes the persons and situations of the drama, and introduces the motives which Wagner ever after used so freely, — among them the curse resting upon the Dutchman, the restless motion of the sea, the message of the Angel of Mercy personified in Senta, the personification of the Dutchman, and the song of Daland's crew. The first act opens with an introduction representing a storm, and a characteristic sailors' chorus, followed by an exquisite love-song for tenor ("Mit Gewitter und Sturm"), and a grand scena for the Dutchman ("Die Frist ist um"), which lead up to a melodious duet between the Dutchman and Daland. The act closes with the sailors' chorus as the two vessels sail away.

After a brief instrumental prelude, the second act opens in Daland's home, where the melancholy Senta sits surrounded by her companions, who are spinning. To the whirring accompaniment of the violins they sing a very realistic spinning song ("Summ' und brumm du gutes Mädchen"), interrupted at intervals by the laughter of the girls as they rally Senta upon her melancholy looks. Senta replies with a weird and exquisitely melodious ballad ("Johohae! träfft ihr das Schiff im Meere an"), in which she tells the story of the Flying Dutchman, and anticipates her own destiny. The song is full of intense feeling, and is characterized by a motive which frequently recurs in the opera, and is the key to the whole work. A duet follows between Eric and Senta, the melodious character of which shows that Wagner was not yet entirely freed from Italian influences. A short duet ensues between Senta and her father, and then the Dutchman appears. As they stand and gaze at each other for a long time, the orchestra meanwhile supplying the supposed emotions of each, we have a clue to the method Wagner was afterwards to employ so successfully. A duet between Senta and the Dutchman ("Wie aus der Ferne") and a terzetto with Daland close the act.

The third act opens with another sailors' chorus ("Steuermann, lass die Wacht"), and a brisk dialogue between them and the women who are bringing them provisions. The latter also hail the crew of the Dutchman's vessel, but get no reply until the wind suddenly rises, when they man the vessel and sing the refrain with which the Dutchman is continually identified. A double chorus of the two crews follows. Senta then appears, accompanied by Eric, who seeks to restrain her from following the stranger in a very dramatic duet ("Wass muss ich hören?"). The finale is made up of sailors' and female choruses, and a trio between Senta, Daland, and the Dutchman, which are woven together with consummate skill, and make a very effective termination to the weird story. There are no points in common between "The Flying Dutchman" and "Rienzi," except that in the former Wagner had not yet clearly freed himself from conventional melody. It is interesting as marking his first step towards the music of the future in his use of motives, his wonderful treatment of the orchestra in enforcing the expression of the text, and his combination of the voices and instrumentation in what he so aptly calls "The Music-Drama."

TANNHÄUSER

"Tannhäuser und der Sängerkrieg auf Wartburg" ("Tannhäuser and the Singers' Contest at the Wartburg"), romantic opera in three acts, text by the composer, was first produced at the Royal Opera, Dresden, October 20, 1845, with the following cast:

Tannhäuser	Herr TICHATSCHEK.
Wolfram	Herr MITTERWURZER.
Walther	Herr SCHLOSS.
Beterolf	Herr WACHTER.
Elizabeth	Frl. WAGNER.
Venus	Mme. SCHRÖDER-DEVRIENT.

Its first performance in Paris was on March 13, 1861; but it was a failure after three presentations, and was made the butt of Parisian ridicule, even Berlioz joining in the tirade. In England it was brought out in Italian at Covent Garden, May 6, 1876, though its overture was played by the London Philharmonic Orchestra in 1855, Wagner himself leading. Its first performance in New York was on April 4, 1859.

In the Spring of 1842 Wagner returned from Paris to Germany, and on his way to Dresden visited the castle of Wartburg, in the Thuringian Valley, where he first conceived the idea of writing "Tannhäuser." The plot was taken from an old German tradition, which centres about the castle where the landgraves of the thirteenth century instituted peaceful contests between the Minnesingers and knightly poets. Near this castle towers the Venusberg, a dreary elevation, which, according to popular tradition, was inhabited by Holda, the Goddess of Spring. Proscribed by Christianity, she took refuge in its caverns, where she was afterwards confounded with the Grecian Venus. Her court was filled with nymphs and sirens, who enticed those whose impure desires led them to its vicinity, and lured them into the caverns, from which they were supposed never to return. The first act opens in this court, and reveals Tannhäuser, the knight and minstrel, under the sway of Venus. In spite of her fascinations he succeeds in tearing himself away, and we next find him at the castle of Wartburg, the home of Hermann the Landgrave, whose daughter Elizabeth is in love with him. At the minstrel contest he enters into the lists with the other Minnesingers, and, impelled by a reckless audacity and the subtle influence of Venus, sings of the attractions of sensual pleasures. Walter, of the Vogelweide, replies with a song to virtue. Tannhäuser breaks out in renewed sensual strains, and a quarrel ensues. The knights rush

Charles Adams as *Tannhäuser*

Ternina as *Elizabeth*
Copyright, Aimé Dupont

upon him with their swords, but Elizabeth interposes and saves his life. He expresses his penitence, makes a pilgrimage to Rome and confesses to the Pope, who replies that, having tasted the pleasures of hell, he is forever damned, and, raising his crosier, adds: "Even as this wood cannot blossom again, so there is no pardon for thee." Elizabeth prays for him in her solitude, but her prayers apparently are of no avail. At last he returns dejected and hopeless, and in his wanderings meets Wolfram, another minstrel, also in love with Elizabeth, to whom he tells the sad story of his pilgrimage. He determines to return to the Venusberg. He hears the voices of the sirens luring him back. Wolfram seeks to detain him, but is powerless until he mentions the name of Elizabeth, when the sirens vanish and their spells lose their attraction. A funeral procession approaches in the distance, and on the bier is the form of the saintly Elizabeth. He sinks down upon the coffin and dies. As his spirit passes away his pilgrim's staff miraculously bursts out into leaf and blossom, showing that his sins have been forgiven.

The overture to the opera is well known by its frequent performances as a concert number. It begins with the music of the Pilgrims' Chorus, which, as it dies away, is succeeded by the seductive spells of the Venusberg and the voices of the sirens calling to Tannhäuser. As the whirring sounds grow fainter and fainter, the Pilgrims' Song is again heard, and at last closes the overture in a joyous burst of harmony. The first act opens with the scene in the Venusberg, accompanied by the bacchanale music, which was written in Paris by Wagner after the opera was finished and had been performed. It is now known as "the Parisian Bacchanale." It is followed by a voluptuous scene between Tannhäuser and Venus, a long dialogue, during which the hero, seizing his harp, trolls out a song ("Doch sterblich, ach!"), the theme of which has already been given out by the overture, expressing his weariness of her companionship. The second scene transports us to a valley, above which towers the castle of Wartburg. A young shepherd, perched upon a rock, sings a pastoral invocation to Holda ("Frau Holda kam aus dem Berg hervor"), the strains of his pipe, an oboe obbligato, weaving about the stately chorus of the elder Pilgrims ("Zu dir wall' ich, mein Herr und Gott") as they come along the mountain paths from the castle. The scene, which is one of great beauty, closes with the lament of Tannhäuser ("Ach! schwer drückt mich der Sünden Last"), intermingled with the receding song of the Pilgrims, the ringing of church-bells in the distance, and the merry notes of hunters' horns as the Landgrave and his followers approach. The meeting with Tannhäuser leads to an expressive septet, in which Wolfram has a very impressive solo ("Als du in kühnem Sange").

The second act opens in the singers' hall of the Wartburg. Elizabeth, entering joyfully, greets it in a recitative ("Froh grüss ich dich, geliebter Raum"), which is characterized by a joyous but dignified dramatic appeal, recalling the scenes of her youth. The interview between Tannhäuser and Elizabeth, which follows, gives rise to a long dialogue, closing with a union of the two voices in the charming duet, "Gepriesen sei die Macht." Then follows the grand march and chorus ("Freudig begrüssen wir die edle Halle") announcing the beginning of the song contest. The stirring rhythm and bold, broad outlines of this march are so well known that it is needless to dwell upon it. The scene of the contest is declamatory throughout, and full of animation and spirit; its most salient points being the hymn of Wolfram ("O Himmel lasst dich jetzt erflehen") in honor of ideal love, and Elizabeth's appeal to the knights to spare Tannhäuser ("Zurück von ihm "), which leads up to a spirited septet and choral ensemble closing the act.

In the third act we are once more in the valley of the Wartburg. After a plaintive song by Wolfram (" Wohl wusst' ich hier sie im Gebet zu finden "), the chorus of the returning Pilgrims is heard in the distance, working up to a magnificent crescendo as they approach and cross the stage. Elizabeth, who has been earnestly watching them to find if Tannhäuser be of their number, disappointed, sinks upon her knees and sings the touching prayer, " Allmächt'ge Jungfrau, hör mein Flehen." As she leaves the scene, Wolfram takes his harp and sings the enchanting fantasy to the evening star (" O, du mein holder Abendstern ") — a love song to the saintly Elizabeth. Tannhäuser makes his appearance. A long declamatory dialogue ensues between himself and Wolfram, in which he recites the story of his pilgrimage. The scene is one of extraordinary power, and calls for the highest vocal and dramatic qualities in order to make it effective. From this point on, the tragedy hastens. There is the struggle once more with the sirens, and amid Wolfram's touching appeals and Tannhäuser's exclamations is heard the enticement of the Venus music. But at the name " Elizabeth " it dies away. The mists grow denser as the magic crew disappears, and through them a light is seen upon the Wartburg. The tolling of bells and the songs of mourners are heard as the cortege approaches. As Tannhäuser dies, the Pilgrims' Chorus again rises in ecstasy, closing with a mighty shout of " Hallelujah ! " and the curtain falls.

Lohengrin

" Lohengrin," romantic opera in three acts, words by the composer, was first produced at Weimar, August 28, 1850, the anniversary of Goethe's birthday, under the direction of Franz Liszt, and with the following cast of the leading parts:

Lohengrin	Herr BECK.
Telramund	Herr MILDE.
King	Herr HOFER.
Elsa	Frau AGATHE.
Ortrud	Frl. FASTLINGER.

"Lohengrin" was begun in Paris, and finished in Switzerland during the period in which Wagner was director of the musical society as well as of the orchestra at the city theatre of Zurich, whither he had fled to escape the penalties for taking part in the political agitations and subsequent insurrection of 1849. Though it manifests a still further advancement in the development of his system, it was far from being composed according to the abstract rules he had laid down. He says explicitly on this point, in his "Music of the Future": "The first three of these poems — 'The Flying Dutchman,' 'Tannhäuser,' and 'Lohengrin' — were written by me, their music composed, and all (with the exception of 'Lohengrin') performed upon the stage, before the composition of my theoretical writings."

The story of Lohengrin, the son of Parsifal, upon which Wagner has based his drama, is taken from many sources, the old Celtic legend of King Arthur, his knights, and the Holy Grail being mixed with the distinctively German legend of a knight who arrives in his boat drawn by a swan. The version used by Wagner is supposed to be told by Wolfram von Eschenbach, the Minnesinger, at one of the Wartburg contests, and is in substance as follows: Henry I., King of Germany, known as "the Fowler," arrives at Antwerp for the purpose of raising a force to help him expel the Hungarians, who are threatening his dominions. He finds Brabant in a condition of anarchy. Gottfried, the young son of the late Duke, has mysteriously

Kraus as *Lohengrin*
Copyright, Aimé Dupont

Emma Eames as *Elsa*
Copyright, Aimé Dupont

disappeared, and Telramund, the husband of Ortrud, daughter of the Prince of Friesland, claims the dukedom. The claimant openly charges Elsa, sister of Gottfried, with having murdered him to obtain the sovereignty, and she is summoned before the King to submit her cause to the ordeal of battle between Telramund and any knight whom she may name. She describes a champion whom she has seen in a vision, and conjures him to appear in her behalf. After a triple summons by the heralds, he is seen approaching on the Scheldt, in a boat drawn by a swan. Before the combat Lohengrin and Elsa are betrothed, he naming the condition that she shall never question him as to his name or race. She assents, and the combat results in Telramund's defeat and public disgrace.

In the second act the bridal ceremonies occur, prior to which, moved by Ortrud's entreaties, Elsa promises to obtain a reprieve for Telramund from the sentence which has been pronounced against him. At the same time Ortrud takes advantage of her success to instil doubts into Elsa's mind as to her future happiness and the faithfulness of Lohengrin. In the next scene, as the bridal cortege is about to enter the minster, Ortrud claims the right of precedence by virtue of her rank, and Telramund publicly accuses Lohengrin of sorcery. The faith of Elsa, however, is not shaken. The two conspirators are ordered to stand aside, the train enters the church, and Elsa and Lohengrin are united.

The third act opens in the bridal chamber. The seeds of curiosity and distrust which Ortrud has sown in Elsa's mind have ripened, and in spite of her conviction that it will destroy her happiness, she questions Lohengrin with increasing vehemence, at last openly demanding to know his secret. At this juncture Telramund breaks into the apartment with four followers, intending to take the life of Lohengrin. A single blow of the knight's sword stretches him lifeless. He then places Elsa in the charge of her ladies and orders them to take her to the presence of the King, whither he also repairs. Compelled by his wife's unfortunate rashness, he discloses himself as the son of Parsifal, Knight of the Holy Grail, and announces that he must now return to its guardianship. His swan once more appears, and as he steps into the boat he bids Elsa an eternal farewell. Before he sails away, however, Ortrud declares to the wondering crowd that the swan is Elsa's brother, whom she has changed into this form, and who would have been released but for Elsa's curiosity. Lohengrin at once disenchants the swan, and Gottfried appears and rushes into his sister's arms. A white dove flies through the air and takes the place of the swan, and Lohengrin sails away as Elsa dies in the embrace of her newly found brother.

The Vorspiel, or prelude, to the opera takes for its subject the descent of the Holy Grail, the mysterious symbol of the Christian faith, and the Grail motive is the key to the whole work. The delicious harmonies which accompany its descent increase in warmth and power until the sacred mystery is revealed to human eyes, and then die away to a pianissimo, and gradually disappear as the angels bearing the holy vessel return to their celestial abode. The curtain rises upon a meadow on the banks of the Scheldt, showing King Henry surrounded by his vassals and retainers. After their choral declaration of allegiance, Telramund, in a long declamatory scena of great power ("Zum Sterben kam der Herzog von Brabant"), tells the story of the troubles in Brabant, and impeaches Elsa. At the King's command, Elsa appears, and in a melodious utterance of extreme simplicity and sweetness, which is called the dream motive ("Einsam in trüben Tagen"), relates the vision of the knight who is to come to her assistance. The summons of the heralds preludes the climax of the

Schumann–Heink as *Ortrud*

Copyright, Aimé Dupont.

act. Amid natural outcries of popular wonderment Lohengrin appears, and as he leaves his boat, bids farewell to his swan in a strain of delicate beauty ("Nun sei gedankt, mein lieber Schwan"). The preparations for the combat are made, but before it begins, the motive of warning is sounded by Lohengrin ("Nie sollst du mich befragen"). The finale of the act takes the form of a powerful ensemble, composed of sextet and chorus, and beginning with the prayer of the King ("Mein Herr und Gott, nun ruf' ich Dich").

The second act opens upon a night scene near the palace, which is merry with the wedding festivities, while the discomfited Telramund and Ortrud are plotting their conspiracy without in a long duet ("Erhebe dich, Genossin meiner Schmach"), which introduces new motives of hatred and revenge, as opposed to the Grail motive. In the second scene Elsa appears upon the balcony and sings a love song ("Euch Lüften, die mein Klagen"), whose tenderness and confidence are in marked contrast with the doubts sown in her mind by Ortrud before the scene closes. The third scene is preluded with descriptive sunrise music by the orchestra, followed by the herald's proclamations, interspersed by choral responses, leading up to the bridal-procession music as the train moves on from the palace to the cathedral, accompanied by a stately march and choral strains, and all the artistic surroundings of a beautiful stage pageant. The progress is twice interrupted; first by Ortrud, who asserts her precedence, and second by Telramund, who, in the scena ("Den dort im Glanz"), accuses Lohengrin of sorcery. When Elsa still expresses her faith, the train moves on, and reaches its destination amid the acclamations of the chorus ("Heil, Elsa von Brabant!").

The third act opens in the bridal chamber with the graceful bridal song by Elsa's ladies ("Treulich gefuhrt, ziehet dahin"), whose melodious strains have accompanied many unions, the world over, besides those of Elsa and Lohengrin. The second scene is an exquisite picture of the mutual outpouring of love, at first full of beauty and tenderness, but gradually darkening as Ortrud's insinuations produce their effect in Elsa's mind. Tenderly Lohengrin appeals to her, but in vain; and at last the motive of warning is heard. The fatal questions are asked, the tragedy of Telramund follows, and all is over. The last scene introduces us once more to the meadow on the Scheldt, where Lohengrin appears before the King and his vassals. In their presence he reveals himself as the son of Parsifal, in a scena of consummate power ("In fernem Land, unnahbar euren Schritten"), wherein the Grail motive reaches its fullest development. It is followed by his touching farewell ("O Elsa! nur ein Jahr an deiner Seite"), the melody of which can hardly be surpassed in dignity and impressiveness. The denouement now hastens, and Lohengrin disappears, to the accompaniment of the Grail motive.

TRISTAN UND ISOLDE

"Tristan und Isolde," opera in three acts, words by the composer, was first produced at Munich, June 10, 1865, under the direction of Hans von Bülow, with the following cast of characters:

Tristan	Herr LUDWIG SCHNORR VON CAROLSFELD.
Kurwenal	Herr MITTERWURZER.
King Mark	Herr ZOTTMAYER.
Isolde	Mme. SCHNORR VON CAROLSFELD.
Brangoena	Mlle. DEINET.

The opera was first produced in New York, December 1, 1887, with the following cast:

Tristan	Herr NIEMANN.
Kurwenal	Mr. ROBINSON.
King Mark	Herr FISCHER.
Isolde	Frl. LILLI LEHMANN.
Brangaena	Frl. MARIANN BRANDT.

"Tristan und Isolde" was commenced in 1857 and finished in 1859, during the period in which Wagner was engaged upon his colossal work, "The Ring of the Nibelung." As early as the middle of 1852 he had finished the four dramatic poems which comprise the cyclus of the latter, and during the next three years he finished the music to "Das Rheingold" and "Die Walküre." In one of his letters he says: "In the Summer of 1857 I determined to interrupt the execution of my work on the Nibelungen and begin something shorter, which should renew my connection with the stage." The legend of Tristan was selected. It is derived from the old Celtic story of "Tristram and Iseult," the version adopted by Wagner being that of Gottfried of Strasburg, a bard of the thirteenth century, though it must be said he uses it in his own manner, and at times widely departs both from the original and the mediæval poem.

In "Tristan and Isolde" Wagner broke completely loose from all the conventional forms of opera. It has nothing in common with the old style of lyric entertainment. As Hueffer says, in his recent Life of Wagner: " Here is heard for the first time the unimpaired language of dramatic passion intensified by an uninterrupted flow of expressive melody. Here also the orchestra obtains that wide range of emotional expression which enables it, like the chorus of the antique tragedy, to discharge the dialogue of an overplus of lyrical elements without weakening the intensity of the situation, which it accompanies like an unceasing passionate undercurrent." In an opera like this, which is intended to commingle dramatic action, intensity of verse, and the power and charm of the music in one homogeneous whole, the reader will at once observe the difficulty of doing much more than the telling of its story, leaving the musical declamation and effect to be inferred from the text. Even Wagner himself in the original title is careful to designate the work "Ein Handlung" (an action).

The vorspiel to the drama is based upon a single motive, which is worked up with consummate skill into various melodic forms, and frequently appears throughout the work. It might well be termed the motive of restless, irresistible passion. The drama opens on board a ship in which the Cornish knight, Tristan, is bearing Isolde, the unwilling Irish bride, to King Mark of Cornwall. As the vessel is nearing the land, Isolde sends Brangaena to the Knight, who is also in love with her, but holds himself aloof by reason of a blood-feud, and orders him to appear at her side. His refusal turns Isolde's affection to bitterness, and she resolves that he shall die, and that she will share death with him. She once more calls Tristan, and tells him that the time has come for him to make atonement for slaying her kinsman, Morold. She directs Brangaena to mix a death-potion and invites him to drink with her, but without her knowledge Brangaena has prepared a love-potion, which inflames their passions beyond power of restraint. Oblivious of the landing, the approach of the royal train, and all that is going on about them, they remain folded in mutual embrace.

The second act opens in Cornwall, in a garden which leads to Isolde's chamber, she being already wedded to King Mark. With Brangaena she is waiting for Tristan. The King goes out upon a night hunt, and no sooner has he disappeared than Isolde gives the signal for his approach, while Brangaena goes to her station to watch. The second scene is a most elaborate love-duet between the guilty pair, the two voices at first joining ("Bist du mein? Hab' ich dich wieder?"). A passionate dialogue ensues, and then the two voices join again ("O sink' hernieder, Nacht der Liebe"). After a brief dialogue Brangaena's warning voice is heard. Absorbed in each other, they pay no heed,

Bispham as *Kurwenal*
Copyright, Aimé Dupont

Jean de Reszke as *Tristan*
Copyright, Aimé Dupont

Edouard de Reszke as *King Mark*
Copyright, Aimé Dupont

and once more they join in the very ecstasy of passion, so far as it can be given musical form, in the finale of the duet ("O süsse Nacht! Ew'ge Nacht! Hehr erhabne Liebes-Nacht"). The treachery of Sir Melot, Tristan's pretended friend, betrays the lovers to the King. Tristan offers no explanations, but touched by the King's bitter reproaches provokes Sir Melot to combat and allows himself to be mortally wounded.

The third act opens in Brittany, whither Kurwenal, Tristan's faithful henchman, has taken him. A shepherd lad watches from a neighboring height to announce the appearance of a vessel, for Kurwenal has sent for Isolde to heal his master's wound. At last the stirring strains of the shepherd's pipe signal her coming. In his delirious joy Tristan tears the bandages from his wounds, and has only strength enough left to call Isolde by name and die in her arms. A second vessel is seen approaching, bearing King Mark and his men. Thinking that his design is hostile, Kurwenal attempts to defend the castle, but is soon forced to yield, and dies at the feet of his master. The King exclaims against his rashness, for since having heard Brangaena's story of the love-potion he had come to give his consent to the union of the lovers. Isolde, transfixed with grief, sings her last farewell to her lover ("Mild und leise wie er lächelt"), and expires on his body. The dying song is one of great beauty and pathos, and sadly recalls the passion of the duet in the second act, as Isolde's mournful strains are accompanied in the orchestra by the sweetly melodious motives which had been heard in it, the interweaving of the two also suggesting that in death the lovers have been reunited.

THE MASTERSINGERS

"Die Meistersinger von Nürnberg," comic opera in three acts, words by the composer, was first produced at

Munich, June 21, 1868, under the direction of Hans von Bülow, with the following cast:

Hans Sachs	Herr BETZ.
Walter	Herr NACHBAUER.
Beckmesser	Herr HÖLZEL.
David	Herr SCHLOSSER.
Eva	Mlle. MALLINGER.
Magdalena	Mme. DIETZ.

The opera was first produced in New York, January 4, 1885, upon which occasion Emil Fischer was the Hans Sachs.

The plan of "The Mastersingers" was conceived about the same time as that of "Lohengrin," during the composer's stay at Marienbad, and occupied his attention at intervals for twenty years, for it was not finished until 1867. As is clearly apparent both from its music and text, it was intended as a satire upon the composer's critics, who had charged that he was incapable of writing melody. It is easy to see that these critics are symbolized by the old pedant Beckmesser, and that in Walter we have Wagner himself. When he is first brought in contact with the Mastersingers, and one of their number, Kothner, asks him if he gained his knowledge in any school, he replies, "The wood before the Vogelweid, 't was there I learnt my singing"; and again he answers:

> "What winter night,
> What wood so bright,
> What book and nature brought me,
> What poet songs of magic might
> Mysteriously have taught me,
> On horses' tramp,
> On field and camp,
> On knights arrayed
> For war parade,
> My mind its powers exerted."

The story is not only one of love as between Walter and Eva, but of satirical protest as between Walter and

Bispham as *Beckmesser*
Copyright, Aimé Dupont

Van Rooy as *Hans Sachs*
Copyright, Aimé Dupont

Beckmesser, and the two subjects are illustrated not only with delicate fancy but with the liveliest of humor. The work is replete with melody. It has chorales, marches, folk-songs, duets, quintets, ensembles, and choruses, and yet the composer does not lose sight of his theories; for here we observe as characteristic a use of motives and as skilful a combination of them as can be found in any of his works. Thoroughly to comprehend the story, it is necessary to understand the conditions one had to fulful before he could be a "mastersinger." First of all he must master the "Tabulatur," which included the rules and prohibitions. Then he must have the requisite acquaintance with the various methods of rhyming verse, and with the manner of fitting appropriate music to it. One who had partially mastered the Tabulatur was termed a "scholar"; the one who had thoroughly learned it, a "schoolman"; the one who could improvise verses, a "poet"; and the one who could set music to his verses, a "mastersinger." In the test there were thirty-three faults to be guarded against; and whenever the marker had chalked up seven against the candidate, he was declared to have oversung himself and lost the coveted honor.

The vorspiel is a vivid delineation of mediæval German life, full of festive pomp, stirring action, glowing passion, and exuberant humor. The first act opens in the Church of St. Katherine, at Nuremberg, with the singing of a chorale to organ accompaniment. During the chorale and its interludes a quiet love scene is being enacted between Eva, daughter of the wealthy goldsmith, Veit Pogner, and Walter von Stolzing, a noble young knight. The attraction is mutual. Eva is ready to become his bride, but it is necessary that her husband should be a mastersinger. Rather than give up the hand of the fair Eva, Walter, short as the time is, determines to master the precepts and enter the lists. As Eva and her attendant,

Magdalena, leave the church, the apprentices enter to arrange for the trial, among them David, the friskiest of them all, who is in love with Magdalena. He volunteers to give Walter some instructions, but they do not avail him much in the end, for the lesson is sadly disturbed by the gibes of the boys, in a scene full of musical humor. At last Pogner and Beckmesser, the marker, who is also a competitor for Eva's hand, enter from the sacristy. After a long dialogue between them the other masters assemble, Hans Sachs, the cobbler-bard, coming in last. After calling the roll, the ceremonies open with a pompous address by Pogner ("Das schöne Fest, Johannis-Tag"), in which he promises the hand of Eva, "with my gold and goods beside," to the successful singer on the morrow, which is John the Baptist's Day. After a long parley among the gossiping masters, Pogner introduces Walter as a candidate for election. He sings a charming song ("So rief der Lenz in den Wald"), and as he sings, the marker, concealed behind a screen, is heard scoring down the faults. When he displays the slate it is found to be covered with them. The masters declare him outsung and rejected, but Hans Sachs befriends him, and demands he shall have a chance for the prize.

The second act discloses Pogner's house and Sachs's shop. The apprentices are busy putting up the shutters, and are singing as they work. Walter meets Eva and plots an elopement with her, but Sachs prevents them from carrying out their rash plan. Meanwhile Beckmesser makes his appearance with his lute for the purpose of serenading Eva and rehearsing the song he is to sing for the prize on the morrow. As he is about to sing, Sachs breaks out into a rollicking folk-song ("Jerum, jerum, halla, halla, he!"), in which he sings of Mother Eve and the troubles she had after she left Paradise, for want of shoes. At last he allows Beckmesser a hearing, provided

Winklemann as *Walter*

he will permit him to mark the faults with his hammer upon the shoe he is making. The marker consents, and sings his song ("Den Tag seh' ich erscheinen"), accompanied with excruciating roulades of the old-fashioned conventional sort; but Sachs knocks so often that his shoe is finished long before Beckmesser's song. This is his first humiliation. Before the act finishes he is plunged into still further trouble, for David suspects him of designs upon Magdalena, and a general quarrel ensues.

The third act opens upon a peaceful Sunday-morning scene in the sleepy old town, and shows us Sachs sitting in his armchair at the window reading his Bible, and now and then expressing his hopes for Walter's success, as the great contest is soon to take place. At last he leans back, and after a brief meditation commences a characteristic song ("Wahn! wahn! Ueberall wahn!"). A long dialogue ensues between him and Walter, and then as Eva, David, Magdalena, and Beckmesser successively enter, the scene develops into a magnificent quintet, which is one of the most charming numbers in the opera. The situation then suddenly changes. The stage setting represents an open meadow on the banks of the Pegnitz. The river is crowded with boats. The plain is covered with tents full of merrymakers. The different guilds are continually arriving. A livelier or more stirring scene can hardly be imagined than Wagner has here pictured, with its accompaniment of choruses by the various handicraftsmen, their pompous marches, and the rural strains of town pipers. At last the contest begins. Beckmesser attempts to get through his song and dismally fails. Walter follows him with the beautiful prize-song ("Morgenlich leuchtend in rosigem Schein"). He wins the day and the hand of Eva. Exultant Sachs trolls out a lusty lay ("Verachtet mir der Meister nicht"), and the stirring scene ends with the acclamations of the people ("Heil Sachs! Hans Sachs! Heil Nürnberg's theurem Sachs!").

THE RING OF THE NIBELUNG

"Der Ring der Nibelungen," trilogy, the subject taken from the Nibelungen Lied and freely adapted by the composer, was first conceived by Wagner during the composition of "Lohengrin." The four dramatic poems which constitute the cyclus were written as early as 1852, which will correct the general impression that this colossal work was projected during the closing years of his life. On the contrary, it was the product of his prime. Hueffer, in his biographical sketch of Wagner, says that he hesitated between the historical and mythical principles as the subjects of his work, — Frederick the First representing the former, and Siegfried, the hero of Teutonic mythology, the latter. Siegfried was finally selected. "Wagner began at once sketching the subject, but gradually the immense breadth and grandeur of the old types began to expand under his hands, and the result was a trilogy, or rather tetralogy, of enormous dimensions, perhaps the most colossal attempt upon which the dramatic muse has ventured since the times of Æschylus." The trilogy is really in four parts, — "Das Rheingold" (The Rhinegold); "Die Walküre" (The Valkyrie); "Siegfried"; and "Die Götterdämmerung" (The Twilight of the Gods), "The Rhinegold" being in the nature of an introduction to the trilogy proper, though occupying an evening for its performance. Between the years 1852 and 1856 the composer wrote the music of "The Rhinegold" and the whole of "The Valkyrie"; and then, as he says himself, wishing to keep up his active connection with the stage, he interrupted the progress of the main scheme, and wrote "Tristan and Isolde," which occupied him from 1856 to 1859. During its composition, however, he did not entirely neglect the trilogy. In the Autumn of 1856 he began "Siegfried," the composition of which was not finished until 1869, owing to many other objects which engaged his attention during this period, one of which was the composition of "The Mastersingers," which he wrote at intervals between 1861 and 1867. From the latter year until 1876, when the trilogy was produced at Baireuth, he gave himself wholly to the work of completing it and preparing it for the stage.

Prior to the production of the completed work, separate parts of it were given, though Wagner strongly opposed it. "The Rhinegold," or introduction, came to a public dress rehearsal at Munich, August 25, 1869, and "The Valkyrie" was performed in a similar manner in the same city, June 24, 1870, with the following cast:

Wotan	Herr KINDERMANN.
Siegmund	Herr VOGL.
Hunding	Herr BAUSERWEIN.
Brünnhilde	Frl. STEHLE.
Sieglinde	Frau VOGL.
Fricka	Frl. KAUFFMANN.

The "Siegfried" and "Götterdämmerung," however, were not given until the entire work was performed in 1876. Upon the completion of his colossal task Wagner began to look about him for the locality, theatre, artists, and materials suitable for a successful representation. In the circular which he issued, narrating the circumstances which led up to the building of the Baireuth opera house, he says: "As early as the Spring of 1871 I had, quietly and unnoticed, had my eye upon Baireuth, the place I had chosen for my purpose. The idea of using the Margravian Opera House was abandoned so soon as I saw its interior construction. But yet the peculiar character of that kindly town and its site so answered my requirements, that during the wintry latter part of the Autumn of the same year I repeated my visit, — this time, however, to treat with the city authorities. . . . An unsurpassably beautiful and eligible plat of ground at no great distance from the town was given me on which to build the proposed theatre. Having come to an understanding as to its erection with a man of approved inventive genius, and of rare experience in the interior arrangement of theatres, we could then intrust to an architect of equal acquaintance with theatrical building the further planning and the erection of the provisional structure. And despite the great difficulties which attended the arrangements for putting under way so unusual an undertaking, we made such progress that the laying of the corner-stone could be announced to our patrons and friends for May 22, 1872." The ceremony took place as announced, and was made still further memorable by a magnificent performance of Beethoven's Ninth or Choral Symphony, the chorus of which, the "Ode to Joy," was sung by hundreds of lusty German throats. In addition to the other contents of the stone, Wagner deposited the following mystic verse of his own:

> "I bury here a secret deep,
> For centuries long to lie concealed;
> Yet while this stone its trust shall keep,
> To all the secret stands revealed."

He also made an eloquent address, setting forth the details of the plans and the purposes of the new temple of art. The undertaking was now fairly inaugurated. The erratic King of Bavaria had from the first been Wagner's steadfast friend and munificent patron; but not to him alone belongs the credit of the colossal project and its remarkable success. When Wagner first made known his views, other friends, among them Tausig, the eminent pianist, at once devoted themselves to his cause. In connection with a lady of high rank, Baroness von Schleinitz, he proposed to raise the sum of three hundred thousand thalers by the sale of patronage shares at three hundred thalers each, and had already entered upon the work when his death for the time dashed Wagner's hopes. Other friends, however, now came forward. An organization for the promotion of the scheme, called the "Richard Wagner Society," was started at Mannheim. Notwithstanding the ridicule which it excited, another society was formed at Vienna. Similar societies began to appear in all the principal cities of Germany, and they found imitators in Milan, Pesth, Brussels, London, and New York. Shares were taken so rapidly that the success of the undertaking was no longer doubtful. Meanwhile the theatre itself was under construction. It combined several peculiarities, one of the most novel of which was the concealment of the orchestra by the sinking of the floor, so that the view of the audience could not be interrupted by the musicians and their movements. Private boxes were done away with, the arrangement of the seats being like that of an ancient amphitheatre, all of them facing the stage. Two prosceniums were constructed which gave an indefinable sense of distance to the stage-picture. To relieve the bare side walls, a row of pillars was planned, gradually widening outward and forming the end of the rows of seats, thus having the effect of a third proscenium. The stage portion of the theatre was twice as high as the rest of the building, for all the scenery was both raised and lowered, the incongruity between the two parts being concealed by a *façade* in front. "Whoever has rightly understood me," says Wagner, "will readily perceive that architecture itself had to acquire a new significance under the inspiration of the genius of Music, and thus that the myth of Amphion building the walls of Thebes by the notes of his lyre has still a meaning."

The theatre was completed in 1876, and in the month of August (13–16) Wagner saw the dream of his life take the form of reality. He had everything at his command, — a theatre specially constructed for his purpose; a stage which in size, scenery, mechanical arrangements, and general equipment, had not then its equal in the world; an array of artists the best that Europe could produce; an orchestra almost literally composed of virtuosi. The audience which gathered at these performances — composed of princes, illustrious men in every department of science and culture, and prominent musicians from all parts of the world — was one of which any composer might have been proud, while the representation itself marked an epoch in musical history, and promulgated a new system of laws which have more or less dominated operatic composition ever since.

The casts of the various portions of the trilogy upon this memorable occasion were as follows:

DAS RHEINGOLD (PRELUDE)

Wotan	Gods	Herr BETZ.
Donner		Herr GURA.
Froh		Herr UNGER.
Loge		Herr VOGL.
Fasolt	Giants	Herr EILERS.
Fafner		Herr VON REICHENBERG.
Alberich	Nibelungs	Herr HILL.
Mime		Herr SCHLOSSER.
Fricka	Goddesses	Frau VON GRÜN-SADLER.
Freia		Frl. HAUPT.
Erda		Frau JAIDA.
Woglinde	Rhine-daughters	Frl. LILLI LEHMANN.
Wellgunde		Frl. MARIE LEHMANN.
Flosshilde		Frl. LAMMERT.

DIE WALKÜRE

Siegmund	Herr NIEMANN.
Hunding	Herr NIERING.
Wotan	Herr BETZ.
Sieglinde	Frl. SCHEFZKY.
Brünnhilde	Frau FRIEDRICH-MATERNA.
Fricka	Frau VON GRÜN-SADLER.

SIEGFRIED

Siegfried	Herr UNGER.
Mime	Herr SCHLOSSER.
Der Wanderer	Herr BETZ.
Alberich	Herr HILL.
Fafner	Herr VON REICHENBERG.
Erda	Frau JÄIDA.
Brünnhilde	Frau FRIEDRICH-MATERNA.

DIE GÖTTERDÄMMERUNG

Siegfried	Herr UNGER.
Gunther	Herr GURA.
Hagen	Herr VON REICHENBERG.
Alberich	Herr HILL.
Brünnhilde	Frau FRIEDRICH-MATERNA.
Gutrune	Frl. WECKERLIN.
Waltraute	Frau JÄIDA.

The motive of the drama turns upon the possession of a ring of magic qualities, made of gold stolen from the Rhine-daughters by Alberich, one of the Nibelungs, who dwelt in Nebelheim, the place of mists. This ring, the symbol of all earthly power, was at the same time to bring a curse upon all who possessed it. Wotan, of the race of the gods, covetous of power and heedless of the curse which follows it, obtained the ring from Alberich by force and cunning, and soon found himself involved in calamity from which there was no apparent escape. He himself could not expiate the wrong he had done, nor could he avert the impending doom, the "twilight" of the gods, which was slowly and surely approaching. Only a free will, independent of the gods, and able to take upon itself the fault, could make reparation for the deed. At last he yields to despair. His will is broken, and instead of fearing the inevitable doom he courts it. In this sore emergency the hero appears. He belongs to an heroic race of men, the Volsungs. The unnatural union of the twins,

Seigmund and Sieglinde, born of this race, produces the real hero, Siegfried. The parents pay the penalty of incest with their lives; but Siegfried remains, and Wotan watches his growth and magnificent development with eager interest. Siegfried recovers the ring from the giants, to whom Wotan had given it, by slaying a dragon which guarded the fatal treasure. Brünnhilde, the Valkyrie, Wotan's daughter, contrary to his instructions, had protected Siegmund in a quarrel which resulted in his death, and was condemned by the irate god to fall into a deep sleep upon a rock surrounded by flames, where she was to remain until a hero should appear bold enough to break through the wall of fire and awaken her. Siegfried rescues her. She wakens into the full consciousness of passionate love, and yields herself to the hero, who presents her with the ring, but not before it has worked its curse upon him, so that he, faithless even in his faithfulness, wounds her whom he deeply loves, and drives her from him. Meanwhile Gunther, Gutrune, and their half-brother Hagen conspire to obtain the ring from Brünnhilde and to kill Siegfried. Through the agency of a magic draught he is induced to desert her, after once more getting the ring. He then marries Gutrune. The curse soon reaches its consummation. One day, while traversing his favorite forests on a hunting expedition, he is killed by Hagen, with Gunther's connivance. The two murderers then quarrel for the possession of the ring, and Gunther is slain. Hagen attempts to wrest it from the dead hero's finger, but shrinks back terrified as the hand is raised in warning. Brünnhilde now appears, takes the ring, and proclaims herself his true wife. She mounts her steed, and dashes into the funeral pyre of Siegfried after returning the ring to the Rhine-daughters. This supreme act of immolation forever breaks the power of the gods, as is shown by the blazing Walhalla in the sky; but at the same time justice has been satisfied, reparation has been made for the original wrong, and the free will of man becomes established as a human principle.

Such are the outlines of this great story, which will be told more in detail when we come to examine the component parts of the trilogy. Dr. Ludwig Nohl, in his admirable sketch of the Nibelungen poem, as Wagner adapted it, gives us a hint of some of its inner meanings in the following extract: "Temporal power is not the highest destiny of a civilizing people. That our ancestors were conscious of this is shown in the fact that the treasure, or gold and its power, was transformed into the Holy Grail. Worldly aims give place to spiritual desires. With this interpretation of the Nibelungen myth, Wagner acknowledged the grand and eternal truth that this life is tragic throughout, and that the will which would mould a world to accord with one's desires can finally lead to no greater satisfaction than to break itself in a noble death. . . . It is this conquering of the world through the victory of self which Wagner conveys as the highest interpretation of our national myths. As Brünnhilde approaches the funeral pyre to sacrifice her life, the only tie still uniting her with the earth, to Siegfried, the beloved dead, she says:

> ' To the world I will give now my holiest wisdom;
> Not goods, nor gold nor godlike pomp,
> Not house, nor lands, nor lordly state,
> Not wicked plottings of crafty men,
> Not base deceits of cunning law, —
> But, blest in joy and sorrow, let only love remain.' "

We now proceed to the analysis of the four divisions of the work, in which task, for obvious reasons, it will be hardly possible to do more than sketch the progress of the action, with allusions to its most striking musical features. There are no set numbers, as in the Italian opera; and merely to designate the leading motives and trace their relation to each other, to the action of the *dramatis personæ*, and to the progress of the four movements, not alone towards their own climaxes but towards the ultimate denouement, would necessitate far more space than can be had in a work of this kind.

DAS RHEINGOLD

The orchestral prelude to "The Rhinegold" is based upon a single figure, the Rhine motive, which in its changing developments pictures the calm at the bottom of the Rhine and the undulating movement of the water. The curtain rises and discloses the depths of the river, from which rise rugged ridges of rock. Around one of these, upon the summit of which glistens the Rhinegold, Woglinde, a Rhine-daughter, is swimming. Two others, Wellgunde and Flosshilde, join her; and as they play about the gleaming gold, Alberich, a dwarf, suddenly appears from a dark recess and passionately watches them. As they are making sport of him, his eye falls upon the gold and he determines to possess it. They make light of his threat, informing him that whoever shall forge a ring of this gold will have secured universal power, but before he can obtain that power he will have to renounce love. The disclosure of the secret follows a most exultant song of the Undines ("Rheingold! leuchtende Lust! wie lachst du so hell und hehr!"). In the announcement made by them the motive of the ring also occurs. The Rhine-daughters, who have fancied that Alberich will never steal the gold because he is in love with them, are soon undeceived, for he curses love, and snatches the gold and makes off with it, pursued by the disconsolate maidens, whose song changes into a sad minor, leading up to the next scene. As they follow him into the dark depths the stream sinks with them and gives place to an open district with a mountain in the background, upon which is the

Mme. Amalie Friedrich-Materna

Copyright, Falk

WAGNER

glistening Walhalla, which the giants have just built for the gods. Wotan and Fricka are discovered awakening from sleep and joyfully contemplating it, the latter, however, with much apprehension lest the giants shall claim Freia, the goddess of love, whom Wotan has promised to them as the reward for their work. Loge, the god of fire, however, has agreed to obtain a ransom for her. He has searched the world over, but has been unable to find anything that can excel in value or attraction the charm of love. As the gods are contemplating their castle Loge appears, and in a scene of great power, accompanied by music which vividly describes the element he dominates ("Immer ist Undank Loge's Lohn"), he narrates the tidings of his failure. The giants, however, have heard the story of the Rhinegold, and as they carry off the weeping Freia agree to release her whenever the gods will give to them the precious and all-powerful metal. As love departs, the heavens become dark and sadness overcomes the gods. They grow suddenly old and decrepit. Fricka totters and Wotan yields to despair. Darkness and decay settle down upon them. The divine wills are broken, and they are about to surrender to what seems approaching dissolution, when Wotan suddenly arouses himself and determines to go in quest of the all-powerful gold. Loge accompanies him, and the two enter the dark kingdom of the gnomes, who are constantly at work forging the metals. By virtue of his gold Alberich has already made himself master of all the gnomes, but Wotan easily overpowers him and carries him off to the mountain. The Nibelung, however, clings to his precious gold, and a struggle ensues for it. In spite of his strength and the power the ring gives to him it is wrenched from him, and the victorious Wotan leaves him free to return to his gloomy kingdom. Infuriated with disappointment over his loss and rage at his defeat, Alberich curses the ring and invokes misfortune upon him who possesses it. "May he who has it not, covet it with rage," cries the dwarf, "and may he who has it, retain it with the anguish of fear"; and with curse upon curse he disappears. Now that he has the ring, Wotan is unwilling to give it up. The other gods implore him to do so, and the giants demand their ransom. He remains inflexible; but at last Erda, the ancient divinity, to whom all things are known, past, present, and future, appears to Wotan and warns him to surrender the ring. She declares that all which exists will have an end, and that a night of gloom will come upon the gods. So long as he retains the ring a curse will follow it. Her sinister foreboding so alarms him that at last he abandons the gold. Youth, pride, and strength once more return to the gods.

The grand closing scene of the prelude now begins. Wotan attempts to enter Walhalla, but it is veiled in oppressive mist and heavy clouds. The mighty Donner, accompanied by Froh, climbs a high rock in the valley's slope and brandishes his hammer, summoning the clouds about him. From out their darkness its blows are heard descending upon the rock. Lightning leaps from them, and thunder-crashes follow each other with deafening sounds. The rain falls in heavy drops. Then the clouds part, and reveal the two in the midst of their storm-spell. In the distance appears Walhalla bathed in the glow of the setting sun. From their feet stretches a luminous rainbow across the valley to the castle, while out from the disappearing storm comes the sweet rainbow melody. Froh sings, "Though built lightly it looks, fast and fit is the Bridge." The gods are filled with delight, but Wotan gloomily contemplates the castle as the curse of the ring recurs to him. At last a new thought comes in his mind. The hero who will make reparation is to come from the new race of mortals of his own begetting. The thought

Louise Homer as *Erda*

Copyright, Aimé Dupont

appears in the sword motive, and as its stately melody dies away, Wotan rouses from his contemplation and hails Walhalla with joy as "a shelter from shame and harm." He takes Fricka by the hand, and leading the way, followed by Froh, Freia, Donner, and Loge, the last somewhat reluctantly, the gods pass over the rainbow bridge and enter Walhalla, bathed in the light of the setting sun and accompanied by the strains of a majestic march. During their passage the plaintive song of the Rhine-daughters mourning their gold comes up from the depths. Wotan pauses a moment and inquires the meaning of the sounds, and bids Loge send a message to them that the treasure shall "gleam no more for the maids." Then they pass laughingly and mockingly on through the splendor to Walhalla. The sad song still rises from the depths of the Rhine, but it is overpowered by the strains of the march, and pealing music from the castle. The curtain falls upon their laments, and the triumphant entrance of the gods into their new home.

Die Walküre

In "Die Walküre," the human drama begins. Strong races of men have come into existence, and Wotan's Valkyries watch over them, leading those who fall in battle to Walhalla, where, in the gods' companionship, they are to pass a glorious life. According to the original legend, Wotan blessed an unfruitful marriage of this race by giving the pair an apple of Hulda to eat, and the twins, Siegmund and Sieglinde, were the result of the union. When the first act opens, Siegmund has already taken a wife and Sieglinde has married the savage warrior Hunding, but neither marriage has been fruitful. It is introduced with an orchestral prelude representing a storm. The pouring of the rain is audible among the violins and the rumbling of the thunder in the deep basses. The curtain rises, disclosing the interior of a rude hut, its roof supported by the branches of an ash-tree whose trunk rises through the centre of the apartment. As the tempest rages without, Siegmund rushes in and falls exhausted by the fire. Attracted by the noise, Sieglinde appears, and observing the fallen stranger bends compassionately over him and offers him a horn of mead. As their eyes meet they watch each other with strange interest and growing emotion. While thus mutually fascinated, Hunding enters and turns an inquiring look upon Sieglinde. She explains that he is a guest worn out with fatigue and seeking shelter. Hunding orders a repast and Siegmund tells his story. Vanquished in combat by a neighboring tribe, some of whose adherents he had slain, and stripped of his arms, he fled through the storm for refuge. Hunding promises him hospitality, but challenges him to combat on the morrow, for the victims of Siegmund's wrath were Hunding's friends. As Sieglinde retires at Hunding's bidding, she casts a despairing, passionate look at Siegmund, and tries to direct his attention to a sword sticking in the ash-tree, but in vain. Hunding warns her away with a significant look, and then taking his weapons from the tree leaves Siegmund alone. The latter, sitting by the fire, falls into dejection, but is soon roused by the thought that his sire had promised he should find the sword Nothung in his time of direst need. The dying fire shoots out a sudden flame, and his eye lights upon its handle, illuminated by the blaze. The magnificent sword-melody is sounded, and in a scene of great power he hails it and sings his love for Sieglinde, whom now he can rescue. As the fire and the song die away together, Sieglinde reappears. She has drugged Hunding into a deep sleep, and in an exultant song tells Siegmund the story of the sword. They can be saved if he is strong enough to wrench it from the trunk of the ash. He recognizes his

Nordica as *Brünnhilde*
Copyright, Aimé Dupont

Gadski as *Brünnhilde*
Copyright, Aimé Dupont

WAGNER

sister and folds her passionately in his arms. The storm has passed, and as the moonlight floods the room he breaks out in one of the loveliest melodies Wagner has ever written, the spring song ("Winterstürme wichen dem Wonnemond"), a song of love leading to the delights of spring; and Sieglinde in passionate response declares, "Thou art the spring for which I longed in winter's frosty embrace." The recognition is mutual, not alone of brother and sister but of lover and mistress, — the union which is destined to beget Siegfried, the hero. Seizing her in his arms, Siegmund disappears with her into the depths of the forest, and the curtain falls.

The second act opens in the mountains of the gods, and discloses Wotan with spear in hand in earnest converse with Brünnhilde, his daughter, who is arrayed in the armor of a Valkyrie. He tells her of the approaching combat, and bids her award the victory to Siegmund the Volsung, beloved of the gods. As she disappears among the rocks, shouting the weird cry of the Valkyries, the jealous Fricka, protector of marriage vows, comes upon the scene in a chariot drawn by rams. A stormy dialogue occurs between them, Fricka demanding the death of Siegmund as compensation for the wrong done to Hunding. Wotan at last is overcome, and consents that the Valkyries shall conduct him to Walhalla. As he yields, Brünnhilde's jubilant song is heard on the heights, and Wotan summons her and announces his changed decision. Siegmund must perish. As he stalks gloomily away among the rocks, Brünnhilde falls into deep dejection, and turns away moaning: "Alas! my Volsung! Has it come to this, — that faithless the faithful must fail thee?" As she enters a cave for her horse, the fugitives Siegmund and Sieglinde hurriedly approach, pursued by the infuriated Hunding. They stop to rest, and Sieglinde falls exhausted in his arms. The scene is marked by alternations of passionate love and fear, hope on the one side, despair on the other, vividly portrayed in the instrumentation. As the music dies away and Sieglinde rests insensible in his arms, Brünnhilde, with deep melancholy in her visage, shows herself to Siegmund. In reply to his question, "Who art thou?" she answers, "He who beholds me, to death in the battle is doomed. I shall lead thee to Walhalla." Eagerly he asks, "Shall I find in Walhalla my own father Wälse?" and she answers, "The Volsung shall find his father there." With passionate earnestness he asks, "Shall Siegmund there embrace Sieglinde?" The Valkyrie replies, "The air of earth she still must breathe. Sieglinde shall not see Siegmund there." Siegmund furiously answers, "Then farewell to Walhalla! Where Sieglinde lives, in bliss or blight, there Siegmund will also tarry," and raises his sword over his unconscious sister. Moved by his great love and sorrow, Brünnhilde for the first time is swayed by human emotions, and exultantly declares, "I will protect thee." Hunding's horn sounds in the distance, and soon is heard his defiant challenge to battle. Siegmund rushes to the top of one of the cloudy summits, and the clash of their arms resounds in the mists. A sudden gleam of light shows Brünnhilde hovering over Siegmund, and protecting him with her shield. As he prepares himself to deal a deadly thrust at Hunding, the angry Wotan appears in a stormcloud and interposes his spear. Siegmund's sword is shivered to pieces. Hunding pierces his disarmed enemy, and he falls mortally wounded. Brünnhilde lifts the insensible Sieglinde upon her steed and rides away with her. Wotan, leaning upon his spear, gazes sorrowfully at the dying Volsung, and then turning to Hunding, so overcomes him with his contemptuous glance that he falls dead at his feet. "But Brünnhilde, woe to the traitor. Punishment dire is due to her treason. To horse, then.

Olive Fremstad as *Sieglinde*
Copyright, Aimé Dupont

Burgstaller as *Siegmund*
Copyright, Aimé Dupont

Let vengeance speed swiftly." And mounting his steed he disappears amid thunder and lightning.

The last act opens in a rocky glen filled with the Valkyries calling to each other from summit to summit with wild cries as they come riding through the clouds after the combat, bearing the dead bodies of the warriors on their saddles. The scene is preluded with an orchestral number, well known in the concert-room as the "Ride of the Valkyries," which is based upon two motives, the Valkyries' call and the Valkyrie melody. In picturesque description of the rush and dash of steeds, amid which are heard the wild cries of the sisters, "The Ride" is vividly descriptive. Brünnhilde arrives among the exultant throng in tears, bearing Sieglinde with her. She gives her the fragments of Siegmund's sword, and appeals to the other Valkyries to save her. She bids Sieglinde live, for "thou art to give birth to a Volsung," and to keep the fragments of the sword. "He that once brandishes the sword, newly welded, let him be named Siegfried, the winner of victory." Wotan's voice is now heard angrily shouting through the storm-clouds, and calling upon Brünnhilde, who vainly seeks to conceal herself among her sisters. He summons her forth from the group, and she comes forward meekly but firmly and awaits her punishment. He taxes her with violating his commands; to which she replies, "I obeyed not thy order, but thy secret wish." The answer does not avail, and he condemns her to sleep by the wayside, the victim of the first who passes. She passionately pleads for protection against dishonor, and the god consents. Placing her upon a rocky couch and kissing her brow, he takes his farewell of her in a scene which for majestic pathos is deeply impressive. One forgets Wotan and the Valkyrie. It is the last parting of an earthly father and daughter, illustrated with music which is the very apotheosis of grief. He then conjures Loge, the god of fire; and as he strikes his spear upon the rock, flames spring up all about her. Proudly he sings in the midst of the glare: —

> "Who fears the spike
> Of my spear to face,
> He will not pierce the planted fire," —

a melody which is to form the motive of the hero Siegfried in the next division of the work — and the curtain falls upon a scene of extraordinary power, beauty, and majesty.

SIEGFRIED

The second division of the tragedy, "Siegfried," might well be called an idyl of the forest. Its music is full of joyousness and delight. In place of the struggles of gods and combats of fierce warriors, the wild cries of Valkyries and the blendings of human passions with divine angers, we have the repose and serenity of nature, and in the midst of it all appears the hero Siegfried, true child of the woods, and as full of wild joyousness and exultant strength as one of the fauns or satyrs. It is a wonderful picture of nature, closing with an ecstatic vision of love.

After the death of Siegmund, Sieglinde takes refuge in the depths of the forest, where she gives birth to Siegfried. In her dying moments she intrusts him to Mime, who forged the ring for Alberich when he obtained possession of the Rhinegold. The young hero has developed into a handsome, manly stripling, who dominates the forest and holds its wild animals subject to his will. He calls to the birds and they answer him. He chases the deer with leaps as swift as their own. He seizes the bear and drags him into Mime's hut, much to the Nibelung's alarm. But while pursuing the wild, free life in the forest, he has dreams of greater conquests than those over nature. Heroic deeds shape themselves in his mind, and sometimes they are illuminated with dim and mysterious visions

Van Rooy as *Wotan*

Copyright, Aimé Dupont

of a deeper passion. In his interviews with Mime he questions him about the world outside of the forest, its people and their actions. He tires of the woods, and longs to get away from them. Mime then shows him the fragments of his father's sword, which had been shattered upon Wotan's spear, the only legacy left her son by Sieglinde, and tells him that nothing can withstand him who can weld them together again. Mime had long tried to forge a sword for Siegfried, but they were all too brittle, nor had he the skill to weld together the fragments of Siegmund's sword, Nothung. The only one who can perform that task is the hero without fear. One day Siegfried returns from a hunting expedition and undertakes it himself. He files the fragments into dust and throws it into the crucible, which he places on the fire of the forge. Then while blowing the bellows he sings a triumphant song ("Nothung! Nothung! neidliches Schwert"), which anticipates the climax towards which all the previous scenes have led. As he sings at his work Mime cogitates how he shall thwart his plans and get possession of the sword. He plots to have him kill Fafner, the giant, who has changed himself into a dragon, for the more effectual custody of the Rhine-treasure and the ring. Then when Siegfried has captured the treasure he will drug him with a poisoned drink, kill him with the sword, and seize the gold. Siegfried pours the melted steel into a mould, thrusts it into the water to cool, and then bursts out into a new song, accompanied by anvil blows, as he forges and tempers it, the motive of which has already been heard in the "Rhinegold" prelude, when Alberich made his threat. While Mime quietly mixes his potion, Siegfried fastens the hilt to his blade and polishes the sword. Then breaking out in a new song, in which are heard the motives of the fire-god and the sword, he swings it through the air, and bringing it down with force splits the anvil in twain. The music accompanying this great scene, imitating the various sounds of the forge, the flutter of the fire, the hissing of the water, the filing of the sword, and the blows upon the anvil, is realism carried to the very extreme of possibilities.

The great exploit has been successful, and Siegfried at last has Siegmund's sword. Mime takes him to the cave where Fafner, the giant-dragon, guards the gold. Siegfried slays the monster, and laughs over the ease of the task. His finger is heated with the dragon's blood, and as he puts it to his lips to cool it he tastes the blood, and thus learns the language of the birds. He cares nought for the treasure, and takes only the ring and a magic helmet, which enables the wearer to assume any shape. After the contest he throws himself at the foot of a tree in the forest and dreamily listens to the "Waldweben," the rustle and mysterious stirrings of the woods. Amid all these subtle, soothing sounds, pierced now and then with the songs of the birds, and distant cries in far-away sylvan recesses, he realizes that he is alone, while his old companions of the woods are together. He thinks of the mother whom he has never known, and of that mysterious being whom he has never seen, with whom he could enjoy the companionship he observes among the birds. The passion of love begins to assert itself vaguely and strangely, but full soon it will glow out with ardent flame. A bird flying over his head sings to him. He can understand its song and fancies it his mother's voice coming to him in the bird-notes. It tells him now he has the treasure, he should save the most beautiful of women and win her to himself. "She sleeps upon a rock, encircled with flames; but shouldst thou dare to break through them, the warrior-virgin is thine." The bird wings its flight through the forest, and Siegfried, joyously seizing his sword, follows it with swift foot, for he knows it is guiding

Alvary as *Siegfried* in "Siegfried"

him to Brünnhilde. The time for great deeds has come. The wild, free life of the forest is over.

The third act once more shows us the god Wotan still plunged in gloom. Gazing into a deep abyss, he summons Erda, who knows the destiny of all the world, to question her again as to the twilight of the gods. The mysterious figure appears at his bidding, but has nothing further to communicate. Their doom is certain. The fearless race of men is destined to efface the gods, and Walhalla must disappear. The hero is at hand, and coming rapidly. The despairing Wotan, who appears in this scene as "Der Wanderer" (the wanderer), cries out, "So be it. It is to this end I aspire." He turns gloomily away, and confronts Siegfried bounding from rock to rock like a deer, still following his airy guide. The god angrily tries to bar his way, but in vain. His lance is shattered at a single blow of the sword Nothung, which he himself had once so easily shivered. It is the first catastrophe of the final fate which is approaching. The hero without fear has come, the free will of man has begun to manifest itself. The power of the gods is breaking. Joyously Siegfried rushes on over the rocks. He is soon bathed in the glow of the fire, which casts weird shadows through the wild glen. Now the burning wall of red flames is before him. With a ringing cry of exultation he dashes through them, and before him lies the sleeping maiden in her glistening armor. Mad with her beauty and his own overpowering passion, he springs to her side and wakes her with a kiss. The Volsung and the Valkyrie gaze at each other a long time in silence. Brünnhilde strives to comprehend her situation, and to recall the events that led up to her punishment, while love grows within her for the hero who has rescued her, and Siegfried is transfixed by the majesty of the maiden. As she comes to herself and fully realizes who is the hero before her and foresees the approaching doom, she earnestly appeals to him:

> "Leave, ah, leave,
> Leave me unlost,
> Force on me not
> Thy fiery nearness.
> Shiver me not
> With thy shattering will,
> And lay me not waste in thy love."

What is preordained cannot be changed. Siegfried replies with growing passion, and Brünnhilde at last yields, and the two join in an outburst of exultant song:

> "Away, Walhalla,
> In dust crumble
> Thy myriad towers.
> Farewell, greatness,
> And gift of the gods.
> You, Norns, unravel
> The rope of runes.
> Darken upwards,
> Dusk of the gods.
> Night of annulment,
> Draw near with thy cloud.
> I stand in sight
> Of Siegfried's star.
> For me he was,
> And for me he will ever be."

With this great duet, which is one of the most extraordinary numbers in the trilogy for dramatic power and musical expression of human emotion, this division closes.

Die Götterdämmerung

The last division of the tragedy opens under the shade of a huge ash-tree where the three Fates sit spinning and weaving out human destinies. As they toss their thread from one to the other, — the thread they have been spinning since time began, — they foresee the gloom which is coming. Suddenly it snaps in their fingers, whereupon

Reiss as *Mime*
Copyright, Aimé Dupont

Bispham as *Alberich*
Copyright, Aimé Dupont

the dark sisters crowding closely together descend to the depths of the earth to consult with the ancient Erda and seek shelter near her. Meanwhile as day breaks Siegfried and Brünnhilde emerge from the glen where they have been reposing in mutual happiness. Brünnhilde has told her lover the story of the gods and the secrets of the mystic runes, but he is still unsatisfied. His mission is not yet fulfilled. He must away to perform new deeds. Before he leaves her he gives her the ring as his pledge of fidelity, and they part, after exchanging mutual vows of love and constancy.

In his search for further exploits, Siegfried arrives at the dwelling of Gunther, a powerful Rhenish chief, head of the Gibichungen, another race of heroes, where also resides Gutrune, his fascinating sister, and the evil Hagen, begotten by Alberich of Crimhilda, Gunther's mother, who was the victim of his gold. Alberich's hatred of the gods and all connected with them is shared by his son, who has been charged by the Nibelung to recover the gold. From this point the tragic denouement rapidly progresses. Siegfried's horn is heard in the distance, and he soon crosses Gunther's threshold, where his ruin is being plotted by the sinister Hagen. He is hospitably received, and at Hagen's bidding Gutrune pours out and offers him a draught so cunningly mixed that it will efface all past remembrances. He is completely infatuated with the girl's beauty, and as the potion takes effect, the love for Brünnhilde disappears. He demands Gutrune in marriage, and Hagen promises her upon condition that he will bring Brünnhilde as a bride for Gunther. Siegfried departs upon the fatal errand, and after taking from her the ring drags her by force to deliver her to Gunther. The Valkyrie rises to a sublime height of anger over her betrayal, and dooms Siegfried to death in the approaching hunt, for by death alone she knows that she can regain his love.

The last act opens in a rocky glen on the banks of the Rhine, the ripple of whose waters is repeated in the melody of "The Rhinegold." Siegfried is separated from his companion, and while alone, the song of the Rhine-daughters is heard. They rise to the surface of the gleaming water and demand their gold, but Siegfried refuses to restore it. They warn him again to flee from the curse, but he proudly exclaims that his sword is invincible and can crush the Norns. Sadly they float away to the sound of harps shimmering over the water. Gunther's horn is heard among the hills, and Siegfried exultantly answers it. The huntsmen assemble and prepare for a feast. Siegfried relates his adventure with the Rhine-daughters, and when Hagen asks him if it is true that he can understand the language of the birds, he tells the whole story of his life in the "Rheinfahrt" (Rhine journey), — a song built up of all the motives which have been heard in the "Siegfried" division, — the melody of the sword, the stir of the woods, the song of the mysterious bird, Mime's enticement, the love of Brünnhilde, and the flaming fire following each other in rapid and brilliant succession through the measures of the picturesque description. As the song dies away, two ravens, messengers of ill omen, fly across the stage. The curse motive sounds gloomily through the orchestra. Hagen springs to his feet and suddenly and treacherously plunges his spear into Siegfried's back, then suddenly turns and disappears among the rocks. The hero falls to the earth and dies breathing Brünnhilde's name, for in the last supreme moment the spell of Hagen's draught passes away. With his last breath he breaks out in a death-song of surpassing beauty and majesty, in which the motives are those of the Volsung and the Valkyrie, as well as of the destiny which is to reunite them in death. Once more he murmurs the name of Brünnhilde, and then his companions tenderly

Jean de Reszke as *Siegfried* in " Die Götterdämmerung "

Copyright, Aimé Dupont

place him upon his shield, and lifting him upon their shoulders carry him to the misty summits and disappear in the cloud, to the mighty and impressive strains of a funeral march, built up on the motives of Siegmund, the love-duet of Siegmund and Sieglinde, the sword and Volsung's motives, and Siegfried's great theme. In the interweaving of these motives and their sombre coloring, in massive fortissimo and crescendo effects, in expressive musical delineation, and in majestic solemnity, the Siegfried funeral march must take precedence of all other dirges. In truth it is a colossal and heroic funeral poem fit to celebrate the death of a demigod. In the last scene Siegfried's body is borne back to the hall of the Gibichungs amid loud lamenting. When Gutrune learns what has occurred, she bitterly curses Hagen and throws herself on Siegfried's corpse. Hagen and Gunther quarrel for the possession of the ring, and Gunther is slain; but when Hagen tries to take the ring, the hand of the dead hero is raised in warning. Then Brünnhilde solemnly and proudly advances in the light of the torches and bids the empty clamor cease, for "this is no lamenting worthy of a hero." She orders a funeral pyre to be built, and Siegfried is laid thereon. She contemplates the dead hero with passionate love and sadness, and then solemnly turning to those about her, exclaims: "Those who efface the fault of the gods are predestined to suffering and death. Let one sacrifice end the curse. Let the Ring be purified by fire, the waters dissolve it forever. The end of the gods is at hand. But though I leave the world masterless, I give it this precious treasure. In joy or in suffering, happiness can alone come from love." She seizes a burning brand, and invoking Loge, god of fire, flings it upon the pyre. Her horse is brought to her, and she proudly mounts it:

"Grane, my horse,
  Hail to thee here!
  Knowest thou, friend,
  How far I shall need thee?
  Heiaho! Grane!
  Greeting to him.
  Siegfried! See, Brünnhilde
  Joyously hails thee, thy bride."

She swings herself upon her steed and dashes into the furious flames. At last they die away, and the Rhine rushes forward from its banks and covers the pyre. The exultant Rhine-daughters are swimming in the flood, for Brünnhilde has thrown them the ring. Hagen makes a last desperate effort to clutch it, but Woglinde and Wellgunde wind their arms about him, and as they drag him into the depths Flosshilde holds the ring above the waters, and the exultant song of the Rhine-daughters is heard above the swelling tide, while far in the distance a red flame spreads among the clouds. Walhalla is blazing in the sky. The dusk of the gods has come. Reparation has been made. The hero without fear is victorious. Free will, independent of the gods, will rule the world, and the gods themselves are lost in the human creation. Love is given to men, and conquers death.

Parsifal

"Parsifal," a "Bühnenweihfestspiel" (festival acting-drama), words by Wagner, was concluded in 1879, and first produced at Baireuth, July 22, 1882, only about seven months before the distinguished composer's death, with Mme. Friedrich-Materna as Kundry, Herr Winckelmann as Parsifal, and Herr Scaria as Gurnemanz.

The theme of the opera is taken from the cycle of Holy Grail myths to which "Lohengrin" also belongs. The reader will remember that Lohengrin in his final address declares himself son of Parsifal, the King of the Grail; and it is with this Parsifal that Wagner's last work is concerned.

WAGNER

Parsifal, like Siegfried, represents free human nature in its spontaneous, impulsive action. He is styled in the text, "Der reine Thor" (the guileless fool), who, in consonance with the old mythological idea, overcomes the evil principle and gains the crown by dint of pure natural impulse. The opera differs widely from "The Nibelung Ring." The composer has used the free instead of the alliterative form of verse, which he then contended was best adapted to musical setting. In "The Ring" the chorus is not introduced at all until the last division is reached, while in "Parsifal" it plays an important part in every act, in the second scene of the first act there being three choirs on the stage at a time. Still there is no trace of the aria, the duet, or the recitative in the Italian style, though there is plenty of concerted music, which grows out of the dramatic necessities of the situations. When these necessities are not urgent the music flows on in dialogue form, as in "The Ring."

The vorspiel is based upon three motives connected with the mystery of the Grail, which forms the keynote of the opera, though in a different aspect from that which the Grail assumes in "Lohengrin," where it can only be visible to the eye of faith, while in "Parsifal" it distinctly performs its wonders. Let it be remembered that the Grail is the chalice from which Christ drank with his disciples at the Last Supper, and in which his blood was received at the cross. The first of these motives is of the same general character as the Grail motive in the "Lohengrin" vorspiel; the second is an impressive phrase for trumpets and trombones, which will be heard again when the Knights of the Grail are summoned to their duties; and the third is a broad, dignified melody in the chorale form.

The action of the drama occurs in the north of Spain, and in the Vicinity of Monsalvat, the Castle of the Holy

Grail, where this chalice was brought by angels when Christianity was in danger. The curtain rises upon a lovely forest glade on the borders of a lake, at daybreak, and discovers the Grail Knight, Gurnemanz, and two young shield-bearers, guardians of the castle, sleeping at the foot of a tree. Trumpet-calls, repeating the motive first heard in the prelude, arouse them from their sleep; and as they offer up their morning prayer the chorale is heard again. As they wend their way to the castle, they meet two knights preceding a litter upon which the wounded Amfortas, King of the Grail, is carried. In the subsequent dialogue Gurnemanz tells the story of the King's mishap. He is suffering from a wound which refuses to close, and which has been inflicted by the sacred spear, — the spear, according to the legend, with which our Saviour's side was pierced. Klingsor, a magician, had aspired to become a Knight of the Grail, but his application was refused; for only those of holy lives could watch the sacred vessel and perform its ministrations. In revenge, Klingsor studied the magic arts and created for himself a fairy palace, which he peopled with beautiful women, whose sole duty it was to seduce the Knights of the Grail. One of these women, a mysterious creature of wonderful fascinations, Kundry by name, had beguiled Amfortas, who thus fell into the power of Klingsor. He lost his spear, and received from it a wound which will never heal so long as it remains in the hands of the magician. In a vision he has been told to wait for the one who has been appointed to cure him. A voice from the Grail tells him the following mystery:

> "Durch Mitleid wissend,
> Der reine Thor,
> Harre sein'
> Den ich erkor." [1]

[1] "Let a guileless fool only, knowing by compassion, await him whom I have chosen."

Meanwhile, as the shield-bearers are carrying Amfortas towards the lake, the savage, mysterious Kundry is seen flying over the fields. She overtakes Gurnemanz and gives him a balm, saying that if it will not help the King, nothing in Arabia can, and then, refusing to accept thanks or reveal her identity, sinks to the ground in weariness. The King takes the drug with gratitude; but she scorns thanks, and sneers at those about her with savage irony. Gurnemanz's companions are about to seize her, but the old knight warns them that she is living incarnate to expiate the sins of a former life, and that in serving the Order of the Grail she is purchasing back her own redemption. As Gurnemanz concludes, cries are heard in the wood, and two knights, approaching, announce that a swan, the bird sacred to the Grail, which was winging its way over the lake, and which the King had hailed as a happy omen, has been shot. Parsifal, the murderer, is dragged in, and when questioned by Gurnemanz, is unaware that he has committed any offence. To every question he only answers he does not know. When asked who is his mother, Kundry answers for him: " His mother brought him an orphan into the world, and kept him like a fool in the forest, a stranger to arms, so that he should escape a premature death; but he fled from her and followed the wild life of nature. Her grief is over, for she is dead." Whereupon Parsifal flies at her and seizes her by the throat; but Gurnemanz holds him back, and Kundry sinks down exhausted. Parsifal answers to the "Thor," but it remains to be seen whether he is the "reine Thor." Gurnemanz conducts him to the temple where the holy rites of the Grail are to be performed, hoping he is the redeemer whom the Grail will disclose when the love-feast of the Saviour is celebrated.

The scene changes to the great hall of the castle and the celebration of the feast of the Grail. The scene is introduced with a solemn march by full orchestra, including trombones on the stage, accompanied by the clanging of bells as the knights enter in stately procession. They sing a pious chant in unison, the march theme still sounding. As the younger squires and pages enter, a new melody is taken in three-part harmony, and finally an unseen chorus of boys from the extreme height of the dome sing the chorale from the introduction, without accompaniment, in imitation of angel voices. The shield-bearers bring in Amfortas upon his litter, when suddenly from a vaulted niche is heard the voice of Titurel, Amfortas's aged father, and the founder of Monsalvat, now too feeble to perform the holy offices, bidding the Grail to be uncovered. Amfortas, mourning that he, the unholiest of them, should be called, opens a golden shrine and takes out the crystal vessel. Darkness falls upon the hall, but the Grail is illuminated with constantly increasing brilliancy, while from the dome the children's voices sing, "Take My blood in the name of our love, and take My body in remembrance of Me." Parsifal watches the scene with bewildered eyes, but upon saying in reply that he does not understand the holy rite, he is contemptuously ejected from the place.

The second act reveals Klingsor's enchanted palace. The magician, gazing into a mirror, sees Parsifal approaching, and knows he is the redeemer who has been promised. He summons Kundry before him, and commands her to tempt him with her spells. She struggles against the task, for in her soul the powers of good and evil are always contending for the mastery. She longs for eternal sleep, and rest from her evil passions, but Klingsor holds her in his power. Parsifal enters, and the scene changes to a delightful garden filled with girls of ravishing beauty in garments of flowers. They crowd about him, and by their fascinating blandishments seek to gain his love, but

Dippel as *Parsifal*, Act I
Copyright, Aimé Dupont

Dippel as *Parsifal*, Act III
Copyright, Aimé Dupont

in vain. He is still the "guileless fool." Then Kundry appears in all her loveliness, and calls him by name, — the name he had heard his mother speak. He sorrowfully sinks at Kundry's feet. The enchantress bends over him, appeals to him through his longing for his mother, and kisses him. Instantly he comprehends all that he has seen, and he cries, "The wound burns in my heart, oh, torment of love!" Then, quickly rising, he spurns her from him. He has gained the world-knowledge. She flies to him again, and passionately exclaims, "The gift of my love would make thee divine. If this hour has made thee the redeemer, let me suffer forever, but give me thy love." He spurns her again, and cries, "To all eternity thou wouldst be damned with me, if for one hour I should forget my mission," but says he will save her too, and demands to know the way to Amfortas. In rage she declares he shall never find it, and summons the help of Klingsor, who hurls the sacred lance at Parsifal. The weapon remains suspended over his head. He seizes it and makes the sign of the cross. The gardens and castle disappear. Parsifal and Kundry are alone in a desert. She sinks to the ground with a mournful cry, and turning from her, his last words are, "Thou knowest where only thou canst see me again."

In the third act we are again in the land of the Grail. Parsifal has wandered for years trying to find Monsalvat, and at last encounters Gurnemanz, now a very old man, living as a hermit near a forest spring, and the saddened Kundry is serving him. It is the Good Friday morning, and forests and fields are bright with flowers and the verdure of spring. Gurnemanz recognizes him, and in reply to his question what makes the world so beautiful, the aged knight makes answer:

> "The sad repentant tears of sinners
> Have here with holy rain
> Besprinkled field and plain,
> And made them glow with beauty.

> All earthly creatures in delight
> At the Redeemer's trace so bright,
> Uplift their prayers of duty.
> And now perceive each blade and meadow flower,
> That mortal foot to-day it need not dread."

Kundry washes "the dust of his long wanderings" from his feet, and looks up at him with earnest and beseeching gaze. Gurnemanz recognizes the sacred spear, hails him as the King of the Grail, and offers to conduct him to the great hall where the holy rites are once more to be performed. Before they leave, Parsifal's first act as the redeemer is to baptize Kundry with water from the spring. The sound of tolling bells in the distance announces the funeral of Titurel, and the scene changes to the hall where the knights are carrying the litter upon which Amfortas lies, awaiting the funeral procession approaching to the strains of a solemn march. The knights demand he shall again uncover the Grail, but he refuses, and calls upon them to destroy him, and then the Grail will shine brightly for them again. Unobserved by them, Parsifal steps forward, touches the King's wound with the spear, and it is immediately healed. Then he proclaims himself King of the Grail, and orders it to be uncovered. As Amfortas and Gurnemanz kneel to do him homage, Kundry dies at his feet in the joy of repentance. Titurel rises from his coffin and bestows a benediction. Parsifal ascends to the altar and raises the Grail in all its resplendent beauty. A white dove flies down from the dome of the hall and hovers over his head, while the knights chant their praise to God, reëchoed by the singers in the dome, whose strains sound like celestial voices:

> "Miracle of supreme blessing,
> Redemption to the Redeemer"

Olive Fremstad as *Kundry*

Copyright, Aimé Dupont

WAGNER (SIEGFRIED)

SIEGFRIED WAGNER, son of Richard Wagner, was born at Triebscheu, near Lucerne, June 6, 1869. He was first intended for an architect, went to a polytechnic school, and made several meritorious plans for churches. After travelling about the world for a time, however, he decided to devote himself to music, and began its study in his twenty-third year with Kniese and Humperdinck. He made his debut as a conductor August 5, 1893, upon which occasion he directed two acts of "Der Freischütz" and the overture to "Rienzi." After this he travelled as a concert conductor through many continental countries, and also appeared in England with much success. He also conducted the performances of the Nibelung Ring at Baireuth in 1896 and 1899. His compositions include a symphonic poem, "Sehnsucht"; and the operas, "Der Bärenhäuter" (1899); "Herzog Wildfang" (1901); and "Der Kobold" (1904). As the success of these operas is still problematical, brief outlines of two of them only are presented. They are mainly interesting as the work of the son of a great composer.

DER BÄRENHÄUTER

"Der Bärenhäuter," romantic opera in three acts, text by the composer, was first produced at the Hof Theatre, Munich, January 22, 1899, with the following cast:

Hans	Herr KNOTE.
The Devil	Herr SIEGLITZ.
The Stranger	Herr BERTRAM
Louise	Frl. HOFMANN

The libretto is based upon Grimm's story of the Idler, "Bearskin," with some features added from a story by Wilhelm Herz, called "Saint Peter and the Stroller." The "everlasting bonfire" scene in the first act, and the military finale to the third are of the composer's own invention. Wagner himself calls his work a "Volks Oper," though it does not by any means contain folk music. He may have used the term to distinguish the character of his work from his father's semi-mythological subjects.

The "Bärenhäuter" is Hans Kraft, a young soldier. He returns from the Thirty Years' War to find his mother dead, and himself a stranger in his native village. While in distressful mood he meets an engaging fellow, the Devil, who offers him an easy job at good pay, which he accepts. His work is to keep a certain number of kettles hot in the lower region. He is much pleased with his task, especially when he finds the soul of a corporal, who had abused him, simmering in a cauldron. He does his work so faithfully that the Devil leaves him to pursue it undisturbed. One day a visitor in priestly attire, described as "The Stranger," but in reality Saint Peter, enters, and knowing Hans's weak side, proposes to throw dice for the souls he is looking after. Hans accepts and loses all of them. The Devil in a rage devises a novel form of penalty. He transforms Hans into a loathsome figure with claws and covered with a bearskin, smeared with mire and filth. He dooms him to wear this without washing until he can find a maiden who will love him faithfully for three years. Louise, the youngest daughter of the burgomaster, loves him, gives him a ring, and at the end of the three years Hans is restored. The Devil then sends nixies to tempt him. They try in vain to get the ring which Louise has given him. Both are faithful. The Stranger blesses them. Hans goes back to the wars,

Perron as *Amfortas*

Goritz as *Klingsor*
Copyright, Aimé Dupont

WAGNER (SIEGFRIED)

returns covered with laurels for his prowess and claims the happy Louise for his bride.

The music of Siegfried Wagner unmistakably shows the influence of the music of Richard Wagner in its themes, several of which recall motifs in the Nibelung Ring. It bears still more the impress of Weber and of Humperdinck. Its melodies are simple and rhythmical, but never very striking. His strongest effects are orchestral, like the symphonic intermezzo in the second act and the music describing sunrise. The fact, however, that the interest in this opera as well as in the others is dying away in Germany, and that they have not been heard outside of that country would seem to indicate that their life is short and that their interest has been due principally to the curiosity to know whether the mantle of the father had descended to the son.

Der Kobold

"Der Kobold" (The Goblin), opera in three acts, text by the composer, was first produced at the Stadt Theatre, Hamburg, in January, 1904. At the opening of the first act, Seelschen, a goblin, begs Vevena, the sleeping heroine, to redeem him, throws a precious stone, a talisman, into her lap, and then disappears. She is aroused by her attendant Eckhart, and tells him of a dream as well as of her love for Friedrich, a wandering actor. Vevena's mother is opposed to the match, and Friedrich is caught in the toils of a countess who has stolen Vevena's talisman in hopes to win his love. At the close of the act the Count invites Friedrich and his troupe to appear at the castle.

The second act opens with their performance. Vevena, as a nymph, is saved from the fauns by Friedrich, who personifies Eros. The Count, enamored of her, seeks to win her with money, and when he uses force she wounds him with her dagger. To save Vevena, Trutz, a member of the company, accuses himself of the act, and while escaping throws the talisman, which he has secured, into the lake. A small figure dives into the water and floats with the stone into the air. At the same instant the goblin appears lamenting.

In the last act Eckhart tells about the souls of small children who cannot die because they cannot find rest. The Count's followers seek Trutz, but not daring to attack him openly, set fire to the actors' quarters. A fight ensues, and when Friedrich is in immediate danger, Vevena springs between the combatants and receives the fatal blow. By her death the goblin is released.

The story is incoherent and sometimes unintelligible, and is not well adapted for strong dramatic expression. As in "Der Bärenhäuter," the orchestral parts are the strongest.

WALLACE

WILLIAM VINCENT WALLACE was born at Waterford, Ireland, in 1815. He first studied music with his father, a band-leader, who afterwards sent him to Dublin, where he speedily became an excellent performer on the clarinet, violin, and piano. At the early age of fifteen he was appointed organist at the Cathedral of Thurles, and soon afterwards was engaged as a theatre director and concert conductor. At the age of eighteen he had a fit of sickness, and upon his recovery went to Australia for his health, and thence to Van Diemen's Land and New Zealand. He passed some time in the latter country, and then began a long series of wanderings, in the course of which he visited the East and West Indies, Mexico, — where he conducted Italian opera, — and the United States. He remained in New York a considerable period, and gave concerts which were very remunerative. In 1846 he returned to Europe, and shortly afterwards his pretty little opera "Maritana" appeared, and made quite a sensation among the admirers of English opera. In 1847 "Matilda of Hungary" was produced, and met with success. Thirteen years of silence elapsed, and at last, in 1860, he produced his legendary opera, "Lurline," at Covent Garden. It gave great satisfaction at the time, but is now rarely performed. Besides his operas he also wrote many waltzes, nocturnes, studies, and other light works for the piano. After the production of "Lurline" he went to Paris for the purpose of bringing out some of his operas, and while in that city also composed the first act of an opera for London, but his health was too delicate

MARITANA

"Maritana," romantic opera in three acts, words by Fitzball, founded upon the well-known play of "Don Cæsar de Bazan," was first produced at Drury Lane, London, November 15, 1845, and in New York, May 4, 1848. The original cast was as follows:

Maritana	Miss ROMER.
Don Cæsar	Mr. HARRISON.
Lazarillo	Miss POOLE.
Don José	Mr. BORRAIN.
King	Mr. PHILLIPS.

The text follows that of the drama. The first act opens in a public square of Madrid, where a band of gypsies are singing to the populace, among them Maritana, a young girl of more than ordinary beauty and vocal accomplishments. Among the spectators is the young King Charles, who after listening to her is smitten with her charms. Don José, his minister, to carry out certain ambitious plans of his own, resolves to encourage the fascinations which have so attracted the King. He extols her beauty and arouses hopes in her breast of future grandeur and prosperity. At this juncture Don Cæsar de Bazan, a reckless, rollicking cavalier, comes reeling out of a tavern where he has just parted with the last of his money to gamblers. In spite of his shabby costume and dissipated appearance he bears the marks of high breeding. In better days he had been a friend of Don José. While he is relating the story of his downward career to the minister, Lazarillo, a forlorn young lad who has just attempted to destroy himself, accosts Don Cæsar, and tells him a piteous tale of his wrongs. Don Cæsar befriends him, and in consequence becomes involved in a duel, which leads to his arrest; for it is Holy Week, and duelling during that time has been forbidden on pain of death. While Don Cæsar is on his way to prison, Don José delights Maritana by promising her wealth, a splendid marriage, and an introduction to the court on the morrow.

The second act opens in the prison, and discovers Don Cæsar asleep, with his faithful little friend watching by him. It is five o'clock when he wakes, and at seven he must die. Only two hours of life remain for him, but the prospect does not disturb him. On the other hand he is gayer than usual, and rallies Lazarillo with playful mirth. In the midst of his gayety the crafty Don José enters and professes strong friendship for him. When Don Cæsar declares that he has but one last wish, and that is to die a soldier's death instead of being ignominiously hanged, Don José says it shall be gratified upon condition that he will marry. The prisoner has but an hour and three quarters to live, but he consents. He is provided with wedding apparel, and a banquet is spread in honor of the occasion. During the feast Lazarillo brings in a paper to Don José containing the King's pardon for Don Cæsar, but the minister promptly conceals it. Maritana, her features disguised by a veil, is introduced, and as the nuptial rites are performed the soldiers prepare to execute the penalty. At the expiration of the hour Don Cæsar is led out to meet his fate, but Lazarillo has managed to extract the balls from the guns. The soldiers perform their duty, and Don Cæsar feigns death; but as soon as the opportunity occurs, he leaves the prison and hurries to a grand ball given by the Marquis and Marchioness de Montefiori at their palace, while the Marquis, who has his instructions from Don José to recognize Maritana as his long-lost niece, is introducing her as such. Don Cæsar enters and demands his bride. The astonished Don José, perceiving that his scheme to introduce Maritana at court is liable to be frustrated, offers the Marquis a rich appointment if he will induce his wife to play the part he shall suggest. The scheme is soon arranged, and the Marchioness, closely veiled, is presented to Don Cæsar as the Countess de Bazan. Disgusted at "the precious piece of antiquity," as he terms her, and fancying that he has been duped, he is about to sign a paper relinquishing his bride, when he suddenly hears Maritana's voice. He recognizes it as the same he had heard during the marriage rites. He rushes forward to claim her, but she is quickly carried away, and he is prevented from following.

The last act opens in a palace belonging to the King, where Maritana is surrounded with luxury, though she is as yet unaware that she is in the royal apartments. Don José, fancying that Don Cæsar will not dare to make his appearance, as he does not know of his pardon, carries out his plot by introducing the King to her as her husband. She at first rejects him, and as he presses his suit Don Cæsar breaks into the apartment. The King in a rage demands to know his errand. He replies that he is in quest of the Countess de Bazan, and with equal rage inquires who he (the King) is. The King in confusion answers that he is Don Cæsar, whereupon the latter promptly replies, "Then I am the King of Spain." Before further explanation can be made, a messenger arrives from the Queen with the announcement that she awaits the King. After his departure Don Cæsar and Maritana mutually recognize each other, and upon her advice he resolves to appeal to the Queen to save her. He waits for her Majesty in the palace garden, and while concealed, overhears Don José informing her that the King will meet his mistress that night. He springs out, and denouncing him as a traitor to his king slays him, and then returning to Maritana's apartment finds the King there again, and tells him what has occurred. He has saved the King's honor; will the King destroy his? The monarch, overcome with Don

Cæsar's gallantry and loyalty, consigns Maritana to him and appoints him Governor of Granada. The appointment does not suit Don Cæsar, for Granada is too near his creditors. The King, laughing, changes it to Valencia, a hundred leagues away, and thither Don Cæsar conducts his happy bride.

The drama is one which is well adapted to bright, cheerful, melodious music, and the opportunity has been well improved, for "Maritana" is one of the sprightliest and brightest of all the English operas, and contains several ballads which for beauty and expressiveness may well challenge any that Balfe has written. The principal numbers in the first act are Maritana's opening song in the public square ("It was a Knight of princely Mien"); the romanza which she subsequently sings for Don José ("I hear it again, 't is the Harp in the Air"), which is one of the sweetest and most delicate songs in any of the lighter operas; the duet between Maritana and Don José ("Of fairy Wand had I the Power"); Don Cæsar's rollicking drinking-song ("All the World over, to love, to drink, to fight, I delight"); and the tripping chorus ("Pretty Gitana, tell us what the Fates decree"), leading up to the stirring ensemble in the finale, when Don Cæsar is arrested. The first scene of the second act is the richest in popular numbers, containing an aria for alto, Lazarillo's song ("Alas! those Chimes so sweetly pealing"); a charming trio for Don Cæsar, Lazarillo, and Don José ("Turn on, old Time, thine Hour-glass"); Don Cæsar's stirring martial song ("Yes, let me like a Soldier fall"); the serious ballad ("In happy Moments, Day by Day"), written by Alfred Bunn, who wrote so many of the Balfe ballads; and the quartet and chorus closing the scene ("Health to the Lady, the lovely Bride!"). The second scene opens with a pretty chorus in waltz time ("Ah, what Pleasure! the soft Guitar"), followed by an aria sung by the King ("The

Mariner in his Bark"), and introduced by an attractive violin prelude. The finale is a very dramatic ensemble, quintet, and chorus ("What Mystery must now control"). The last act falls off in musical interest, though it is very strong dramatically. It contains a few numbers, however, which are very popular; among them one of the most admired of all English songs ("Scenes that are brightest"), which Maritana sings in the King's apartments at the beginning of the act; the humorous duet between the King and Don Cæsar when they meet; the love duet between Don Cæsar and Maritana ("This Heart with Bliss o'erflowing"); and Don Cæsar's song ("There is a Flower that bloometh"), which is in the sentimental ballad style. The freshness, brightness, and gracefulness of the music of this little opera, combined with the unusual interest and delicate humor of the story, have always commended it to popular admiration.

LURLINE

"Lurline," romantic opera in three acts, text by Fitzball, was first produced at Covent Garden Theatre, London, February 23, 1860. The story closely follows the old legend of the "Lorelei." Count Rudolph, having dissipated his fortune, proposes marriage with Ghiva, daughter of a neighboring baron, to recoup himself. The Baron, however, turns out to be as poor as the Count, and nothing comes of the proposition. Meanwhile Lurline, the Rhine nymph, has seen the Count sailing on the river and fallen in love with him. At the last banquet he and his companions give in the old castle, she appears, weaves spells about him, places a magic ring on his finger, and then disappears. When he comes to his reason, he finds himself enamored of her, follows the notes of her harp on the Rhine, and is engulfed in the whirlpool to which Lurline lures her victims.

The second act opens in Lurline's cavern under the

Rhine, and Rudolph is there by virtue of his magic ring. He hears his friends singing and mourning his loss as they sail on the river, and is so touched by it that he implores permission to return to them for a short time. Lurline consents to his absence for three days, and agrees to wait for him on the summit of the Lurlei-Berg at moonrise on the third evening. She also prevails upon her father, the Rhine King, to give him treasures, with which he embarks in a fairy skiff, leaving Lurline dejected.

In the last act Rudolph discloses to the Baron and his daughter, as well as to his companions, the secret of his wealth. The Baron once more encourages his suit, and the crafty Ghiva steals the magic ring and throws it into the Rhine. In the meantime Lurline waits nightly on the Lurlei-Berg for the return of her lover, and there a gnome brings to her the ring, token of his infidelity. Distracted between grief and anger, she determines to reproach him with his perfidy at a banquet in the castle. She suddenly appears there and demands her ring from him. A scene of bitter reproaches ensues, ending with her denunciation of his companions' treachery. Growing envious of the Count's wealth, they had conspired to destroy him and then plunder the castle. Ghiva and her father, overhearing the plot, reveal it to the Count, and urge him to escape by flight. Rudolph, however, preferring death near Lurline, confronts the assassins. Love returns to Lurline once more. She strikes her harp and invokes the Rhine, which rises and engulfs the conspirators. When the waves subside, the Rhine King appears and gives the hand of his daughter to the Count.

The principal numbers of the first act are Rhineberg's invocation aria ("Idle Spirit, wildly dreaming"); Lurline's beautiful romanzas with harp accompaniment ("Flow on, flow on, O silver Rhine,") and ("When the Night Winds sweep the Wave"); the melodious chorus

("Sail, sail, sail on the Midnight Gale"); the drinking-song ("Drain the Cup of Pleasure"); the quaint tenor song ("Our Bark in Moonlight beaming"); and the vigorous chorus of the gnomes in the finale ("Vengeance, Vengeance"). The second act opens with the gnomes' song ("Behold Wedges of Gold"). The remaining conspicuous numbers are the Count's song ("Sweet Form that on my dreamy Gaze"); Lurline's brilliant drinking-song with chorus ("Take this Cup of sparkling Wine"); Ghiva's ballad for contralto ("Troubadour enchanting"); the breezy hunting-chorus ("Away to the Chase, come away"); Rhineberg's sentimental song ("The Nectar Cup may yield Delight"); and the ensemble in the finale, which is in the genuine Italian style. The third act is specially noticeable for the ballad sung by Rudolph ("My Home, my Heart's first Home"); Lurline's song on the Lurlei-Berg ("Sweet Spirit, hear my Prayer"), which has been a great favorite on the concert stage; the unaccompanied quartet ("Though the World with Transport bless me"); the grand duet ("Lurline, my Naiad Queen"), and the incantation music and closing chorus ("Flow on, thou lovely Rhine").

WEBER

CARL MARIA VON WEBER was born December 18, 1786, at Eutin, and may almost be said to have been born on the stage, as his father was at the head of a theatrical company, and the young Carl was carried in the train of the wandering troupe all over Germany. His first lessons were given to him by Henschkel, conductor of the orchestra of Duke Friedrich of Meiningen. At the age of fourteen he wrote his first opera, "Das Waldmädchen," which was performed several times during the year 1800. In 1801 his two-act comic opera, "Peter Schmoll and his Neighbors," appeared and during these two years he also frequently played in concerts with great success. He then studied with the Abbe Vogler, and in his eighteenth year was engaged for the conductorship of the Breslau opera. About this time his first important opera, "Rubezahl" was composed. At the conclusion of his studies with Volger he was made director of the Opera at Prague. In 1814 he wrote a cantata, "The Lyre and Sword," for a festive occasion, and it was greeted with the wildest enthusiasm. In 1816 he went to Berlin, where he was received with the highest marks of popular esteem, and thence to Dresden as Hofcapellmeister. This was the most brilliant period in his career. It was during this time that he married Caroline Brandt, the actress and singer, who had had a marked influence upon his musical progress, and to whom he dedicated his exquisite "Invitation to the Dance." The first great work of his life, "Der Freischütz," was written at this period. Three other important operas followed,—"Preciosa," "Euryanthe,"

the first performance of which took place in Vienna in 1823, and "Oberon," which he finished in London and brought out there. Weber's last days were spent in the latter city; and it was while making preparations to return to Germany, which he longed to see again, that he was stricken down with his final illness. On the 4th of June, 1826, he was visited by Sir George Smart, Moscheles, and other musicians who were eager to show him attention. He declined to have any one watch by his bedside, thanked them for their kindness, bade them good-bye, and then turned to his friend Fürstenau and said, "Now let me sleep." These were his last words. The next morning he was found dead in his bed. He has left a rich legacy of works besides his operas, — a large collection of songs, many cantatas (of which "The Jubilee," with its brilliant overture, is the finest), some masses, of which that in E flat is the most beautiful, and several concertos, besides many brilliant rondos, polaccas, and marches for the piano.

Der Freischütz

"Der Freischütz," romantic opera in three acts, words by Friedrich Kind, was first produced at Berlin, June 18, 1821. It is one of the most popular operas in the modern repertory. It was first performed in Paris, December 7, 1824, as "Robin des Bois," with a new libretto by Castile Blaze and Sauvage, and many changes in the score, such as divertisements made up of the dance music in "Preciosa" and "Oberon," and of "The Invitation to the Dance," scored by Berlioz. In 1841 it was again given in Paris, with an accurate translation of the text by Pacini, and recitatives added by Berlioz, as "Le Franc Archer." Its first English performance in London was given July 22, 1824, as "Der Freischütz, or, the Seventh Bullet," with several ballads inserted; and its first Italian at Covent

Garden, March 16, 1850, with recitatives by Costa, as "Il Franco Arciero." It was first represented in New York, March 3, 1825. It was so popular in England in 1824 that no less than nine theatres were presenting various versions of it at the same time. The original cast was as follows:

Agatha	Frau CAROLINE SEIDLER.
Annchen	Frl. JOHANNA EUNIKE.
Max	Herr CARL STÜMER.
Caspar	Herr HEINRICH BLUME.
Ottakar	Herr RUBINSTEIN.
Kuno	Herr WANER.
Hermit	Herr GERN.
Kilian	Herr WIEDEMANN.

The text of the opera is taken from a story in "Popular Tales of the Northern Nations," and is founded upon a traditional belief that a demon of the forest furnishes a marksman with unerring bullets cast under magical influences. Kuno, the head ranger to the Prince of Bohemia, too old to longer continue in his position, recommends Max, a skilful marksman, who is betrothed to his daughter Agatha, as his successor. The Prince agrees to accept him if he proves himself victor at the forthcoming hunting-match. Caspar, the master-villain of the play, who has sold himself to the demon Zamiel, and who also is in love with Agatha, forms a plot to ruin Max and deliver him over to Zamiel as a substitute for himself, for the limit of his contract with the Evil One is close at hand. With Zamiel's aid he causes Max to miss the mark several times during the rehearsals for the match. The lover is thrown into deep dejection by his ill luck, and while in this melancholy condition is cunningly approached by Caspar, who says to him that if he will but repeat the formula, " In the name of Zamiel," he will be successful. He does so, and brings down an eagle soaring high above him. Elated with his success, Caspar easily persuades him that he can win the match if he will meet him at midnight in the Wolf's Glen, where with Zamiel's aid he can obtain plenty of magic bullets.

The second act opens in Kuno's house, and discloses Agatha in melancholy mood as she forebodes coming evil. A hermit whom she has met in the woods has warned her of danger, and given her a wreath of magic roses to ward it off. An ancestral portrait falling from the walls also disturbs her; and at last the appearance of the melancholy Max confirms her belief that trouble is in store for her. Max himself is no less concerned. All sorts of strange sounds have troubled him, and his slumbers have been invaded with apparitions. Nevertheless, he goes to the Wolf's Glen; and though spectres, skeletons, and various grotesque animals terrify him, and his mother's spirit appears and warns him away, he overcomes his fright and appears with Caspar at the place of incantation. Zamiel is summoned, and seven bullets are cast, six of which are to be used by Max himself in the forthcoming match, while the seventh will be at the disposal of the demon. Little dreaming the fate which hangs upon the seventh, Caspar offers no objections.

The third act opens, like the second, in Kuno's house, and discovers Agatha preparing for her nuptials, and telling Annchen a singular dream she has had. She had fancied herself a dove, and that Max fired at her. As the bird fell she came to herself and saw that the dove had changed to a fierce bird of ill omen which lay dying at her feet. The melancholy produced by the dream is still further heightened when it is found that a funeral instead of a bridal wreath has been made for her; but her heart lightens up again as she remembers the magic rose-wreath which the hermit had enjoined her to wear on her wedding day. At last the eventful day of trial comes, and the Prince and all his courtiers assemble to witness the match. Max makes six shots in succession which go home to the mark. At the Prince's command he fires the seventh, Zamiel's bullet, at a dove flying past. As he fires, Agatha appears to him as the dove, and he fancies he has slain her. The wreath protects her, however, and Zamiel directs the bullet to Caspar's heart. The demon claims his victim, and Max his bride, amid general rejoicing.

The overture, which is one of the most favorite numbers of its class in the concert room as well as in the opera house, is a masterpiece of brilliant and descriptive instrumentation, and furnishes us with a key to the whole story in its announcement of the leading themes. It opens with an adagio horn passage of great beauty, giving us the groundwork of the entire action; and then follow motives from Max's grand scena in the first act, the Incantation music, Agatha's moonlight scene, and other episodes connected with the action of Max and Caspar. Indeed, the frequent and expressive use of the Leit motif all through the work seem to entitle Weber to the credit of its invention.

The first act opens with a spirited chorus of villagers, followed by a lively march and a comic song by Kilian, in which he rallies Max upon his bad luck. The next number is a trio and chorus, with solos for the principals, Max, Kuno, and Caspar ("O diese Sonne, furchtbar steigt sie mir empor"). Max laments his fate, but Kuno encourages him, while Caspar insinuates his evil plot. The trio is of a sombre cast at the beginning, but as it progresses, the horns and an expressive combination of the chorus give it a cheerful character. It is once more disturbed, however, by Caspar's ominous phrases, but at last Kuno and his men cheer up the despondent lover with a brisk hunting-chorus, and the villagers dance off to a lively waltz tempo. Max is left alone, and the next number is a grand tenor scene. It opens with a gloomy recitative, which lights up as he thinks of Agatha, and then passes into one of the most tender and delicious of melodies ("Durch die Wälder, durch die Auen"), set to a beautiful accompaniment. Suddenly the harmony is clouded by the apparition of Zamiel, but as he disappears, Max begins another charming melody ("Jetzt ist wohl ihr Fenster offen"), which is even more beautiful than the first. As Zamiel reappears the harmony is again darkened; but when despairing Max utters the cry, "Lives there no God!" the wood-demon disappears, and the great song comes to an end. In this mood Caspar meets him, and seeks to cheer him with an hilarious drinking-song ("Hier im ird'schen Jammerthal"), furious in its energy, and intended to express unhallowed mirth. The act closes with Caspar's bass aria of infernal triumph ("Triumph! die Rache, die Rache gelingt"), accompanied by music which is wonderfully weird and shadowy in its suggestions.

The second act opens with a duet ("Schelm! halt fest") in which Agatha's fear and anxiety are charmingly contrasted with the lightsome and cheery nature of Annchen, her attendant, and this in turn is followed by a naive and coquettish arietta ("Kommt ein schlanker Bursch gegangen") sung by the latter. Annchen departs, and Agatha, opening her window and letting the moonlight flood the room, sings the famous scena and prayer, "Leise, leise, fromme Weise," beginning, after a few bars of recitative, with a melody full of prayer and hope and tender longings, shaded with vague presentiment. It is an adagio of exquisite beauty, closing with an ecstatic outburst of rapture ("Alle meine Pulse schlagen") as she beholds her lover coming. The melody has already been heard in the overture, but its full joy and splendid sweep are attained only in this scene. In the next scene we have a trio ("Wie? was? Entsetzen?") between Max, Annchen, and Agatha, in which the musical discrimination of character is carried to a fine point; and the act concludes with the incantation music in the Wolf's Glen, which has never been surpassed in weirdness, mystery, and diablerie, and at times in actual sublimity. Its real power lies in the instrumentation; not alone in its vivid and picturesque presentation of the melodramatic scene with its hideous surroundings, but in its expressiveness and appositeness to the action and sentiment by the skilful use of motives.

The last act has an instrumental prelude foreshadowing the Hunters' Chorus. It opens with a graceful but somewhat melancholy aria of a religious character ("Und ob die Wolke sie verhülle"), sung by Agatha, in which she is still wavering between doubt and hope, and succeeded by another of Annchen's arias, beginning with the gloomy romance, "Einst traumte meiner sel'gen Base," and closing with a lively allegro ("Trübe Augen, Liebchen"), which is intended to encourage her sad mistress. Then the bridesmaids sing their lively chorus ("Wir winden dir den Jungfern-Kranz"), so well known by its English title, "A rosy Crown we twine for Thee." The pretty little number is followed by the Hunters' Chorus ("Was gleicht wohl auf Erden dem Jägervergnügen,") which is a universal favorite. It leads up to a strong dramatic finale, crowded with striking musical ideas, and containing Agatha's beautiful melody in the closing chorus.

Few operas have had such world-wide popularity as "Der Freischütz," and yet it is an essentially German product. The composer's son has aptly characterized it, in his biography of his father: "Weber did not compose 'Der Freischütz'; he allowed it to grow out of the rich soil of his brave German heart, and to expand leaf by leaf, blossom by blossom, fostered by the hand of his talent; and thus no German looks upon the opera as a work of art which appeals to him from without. He feels as if every line of the work came from his own heart, as if he himself had dreamed it so, and it could no more sound otherwise than the rustling of an honest German beech-wood."

OBERON

"Oberon, or, the Elf King's Oath," romantic and fairy opera in three acts, words by J. R. Planché, was first produced at Covent Garden, London, April 12, 1826, in English. Its first Italian performance was given in the same city, July 3, 1860, the recitatives being supplied by Benedict, who also added several numbers from "Euryanthe." It was first sung in New York, October 9, 1829. The original cast was as follows:

Reiza . . . . Miss PATON.
Fatima . . . . Mme. VESTRIS.
Puck . . . . Miss CAWSE.
Huon . . . . Mr. BRAHAM.
Oberon . . . . Mr. BLAND.
Sherasmin . . . . Mr. FAWCETT.
Mermaid . . . . Miss GOWNELL.

The librettist, Planché, in a tribute to Weber, gives the origin of the story of "Oberon." It appeared originally in a famous collection of French romances, "La Bibliothèque Bleue," under the title of "Huon of Bordeaux." The German poet Wieland adopted the principal incidents of the story as the basis of his poem, "Oberon," and Sotheby's translation of it was used in the preparation of the text. The original sketch of the action, as furnished by Planché, is as follows:

"Oberon, the Elfin king, having quarrelled with his fairy partner, vows never to be reconciled to her till he shall find two lovers constant through peril and temptation. To seek such a pair his 'tricksy spirit,' Puck, has ranged in vain through the world. Puck, however, hears the sentence passed on Sir Huon of Bordeaux, a young knight, who having been insulted by the son of Charlemagne, kills him in single combat, and is for this condemned by the monarch to travel to Bagdad to slay him who sits on the Caliph's left hand, and to claim his daughter as his bride. Oberon instantly resolves to make this pair the instruments of his reunion with his queen, and for this purpose he brings up Huon and Sherasmin asleep before him, enamors the knight by showing him Reiza, daughter of the Caliph, in a vision, transports him at his waking to Bagdad, and having given him a magic horn, by the blasts of which he is always to summon the assistance of Oberon, and a cup that fills at pleasure, disappears. Here Sir Huon rescues a man from a lion, who proves afterwards to be Prince Babekan, who is betrothed to Reiza. One of the properties of the cup is to detect misconduct. He offers it to Babekan. On raising it to his lips the wine turns to flame, and thus proves him a villain. He attempts to assassinate Huon, but is put to flight. The knight then learns from an old woman that the princess is to be married next day, but that Reiza has been influenced, like her lover, by a vision, and is resolved to be his alone. She believes that fate will protect her from her nuptials with Babekan, which are to be solemnized on the next day. Huon enters, fights with and vanquishes Babekan, and having spellbound the rest by a blast of the magic horn, he and Sherasmin carry off Reiza and Fatima. They are soon shipwrecked. Reiza is captured by pirates on a desert island and brought to Tunis, where she is sold to the Emir and exposed to every temptation, but she remains constant. Sir Huon, by the order of Oberon, is also conveyed thither. He undergoes similar trials from Roshana, the jealous wife of the Emir, but proving invulnerable she accuses him to her husband, and he is condemned to be burned on the same pile with Reiza. They are rescued by Sherasmin, who has the magic horn. Oberon appears with his queen, whom he has regained by their constancy, and the opera concludes with Charlemagne's pardon of Huon."

The overture, like that of "Der Freischütz," reflects the story, and is universally popular. Its leading themes are the horn solo, which forms the symphony of Sir Huon's vision, a short movement from the fairies' chorus, a martial strain from the last scene in the court of Charlemagne, a passage from Reiza's scene in the second act, and Puck's invocation of the spirits.

The first act opens in Oberon's bower with a melodious chorus of fairies and genii ("Light as fairy Feet can fall") followed by a solo for Oberon ("Fatal Oath"), portraying his melancholy mood, and "The Vision," a quaint, simple melody by Reiza ("Oh! why art thou sleeping?"), which leads up to a splendid ensemble ("Honor and Joy to the True and the Brave"), containing a solo for Oberon, during which the scene suddenly changes from the fairy bower to the city of Bagdad. Huon has a grand scena ("Oh! 't is a glorious Sight"), a composition in several movements beginning with a dramatic bravura illustrative of the scenes of the battlefield, and closing with a joyous, brisk allegretto ("Joy to the high-born Dames of France"). The finale begins with an aria by Reiza ("Yes, my Lord"), in the Italian style, passing into a duet for Reiza and Fatima, and closing with the chorus, "Now the Evening Watch is set."

The second act opens with a characteristic chorus ("Glory to the Caliph"), the music of which has been claimed by some critics as genuinely Moorish, though it is probable that Weber only imitated that style in conformity to the demands of the situation. A little march and three melodramatic passages lead up to an arietta for Fatima ("A lovely Arab Maid") beginning with a very pleasing minor and closing in a lively major. This leads directly to the lovely quartet, "Over the dark blue

Waters," — one of the most attractive numbers in the opera. It is a concerted piece for two sopranos, tenor, and bass, opening with two responsive solos in duet, first for the bass and tenor, and then for the two sopranos, the voices finally uniting in a joyous and animated movement of great power. The music now passes to the supernatural, and we have Puck's invocation to the spirits, whom he summons to raise a storm and sink the vessel in which the lovers have embarked. Puck's recitative is very powerful, and the chorus of the spirits in response, a very rapid presto movement, is in its way as effective as the incantation music in "Der Freischütz." The storm rises, the orchestra being the medium of the description, which is very graphic and effective. Huon has a short prayer ("Ruler of this awful Hour"), which is impressively solemn, and then follows Reiza's magnificent apostrophe to the sea ("Ocean, thou mighty Monster that liest curled like a green Serpent round about the World"). The scene is heroic in its construction, and its effective performance calls for the highest artistic power. It represents the gradual calm of the angry waters, the breaking of the sun through the gloom, and the arrival of a boat to the succor of the distressed Reiza. The immense effect of the scene is greatly enhanced by the descriptive instrumentation, especially in the allegro describing the rolling of the billows and the recitative and succeeding andante picturing the outburst of the sun. The mermaid's song ("Oh! 't is pleasant"), with its wavy, flowing melody, forms a fitting pendant to this great picture of elementary strife; and a delicate and graceful chorus closes the act.

The third act opens with a lovely song for Fatima ("Oh! Araby, dear Araby"), consisting of two movements, — an andante plaintively recalling past memories, and an allegro of exquisite taste. The song, even detached from the opera, has always been greatly admired in concert rooms, and, it is said, was a special favorite also with the composer. It is followed by a duet for Sherasmin and Fatima ("On the Banks of sweet Garonne"), which is of a vivacious and comic nature in Sherasmin's part, and then passes into a tender minor as Fatima sings. The next number is a trio for soprano, alto, and tenor ("And must I then dissemble?"), written very much in the style of the trio in "Der Freischütz," and yet purely original in its effect. Reiza follows with a smooth, flowing, and pathetic cavatina ("Mourn thou, poor Heart"), which is succeeded in marked contrast by a joyous rondo ("I revel in Hope") sung by Sir Huon. The next scene is that of Sir Huon's temptation, a voluptuous passage for ballet and chorus, interrupted at intervals by the energetic exclamations of the paladin as he successfully resists the sirens. The gay scene leads up to the finale. Sir Huon and Reiza are bound to the stake, surrounded by slaves singing a weird chorus. A blast from the magic horn sets them dancing, and a quartet for the four principal characters based upon the subject of the slaves' chorus ensues. Oberon appears and takes his leave after transporting the whole company to the royal halls of Charlemagne. A stirring march opens the scene, a beautiful aria by Huon follows ("Yes! even Love to Fame must yield"), and a chorus by the entire court closes the opera.

EURYANTHE

The opera of "Euryanthe" was written for the Kärnthnerthor Theatre, Vienna, where it was first produced October 25, 1823, though not with the success which afterwards greeted it in Berlin, owing to the Rossini craze with which the Austrian capital was afflicted at that time. The original cast was as follows:

Euryanthe	Frl. SONTAG.
Eglantine	Frau GRÜNBAUM.
Lysiart	Herr FORTI.
Adolar	Herr HEITZINGER.
Ludwig VI	Herr SEIPELT.

The libretto is by Helmine von Chezy, an eccentric old woman who proved a sad torment to the composer. The plot, which is a curious mixture of "Cymbeline" and "Lohengrin," was adapted from an old French romance, entitled "L'Histoire de Gerard de Nevers et de la belle et vertueuse Euryanthe, sa mie," and is substantially as follows :

In the palace of King Louis of France, where a brilliant assemblage is gathered, Count Adolar sings a tribute to the beauty and virtue of Euryanthe, his betrothed. Count Lysiart replies with a sneer and boast that he can gain her favor; but Adolar challenges him to bring a proof. The scene then changes to the castle of Nevers, and discloses Euryanthe longing for Adolar. Eglantine, who is also in love with Adolar, and who is conspiring against Euryanthe, soon joins her, and in their interview the latter rashly discloses the secret of a neighboring tomb known only to herself and Adolar. In this tomb rests the body of Emma, Adolar's sister, who had killed herself, and whose ghost had appeared to Euryanthe and her lover with the declaration that she can never be at peace until tears of innocence have been shed upon the ring which was the agency employed in her death. Lysiart arrives from court with a commission to take Euryanthe to the King, while Eglantine is left behind in possession of the secret.

In the second act Lysiart deplores his failure to obtain the favor of Euryanthe; but his hopes are renewed when he meets Eglantine emerging from the tomb with the ring, and learns from her that it can be made to convict Euryanthe of indiscretion, or at least of breaking her

462   THE STANDARD OPERAS

promise not to reveal the tomb secret. He obtains the ring, confronts Euryanthe with it at the palace, and forces her to admit the broken promise. Adolar, believing that she is guilty, drags her away to a wilderness where it is his intention to kill her; but on the way they are attacked by a serpent. Adolar slays the monster, and then, seized with sudden pity, he abandons his intention of killing her, but leaves her to her fate. She is subsequently found by the King while on a hunting expedition, and to him she relates the story of Eglantine's treachery. The King takes her with him to the palace. Meanwhile Adolar has begun to suspect that Euryanthe has been the victim of her base wiles, and on his way to Nevers to punish Lysiart he encounters the wedding procession of the guilty pair, and challenges him. The King suddenly arrives upon the scene and announces Euryanthe's death, whereupon Eglantine declares her love for Adolar. The furious Lysiart turns upon her and stabs her. Euryanthe is not dead. She has only fainted, and is soon restored to her lover, while Lysiart is led off to the scaffold.

The overture, which is familiar in our concert rooms, gives a sketch of the principal situations in the opera. The first act opens in the great banquet-hall of the King with a flowing and stately chorus ("Dem Frieden Heil") alternating between female and male voices and finally taken by the full chorus. Then follows Adolar's lovely and tender romanza ("Unter blühenden Mandelbäumen"). The next number, a chorus ("Heil! Euryanthe"), with recitatives for Adolar, Lysiart, and the King, leads up to a vigorous trio ("Wohlam! Du kennst"). Euryanthe's idyllic and touching cavatina ("Glöcklein im Thale") is a match in beauty and tenderness for Adolar's romanza. The recitative which follows introduces a sentimental aria for Eglantine ("O mein Leid ist unermessen"), leading to a duet with Euryanthe ("Unter ist mein Stern gegangen"). A scena for Eglantine, characterized by all the hatred and fury of jealousy, introduces the finale, which consists of a vigorous chorus ("Jubeltöne") accompanying Euryanthe's solo ("Fröhliche Klänge").

The second act opens with a powerful recitative and aria for Lysiart ("Wo berg ich mich"), which is full of passion. A duet of a menacing and sombre character between Lysiart and Eglantine ("Komm denn unser Leid zu rächen") stands out in gloomy contrast with Adolar's aria ("Wehen mir Lufte Ruh'") and the duet with Euryanthe ("Hin nimm die Seele mein"), so full of grace and tenderness, which lead up to the finale, a grand quartet ("Lass mich empor zum Lichte"), with powerful chorus accompaniment.

The last act opens with the serpent episode, accompanied by characteristic music, and a recitative scene between Euryanthe and Adolar leads up to a pathetic cavatina for Euryanthe ("Hier am Quell wo Weiden stehn"). The ringing notes of the horns behind the scenes announce the approach of the King's party, who sing a fresh and sonorous hunting chorus ("Die Thale dampfen"). The remaining numbers are a duet for Euryanthe and the King with chorus ("Lasst mich hier in Ruh' erblassen"), a lovely and melodious aria with chorus for Euryanthe ("Zu ihm"), a bright wedding march and scene with chorus, and a duet for Adolar and Lysiart with chorus, leading to the grand quintet and chorus which bring the opera to a close.

PRECIOSA

"Preciosa," romantic drama in four acts, text by Pius Alexander Wolff, after Cervantes's novel, "The Gypsy Maiden," was first produced in Berlin, March 14, 1821. "Preciosa" is not an opera in the strict sense but a drama with incidental music, Weber having composed the music for the songs and dances. The drama was first set to music by Eberwein, but when offered for performance was rejected upon the score of being "likely to create a false interest in the robber bands infesting the neighborhood of Berlin." Some time afterwards, when Wolff and Weber had become close friends, Weber was urged to furnish better music, which he did, although he had decided not to compose incidental music for dramas any more.

The story is a simple one. The child Preciosa is stolen by gypsies and grows up beautiful and accomplished. A young nobleman, Alonzo, falls in love with her and decides to remain with the gypsies and assume their habits for two years to prove his constancy and devotion. In the meantime, Eugenio, son of Don Azevedo, a friend of Don Francesco, Alonzo's father, arouses Alonzo's jealousy with the result that a quarrel follows and Alonzo finds himself in prison. In the last act, Donna Clara, Eugenio's mother, helps to release Alonzo, and for the sake of his father, Preciosa renounces her lover. While bidding them all farewell, she is greatly overcome, but in the end happiness is restored, for Preciosa turns out to be Donna Clara's own daughter, who had been stolen many years before. The denouement of course is Preciosa's union to her faithful lover, Alonzo.

The musical interest of "Preciosa" centres largely in Weber's skilful use of national melodies, especially the gypsy music. The most striking numbers are the overture, which still is a favorite on the concert stage, the Gypsy March, which opens the opera, followed by the chorus ("Hail Preciosa"), the melodramatic soliloquy for Preciosa, the Gypsy Chorus opening the second act with its descriptive accompaniment, and another Gypsy Chorus closing it, the Spanish national dance and the closing dramatic music in the last act. Although the music is incidental, Weber bestowed as much care upon it as if it had been the dominant feature. His son says: "On the 20th of July, the whole score of 'Preciosa' was despatched to Brühl, together with a lengthy notice to Wolff, relative to the nature, meaning, and musical character to be given to each separate piece, the precise introduction of every phrase of the melodramatic music during the declamation, and more especially of the echo, and of the movements and stage business of the gypsy band during the repetition of the voices in the distance." The chief interest, however, which attaches to "Preciosa" is the fact that it was the precursor of "Der Freischütz," and contains in a general way the ideas which were fully developed in that greatest opera in the German romantic school.

APPENDIX

BIBLIOGRAPHY OF AMERICAN OPERA

THE subjoined list of operas written by American composers does not include musical comedies, which are now so much in vogue, nor those very light operettas and musical farces which have been of the most ephemeral character. The compiler of this volume has sought only to make a record of those which can claim some degree of musical ambition and merit. A large number of operas have been written by American composers, but none of them has succeeded in making a permanent place for itself on the stage or securing a position which may be called standard. It cannot be doubted, however, that an American composer of grand opera will appear some day, and that his work will be accepted as worthy of a place by the side of English, French, German, and Italian operas.

The earliest American opera of which mention is made is "The Archers; or, the Mountaineers of Switzerland," written by Benjamin Carr, in 1756. Little is now known about it. The next opera was "The Disappointment; or, the Force of Credulity," by Andrew Barton, the libretto of which was published at Philadelphia in 1767. Mr. O. G. Senneck, Chief of the Music Department of the Congressional Library, in his scholarly monograph, "Francis Hopkinson, the First American Poet-composer," says of it: "'The Disappointment' was the first opera libretto written by a native American and printed in the Colonies. The work is entitled a comic opera for being interspersed with songs." Other early operas were "The Vintage" (1790) and "Edwin and Angelina," by Victor Pellesier (1798). The first operas written in the grand style were "Leonora" and "Notre Dame de Paris" (1863), by William H. Fry of New York, an accomplished musician, critic, and scholar. Both these operas were very successful at the time. In 1855, George F. Bristow also produced his opera, "Rip Van Winkle." It was well received, but it also is now unknown, except in libraries. The general bibliography of American operas is as follows:

ADAMOWSKI, TIMOTHY: "Lord Buncombe's Daughter."
ARONSON, RUDOLPH: "Captain Kidd."
ARTHUR, ALFRED: "The Water Carriers," "The Roundheads and Cavaliers," "Adaline."
BAKER, B. F.: "William Penn."
BARTLETT, HOMER N.: "La Vallière."
BASSFORD, WILLIAM K.: "Cassilda."
BECK, JOHANN H.: "Salammbo."
BIRD, ARTHUR: "Daphne."
BLAKE, CHARLES D.: "The Light Keeper's Daughter."
BONAWITZ, JOHANN H.: "The Bride of Messina," "Ostrolenka."
BUCK, DUDLEY: "Deseret."
BURR, FRANK A.: "Mizpah."
BUTTERFIELD, JAMES A.: "Romance of a Summer."
CHADWICK, GEORGE W.: "Tabasco," "Judith."
COERNE, L. A.: "A Woman of Marblehead."
CONVERSE, FREDERICK S.: "Pipe of Desire."
CROUCH, FREDERICK M.: "The Fifth of November," "Sir Roger de Coverley."
DAMROSCH, WALTER J.: "The Scarlet Letter."
DANKS, HARVEY P.: "Pauline."
DE KOVEN, REGINALD: "The Begum," "Don Quixote," "Robin Hood," "The Fencing Master," "The Knickerbockers," "The Algerian," "Rob Roy," "The Tzigane," "The Mandarin," "The Paris Doll," "The Highwayman," "The Three Dragoons," "Maid Marian," "Papa's Wife," "Foxy Quiller," "Little Duchess," "Red Feather," "Elysia," "The Student King."
EGGERS, ANTON C.: "Nina."

APPENDIX

EICHBERG, JULIUS: "Doctor of Alcantara," "The Rose of Tyrol," "The Two Cadis," "A Night in Rome."

FAIRLAMB, JAMES R.: "Treasured Tokens," "Valerie," "Leonello."

FANCIULLI, FRANCESCO: "Miles Standish."

FLORIO, CARYL (W. J. ROBJOHN): "Inferno," "Les Tours de Mercure," "Suzanne," "Sulda," "Uncle Tom."

GLEASON, FREDERICK G.: "Otho Visconti," "Montezuma."

GOLDBECK, ROBERT: "Soldiers' Return," "Saratoga," "Newport," "The Commodore."

GOTTSCHALK, LOUIS M.: "Charles IV," "Isaura de Salerno."

HAMERIK, ASGER: "Tovelille," "Hjalmar and Ingeborg," "La Vendetta," "The Traveler."

HARRIS, WILLIAM V.: "Mlle. Maie et M. de Lembre."

HENSCHEL, GEORGE: "Love's Stowaway."

HERBERT, VICTOR: "Prince Ananias," "The Wizard of the Nile," "The Serenade," "The Idol's Eye," "The Fortune Teller," "Cyrano de Bergerac," "The Ameer," "The Viceroy," "The Singing Girl," "Babette," "Babes in Toyland," "Mlle. Modiste," "It Happened in Nordland."

HOLST, EDOUARD: "Our Flats."

JORDAN, JULES: "Rip Van Winkle."

KELLY, EDGAR S.: "Puritania."

KIELBLOCK, FRANZ: "Miles Standish."

KLEIN, BRUNO O.: "Keno."

LAVELLE, CALIXO: "The Widow."

LEAVITT, W. J. D.: "Mercedes," "The Adventure Club," "Flowers and Lilies."

LOOMIS, HARVEY W.: "The Maid of Athens," "The Burglar's Bride."

LORENZ, J. M.: "The Pearl of Bagdad."

MARETZEK, MAX: "Hamlet," "Sleepy Hollow."

MERZ, KARL: "Last Will and Testament," "Katie Dean," "The Runaway Flirt."

MILLARD, HARRISON: "Deborah."

MOLLENHAUER, EDWARD: "The Corsican Bride."

NEUENDORFF, ADOLPH: "Rat Catcher of Hamelin," "Don Quixote."

PAGE, N. C.: "The First Lieutenant," "Villiers."

PAINE, JOHN K.: "Azara."

PRATT, SILAS G.: "Zenobia," "Lucille," "Triumph of Columbus," "Antonio."

PRÉVOST, EUGENE: "Esmeralda."

ROWE, G. F.: "Phyllis."

SHELLEY, HARRY R.: "Leila."

SOUSA, JOHN P.: "The Free Lance," "The Smugglers," "Desirée," "The Queen of Hearts," "El Capitan," "The Bride Elect," "The Charlatan," "Chris and the Wonderful Lamp," "Katherine."

STAHL, RICHARD: "Lee-li-nan."

SUSETTE, THOMAS W.: "Priscilla; or, the Pilgrims' Proxy," "Cascabel."

TRAJETTA, PHILIPPE: "The Venetian Maskers."

TRYON, G. W.: "Amy Gassenet."

VANDERSTUCKEN, FRANK: "Vlascla."

WEIL, OSCAR: "Pyramus and Thisbe."

WOOLF, BENJAMIN E.: "Lawn Tennis," "Pounce & Co.," "Westward Ho."

YOUNG, CORINNE: "Onganita."

APPENDIX TO NEW EDITION

SINCE the last edition of "The Standard Operas" appeared several operas not included in that volume have been produced upon the European and American stage. While some of these have met with popular appreciation, it would be premature as yet to accept that appreciation as permanent, much less absolutely to pronounce them "standard." It may be that success in some instances has been due rather to admiration for some operatic star than to the actual merits of the works themselves. But to bring "Standard Operas" down to date they are presented in the form of an appendix, compiled in some cases from the scores, and, where scores have not been available, from the best authorities, thus giving the reader an opportunity to become acquainted with some of the new operas as well as comparatively old operas produced for the first time in this country during the last two or three years.

ALBERT, D'

TIEFLAND

"TIEFLAND" is a musical setting of a well-known and popular Spanish drama, originally written in Catalonian by Angel Guimera, and called "Tevva Baixa." The Spanish dramatist, José Echegaray, next produced a version of it, called "Tierra Baja." An English version has been made familiar to American audiences by the actress, Bertha Kalich, as "Marta of the Lowlands." The libretto of "Tiefland" was adapted from the Catalonian version by Rudolph Lothar.

The opera was first produced in Prague in 1903, but without marked success. It was then revised by D'Albert and brought out in Hamburg in 1907, also in Berlin, and had a long run in both cities. Its first performance in this country took place in New York, Nov. 23, 1908.

The opera is divided into a prologue and three acts. The prologue opens among the Pyrenees Mountains and discloses the shepherd Pedro tending his flocks. He lives in solitude but has dreamed that the Lord will sometime send him a wife. The rich landowner Sebastiano appears and informs Pedro that he has brought the young girl Marta to him for his wife, and that he must leave the mountains and go down to the Lowlands for his wedding. Pedro, thinking his dream is realized, is overjoyed at the prospect, although Marta is unwilling and will not even look at Pedro. Behind Sebastiano's apparently generous proposal, however, is a dark plot. Years before this, Marta, the daughter of a strolling player, had come to the Lowlands where Sebastiano dwelt and had been induced to live with him as his mistress in consideration of his gift of a mill to her father. As Sebastiano is now about to wed an heiress, he has plotted to marry Marta to Pedro, and at the same time continue his illicit relations with her.

The first act is devoted to Pedro's arrival at the Lowland village, where his marriage is to take place at the mill. At first he is unable to understand why the villagers, who are aware of Marta's relations to Sebastiano, make sport of him. After the wedding, Marta, wishing to avoid Sebastiano, does not go to her chamber nor accompany Pedro, all of which mystifies him still more.

In the second act Marta begins to love her husband, but Pedro's persecutions continue and at last he tells her he is going back to the hills. She begs to go with him and tells him her story, whereupon he advances with his knife as if to kill her, but his love is stronger than his rage and they decide to go together. At this moment Sebastiano enters, ejects Pedro, and makes advances to Marta.

In the last act the heiress whom Sebastiano expects to marry rejects him and he renews his advances to Marta, who calls to Pedro for help. He rushes in with his knife, but, seeing that Sebastiano is unarmed, throws it down and strangles him. Catching Marta in his arms, he rushes out with the passionate exclamation, "Back to the mountains, far from the lowlands, to sunshine, freedom and light."

It will be seen from this brief sketch that the plot is of the simplest kind and the story merely one of elemental human passion, ending in the inevitable tragedy. It is of the same type as the subjects chosen by the writers of the modern Italian operas, for instance, Mascagni in "Cavalleria Rusticana" and "Iris," Puccini in "Tosca," and Leoncavallo in "Pagliacci"; in a word, it is the jealousy and sudden passionate fury of the South set forth in this opera in the regular and symphonic Teutonic manner, and its outcome is somewhat incongruous. It resembles these modern

Italian music-dramas, however, in that it contains no formal numbers or sustained melodies. The composer has sought to make his music grow out of the dramatic situation, with the result that it is declamatory rather than lyrical, and yet there are strong and beautiful moments, such as Pedro's recital of the vision of the Virgin; the shepherd's description of his killing of the wolf; and Marta's story as she sits by the fire; as well as the passionate climax, when after the tragedy they leave Tiefland and go back to the mountains. But upon the whole, like "Pagliacci" and "Cavalleria Rusticana," the interest of this opera is dramatic rather than musical. The "Marta of the Lowlands," as presented by Kalich, is much stronger dramatically than the "Tiefland" of D'Albert.

BRETON

La Dolores

THE name of Breton, although he is the most eminent of living Spanish composers, was unknown to this country until about two years ago. Tomas Breton was born, at Salamanca in 1846. It is somewhat curious that he is specially eminent as a composer of chamber music, a department in which the modern Latin composers have never greatly excelled. His quartets and trios are reputed to be masterly in design and very effective in treatment. His fame out of his own country, however, rests upon his lyrical dramas, the only one of which known in this country is "La Dolores," first produced in Madrid in 1895, and in this country in 1909.

The libretto was written by the composer himself and the opera is divided into three acts, the scene being laid in Aragon, and the time the present. Its atmosphere is Spanish throughout, as will be seen by the story and the *dramatis personæ*, which include Dolores, the heroine; Gaspara, an innkeeper; Lazaro, her son; Celemino, the tenor; Melchior, a barber; Patrizio, baritone; Rojas, a sergeant; and the muleteer, a second tenor.

The first act opens in the market-place of Calatayud where Patrizio and Celemino are seated at a table before Gaspara's inn, discoursing of Dolores, whom Patrizio wishes to marry. A troop of soldiers enter, headed by Rojas, who is also in love with Dolores, but the latter as she brings wine flouts them both. Meanwhile, Lazaro, who is being educated for the church, and who is secretly in love with Dolores, comes with a message to her from his mother. Next enters

Melchior, the barber, who has seduced Dolores and is about to marry another. She pleads with him to restore her honor, only to be insulted by him.

The second act opens in the courtyard of the inn, with a song by Lazaro, describing his hopeless passion for Dolores. Patrizio, Rojas, and Celemino next come upon the scene. Patrizio is drnnk and quarrelsome, and Rojas boastful about his exploits in the bull ring. Melchior appears and boasts his love for Dolores. After these have departed, Lazaro enters and declares his passion to Dolores. The people gather for the bull fight, Celemino among them, who jeers at Lazaro, receiving a blow in return. The story of the fight is then told, how Rojas was getting the worst of the encounter, when Lazaro sprang into the arena and killed the bull — an exploit which secures him Dolores' promise of love.

The third act is laid in a room in the inn. Lazaro is chanting the litany, after which Dolores tells him he must not come to her room that evening. Celemino informs Lazaro of Melchior's boast about Dolores to which, however, he pays no heed. Afraid of Melchior's designs, Dolores asks Patrizio and Rojas to come to her room, after she has told Lazaro's mother of her love for him. Melchior at last enters her apartment and insults her. The furious Lazaro bursts in and attacks Melchior, and in the struggle both fall through the window. Lazaro returns with the intention of killing Dolores also, but has hardly locked the door when Celemino, Patrizio, and Rojas demand admission. Dolores refuses to unlock the door, but they break the door and inquire what has happened. Dolores replies that Melchior insulted her and she has killed him. Lazaro exclaims that Dolores is an impure woman and made so by Melchior, and that he himself has killed him.

It will be seen that the action is melodramatic and the atmosphere Spanish throughout. The music is spirited,

APPENDIX 477

dramatic, and full of local color. The prominent numbers are the muleteer's song, the soldier's song by Sergeant Rojas, the chorus of Rondalla, and the Jota, a national dance of Aragon, with couplets, in the first act; the madrigal by Lazaro, and the Toreador song by Rojas, and bull fight description in the second act, which is suggestive of the similar scene in "Carmen," though it does not imitate Bizet's music; and the impressive litany and descriptive accompaniment of the tragic finale, in the third act.

BRUNEAU

L'Attaque du Moulin

BRUNEAU'S opera, "L'Attaque du Moulin," was first produced at the Paris Opera Comique in 1893 and in this country in 1908. The libretto, by M. Gallet, is based upon one of Zola's stories in his "Soirées de Medan." Zola indeed furnished Bruneau with many librettos, that of "L'Attaque du Moulin" being the last one used by Bruneau which was not written by his friend. The original story dealt with an episode in the Franco-Prussian War, but for certain State reasons the story was referred back to the war of 1792. Bruneau's earlier operas met with little success in Paris because of his ardent espousal of the cause of Zola in the Dreyfus affair and some of them were banished from the stage. "L'Attaque du Moulin" itself was not successful at first, for musical rather than political reasons, however, but it gradually overcame Parisian prejudice and the attacks of critics and established itself in favor.

The first act opens with the preparations for the marriage of Françoise, daughter of Merlier, the miller, to Dominique, a native of Flanders, but in the midst of the festivities the town crier announces the declaration of war.

The opening of the second act discloses the mill under attack by the enemy and its capture. Dominique is taken prisoner but is offered his life upon condition that he will guide the enemy's troops to a certain position of strategic importance. He refuses and is left a prisoner in the mill. Françoise finds her way to him, gives him a knife, and tells him to make his escape while she engages the attention of the sentinel.

In the third act Dominique kills the sentinel and escapes into the forest. Thereupon Merlier, the miller, is summoned by the enemy's commander and notified that unless he reveals the hiding place of Dominique, he shall be shot in his stead.

The opening of the fourth act shows Dominique returning by stealth to the mill where he is told by Merlier that he has been pardoned, which is untrue, and is sent by him to hurry the advance of the French troops. The enemy is repulsed, but before the mill is given up, Merlier is shot before the eyes of Françoise just as Dominique enters at the head of the victorious French.

The story is but an episode and the music itself is somewhat episodical. Bruneau was at one time looked upon as Wagner's successor, though his earlier works did not show that feeling for melody or skill in orchestral treatment which entitled him to wear Wagner's mantle. In fact, in those operas, as well as in "L'Attaque du Moulin," he seems to have a contempt for musical beauty. All rules of harmony are disregarded and dissonances are freely used, which led the conservative French critics to declare that his music was all noise and confusion. In the opera under consideration the points in which he resembles Wagner are the continuous melodic recitatives and the individual use of voices. In "L'Attaque du Moulin," however, he relaxes considerably from his former style and is much less severe in his treatment of voices, even allowing them to sing together occasionally, and yet hardly reaching what might be called conventional melody. His purpose in this, as in his other operas, is evidently to express details of action and emotional traits in his music. In an article written by himself he defines the "lyrical drama" in a manner which may sufficiently explain "L'Attaque du Moulin." It is music uniting itself "intimately to the poetry in order to impart life, movement, passionate interest to a human action, the course of which must run uninterruptedly from the rising of the curtain to the last scene." And again, "the orchestra comments upon the inward thoughts of the different characters, makes known the reasons that cause them to act, and whilst depicting their natures, magically evokes before our eyes the subtle and fabulous scenes dreamed of by our fancy." In other words, he is seeking for infinite melody as the basis of realism in music. It is questionable whether he has been successful in his search, or brings before the eyes any scenes which can be explained without a programme.

CATALANI

La Wally

ALFREDO CATALANI, the Italian opera composer, although he died seventeen years ago, in his fifty-sixth year, and for many years was well known in Italy, has but recently been discovered in this country. He was born at Lucca in 1854 and began writing sacred music in his fourteenth year. At seventeen, unlike other Italian composers, he entered the Paris Conservatory, and two years later the Milan Conservatory, in which city he produced his first dramatic work. It was followed by five more operas and a symphonic poem, all of which proved successful. His best known opera, " La Wally," was brought out in Milan in 1892, and a year later its composer died.

" La Wally " at first encountered hostile criticism, but in 1893 it made a great success in Buenos Ayres. It was also heard many times in Europe, where it has steadily gained in favor, and was first produced in this country in 1908. The book, by the well-known Italian librettist, Luigi Illica, is based upon " Geyer-Wally," a German novel, written by the Baroness Wilhelmine Von Hillern in 1873. The action takes place in the Tyrolean Alps early in the nineteenth century, and is distributed over four acts.

The first act opens at the village of Hochstoff, outside of the hut of Stromminger, the hunter, where his friends are celebrating his seventieth birthday. One of these friends is Gellner, a noted marksman, who has a quarrel with Hagenbach, a rival marksman from another village. The latter is also a rival for the hand of Wally, Stromminger's daughter. When the hunter discovers this he becomes infuriated and promises his daughter to Gellner; when she refuses to obey her father, he turns her out of doors.

In the second act Stromminger has died and Wally has inherited his wealth, but will not think of marriage. The two rivals appear upon the scene and Hagenbach flirts with Afra, the innkeeper's daughter. This so enrages Wally that she insults her, whereupon Hagenbach consoles Afra by telling her he will force Wally to give him a kiss, which he accomplishes by asking it as the prize of a dance. The spectators, who are aware of the scheme, jeer at Wally, who then turns to Gellner and demands that he shall kill Hagenbach.

In the third act Gellner meets Hagenbach in a dark place and pushes him over a precipice. Thereupon the fickle Wally is overcome by remorse, climbs down the descent, and helps to rescue Hagenbach.

The fourth act finds Wally in a lonely mountain hut. Hagenbach appears and declares his love for her. Wally now finds herself violently in love with him, and the two become so absorbed with their passion that they do not notice the approach of a violent storm. Hagenbach on his way down the mountain is killed by an avalanche and Wally meets her fate by hurling herself over the precipice.

The story, as will be perceived, has ample opportunities for melodramatic music and Catalani has improved them. It is theatrical, however, rather than lyric in these opportunities and yet the composer has enriched his score with many melodic beauties and with much vivacious dramatic music as well as charming orchestration. The weakest spot in the opera perhaps is the one which should have been the strongest, namely, the Kiss dance. It is hardly above the commonplace, especially when compared with any of the efforts of the Viennese light opera composers in that direction. The most effective passages in the opera are the Edelweiss song by Walter, Hagenbach's hunting song, and Wally's song in the finale of the first act; the duet between Gellner and Wally in the second act in which he pleads his cause and after he is repulsed tells Wally that Hagenbach will soon wed Afra; the recurrence in the third act of the music heard at the close of the first; and the song for Walter and final duet in the fourth act preceding the tragedy.

CHARPENTIER

Louise

CHARPENTIER'S "Louise," an opera in four acts, libretto by the composer, was first produced in Paris in 1900 and in this country in 1909. The story is a simple one. Its background is the life of the gay city of Paris, and in detail the stirring scenes of Montmartre, the home of the composer, which he has portrayed most realistically in others of his works. It is first and last a story of Paris life, like Puccini's "La Bohème," and deals with the same fascinating material. Naturally such a work met with its most enthusiastic greeting at the hands of Parisians to whom every scene was familiar, but notwithstanding its lack of scope and its local color it has commended itself elsewhere by reason of its human quality and effective musical treatment, and especially its orchestral expression. The plot is very simple and turns upon the breaking of home ties in a tragic way by Louise, with the accompaniments of the Paris street life and the revels of Montmartre. Its characters also are few, including only Louise, her father and mother, her Bohemian poet lover Julien, an errand girl, and the King of the Fools in the revels, with pedlers, working people, grisettes, and Bohemians filling in the background.

In the first act, which transpires in the garret home of Louise, it is disclosed that Louise is in love with Julien, the Bohemian poet, whose manner of life does not commend itself to her parents. He has written to them but his letter has not been acknowledged. Louise informs her lover of this and advises him to write a second letter,

APPENDIX

promising to run away with him if it is rejected. The second letter comes. The father is somewhat more lenient, but the mother grows more bitter.

In the second act Julien among his boon companions in Montmartre meets Louise and inquires the fate of his second letter. She informs him it is unfavorable. He reminds her of her promise and begs her to fly with him, but she refuses, fearful of the effect it might have upon her father. The next scene shows Louise at work with other girls in a sewing room. In the courtyard below Julien and his comrades serenade her. The girls at first are delighted with the serenade but at last getting tired of it, they abuse him. Louise, overcome by her emotions, pleads illness, leaves the shop, and her companions see her going away with her lover.

The third act finds Louise and Julien living together at Montmartre. Their friends come to their cottage to crown her as the Muse of Montmartre and decorate the house. She receives a black and silver shawl, the symbol of her office, and the revel begins with gay songs and dances. In the midst of the ceremonies Louise's mother appears, and when alone with her and Julien, informs her that her father is dying, and that Louise's return may save him. She promises Julien that no restraint shall be placed upon her and at last he consents to her departure.

In the last act Louise is at home. Her father upbraids her for her unfilial conduct and begs her to love him as she used to do. But Louise grows bitter and complains that having been promised her liberty she is kept a prisoner. The parents plead with her, but to no purpose, and at last she calls for Julien to come to her, saying all she wants is Julien and Paris. The father in a rage opens the door and bids her begone. She rushes out with a wild cry. The father goes to the window and implores her to return, but it is too late. Shaking his fist at the city, he exclaims, "Oh! Paris," and the curtain falls upon the homely tragedy.

The music of this extraordinary lyric picture of Paris life is realistic in the highest degree, wonderfully expressive of traits of character and Parisian street life, poetic in its feeling, and effective in dramatic skill and rich orchestration. Its striking numbers are Julien's love song in the first act; his serenade in the second act; the duet of Julien and Louise, "Paris, City of Strength," the farandole, address of the King of Fools, and ragman's sombre song in the third act; the father's lullaby and the duet between him and his daughter and the succeeding climax in the fourth act, as well as the workroom chorus, the chorus of the Bohemians, and the street cries which help fill in the musical picture.

CONVERSE

THE PIPE OF DESIRE

"THE Pipe of Desire," an opera, by Frederick S. Converse, was first performed in Boston in the spring season of 1906 and again in New York by the Metropolitan Opera House Company in the spring season of 1910. Its production upon the latter occasion was a notable event, as the opera is the work of an American composer, the performance was in English, and the performers were Americans. Many operettas by De Koven, Herbert, Sousa, Maretzek, and others have been given in English, and Mr. Walter Damrosch a few years ago produced his "Scarlet Letter" in one of his own seasons, but the recent performance of "The Pipe of Desire" in New York marks the first time that a grand opera has been brought forward in English in the regular season since the days of Fry's "Leonora" and "Hunchback of Notre Dame," and Bristow's "Rip Van Winkle."

"The Pipe of Desire" is in one act, the libretto by George E. Barton. Its story is symbolic and in a certain sense philosophical. In a word, it is the old story of free will and fate. The characters are few, including only a peasant, Iolan, his betrothed, Naoia, and the Old One, who is the King of the elves and the sylphs, and keeper of the Pipe of Desire, which is the symbol of unchangeable law.

The curtain rises upon a glade in springtime in which the sylphs and elves are engaged in the service of the Old One, their King. Iolan, the peasant, makes his appearance. He has returned from a successful quest for fortune that he may marry Naoia. He enters singing an exultant strain to which the elves make response. The Old One reminds them this is forbidden, but they protest they have the privilege as it is the first day of Spring. As Iolan hears their call he invites them to his wedding. Observing the Old One with the pipe hanging from his neck, he asks what it is for, and upon being told that it signifies the sceptre of the world, he laughs at them and declares it is only fit for the dance. The elves, availing themselves of their privilege, call for the dance, but the Old One, knowing the penalty which must follow, entreats them to wait until Iolan has gone. They decline to do so and he plays the Dance of Spring. Iolan mocks the power of the pipe, but they tell him it can make him dance also. They demand that the Old One shall play again. He does so and Iolan is forced to dance. Infuriated, he snatches the pipe and plays it himself to make the Old One dance. He produces only most discordant sounds, however. Then he expresses the desire that the pipe shall play the emotions in his own heart. He sees the object of his desire and calls upon Naoia to meet him in the forest. The Old One warns him of the penalty, but he plays again and this time sees Naoia desperately ill in her cottage. He also sees her listening to his call, rising from her bed in delirium, searching for him in the forest, and at last falling and dying from fatigue and exposure. He throws away the pipe and curses God, but the Old One reminds him it was his own and not God's will which has brought about this sorrow. His anger then turns to remorse and regret. In pity, the elves implore the Old One to play the song of Autumn and Winter. As he does so, Iolan feels himself growing old and overtaken by the chill of death. In his last moment he sees the vision of Naoia waiting above for him to come to her. He hastens to meet her and begins the new life.

The music is after the manner of Wagner in the use of

APPENDIX

motives, four of them being employed, the first representing the pipe; the second, unchanging law; the third, Iolan, and the fourth his love feeling for Naoia. It is also after the manner of Debussy in having no set vocal melodies but musical declamations skilfully accompanied. As "The Pipe of Desire" may be a long time in penetrating Western wilds, some extracts from the leading New York criticisms on the morning following its recent performance may prove of interest. Mr. Krehbiel of the *Tribune* says of the book:

The Old One, as the King is called, is a mixture of Wagner's Wotan and Ambroise Thomas's Harper; the First Salamander is an absurd caricature of Loge, the First Gnome of Mme. Naoia, the mortal woman goes mad like Lucia and Marguerite and dies stricken like Mireille. The pipe is Oberon's horn, Tamino's flute, and Papageno's bells, though it fails to discourse music of the kind that its nature and magic power would seem to invite. The elves dance about Iolan, the shepherd, like the flower maidens around Parsifal. The gnomes and salamanders burst through the ranks of the dancers like the satyrs in the bacchanalian scene in "Tannhäuser."

Mr. Aldrich of the *Times* says of the music:

Mr. Converse in this music, as in other music of his that has been heard here, is entirely a modern, in his harmonies, in the quality of his invention. He uses no set forms; his orchestra has a free and spontaneous utterance, a perfectly independent function of its own. The orchestration is skilful, that of one who has something more than the facility that comes of training, and whose ideas are cast naturally in the orchestral mould, conceived with orchestral color.

Mr. Finck of the *Evening Post* says generally:

Mr. Converse was sadly handicapped by this text, yet his score also gives evidence of a plentiful lack of experience as a maker of operas. He does not know how to write effectively and idiomatically for the voices, and he lacks the gift of originating vocal melodies, the result being that although the opera lasts only an hour and ten minutes, and all the numbers are short, it seems too long, and for the most part dull. By far the best portions are the choruses, which are well conceived and effective, though not in the least elfish, as Weber or Mendelssohn would have made them. The orchestral music is undisguisedly Wagnerian; starting with "Götterdämmerung," we have reminiscences of "Die Meistersinger," "Siegfried," "Parsifal," and, in the death scene, of "Tristan."

DEBUSSY

Pelléas and Mélisande

THE "opera" of "Pelléas and Mélisande" is not an opera in the conventional sense. It is usually classified as a "lyrical drama," but if by this term it is implied that it contains lyrics, the classification is not accurate. Perhaps it would be correct to call it an impressionist tone-picture. It is based upon the drama of the same name, written by Maurice Maeterlinck in 1892 and first performed in Paris in 1893. Mrs. Patrick Campbell familiarized American audiences with the play in 1902.

The musical setting of the drama was first given in Paris in 1902 with Mary Garden and M. Jean Périer in the title roles. It was heard in Brussels and Frankfort in 1907 and in this country in 1909. The score, sometimes called a "revolutionary score," is arranged in five acts and twelve scenes. The libretto was adapted by Debussy himself, and owing to numerous excisions provoked a bitter quarrel between the dramatist and composer.

The first act opens in a forest. Golaud, the hunter, has been led astray by his dogs and while trying to find his way meets Mélisande weeping by a spring. She also has been lost but refuses to reveal her identity to Golaud. She is weeping because she has lost her crown in the water. He offers to recover it but she says she will have no more of it. He at last prevails upon her to leave the forest with him. The next scene reveals the castle where Golaud, his mother Geneviève, his son Yniold, child of his first wife, his half brother Pelléas, and his old father Arkël, King of Allemande, reside. Geneviève is reading a letter sent to Pelléas by

Golaud in which he announces his marriage to Mélisande and asks her to intercede with Arkël to receive her as his daughter. The intercession is favorable. The next scene shows Mélisande and Geneviève walking in the gardens, joined by Pelléas. The interview shows that Pelléas is in love with Mélisande.

The second act discloses Pelléas and Mélisande sitting by a fountain in the park. Mélisande is playing with the wedding ring and at last tosses it up and it falls into the water. Pelléas advises her to tell the truth if Golaud questions her about it. In the next scene Golaud has been injured while hunting. Mélisande, while tending him, confesses she is unhappy but does not tell her husband why. When he notices the absence of the ring and inquires about it she declares she lost it in a grotto by the shore. He requests that she and Pelléas shall go and search for it. The next scene reveals the two in the grotto in a state of agitation.

In the opening of the third act Mélisande is standing at the tower window singing and combing her hair. As she leans out to greet Pelléas her loosened tresses fall about him. He twines them about his arm, threatening thus to hold her a prisoner the night long. Golaud discovers them and his jealousy is at last aroused. His suspicions are confirmed by the little child Yniold who relates what he has seen passing between his mother and uncle.

In the fourth act Pelléas, about to travel, begs a meeting with Mélisande at the fountain, which she grants. Pelléas keeps his tryst and the two exchange love vows. While embracing one another, Golaud suddenly rushes upon them with drawn sword and kills Pelléas. Mélisande flees in terror pursued by Golaud.

The last act reveals Mélisande dying. On her deathbed she had been delivered of a child and Golaud, who had sought to kill himself with the same sword that slew Pelléas, is filled with remorse for killing her without cause. She calls for Golaud and confesses she had loved Pelléas, but it was not a guilty love. The new-born babe is brought in to her but she is too weak to take it. As she passes away the servants fall upon their knees. Golaud sobs aloud, but Arkël bids them all go and leave the dead mother with the child.

It would be impossible to call attention to this or that number or to analyze numbers where there are none. The listener will listen in vain for melodies. In answer to his critics at the time of the first performances Debussy said, "I have been reproached because in my score the melodic phrase is always in the orchestra, never in the voice. I tried, with all my strength and all my sincerity, to identify my music with the poetical essence of the drama." The result of this to the hearer untutored in impression is something shadowy and mystical, and because it is shadowy and mystical throughout therefore it is monotonous. To appreciate it and enjoy it one must not merely understand the use of the leit-motif and continuous melody, but he must have senses keenly attuned to the poetic significance of the drama and a musical knowledge delicate enough to understand how this poetic significance is interpreted musically. He must abandon all conventional ideas of melody, all purely musical emotion, all symphonic development of orchestration, and listen to what has been called "sound wraiths," as so-called melody which is intangible, and to many a passage which is too subtle for appreciation. As to the characters, they were called by Debussy's critics "stammering phantoms," as indeed they are in most of the "revolutionary music." Would not "Pelléas and Mélisande have been just as effective if the composer had left voices out entirely and scored the drama as he has done his "Prélude à l'Après-midi d'un Faune"? Debussy is a school in himself. Some day the world may come to know him. It is idle to affirm or deny anything in these days of musical transition.

FRANCHETTI

Germania

THE name of Franchetti is not an unfamiliar one in the American concert-room and opera house. More than twenty years ago Theodore Thomas included one of his symphonies in a New York Philharmonic programme, and in the following year produced the prelude to his opera "Asraële," the entire opera being given in New York in the season of 1890–91. "Germania," his last important work, was brought out for the first time in Milan in 1902, and in this country in 1909–10. The composer is of the Rothschild family on his mother's side, a baron by rank and very wealthy, but notwithstanding these drawbacks has shown himself a serious, industrious, and talented musician. He belongs neither to the advanced young Italian school nor to the Wagner school. In this regard he may be reckoned an independent composer, though in Italy he is regarded as the Italian Meyerbeer, probably from his love for the spectacular and great masses of sound.

The libretto of "Germania" was written by Luigi Illica, and its incidents are taken from the days of the Napoleonic invasion of Germany. It is peculiarly interesting for its array of historical characters, including Johann Philipp Palm, the printer whom Napoleon ordered shot; Karl Theodore Körner, the poet, and Baron Lützow; Carl Maria von Weber, Schlegel, Fichte, and Queen Louise.

The opera is arranged in a prologue, two acts, and epilogue. The prologue opens in an old Nuremberg mill, the hiding place of Palm, and also the place where the incendiary literature is printed. Several of the student patriots are gathered there and in their midst suddenly appears

Ricke, who has been wronged by Karl Worms, one of the students, and is in love with Frederick Loewe, another of the band who is at the front. Loewe returns, however, and implores Ricke to become his bride, just as the police enter the mill and arrest Palm.

The opening of the first act discloses a hut in the Black Forest, where Loewe and Ricke are in concealment, and are to be married that day. At the conclusion of the ceremony Worms arrives, fatigued with his wandering, and asks for shelter, but departs as he recognizes the married couple. Ricke, overcome by remorse, leaves her husband.

The second act opens in the secret resort of the Louise band, a patriotic order in Königsberg. Karl Worms is the leader, and in the midst of their discussions a voice is raised against Worms. When he discovers it is that of Loewe, insults are exchanged and a duel is only prevented by the sudden appearance of Queen Louise, leading Prince William. She interposes and peace is preserved.

The epilogue discloses the battlefield at Leipsic. Ricke, wandering over the field, discovers Loewe mortally wounded. He declares to her that he knows she is innocent and pleads with her to forgive Worms, who fell near him. She discovers the latter's body, and as she stands there Napoleon and his army appear in retreat. Loewe raises himself, apostrophizes Germany, and falls back dead.

The spectacular nature of the story and the large number of persons engaged upon the stage afford Franchetti the opportunity for just such a score as is best suited to his talent. While not appealing deeply to the emotions nor impressing by its elevation or nobility, still it is music written in a skilful and scholarly manner and shows the effect of his early German training, — an unusual quality in an Italian musician. One of the most impressive passages in the opera is that of the singing of the hymn of liberty by the patriots.

GIORDANO

Andrea Chenier

THE opera of "Andrea Chenier" by Umberto Giordano was first produced in Milan in 1896. The libretto is by Luigi Illica, the place Paris, and the time that of the French Revolution. The opera is arranged in four acts.

The first act opens in the ballroom of the Château de Coigny and discloses Gerard, who is a revolutionary and anixous to escape from domestic service, setting the ballroom to order. The Countess enters with Maddalena and Bersi her maid, and is followed by guests, among them the Abbé, Fléville, and Chenier, a poet. After some gay chatter the music strikes up for the dance and is interrupted by Gerard, who appears at the head of a forlorn-looking crowd, who are ordered out by the Countess, while Gerard's father intercedes for him.

The second act opens in the Café Hottot and reveals Chenier sitting at one table and Bersi and a spy at another. The spy is watching both of them. At this moment a friend brings Chenier his passport and urges him to quit Paris as he is to meet that day an unknown lady with whom he is in love. A mob headed by Robespierre passes the *café*, after which Bersi requests Chenier to await a lady called "Speranza." In the darkness Maddalena, watched by the spy, comes to meet Chenier. As she throws back her disguise he recognizes her and the spy goes to report to Gerard. They declare their love and are about to fly when Gerard intercepts them and tries to seize her. In the encounter which ensues, Gerard is wounded but warns Chenier he is proscribed and implores him to save Maddalena. Chenier flies and the mob surrounds Gerard, who pretends he does not know who wounded him.

The third act opens in the Revolutionary Tribunal. While a member is addressing it, Gerard, though suffering from his wound, appears and pleads for money for the cause. The spy notifies Gerard that Chenier has been arrested and that Maddalena is near by. He also urges Gerard to inform against Chenier, who signs the necessary papers. At this moment Maddalena appears. Gerard declares that Chenier is in prison and avows his love for her. Maddalena seeks to escape and offers her honor for Chenier's life, but Chenier is summoned for trial and denounced as a traitor. He denies the charge and as he is making his defence Gerard cries out that he had made his accusations from motives of jealousy. The mob, however, demands vengeance, and Chenier is led away.

The last act opens at midnight in the prison of Saint Lazare, where Chenier sits writing. Ronches, his friend, is with him and Chenier reads his poem to him. Maddalena enters with Gerard and bribes the jailer to put her name on the death list in place of another woman, that she may die with her lover. They go to the executioner together.

It is about thirteen years ago that "Andrea Chenier" was first given in this country, and when it was revived last year it still preserved its charm. The text is thoroughly dramatic and the music suits it. It abounds in melodic passages and is also enlivened by the introduction of the "Marseillaise," the "Ça Ira," and "Carmagnola," the war calls of the Revolution. The most striking points of the opera are Gerard's monologue in the Tribunal Chamber and the subsequent duet with Maddalena, the Shepherd's Song in the first act, Chenier's solos both in the first and second acts, and the love duet with Maddalena.

APPENDIX

GOLDMARK

Cricket on the Hearth

"HEIMCHEN AM HERD," or the "Cricket on the Hearth," was written by Carl Goldmark, the text by Willner, and was first produced at Berlin in 1896, but it did not find its way to this country until the present year. It is divided into three acts, the story closely following Dickens' well-known tale.

The first act opens in the home of John Peerybingle with a prologue by the elves, followed by a song by the cricket, the dweller on the hearth. Dot tells the cricket the secret of the child. May, the orphan, lamenting her departed lover, grieves over her coming marriage to old Tackleton. Meanwhile John comes home, bringing Edward, her lover, in the disguise of a sailor.

The second act transpires in a garden, disclosing May and Tackleton at supper, the latter very jealous of this mysterious newcomer. Edward reveals himself to Dot, and John in turn becomes so jealous of him that he is bent upon killing himself. But the cricket charms him to sleep and in his sleep he dreams that he is in a garden peopled by elves and that he is to be a happy father.

The third act opens in John's home, and May, convinced of Edward's loyalty, leaves with him for the marriage ceremony, in spite of Tackleton's effort to prevent it. Dot tells John her secret and he too is reconciled, and a tableau of the happy quartet closes the scene.

As compared with the operas of impression and the efforts of the advanced composers to make the orchestration tell the story without the aid of the conventional melody, the "Cricket on the Hearth" seems old-fashioned enough. It is a simple, charming story, illustrated by simple, charming, tuneful music that appeals to the heart rather than to the head. It is all fresh and spontaneous from beginning to end, and story and music are perfectly blended. The special points of interest are the chorus of elves, the cricket's song, "I am the Cricket," and the home song in the first act; the quintet, Dot's dance, and cricket's song in the second; and the prelude, the basis of which is a German folk-song, Edward's song of the sea, and the marriage choruses in the finale of the third.

LEHAR

The Merry Widow

FRANZ LEHAR'S " Die lustige Witve " (" The Merry Widow ") was first produced in Vienna in 1908 and almost immediately started upon a tour of Europe, reaching this country in the same year, where the reception of the fascinating little operetta was no less enthusiastic than it had been abroad. Like the operettas of Sullivan and Gilbert it overshadowed everything else for the time being and it still holds the stage, though not so absorbingly as of yore. Probably its success will prove evanescent, but as a phenomenal event it deserves chronicling in these pages.

The principal personages in this story are Prince Danilo of Marsovia and Sonia, a peasant's daughter. Some time before the beginning of the action, the Prince had been in love with Sonia, but to break off the affair he is sent to Paris by his uncle, the King, as a diplomatic *attaché*, and there he plunges into dissipation to forget his troubles. In the meantime Sonia solaces herself by marrying a rich banker who dies and leaves his millions to her. She betakes herself to Paris and becomes a merry widow, professing to care no longer for the Prince and rejecting all offers of marriage with contempt. In the midst of her dissipations she meets her old lover who has been spending his days and nights at Maxim's, and is hardly sober. She still loves him, but when he begins to grow affectionate she turns cold as she fancies that he is attracted only by her money. This so offends the Prince that he declares nothing on earth shall make him say again that he loves her. At last,

APPENDIX 501

however, in a moment of repentance she selects him as a partner in a dance, but he sells her choice to another for some thousands of dollars. At last when the Prince positively refuses to dance with her she begins an old Marsovian waltz which so fascinates him that he is forced to join her. But the Prince leaves her disconsolate.

In a subsidiary plot Natalie, wife of Baron Popoff, is in an intrigue with the Viscomte de Jolidon. The baron, who has confidence in his wife, sees a man and woman entering a pavilion, and, moved by curiosity, peeps through the keyhole and beholds the Viscomte kissing a woman who he is quite sure is his wife. Sonia improves the opportunity to slip into the pavilion and take the woman's place, and then, to save the Viscomtesse and further inflame the jealousy of the Prince, comes out leaning upon the Viscomte's arm. In dire rage the Prince rushes off declaring he has done with her forever, but Sonia is quite sure that she has his love. A fan with the words "I love you" written upon it finds its way into the Prince's hands and Sonia concludes he has written them. Finally he confesses that he really loves her after she tells him that if she marries again she will lose her fortune.

The operetta is arranged in three acts, the first at the Marsovian embassy in Paris, the second in Sonia's gardens, and the the third in the Café Maxim, though the third act has little or only a forced connection with the story, the scene in Maxim's evidently having been added for spectacular effect. There are a few pretty lyrics like Sonia's Marsovian song, Danilo's Maxim song, the duet in the second act for Sonia and Danilo, and the opening chorus of the third act, but the real fascination of the operetta is saltatory. Without the Merry Widow Waltz, simple as it is in construction, and the quaint Hungarian dance in Sonia's gardens, the work would lose its principal interest. The rage for the Merry Widow Waltz was equalled only by the rage for the Merry Widow hat and other monstrous headgear which it introduced. It is interesting to note that Lehar is now engaged upon a serious opera, "Love of a Soldier," which is to have its first performance in the Autumn of 1910 at Budapest.

MANCINELLI

Ero e Leandro

LUIGI MANCINELLI is better known as a conductor than as a composer. His professional career began about forty years ago. An accident placed him at the conductor's desk in Rome in 1874, where he served with such eminent ability that engagements for opera, festivals, and concerts poured in upon him and he soon found himself famous. Beginning with Rome, he filled engagements season after season at Bologna, London, Norwich, Madrid, New York, and other cities. He has written sketches, suites, oratorios, and operas, but of all his works, the opera " Ero e Leandro " is unquestionably his masterpiece.

The author of the libretto was Boito, the composer, who conceived the idea of setting the old familiar classic story as an opera, but abandoned it for the subject of " Mefistofele." The libretto at last came into the hands of Mancinelli and was utilized by him. The opera was first produced in concert form at the Norwich (England) Festival of 1896, then in its dramatic form at Madrid in 1897, and at Covent Garden, London, in 1898. Its first performance in this country was in 1899, the composer conducting it.

The story, as Boito tells it, has many variations on the original theme as well as additions. Ariofarno, the archon, is in love with Hero, and to gratify his desires, plots to engage her in a service which will remove her from the temple of Venus. In her alarm Hero consults the oracle in a seashell and a vision of her fate appears. She seeks the statue of Apollo for confirmation and it answers " death," but the voice, unknown to her, is that of the archon in concealment.

Ariofarno further develops his scheme by appointing Hero to the position of watching for storms, but offers to save her from this diversion of duty if she will yield to him. She spurns his advances and Leander comes to her support. For this he is banished to the opposite shore. In the finale, which corresponds more nearly with the original, Hero holds the light as the guide for Leander. He throws himself into the sea. The tempest rises. Hero has sounded no warning. When Ariofarno discovers her neglect he condemns her to death. But his condemnation is needless. Leander is drowned in the storm, and as Hero sees his body hurled upon the rocks she falls dead and the hapless lovers are reunited. The most striking passages in the opera are Hero's invocation of the shell, a love-duet in the first act; the stirring choral, "Io paean," in the second; and the final duet and storm music in the third.

MASSENET

GRISELIDIS

"GRISELIDIS," an opera, with prologue and three acts, libretto by Armand Silvestre and Eugene Morand, was first produced in Paris in 1901 and in this country in 1909. It is based upon a mystery play.

The prologue opens with a scene in southern France with Alain, the shepherd, singing of his love for Griselidis. The Marquis Saluzzo, lord of the region, sees her, takes her away from Alain, and marries her. In the first act the Marquis, about to depart for the Crusades, is warned by the Prior that the Devil will tempt his wife to be unfaithful while he is away, but he has such faith in her that he dares the Devil to do his worst. The latter wagers he will be successful and the Marquis accepts the wager and gives him the wedding ring as a pledge.

The second act opens on the terrace by the castle. The Devil appears with his wife Flamina, who is jealous of him, and spiteful against all wives. She is aiding her husband, therefore, in his villanous plot and is more than willing to ruin Griselidis, and, to carry out her part, appears as a slave. They inform her that the Marquis has ordered Flamina to be the head of the house. She consents and the Devil then brings Alain with his declaration of love, hoping that Griselidis will accept him and thus solace herself for the Marquis' supposed affront. She is about to do so when her little boy Loys appears and saves her. The infuriated Devil seizes the boy and carries him away.

The third act discloses Griselidis praying at the shrine of Saint Agnes from which the Devil has removed the image.

The Devil is at her side and tells her a pirate has her boy, but that he will be restored to her for a kiss. She starts to find Loys and meets the Marquis returning from the wars. The plot of the Devil is foiled when the Marquis informs her that he never sent any one to be her mistress, and they are speedily reunited. The Devil then returns and taunts the Marquis with the loss of the child. In a rage he attempts to seize his sword, but the weapons on the wall disappear as if by magic. They kneel before the altar of Saint Agnes imploring help. Suddenly the cross upon it changes to a flaming sword. Griselidis appeals again for help and to the accompaniment of a peal of thunder the candles are lighted and the triptych of the altar opens, disclosing the boy at the feet of the saint, whereupon the Devil disappears, vanquished.

The music of the opera abounds in melodic beauty and thrilling episodes. Its leading features are the opening song of Alain, the invocation scene of the Devil in the forest with the responses of the unseen choir, the temptation scene in the garden, Griselidis' solo in the second act with a beautiful viola accompaniment, Satan's satirical song, and the climax of the miracle in the oratory. The choral parts are delightful throughout and the chorus is always invisible, which adds the feeling of mystery. The orchestration lends itself to the same feeling and contains many beautiful solo effects. Though the situations might suggest it, it is never theatrical, but always adapts itself to the mysterious and sometimes supernatural mood.

HERODIADE

"Herodiade" is one of Massenet's earlier works, having been written in 1877. It was first intended for production in Milan in the Spring of 1881, but was postponed and was not given until December of that year, in Brussels.

//
APPENDIX

Massenet then made some changes in it for production in Paris in 1884. In 1903 it was revived in Paris and was then taken to London where after many alterations of the text by the Lord Chamberlain it was produced as "Salome." The original libretto by Zanardini was made over in most absurd, inconsistent, and incongruous fashion by Milliet and Gremiet, and in this form it was produced in this country in 1908.

The opera is arranged in four acts. The first opens in a court of the palace of Herod where Phanuel, an astrologer, is berating some merchants for not expelling the Romans. Salome enters and tells Phanuel that she is following John, whom she met in the desert where she was abandoned by her mother. After her exit Herod enters with a declaration of his love for Salome but is interrupted by Herodias' demand of vengeance upon John for denouncing her. John next appears and repeats his denunciation, whereupon Herod and Herodias leave. Salome appears again and declares her love for John, who bids her forget love and think of higher things.

The second act transpires in Herod's apartments. He declares to Phanuel he will expel the Romans and avail himself of John's influence to make himself king. In the next scene he urges the populace to rise, but upon the appearance of Vitellius, the Roman proconsul, the people follow him. John next appears, followed by Salome and Canaanite women who greet the Proconsul enthusiastically, while Phanuel draws Herod away.

The third act opens in Phanuel's house, where Herodias requests him to point out for her the star of the woman who has stolen Herod's love from her. He does so and while Herodias is uttering threats of vengeance Phanuel shows her Salome entering the Temple. In the change of scene Salome falls exhausted as Herod enters. He declares his love for her and is spurned, whereupon he threatens to find his rival and send them both to the executioner. The priests meanwhile are importunate in their demands that John shall be sacrificed. He is brought in, and Herod offers to save him if he will abet him in his plans. He refuses, and again the priests clamor for his blood. Salome throws herself at his feet asking that she may share his fate. Herod, recognizing John as his rival, orders the execution of both.

The last act opens in a subterranean vault of the Temple. Salome has been pardoned by Herod, but she suddenly appears with the declaration to John that she has come to die with him. The last scene transpires in the Proconsul's banquet-hall. Salome is there and appeals to Herod and Herodias for John's life. "If you are a mother, have pity," she exclaims. At this word Herodias is seized with remorse and begins to relent, but when the executioner appears with a bloody sword, Salome draws a dagger and with the cry, "You have killed him," hurls herself upon Herodias who exclaims, "Pity me! I am your mother." The revelation comes too late. Herodias is killed.

From this rough sketch of the outline it will be seen how absurd, if not irreverent, the story is. One of Massenet's critics says, "He lacks the depth of thought and strength to grapple with Biblical subjects." He was certainly aided and abetted by his librettists in their effort to make a commonplace operatic love story out of the Biblical narrative. To add to the general incongruity, the work abounds in sensuous melodies and a general condition of mellifluousness unbecoming the Scriptural story and better adapted to the Songs of Solomon than to the fate of John the Baptist. And yet the music in itself has great charm. The duets of John and Salome are alluring. Salome's aria, "Il est doux, il est bon," and Herod's beautiful aria, "Vision fugitive," are, and will long remain, prime favorites in the concert-room. The concerted effects also, like the scene in the Temple, with the religious service and intonings, the entrance of the Proconsul with the stately fanfares of trumpets and martial music, followed by the Canaanites singing hosannahs, and the fascinating ballet of the Babylonian dancers, form ensembles that irresistibly appeal to eye and ear, and make one unmindful of the absurd story.

WERTHER

The opera of "Werther," or lyrical drama, as it is usually styled, was written in 1887, but it was not produced until 1892. It was while Massenet was in Vienna superintending rehearsals of his "Manon" that he was requested to bring out "Werther" at the Imperial Opera House. It proved to be such a great success that it was performed in the following year at the Opera Comique, Paris, and its success was repeated there. It was first given in this country in 1894, and has also been produced in several seasons since that time.

"Werther" is arranged in three acts, the time 1772, and the place near Wetzlar. The text, founded upon Goethe's "Sorrows of Werther," is by Edouard Blau, Paul Millet, and Georges Hartmann. The first act opens at the house of the Bailiff, the heroine's father, where Charlotte, Sophie her sister, and others are preparing for a ball. Before leaving, Charlotte "cuts the bread and butter" for the children. The Bailiff presents Werther to her and they all go to the ball. Albert, her affianced, in the meantime comes back from a journey and goes to the inn intending to meet her in the morning. When Werther and Charlotte return from the ball, he is so violently in love with her that he makes a proposal which she at first refuses, and then she displays great agitation as she reflects upon what she has done. Werther leaves disheartened.

In the second act Charlotte and Albert have been married three months. Werther sees them entering church and is so overcome that he falls to the ground. Albert rushes to him, assures him he understands it all, and forgives him. Werther thanks him and asks for his friendship. Sophie now appears with flowers for him, and Albert vainly urges him to pay his attentions to her. Charlotte at last convinces him that she is true to her husband, which adds to the "sorrows of Werther," as well as to those of Sophie.

The third act opens in Charlotte's home. She has discovered that she really loves Werther and fears for herself as she reads his letters hinting at self-destruction. In Albert's absence the distracted Werther appears at her door. They have a long interview in which she does not deny her love but says it is in vain and flees from him. He takes Albert's pistol and leaves, and in the end kills himself. Before he dies Charlotte reaches him again, confesses her love, and begs his forgiveness as he expires in her arms in a denouement somewhat different from that described by Thackeray in his well-known verse:

> Charlotte, having seen his body
> Borne before her on a shutter,
> Like a well-conducted person
> Went on cutting bread and butter.

Notwithstanding the morbid character of the text and the tiresome nature of Werther's surging passion with its suicidal ending, Massenet's score is characterized by refinement, beauty, and tenderness instead of the languorous and sensuous touches one might naturally expect in his treatment of such a tempting subject. Like Gounod he is fond of sentimental scenes and is somewhat feminine in his treatment of them. He once said: "We musicians, like the poets, must be the interpreters of true emotion. To feel, to make others feel, therein lies the whole secret." He has succeeded in doing this in his "Werther." It abounds in graceful, refined, melodic beauty. The Christmas Carol and Werther's two songs in the first act, Sophie's gladsome aria and Werther's closing song in the second, and the duets of Charlotte and Werther in the third illustrate this.

"Cendrillon" and "Sapho"

"Cendrillon" and "Sapho," although they have been brought forward in this country within the last two years, are comparatively of little consequence as musical works and are not likely to become standard. They may be heard infrequently as curiosities or to display the talent of some special singer, consequently their stories may be of some interest. "Cendrillon" was first produced at the Opera Comique, Paris, in 1899, and the libretto, based upon the fairy tale of Cinderella, was written by Henri Cain. The opera is arranged in four acts.

The first act opens at the home of Madame de la Halliere, who is preparing to take her two daughters to the ball at which the young prince is to select his wife. Cendrillon is the daughter of her husband, Pandolph, by his first wife, and is left at home while her father, the madame, and her two daughters go to the ball. After they are gone the fairy godmother appears, dresses Cendrillon in finery, and sends her to the festivity.

In the second act Prince Charming is revealed in the palace gardens wandering about dejectedly. His father appears and tells him that he must select a wife as the remedy for his ennui. Many ladies show off their graces before him, among them Madame de la Halliere's daughters, but their appeals are useless. At last he espies Cendrillon and falls in love with her at first sight, but at the stroke of the midnight bell she obeys the fairy godmother's instruction and disappears, leaving her glass slipper behind her as the only consolation for the Prince.

The third act discloses Cendrillon about to end her unhappy life at the Fairies' Oak and the Prince arriving there for the same purpose. The fairies render them invisible to one another and they fall asleep. In the last act Cendrillon imagines that her adventure was only a dream, but gives up the delusion when she learns that the Prince is seeking for the owner of the slipper. In the finale it is tried on and fits her and she becomes the Princess, much to her delight and that of her father and the discomfiture of the madame and her two daughters.

"Sapho" was first produced at the Opera Comique, Paris, in 1897, and is based upon Alphonse Daudet's well-known novel of the same name, the libretto written by Cain and Bernede. It is arranged in five acts.

The first act discloses the meeting of Jean Gaussin with Fanny Legrand, known among the artists as "Sapho," at a masked ball given by the sculptor Coandal. Sapho becomes fascinated by the young fellow and lures him away from the ball while the other guests are going to supper.

In the second act Jean is disclosed in his lodgings with his parents who are establishing him in a new studio. After they are gone Sapho enters and makes herself mistress both of Jean and his apartment.

In the third act the two are at a restaurant attending an artists' dinner. Then Jean accidentally learns that Sapho is a notorious model with a notorious past, whereupon he leaves the restaurant without her and at the same time leaves her in a rage.

The fourth act transpires in Provence at his old home. Jean has gone back seeking forgiveness and obtains it. Just when he fancies he shall be happy once more Sapho appears there with the purpose of reclaiming him, but he repels her and she departs.

In the last act Jean is overcome by the old fascination and seeks Sapho in her Paris lodgings. She begs him to leave her, but he refuses and is ready to make any sacrifice for her. He falls asleep from weariness, and she, knowing that she cannot possess him, steals away and leaves him forever.

Thaïs

"Thaïs," a lyric opera, the libretto by Gallet, was first produced in Paris in 1894. It is arranged in four acts and the scene is laid at Thebes and in the desert, during the Greek occupation of Egypt.

The first act opens beside the Nile and discloses the monks at supper. Athanaël, a young monk, who has been to Alexandria to protest against Grecian luxury and corruption, returns disheartened by his task, having found that city given over to the influences of Thaïs, a courtesan of great beauty. After their separation for the night Athanaël dreams of Thaïs appearing before the people as Venus. The next scene is laid at the house of Nicias in Alexandria, whither Athanaël has gone to resume his exhortations. Nicias greets him, and Athanaël questions him as to Thaïs. He confesses he has been ruined by her and laughs at Athanaël's determination to reclaim her. To afford him the opportunity Nicias gives a supper for her at which Athanaël, handsomely arrayed, is present. He attracts the admiration of Thaïs, and while he is bent upon his purpose she seeks to allure him with her charms. Athanaël denounces her and flees from the house when she once more prepares to pose as Venus.

The second act opens in the house of Thaïs. While she is regarding her charms in the mirror, Athanaël appears at the door, prays for her, and tells her he loves her with his spirit. As she listens to him she places incense in a burner and invokes Venus. Athanaël commands her to follow him, but hears the distant voice of Nicias calling her. She hesitates, and Athanaël says he will wait until the dawn. He sleeps upon the pavement where at last Thaïs appears with a lamp and a little image of Eros which Nicias had given her. She says she is prepared to follow him, and asks permission to take the image with her. He dashes the image to pieces on the stones and they enter the house together. Nicias and his friends appear, and revelry begins. As it proceeds Athanaël fires the house and Thaïs, clad in a woollen garment, follows him away amid the execrations of Nicias' followers.

The opening scene of the third act is laid at an oasis, where Thaïs and Athanaël appear, overcome with fatigue. Athanaël consoles her, then leads her to a convent and leaves her in charge of the abbess, after she has bidden him a last farewell. In the next scene a storm arises and Athanaël appears among the monks in a dejected condition. He confesses that since he has reclaimed Thaïs he has been haunted by impure dreams. A vision of Thaïs comes before him, whereupon he rushes out into the storm.

The last act shows the gardens of the monastery. Thaïs lies dying with the nuns by her side, when Athanaël enters inquiring for her. The nuns lead him to her and he kneels by her side as she tells him of her conversion. Athanaël, however, still under the influence of his love for her, tries to divert her mind to earthly things, but Thaïs points to the sky where angels are awaiting her. As she dies Athanaël falls to the earth with a cry of despair.

The music of "Thaïs" is brilliant, impassioned, dramatic throughout, especially the instrumental part, as in the meditation music of the second act and the Oriental music which accompanies the scenes in Alexandria. Among the most striking vocal numbers are Athanaël's solo, as he awakes from his dream of Thaïs; her love song and incantation and the dance music of the second act; the exquisite duet for Thaïs and Athanaël as he brings her water in the desert; and the celestial song of Thaïs, "Heaven opens its gates," in the finale of the last act.

LE JONGLEUR DE NOTRE DAME

"Le Jongleur de Notre Dame" ("Our Lady's Juggler") entitled a miracle play, was first produced at Monte Carlo in 1892, in Paris in 1904, and in this country in 1908. It is arranged in three acts and is based upon a mediæval legend, as told in Anatole France's "Etui de Nacre," the libretto by Maurice Lena.

The story is mainly concerned with Jean, a strolling mendicant juggler. In the first act he appears outside the gates of the monastery of Cluny seeking a meal by exhibiting his tricks to the people on market day. As he is singing a drinking-song the prior passes and censures him, at the same time soliciting him to enter the monastery and become a monk. Moved by the prior's admonitions and at the same time by the appearance of the monastery cook and his donkey laden with provisions, he enters.

The second act opens upon preparations in the monastery for the celebration of the Feast of the Assumption. Jean beholds the artists among the monks preparing an image of the Virgin and realizes that he alone of all his companions is doing nothing in her honor. After they leave he finds himself alone with Boniface, the cook, to whom he confides his anxiety to do something. Boniface relieves him with the assurance that anything he does will be pleasing to the Virgin.

The third act reveals Jean in the chapel at night practising his songs and dances before the new image of the Virgin. The Prior and the monks suddenly enter and are scandalized at his antics. They are about to sieze him and drag him from the chapel when suddenly the image is illuminated with a bright glow and the Virgin stretches her hands above him with a smile. The monks are overcome by the miracle and Jean sinks to the floor and expires while celestial voices are heard commending him.

The subject is one which is admirably adapted to Massenet's style. He has invested it with a mediæval atmosphere and has added to the mystic feeling by the use of the Gregorian Chant and the old folk-song. There is no passionate fervor nor dramatic outburst. The music flows along quietly, simply, and melodiously, and preserves the mystic character of the story it illustrates. Its most effective numbers are the prelude to the first act, the wine song by Jean ("Alleluia du Vin"), Boniface's melody which is jovially ecclesiastic, as he appears with his donkey, the prelude to the second act, Boniface's song in which he tells the story of the Sage Brush, Jean's songs before the Virgin and his address to her, and the climax of the miracle at the close with the celestial chorus.

Don Quixote [1]

"Don Quixote," the last opera from the fertile pen of the veteran Massenet, was performed at Monte Carlo for the first time in January, 1910. The librettist is Henri Cain, who has drawn his situations more liberally from a play by Le Lorrain, a French poet, than from Cervantes' romance. Don Quixote is represented as a pattern of kindness and magnanimity instead of the fantastic, serio-comic knight, and Dulcinea in place of a rustic appears as a gay courtesan, while Sancho Panza retains his original qualities. The relations between Don Quixote and Dulcinea are romantic. He seeks to win her from her course of life and would even wed her, but she refuses his offer because she would not disturb his ideals. Among the knight's adventures are the encounters with the windmill, the giants, and the brigands,

[1] The accompanying brief sketch of "Don Quixote" is compiled from notices of the new opera by French reviewers. The score of the opera has not yet reached this country, but it is announced for performance during the season of 1911.

APPENDIX 517

the farewell to Sancho, and the death of Don Quixote, while leaning in full armor upon his lance and gazing at the stars. The music is said to run mostly in melodious declamation, interspersed with short arias, and accompanied by instrumentation of a fine delineative character and vivid coloring. The reviewers are agreed that the opera is worthy of Massenet's finest talent and recalls much of the distinction of his "Manon" and "Werther."

NEVIN

POIA [1]

THE opera of "Poia," by Arthur Nevin, was first produced in Berlin, April 24, 1910. The libretto which is based upon a Blackfoot legend, was written by Randolf Hartley, and the opera is arranged in three acts. As no score of the work has been yet published it is possible only to give a sketch of the story. Special interest attaches to this opera as its subject is American, its composer an American, and the work itself the first of its kind produced in Germany.

Poia, a young Blackfoot Indian, is the hero of the story. The opening of the first act reveals that he is in disfavor in his tribe because of some mystery attached to his birth, and also that he is an object of ridicule because his face is disfigured by a scar. Poia is in love with Natoya, a chieftain's daughter, but Natoya is in love with Sumatsi, the

---

[1] "Poia" was first produced at the Royal Opera House, Berlin, April 24, 1910, under the auspices of the Emperor of Germany and Count Von Hulsen, the intendant of the opera. Although the composer and librettist were called out five times at the end of the second act and eight times at the close of the opera, the German critics with one or two exceptions were severe in their strictures. The two extremes are represented by the *Lokal Anzeiger* which said: "The opera is not worth while exciting oneself about. The legends recall German folklore. The music, apart from the Indian melodies, reminds one of Strauss and Verdi in their weaker moments." The *National Zeitung* said: "The music in various parts is charming in melody, rhythm, and instrumentation." According to despatches the opera went much better at the second performance, and the Emperor had ordered a special performance upon the occasion of Ex-President Roosevelt's visit to Berlin.

APPENDIX

warrior, and to rid herself of Poia, declares she will never accept him until his scar is removed. Poia is informed by Nenahu, the medicine woman, that the Sun God placed the scar there and only he can remove it, whereupon Poia sets out for the Sun God's home.

The second act discloses Poia in the forest almost exhausted, but at last he finds the Sun God in his court and remains there as an attendant, winning the Sun God's favor by saving the life of Morning Star, his son. In gratitude for this service the Sun God removes the scar and sends Poia back to the Blackfeet to teach them the worship of the sun, moon, and morning star. He is guided by Morning Star along the Milky Way and is given a magic flute which will help him win any maiden he loves.

The third act shows the Blackfeet in trouble, and Natoya is blamed for it. During an interview between her and Sumatsi, Poia's flute is heard. She falls in love with the player and in hate with Sumatsi. When Poia makes his appearance he is welcomed by his tribe, whereupon the jealous Sumatsi attempts to kill him. Natoya shields him and receives her death wound. The sky thereupon opens, a bright shaft of light strikes down Sumatsi, and Poia ascends to the home of the Sun God bearing the dying Natoya in his arms.

OFFENBACH

Les Contes De Hoffmann

"LES Contes De Hoffmann" ("Tales of Hoffmann"), a lyric opera arranged in prologue, three acts or scenes, and epilogue, was first produced in Paris in 1880. The libretto is by Jules Barbier and is based upon the well-known tales by Hoffmann. The opera is a remarkable one in two respects. First, it is the only lyric work by Offenbach, all his other dramatic compositions being extravaganzas in the form of operas bouffes. Second, it is so constructed that the leading soprano appears in four different roles, those of the mistresses of Hoffmann, and the leading baritone in three, those of Hoffmann's enemies. The story itself is unique.

The prologue reveals that the wealthy Lindorf is in love with the singer, Stella, with whom Hoffmann had also been in love at Milan. When she once more sees the latter her passion for him is rekindled and she writes him a letter making an appointment to meet him. By bribery Lindorf secures this letter and plots to make Hoffmann drunk so that Stella will be disgusted with him. Lindorf succeeds, and Hoffmann while intoxicated tells his companions the story of his three love adventures.

In the first scene Hoffmann is in love with the automaton, Olympia. This automaton has been constructed by Spalanzani, aided by Coppelius, and is exhibited as his daughter. Hoffmann is so enamoured of her that he writes her a letter making an appointment. The secret of the irresponsive antomaton is revealed to him by Coppelius.

The second scene shows the beautiful Giulietta entertaining her admirers in Venice, the favorite among them being Schlemihl, the man without a shadow. Hoffmann falls violently in love with her. His enemy, Dapertutto, who owns Schlemihl's shadow, connives with Giulietta who induces Hoffmann to exchange his shadow for her love. She then violates her promise and betrays him to his enemies.

In the third scene, the inamorata is Antonie, the daughter of Krespel, whose mother had been a famous singer and whose death was occasioned by Dr. Mirakel, who closely resembles the character of Svengali. As Antonie is in failing health her father forbids her to sing. Hoffmann falls in love with her, but Krespel, fearing he will encourage her to sing, opposes his suit. In this juncture a quarrel ensues between Krespel and Dr. Mirakel, in the course of which the latter summons the spirit of the mother who requests Antonie to sing. She attempts it and dies, and Hoffmann thus loses his bride.

These are the stories which Hoffmann relates in his intoxicated condition. In the epilogue he sings a song to Stella and he is left with his bottle, "all I have to embrace."

The opera is replete with beautiful melodies, such as the drinking-songs, the love song of Hoffmann, the waltz movement of the automaton, the duet between Antonie and Hoffmann, the passionate music of Antonie in her death scene, and the exquisite barcarole, "Fair night, O night of love," one of the best known and most popular of all of Offenbach's many popular lyrics. The sorrowful feature of this opera is that Offenbach did not live to hear his own work in which he made so wide a departure from his opera bouffe style.

PUCCINI

Madame Butterfly

"MADAME BUTTERFLY," the text by L. Illica and G. Giacoso, is founded upon the story of the same name by John Luther Long and the drama by David Belasco. It is arranged in three acts and was first given at Milan in 1904 and in this country in 1906.

The story is infinitely pathetic. The first act opens near Nagasaki. Lieut. Pinkerton of the United States Navy has arranged through a marriage broker to wed Cho-Cho-San (Madame Butterfly) and is disclosed inspecting a house he has leased, and with him Sharpless, the American Consul, who seeks to dissuade him from the marriage. During their interview the bride and her friends arrive and the situation is further complicated by Madame Butterfly's announcement to the Consul that she has abjured her faith and will entrust her future to her husband. The marriage contract is signed, but as the celebration begins Madame Butterfly's uncle, a priest, arrives and curses her for her renunciation, whereupon Pinkerton turns him and the rest of the Japanese out of the house. A passionate scene with Madame Butterfly follows.

Three years are supposed to elapse. Pinkerton has long since been recalled to America and Madame Butterfly patiently and bravely awaits his return. Meanwhile Pinkerton has informed the Consul that he is now married to an American wife and is about to return to Nagasaki. The Consul comes to break this news to her, but finds it a difficult task to undeceive her. Meanwhile Yamadori, a wealthy Japanese suitor, visits her, but she will not listen to

APPENDIX

his proposal, upon the ground that she is already married to Pinkerton. As he departs the Consul again tries to convince her of the truth of his message, but she only answers him by bringing in her baby boy. As he departs, guns announce the arrival of Pinkerton's ship and Madame Butterfly is in a transport of joy. She and her maid decorate the house for his reception and they watch for his approach. The tired maid and the baby go to sleep, but Madame Butterfly still watches.

The third act opens with the vision of Madame Butterfly still watching for her husband. At last he appears, approaching the house with his American wife upon his arm. As he realizes the tragedy of the situation he rushes away, leaving the Consul to explain. The latter induces the maid to tell the whole truth to Madame Butterfly and also to urge her to give the baby to the American lady to be brought up. When the former learns the full truth she wishes the American lady happiness and sends word to Pinkerton she will soon find peace. A little later Pinkerton and the Consul return, only to find her dead. She has killed herself with her father's dagger.

The music is thoroughly in keeping with the movements of this sad tragedy. It abounds in melodious recitative and has many movements of deepest pathos as well as of fascinating grace and brilliancy. Its most prominent numbers are the Oriental music which accompanies the first appearance of Madame Butterfly and her friends; the exquisite love duet in the first act; the finale to the same act, "Ah! Night of Rapture"; Madame Butterfly's lament in the second act; and her closing music in the third, which is marked by tender pathos, love, and resignation to her fate.

MANON LESCAUT

"Manon Lescaut," the third of Puccini's operas, was first produced in Milan in 1893 and had its first performance in this country in 1894. The text is based upon Prevost's "Manon Lescaut" and the opera is arranged in four acts so that each act constitutes a scene.

The first act opens before an inn where students are singing and waiting for the girls to come from work. Des Grieux enters but does not join them. Manon and Lescaut, her brother, alight from a coach and Des Grieux accosts her. She is on her way to a convent but promises to meet him later. Geronte, another admirer of Manon, and an old *roué*, plans to carry her off, but Edmund, a student, overhears his plan and advises Des Grieux to take Manon away in Geronte's postchaise, which he does, followed by Lescaut and Geronte.

The opening of the second act reveals that Manon has become Geronte's mistress. She is installed in his Paris apartment, but is sad as she remembers Des Grieux. A dance follows, after which, in Geronte's absence, Des Grieux appears. In the midst of their loving interview Geronte suddenly returns, pretends to give them their freedom, and leaves them. Her brother urges them to fly but as they attempt to do so the door is locked by Geronte's orders, and a squad of soldiers appears. Manon is arrested and taken away, Des Grieux vainly attempting to follow.

The third act opens in a square at Havre. Manon is in prison but tells Lescaut and Des Grieux through the bars that she is to be exiled to America. Their attempts at rescue are thwarted. At last Manon, amid a crowd of women who are also to be deported, is escorted by the guards to a vessel. Des Grieux seeks to walk by her side but the sergeant roughly pushes him away. The captain of the vessel, however, sympathizing with him, manages to smuggle him aboard.

The fourth act reveals a desert place near New Orleans (!) where Manon and Des Grieux are wandering about exhausted, and vainly seeking shelter. As Des Grieux is long absent seeking for water, she thinks he has deserted her, abandons all hope and lies down to die. Des Grieux returns, but too late for she dies in his arms.

The most striking passages of the opera are the duet for the two lovers and the beautiful romanza for Des Grieux in the first act; the graceful minuet and madrigal and the passionate duet of the lovers in the second act; the orchestral intermezzo called "Journey to Havre" between the second and third acts; the tenor solo, in which Des Grieux pleads for Manon and the very dramatic climax in the finale of the third, punctuated with the sergeant's roll-call as the unfortunate women are deported. The fourth act is a long, monotonous, and somewhat dreary duet between Manon and Des Grieux.

Le Villi

"Le Villi," an opera in two acts, libretto by Ferdinando Fortuna, is interesting as the first dramatic work of a composer now world-famous. It was written by Puccini while he was a student at the Milan Conservatory, in competition for a prize, but was rejected by the Committee. Subsequently, with the help of Boito, the young composer revised it and expanded it from one act to two and in this form it was produced in Milan in 1884 and achieved a success. The source of the story used by the librettist is legendary, being both Slavic and Teutonic. The legends agree in the main, the Villi, or Wilis, being the ghosts of maidens deserted by their lovers, who take revenge by waylaying their betrayers and whirling them to death in the dance.

There are but three principal characters in "Le Villi" — Wulf, the mountaineer; Anna, his daughter; and Robert, the faithless lover. The scene is laid in the Black Forest. The first act opens upon the betrothal feast of Robert and Anna. The former is about to depart upon a journey and assures the disconsolate Anna he will remain faithful to her. All join in prayer and he takes his farewell.

The second act reveals that Robert has forgotten his promises. He devotes himself to wild orgies in Mayence and is led astray by an evil woman upon whom he squanders his money. Despairing of his return Anna is taken ill and dies. Robert returns to his native village, a broken-down man, but as he is passing through the forest the Wilis dance about him. He reaches Anna's cottage and hears strange sounds — the funeral chant. The witch dancers reappear and among them is the apparition of Anna. She upbraids him. He tries to escape but she seizes him by the arm and the Wilis surround him and whirl him about. With a last appeal to Anna he falls dead and Anna vanishes, while the chorus sings a derisive "Hosanna."

The music of "Le Villi" derives its main interest from the fact that it reveals the beginnings of the genius displayed in "Le Bohème" and "Manon Lescaut," and yet there are numbers which are very attractive, among them the betrothal music, prayer, and waltz in the first act; and the symphonic prelude to the second act, "L'Abbandono," and its second part after the passage of the funeral procession "La Tregenda," accompanying the dances of the Wilis. Streatfeild, analyzing the work of Puccini, says: "The music is the work of a man of imagination. It is thoroughly Italian in character and there is little attempt at local color. In the supernatural part the composer is completely successful. His Wilis have a character of their own, entirely distinct from that of other operatic spectres. There is a fiendish rapture in their gambols which Puccini has been very happy in conveying."

SMETANA

The Bartered Bride

"PRODAÑA Nevesla" ("The Bartered Bride") was first produced at Prague in 1866; at the Vienna exposition in 1892; in London in 1895; and in this country in 1908, though the overture had been frequently played in American concert-rooms before that time. The libretto was written by Sabina and the opera is arranged in three acts. The saddest event connected with the work is the fact that while it is the composer's masterpiece he died in an insane asylum without even hearing it.

The first act opens in a Bohemian village where the Kirmess festival is in progress. Mary, daughter of a rich peasant, is there but takes no part in it. Her parents have arranged her marriage to Wenzel, son of Micha, another rich peasant, whom she has never seen, and while she is in love with Hans, a servant of her father's. Following the Bohemian practice, Wenzel has not proposed to Mary but left the business to Kezul, a professional marriage broker, who has carried on the negotiations. When the broker approaches Mary, however, and acquaints her with Wenzel's proposal she rejects it and declares her love for Hans.

In the second act Wenzel makes a personal offer. Mary not only rejects him but upbraids him for offering to marry a girl whom he does not love and at last makes him promise to abandon the idea of marriage with her. Kezul in the meantime has offered Hans money if he will give Mary up. When he learns that his rival is Micha's son he agrees to sign a contract providing that none other than Micha's son shall marry Mary. Kezul agrees and pays Hans his price and the latter publicly renounces all claim upon her.

The third act opens with a tight rope performance and dance. Wenzel falls in love with Esmeralda, a Spanish dancer, and to be near her accepts an offer of the manager to take the part of a dancing bear. As he is assuming his costume his parents appear and demand that he shall sign the marriage contract with Mary which he refuses to do. Mary in the meantime is overcome with sorrow, for Kezul has shown her Hans' deed of renunciation. She still refuses to marry any one else although Wenzel, tired of the dancing bear business, has renewed his advances. Hans now appears and she upbraids him for his faithlessness but he summons the villagers and tells them it is his wish she shall marry Micha's son. Mary is now in despair and declares she will marry Wenzel as her parents and Hans desire. Hans then steps before Micha who recognizes him as his son by a former marriage. Disgusted at the prospect of a step-mother, Hans had left home and gone into service with Mary's father. He claims Mary upon the ground that under his contract with Kezul she belongs to him. They are married and live happily ever after. Wenzel returns to his antics as a show bear and is killed in one of them.

"The Bartered Bride" is one of the most delightful of comic operas. It abounds in Bohemian folk-songs and is replete with melodies. It is lively and vivacious throughout and notwithstanding its strong local color, has been enjoyed wherever it has been performed, especially in Germany. With regard to Smetana's earlier operas the critics had claimed that he could write only Czech music. It is said that he wrote "The Bartered Bride" to disprove this accusation. He certainly succeeded for its most enthusiastic successess were achieved in Vienna and Berlin.

STRAUSS, R.

SALOME

THE score of "Salome" was finished by Strauss in June, 1905, and was first produced in the same year in Dresden. It was first heard in this country in New York in 1907. The text is a translation of Oscar Wilde's play of the same name, made by Hedwig Lachmann. It is arranged in one act and the leading characters are Herod, tetrarch of Judaea; Jokanaan, the Prophet; Narraboth, captain of the guard; Naaman, executioner; Herodias, wife of Herod; and Salome, daughter of Herodias; these are set against a background of slaves, soldiers, Jews, and Nazarenes.

The story is repulsive, unclean, and sensual. There is but one scene, a terrace above the banquet hall of Herod. Narraboth, the captain of the guard, looking down into the hall discourses to his companions upon the beauty of Salome, who is sitting at the feast with Herod and his courtiers. A page of Herodias warns him against her and as he utters his warning Salome appears in the doorway. As she stands looking out upon the night, Narraboth is spellbound. His reverie is broken in upon by the voice of an invisible man. In answer to Salome's inquiry she is informed that it is the voice of a man imprisoned in a cistern, — Jokanaan's (John the Baptist's) dungeon, — who is known as "The Baptist" and by some is regarded as a Prophet. She remembers it was this man who denounced her mother and she has a wild desire to see him. Narraboth thereupon orders him brought out. Salome no sooner beholds him then she falls violently in love with him but he indignantly repels her sensual advances. Narraboth in a fit of jealousy kills himself, after Jokanaan has been returned to the cistern. At this juncture Herod, Herodias, and the courtiers appear upon the terrace to see why she has not obeyed his order to return to the banquet. He displays passion for his step-daughter, but Salome, longing for Jokanaan, pays no heed to him. The Prophet's denunciation is heard again and Herodias demands that Herod shall silence him but he is afraid to do so. He even refuses to surrender him to the Jews and another denunciation is heard. Herod refuses again to order his execution but instead bids Salome dance for him, offering her anything she may ask if she will do so. She consents at last and when the dance is concluded, demands the head of Jokanaan upon a charger. He demurs at first but she insists and at last he gives the order. The executioner descends into the cistern and in a moment his arm is thrust out and the ghastly head of the Prophet is before her upon a silver shield. As she seizes it and lavishes kisses and caresses upon it Herod orders his soldiers to kill her. They close about her and crush her under their shields, her last words being: "Ah! I have kissed thy mouth, Jokanaan. There was a bitter taste on thy lips. Was it the taste of blood? But perchance it is the taste of love. They say that love hath a bitter taste. But what of that? What of that? I have kissed thy mouth Jokanaan, I have kissed thy mouth." And thus the ghastly, sensual story ends.

"Salome" is neither opera, music drama, nor symphonic poem, according to Strauss. He simply calls it "drama." It begins abruptly without overture, or even prelude, by the announcement of one of Salome's motives. Motives, forty or more, are closely interwoven with the movement of the drama. If we may except the "Dance of the Seven Veils" which is very effective as a concert number, there are no melodious numbers to be indicated. Dissonance is conspicuous throughout. New and unexpected tone effects abound. The voices have no opportunities. The people on the stage are only necessary for the physical action. The *dramatis personæ* declaim and sometimes so unmusically that it is mere talk. Strauss himself at a rehearsal remarked that no consideration had been paid to the singers. The immense orchestra of one hundred and twelve pieces, often most minutely subdivided, bears the heat and burden of this orgy of strange technic and complex cacophony. At another rehearsal Strauss admonished the orchestra: "You play too gently. This music is not civilized, it must crash." The orchestra is subsidized for all manner of strange work and sometimes ludicrous description of the action, the words, looks, and even gestures of those on the stage. The outcome of it all is a riotous squandering of extraordinary genius in orchestration and constructive musicianship, upon dramatic rottenness. For rottenness it is, notwithstanding the composer's weak averment: "In art there is never the moral or the immoral; such conceptions are incompatible with the conception of art. The artist refuses to answer the question, 'Is your art moral?'" Even the artist cannot touch pitch and remain undefiled.

Elektra

"Elektra," Strauss' latest opera, if "opera" be the correct term, was first produced at Dresden in 1909 and in this country in 1910. The story is based upon Von Hofmannstahl's drama of "Elektra." The characters are the same but the action diverges radically from that of the old Greek drama. The first production in this country was in French from a version by Henry Gauthier-Villars.

The German drama is not merely a tragedy but a tragedy of insanity and horror. If "Salome" is an orgy of sensuality, "Elektra" is an orgy of bloodthirstiness and insane fury, in which Elektra is the central figure. When Agamemnon, Elektra's father, went to the Trojan War, he confided his wife, Clytemnestra, and his home to Ægisthus, the murderer of Agamemnon's father. His confidence is abused and when he returns he is slain in his bath by Ægisthus and Clytemnestra. The opening of the drama reveals Elektra crazed with grief and rage over her father's murder and the banishment of her brother, Orestes, whom she believes to be dead. She rushes about the palace shrieking vengeance. She meets her mother and denounces her. She also denounces her sister, Crysothenus, whom she believes to have been concerned in the murder. Orestes suddenly appears and when he learns what has occurred he determines to execute speedy vengeance in which he is aided by his sister. She scratches up the earth in which the murderer's hatchet is buried. Orestes rushes into the palace and Clytemnestra's screams announce her fate. Ægisthus, returning from the hunt, has forebodings of his own fate and is soon uselessly shrieking for help. These two out of the way and her vengeance complete, Elektra executes a diabolical, frenzied dance, until at last she swoons, and loses her reason. Then all is quiet in this mad house.

A general analysis of the music of "Elektra" would follow closely on the lines of that of "Salome." The same lack of consideration for the voices obtains. Motives are just as abundant and as complicated in their interweaving. There is if possible less of melody. A simple chord serves as prelude. There is even more vociferation and shriek. The orchestra is just as colossal.

Some references to outside criticism may be of interest. One critic calls its atmosphere "mad and morbid," another characterizes it as "a panorama of neurotic, decadent, pathological humanity, reeking with morbid, maniacal, unnatural instincts." The *London Spectator* said: "Elektra is a sickening disappointment to those who have hoped Strauss would still extricate his great talent from the slough of calculated eccentricity in which it has been too long submerged." The *Saturday Review* said: "One rarely chances on genuine pregnant themes. But it must be admitted Strauss shows fiendish cleverness in spinning a continuous web of tone out of the least promising subjects. 'Elektra' is not a masterpiece but just what a supernaturally clever professor might write to show his pupils how students' music should be written, or a similarly gifted but more artistic professor might write to show how real music should not be written." Mme. Schumann-Heink, who was the original Clytemnestra at the Dresden performance says: "I will never sing it again. *Es war furchtbar!* We were a set of mad women. The music is maddening. . . . There is nothing beyond 'Elektra.' It can go no further. One has lived and reached the uttermost of that art — Wagner. He has made use of the furthest outlines in vocal writing. Richard Strauss goes beyond him, and his singing voices are lost. We have come to a full stop. I believe Strauss himself sees it." Perhaps he does. He is now writing a comic opera, "Der Rosenkavalier," of which he himself says: "It is written in a very simple musical manner, consisting of separate songs and waltzes."

Der Rosenkavalier

Strauss is now engaged in the composition of a new opera in comedy style, called "Der Rosenkavalier." The text is by Von Hofmannsthal, the librettist of his "Elektra." The story is told by the composer as follows:

"The action is in the time of Empress Maria Theresa in Vienna, and begins with pleasing and amusing vivacity in a scene in the sleeping apartment of the Countess Werdenberg, wife of the Field Marshal, Count Werdenberg. On the couch in a somewhat careless attitude, Octavien, a gay youth of seventeen, of distinguished family, gives himself up to protestations of love. This Octavien, a fascinating but well-bred boy, a sort of cherub, and his opponent in the field of love, the Baron Ochs von Lerchenau, who, in spite of his noble lineage, is a brutal, arrogant boaster, are the two principal characters of the comedy. At this early hour in the forenoon the baron forces his way unbidden into the presence of the countess, his cousin, and Octavien, to avoid compromising the lady of his heart, slips into the dress of a chambermaid, in which character he is drawn into the snares of the baron.

"Ochs von Lerchenau informs the countess that he has condescended to become engaged to Sophie von Farinal, the daughter of a wealthy but newly titled man, and he asks the countess to provide for him a Rosenkavalier, a nobleman to woo for him, and, as the custom is, to present to the bride in the name of the bridegroom the rose of betrothal. Octavien is chosen as Rosenkavalier. The bride-to-be, repelled by the over-eagerness of the baron, falls in love with the wooer, who, under the stress of noble emotion, gives the bridegroom-baron a sword-thrust, because of the ever-increasing amorousness with which he pursues his *fiancée*. A strategy saves the girl from the proposed marriage. The baron receives a tender message from the chambermaid, *i. e.*, from the Rosenkavalier, Octavien; they meet in a secluded chamber and the baron is boldly duped and unmasked. He goes away empty-handed and the Rosenkavalier leads home his bride."

As to the music, Strauss himself says: "Hofmannsthal's text has a charming and decided rococo tone, and it now became my task to convey this atmosphere to the musical setting. The spirit of Mozart involuntarily rose before me, but in spite of this I remained true to myself. The orchestration is not so heavy as in 'Salome' or 'Elektra,' but it is by no means treated after the modern manner of performing Mozart with small orchestra; the 'Rosenkavalier'

APPENDIX

is composed for complete orchestra. Mozart's own ideas did not at all incline toward a small orchestra; once when an English Mæcenas had one of his symphonies played with a hundred violins, Mozart was very enthusiastic over the effect produced.

"I have not departed from the path of the text's gay vivacity, which, however, never oversteps the bounds of grace and elegance; the second act ends with a genuine Vienna waltz and the duet between the chambermaid, Octavien, and the Baron Ochs in the secluded chamber is made up entirely of waltz motives The part of the Rozenkavalier is to be sung by a lady, a mezzo-soprano, and that of the baron by a bass-buffo. Besides six other important roles, the 'comedy for music' contains fourteen smaller solo parts."

TSCHAIKOWSKY

Dame de Pique

"DAME de Pique" ("Queen of Spades") was first produced in Moscow in 1890, three years before the composer's death, and for the first time in this country in 1910. The libretto, based upon a tale by Poushkin, was written by the composer's brother, Modeste Ilich Tschaikowsky, and the opera is arranged in four acts. The music was written at first for another libretto based upon "The Captain's Daughter," also a Poushkin story, but for some reason the composer abandoned it after progressing through a considerable portion of the score.

The opening scene is laid in the Winter Garden at St. Petersburg where Hermann, a young officer, tells his friend Tomski of his love for Lisa, granddaughter of an old Countess who had been a famous beauty in her youth. Hermann, thinking that he cannot win the hand of Lisa without money, is in despair. Tomski tells him the story of the past life of the Countess, who was so infatuated with gambling that she gave up all her suitors and became known as the Queen of Spades. One of these suitors, the Count St. Germain, offered to tell her the run of three cards which would always be successful if she would accept him and to this she agreed, but that night a spectre told her she would die if a lover should ever demand from her the secret of the three cards.

In the second act Hermann makes love to the Countess and asks her the secret of the cards. She refuses to tell him. Whereupon he threatens her with a pistol and so alarms her that she falls dead. Later, her funeral proces-

APPENDIX 537

sion passes his barracks and her ghost appears to him, announcing the secret of the cards and at the same time his fate.

The third act reveals Lisa on the banks of the Neva waiting for Hermann to come to her. Infatuated with gambling and excited with the knowledge of the Countess' secret, he forgets Lisa who in her despair over her abandonment throws herself into the river.

The last act discloses Hermann still in the gambling house, winning steadily with the aid of the secret. In an unfortunate moment he turns the Queen of Spades and loses all he has won. The ghost of the Countess appears to him again, demanding his life. The warning by the spectre who had appeared to the Countess when she obtained the secret is fulfilled, for Hermann stabs himself.

There is little set melody in the opera, its music being mainly dramatic and passionate recitative marked by that tinge of melancholy which characterizes so much of Tschaikowsky's music. Its leading numbers are the quintet by Hermann's friends in the garden scene, Tomski's song describing the past life of the Countess with the three card refrain, and the passionate duet between Lisa and Hermann in the first act; the masked ball with the music of the shepherds and shepherdesses and minuet, written in Mozartean manner, and the scene in the Countess' chamber when Hermann seeks to obtain the secret, in the second; the ghost scene with the storm accompaniment and the closing duet of Hermann and Lisa in the third; and the climax of Hermann's death in the gambling house.

INDEX

INDEX

A

Achard, M., 341
"Adaline," Arthur, 468
Adam, Adolph, Boieldieu's pupil, 50
Adam, Adolphe Charles, sketch of, 1
Adamowski, Timothy, 468
"Adelson e Salvino," Bellini, 30
Agathe, Frau, 394
"Aïda," outline of, 368–371
Albani, Emma, 76
Alboni, Mme., 5, 187
"Alceste," Gluck, 101
Aldighieri, Sig., 252
"Alessandro Stradella," 95
Alexi, Herr, 110
"Ali Baba," Cherubini, 59
"Ali Pascha von Janina," Lörtzing, 154
"Almanzar," Meyerbeer, 185
Alvary, Herr, 113
American Opera Company, 69, 106, 172, 282
American Opera Troupe, 102
Amodio, Sig., 361
"Am Runenstein," Genée and Flotow, 98
"Amy Gassenet," Tryon, 470
"Anacreon," Cherubini, 59
Ancona, Sig., 151
Ander, Herr, 92
"Anecdotes," Crowest, quoted, 81
"A Night in Rome," Eichberg, 469
"Anna Bolena," Donizetti, 73
Anthes, Herr, 245
"Antonio," Pratt, 469
Arditi, Sig., 386
Arimondi, Sig., 375
"Armida," Rossini, 269
"Armide," Gluck, 102
Arnoldson, Mme., 151
Aronson, Rudolph, 468
Arthur, Alfred, 468
"Ascanio," Saint-Saëns, 287
Aterrier, M., 144
"Attila," Verdi, 350

Auber, Daniel F. E., sketch of, 5
"Aureliano in Palmira," Rossini, 269
"A Woman of Marblehead," Coerne, 468
"Azara," Paine, 469

B

"Babes in Toyland," Herbert, 469
"Babette," Herbert, 469
Bache, Constance, 138
Baglioni, Sig., 218
Baireuth theatre, 407–410
Baker, B. F., 468
Balanqué, M., 118
Balderi, M., 361
Balfe, Michael William, sketch of, 17
Bandrowski, Mr. von, 245
"Barbe Bleue," Offenbach, 236
Barbier, Jules M., 118, 121, 123, 169, 172, 198, 214, 282, 340, 345
Barbot, M., 118
Barlandini, Sig., 252
Barnett, Alice, 316, 319
Baroelhst, M., 76
Barrington, Rutland, 311, 316, 319
Bars, Jacques, 138, 259
Bartlett, Homer N., 468
Barton, Andrew, 467
Bassford, William K., 468
Bassi, Sig. Luigi, 218
"Bastien und Bastienne," Mozart, 212
Bataille, M., 341
Batteo, Mlle. Marie, 205
Battu, M., 171
Baucardé, M., 361
Bauserwein, Herr, 407
Bayard, M., 74
"Beatrice di Tenda," Bellini, 30
Beaucarde, Sig., 354
Beck, Herr, 394
Beck, Johann H., 468
Beethoven, Ludwig van, sketch of,

INDEX

25; his estimate of "The Magic Flute," 227
Behrens, Conrad, 62
Bellamy, Mr., 142
Bellinconi, Gemma, 162
Bellini, Vincenzo, sketch of, 30
"Bellmann," Suppé, 333
Belval, M., 205
Benedict, Julius, sketch of, 39
Bensberg, Kate, 107
Bentham, Mr., 309
Benucci, Sig., 213, 216
Berthold, Barron, 62
Bertram, Herr, 437
Betts, Miss, 18
Betz, Herr, 402, 410, 411
"Bianca," Brüll, 56
"Bianca e Faliero," Rossini, 269
"Bianca e Fernando," Bellini, 30
Biancolini, Sig., 252
Bird, Arthur, 468
Bis, Hippolyte, 277
Bispham, Mr., 245
Bizet, Georges, sketch of, 43
Blake, Charles D., 468
Bland, Mr., 456
Blass, Mr., 245
Blau, M., 177, 182, 262
Bloch, Mme., 288
Blume, Herr Heinrich, 451
"Boccaccio," outline of, 336, 337
Boieldieu, François Adrien, 1, 48
Boito, Arrigo, sketch of, 52; 251, 372, 375
Bonawitz, Johann H., 468
Bondini, Signora, 218
Bond, Miss J., 311, 319
Borghi-Mamo, Mme., 361
Borrain, Mr., 442
Borrani, Mr., 13, 18
Bosio, Mme., 6, 354
Bosman, Mme., 262
Botticelli, Sig., 270
Boucicault, Dion, 39
Bouilly, M., 59
Boussa, M., 262
Bouvet, M., 182
Braham, John, 9, 456
Braham, Leonora, 316, 319
Brandt, Frl. Mariann, 110, 113, 398
Brani, Miss Cecile, 138
Brignoli, Sig., 361
Bristow, George F., 468
Brüll, Ignaz, sketch of, 56
Brunswick, Mr., 2
Buck, Dudley, 468

Bunge, Rudolph, 229
Bunn, Alfred, 18, 95
Burgmuller, Herr, 92
Burr, Frank A., 468
Bursch, Herr, 113
Bussani, Signora, 213
Bussani, Sig., 213
Butterfield, James A., 468.

C

Cabel, Mme. Marie, 198, 341
Cache, Herr, 26
"Cagliostro," Adam, 1
Calzabigi, Sig., 202
"Camargo," Lecocq, 144
Cammarano, M., 81, 361
Campbell, Miss, 162
Candidus, Mr., 282
"Captain Kidd," 468
Carafa, M., 274
Carl Rosa English Opera Troupe, 257
"Carmen," 43; outline of, 44-47
Caron, Mme. Rose, 262
Carr, Benjamin, 467
Carré, M., 118, 121, 123, 169, 172, 198, 214, 340, 345
Carte, D'Oyly, 309
"Cascabel," Susette, 470
"Cassilda," Bassford, 468
Castellan, Mme., 187
"Catarina Comaro," Donizetti, 73
"Catharine Grey," Balfe, 17
"Cavalleria Rusticana," outline of, 162-165
Cawse, Miss, 456
"Cenerentola," Rossini, 269
Chadwick, George W., 468
Chapuy, Mlle., 44
"Charles IV.," Gottschalk, 469
"Charles VI.," Halévy, 126
"Charles de France," Boieldieu and Herold, 132
Chavanne, Frl. von, 245
Cherubini, Maria Luigi C. Z. S., sketch of, 59
"Chris and the Wonderful Lamp," Sousa, 470
"Cinq-Mars," Gounod, 117
Cinti-Damoreau, Mme., 194
Clairville, M., 147, 248
"Clari," Halévy, 126
Clifford, Mr., 311
Coerne, L. A., 468

INDEX

Coletti, Sig., 354
Conders, M., 341
Converse, Frederick S., 468
"Coppelia," ballet, Delibes, 69
Cordier, Mlle., 198
Costa, Sig., 368
"Cox and Box," Sullivan, 308, 309
Cremieux, M., 241
Cremonini, Sig., 259
"Crispino," outline of, 266–268
Crouch, Frederick M., 468
Crowest, "Anecdotes," quoted, 81
"Cyrano de Bergerac," Herbert, 469
"Czar and Carpenter," outline of, 154–156

D

Dabodie, M., 277
Dabodie, Mme., 277
Damoreau-Cinti, Mme., 9, 277
Damrosch, Walter J., sketch of, 62; 288
Danks, Harvey P., 468
"Daphne," Bird, 468
Da Ponte, Lorenzo, 213, 218
"Das Glück von Edenhall," Humperdinck, 137
"Das Goldene Kreuz." *See* "The Golden Cross"
"Das Mädchen vom Lande," Suppé, 333
"Das Rheingold," outline of, 414–417
"Das Spitzentuch der Königin," Johann Strauss, 296
"Das Steinerne Herz," Brüll, 56
"Das Waldmädchen," Weber, 449
"Deborah," Millard, 469
De Gramont, M., 182
Deinet, Mlle., 398
De Koven, Reginald, sketch of, 64
Delavigne, 9, 194, 195
Deldeves, M., 92
De Leuven, M., 2
Delibes, Leo, sketch of, 69
De Puente, Sig., 162
De Lucia, Sig., 151, 259
De Meric, Mme., 194
Demmer, Herr, 26
"Démophon," Cherubini, 59
Dennery, M., 177
"Der Bärenhäuter, outline of, 437–439
"Der Bettler von Samarkand," Brüll, 56

Dereim, M., 290
De Reszke, Edouard, 177
De Reszke, Jean, 177
"Der Freischütz," outline of, 450–456
"Der Geiger aus Tirol," Genée, 98
"Der Husar," Brüll, 56
Derivis, M., 186
"Der Kobold," outline of, 439, 440
"Der Kyffhaüser Berg," Marschner, 157
"Der Landfriede," Brüll, 56
"Der Lustige Krieg," Johann Strauss, 296
"Der Müller von Meran," Flotow, 91
"Der Rattenfänger von Hameln," Nessler, 229
"Der Regimentstambour," Millöcker, 209
"Der Seekadett," Genée, 98
"Der Templer," Nicolai, 233
"Der Templer und die Jüdin," Marschner, 157
"Der Trompeter von Säkkingen." *See* "The Trumpeter of Sakkingen"
"Der Vampyr," Marschner, 157
"Der Waffenschmied," Lörtzing, 154
"Der Wasserträger," Cherubini, 59
"Der wilde Jäger," Nessler, 229
"Der Wildschütz," Lörtzing, 154
"Der Zigeunerbaron," Johann Strauss, 296
Deschamps, M., 186
Deschamps, Mme., 262
"Deseret," Buck, 468
"Desirée," Sousa, 470
Detmer, Herr, 380
Détroyat, M., 290
"Deux Sous de Carbon," Delibes, 69
Devrient, Edouard, 157
Devries, M., 262
"Die Afrikareise," Suppé, 333
"Die beiden Schützen," Lörtzing, 154
"Die Dreizehn," Genée, 98
"Die Entführung aus dem Serail," Mozart, 213
"Die Fledermaus," outline of, 298, 299
"Die Fraueninsel," Millöcker, 209
"Die Generalprobe," Genée, 98
"Die Gotterdämmerung," outline of, 426–430

INDEX

"Die Göttin der Vernunft," Johann Strauss, 296
"Die Grossfürstin," Flotow, 91
"Die Heimkehr des Verbannten," Nicolai, 233
"Die Hochzeit des Figaro." *See* "The Marriage of Figaro"
"Die ländliche Hochzeit," 110
"Die Matrosen" ("Le Naufrage de la Méduse"), 91
"Die Piraten," Genée, 98
"Die Roland's Knappen," Lörtzing, 154
Dietz, Mme., 402
"Die Walküre," outline of, 417-422
"Die Wallfahrt nach Kevelaar," Humperdinck, 137
"Die Zauberflöte," 213. *See* "The Magic Flute"
Dilthey, Minnie, 102
Di Murska, Mlle., 386
"Dinorah," outline of, 198-201
"Djamileh," Bizet, 43
"Docteur Miracle," Bizet, 43
"Doctor of Alcantara," Eichberg, 469
Donatelli, Mme., 358
"Don Carlos," Verdi, 350
"Don Giovanni," 213; outline of, 218-223
Donizetti, Gaetano, sketch of, 73
"Donna del Lago," Rossini, 269
"Don Pasquale," outline of, 79-81
"Don Quixote," De Koven, 64
"Don Quixote," Neuendorff, 469
"Don Sebastien," Donizetti, 73, 81
Donzelli, Sig., 31
Dormoy, M., 80
"Dornröschens Brautfahrt," Nessler, 229
Dorus-Gras, Mme., 9, 127, 186, 194
Douste, Miss Jeanne, 138
"Drei Paar Schuhe," Millöcker, 209
Dubreul, M., 172
"Duc de Guise," Flotow, 92
Duclos, Mme., 118
Dufriche, Sig., 259
Du Locle, M., 262
Dupont, M., 277
Duprez, M., 76, 81, 277
Durnset, Mr., 18

E

"Echo et Narcisse," Gluck, 102
"Edgar," Puccini, 256
"Edwin and Angelina," Pellesier-468
Eggers, Anton C., 468
Eichberg, Julius, 469
Eilers, Herr, 410
"Ein Abenteuer in Wien," Millöcker, 209
"Eine Nacht in Venedig," Johann Strauss, 296
"Ein Feldlager in Schlesien," Meyerbeer, 186
Elba, Miss Marie, 138
"El Capitan," Sousa, 470
"Elysia," De Koven, 468
"Emma di Resburgo," Meyerbeer, 185
"Enchanteresse," Flotow, 91
"Enrico di Borgogna," Donizetti, 73
"Erminie," outline of, 142, 143
"Ernani," outline of, 351-354
"Erostrate," Reyer, 262
"Esclarmonde," outline of, 182-184
"Esmeralda," Prévost, 469
"Esule di Granata," Meyerbeer, 185
"Étienne Marcel," Saint-Saëns, 287
"Eugen Onégin," outline of, 347-349
Eunike, Frl. Johanna, 451
"Euryanthe," outline of, 460-463
Everard, Miss, 311
Evers, Signora, 354

F

Fairlamb, James R., 469
Faivre, Mlle., 118
Falcon, Mlle. Cornelia, 127, 186
Falconer, M., 22
"Falstaff," Balfe, 17
"Falstaff," outline of, 375-378
"Famille Suisse," Boieldieu, 48
Fanciulli, Francesco, 469
"Faniska," Cherubini, 59
Fastlinger, Frl., 394
"Fatinitza," outline of, 333-335
Faure, M., 198, 205, 345
"Faust," outline of, 118-121
Fawcett, Mr., 456
"Feldlager in Schlesien," Meyerbeer, 191
Ferenczy, M., 288
Fessenden, W. H., 107, 282
"Feuersnot," outline of, 304-307
"Fidelio," outline of, 26-29
Fidès-Devriès, Mme., 177

INDEX 545

Fischer, Emil, 110, 113, 398, 402
Fitzball, M., 442, 446
Flécheux, Mlle., 186
"Fleur de Thé," Lecocq, 144
"Fleurette," Nessler, 229
Florio, Caryl, 469
Flotow, Friedrich von, sketch of, 91
"Flotte Bursche," Suppé, 333
"Flowers and Lilies," Leavitt, 469
Foli, Sig., 386
Formes, Carl, 92
Fornari, Sig., 372
Forti, Herr, 461
"Foxy Quiller," De Koven, 468
"Fra Diavolo," outline of, 6-9
"Francesca di Rimini," Goetz, 106
"Francis Hopkinson, the First American Poet-Composer," Senneck, quoted, 467
"Françoise de Rimini," Thomas, 340
"Franz Schubert," Suppé, 333
Fraschini, M., 365
"Fredegonde," Guiraud and Saint-Saëns, 287
Frezzolini, Mme., 361
Friedrich-Materna, Frau, 410, 411, 430
Fry, William H., 468
"Furstin Ninetta," Johann Strauss, 296

G

Gabet, M., 248
Gadski, Johanna, 62
"Galatée," Massé, 169
Gallet, Luigi, 175, 177
Galli-Marie, Mme., 44, 341
Galli, Sig., 274
Garbin, M., 375
Garcia, Sig., 270, 271
Gardoni, Sig., 6, 350
Gayarro, Sig., 252
"Gazza Ladra," Rossini, 269
"Gemma di Vergi," Donizetti, 73
Genée, Franz F. R., 98, 209, 297, 298, 333, 336, 337
"Genevieve de Brabant," Offenbach, 236
Gern, Herr, 451
"Giacinta ed Ernesto," Benedict, 39
Giacosa, M., 256, 259
Gibert, M., 182
Gilbert, W. S., 308, 309, 311, 314, 316, 319, 321, 324, 326, 328, 330
Gilibert, Sig., 259

"Gille et Gillotin," Thomas, 340
Gille, M., 180
"Giroflé-Girofla," outline of, 144-147
Gleason, Frederick G., 469
"Gli Ugonotti" ("The Huguenots"), 186
Gluck, Christoph Willibald, sketch of, 101
Goeffoel, M., 262
Goethe's influence on Boito's work, 52
"Goethe's Jugendzeit," Meyerbeer, 186
Goetz, Hermann, sketch of, 106
Goggi, Mme., 361
Goldbeck, Robert, 469
Goldmark, Karl, sketch of, 110
Gordon, Miss Alice, 138
Gorl, Frau, 223
Gotlieb, Frl., 223
Gottlieb, Frau, 213
Gottschalk, Louis M., 469
Gounod, Charles François, sketch of, 117
Gownell, Miss, 456
Graziani, M., 358
Gresse, M., 262
"Gringoire," Brüll, 56
Grisi, Mme., 31, 36, 77, 79
Gromzeski, Sig., 151
Grossi, Signora, 368
Grossmith, Mr. George, 309, 311, 316, 319
Grünbaum, Frau, 461
Gruneisen's memoir of Meyerbeer, quoted, 194
Guaymat, Mme., 345
Guerrini, Signora, 375
Guetary, Sig., 151
"Guglielmo Ratcliff," Mascagni, 162
Guicciardi, M., 361
"Guido et Ginevra," Halévy, 126
Guille, M., 162
"Guntram," Richard Strauss, 303, 307
Gura, Herr, 410, 411

H

"Haddan Hall," Sullivan, 309
Haffner, M., 298
Halévy, Jacques F. F. E., sketch of, 126
Halevy, M., 44, 237, 239

35

INDEX

Hamerik, Asger, 469
Hamilton, W. H., 107, 282
"Hamlet," Maretzek, 469
"Hamlet," outline of, 345, 346
"Hansel and Gretel," outline of, 138–141
"Hans Heiling," outline of, 158–160
Hanslick, and "Robert le Diable," 198
"Happy Land," De Koven, 64
"Harmonicon, The," printed analysis of "Semiramide," 274, 276
Harris, Mr., 22
Harris, William V., 469
Harrison, William, 13, 15, 18, 198, 442
Hastreiter, Helene, 102
Haupt, Frl., 410
Heberlé, Mlle., 194
Heilbronn, Mme., 180
Heinrich, Herr, 113
"Heinrich IV," Marschner, 157
Heitzinger, Herr, 461
"Henry VIII," outline of, 290–293
Henschel, George, 469
Herbert, Victor, 469
"Hermione," Halévy, 126
"Hérodiade," Massenet, 174
Herold, Louis J. F., sketch of, 132
Hervey's biography of Massenet, quoted, 176, 181
"Herzog Wildfang," Siegfried Wagner, 437
"Hilda," Flotow, 91
Hill, Mr., 410, 411
"Hjalmar and Ingeborg," Hamerik, 469
"H. M. S. Pinafore," outline of, 311–314
Hofer, Frau, 223
Hofer, Herr, 394
Hofmann, Frl., 437
Holst, Edouard, 469
Hölzel, Herr, 402
Homer, Mme., 245
Horncastle, Mr., 13
Howson, John, 107
Howson, Miss E., 311
Hueffer's life of Wagner, quoted, 399
Hugo, Victor, and "Lucrezia Borgia," 86
Humperdinck, Engelbert, sketch of, 137

I

"I Capuletti ed i Montecchi," Bellini, 30
"Idomeneo," Mozart, 213
"Il Crociato in Egitto," Meyerbeer, 185
"Il Diavolo a Quattro," Ricci, 266
"Il Falegname de Livonia," Donizetti, 73
"Il Figliuol Prodigo," Ponchielli, 251
"Il Flor d'Harlem," Flotow, 91
"Il Furioso," Donizetti, 73
"I Lituani," Ponchielli, 251
Illica, Luigi, 165, 256, 259
"I Lombardi," Verdi, 350
"Il Pirata," Bellini, 30
"Il Poliuto," Donizetti, 73
"Il Talismano," Balfe, 18
"Il Trovatore," outline of, 361–365
"Il Turco in Italia," Rossini, 269
"I Masnadieri," Verdi, 350
"I Medici," Leoncavallo, 150
"Indigo," Johann Strauss, 296
"Indra," Flotow, 91
"Inferno," Florio, 469
"In Filanda," Mascagni, 161
"Iolanthe," outline of, 319–321
"Iolanthe," Tschaikowsky, 347
"I Pagliacci," outline of, 151–153
"Iphigénie en Aulide," Gluck, 101
"Iphigénie en Tauride," Gluck, 102
"I Promessi Sposi," Ponchielli, 251
"I Puritani," 30; outline of, 36–38
"I Rantzau," Mascagni, 162
"Irene" ("La Reine de Saba"), 117
"Iris," outline of, 165, 166
"Isaura de Salerno," Gottschalk, 469
"Italian Wagner" (Boito), 52
"It Happened in Nordland," Herbert, 469
"Ivanhoe," Sullivan, 309
"I Vespri Siciliani," Verdi, 350

J

"Jabuka," Johann Strauss, 296
Jahn's criticism of "The Magic Flute," 227, 228
Jäida, Frau, 410, 411
Jakobowski, Edouard, sketch of, 142
"Jean de Paris," Boieldieu, 48
"Joan of Arc," Balfe, 17

INDEX

Johnston, Miss Edith, 138
Jordan, Jules, 469
Jourdain, M., 262
Jouy, Etienne, 277
Juch, Emma, 102, 282
"Judith," Chadwick, 468

K

Kammer, Frl., 245
Kashkin, M., 347
"Katherine," Sousa, 470
"Katie Dean," Merz, 469
Kauffmann, Frl., 407
Kellogg, Clara Louise, 76, 172, 344, 386
Kelly, Edgar S., 469
Kelly's "Reminiscences," quoted, 214, 216
Kemlitz, Herr, 113
"Keno," Klein, 469
Kielblock, Franz, 469
Kindermann, Herr, 407
Kind, Friedrich, 450
Klein, Bruno O., 469
Knote, Herr, 437
Konig, Herr, 147
"Königin Mariette," Brüll, 56
Kramer-Weidl, Frau, 110
Krauss, Mlle., 290
Kronold, Mme., 162
Krull, Frl., 245

L

Labarre, Boieldieu's pupil, 51
"La Belle Hélène," outline of, 239–241
"La Bergère Châtelaine," Auber, 5
Lablache, Sig., 36, 79, 81, 350
"La Bohème," outline of, 256–258
"La Bohémienne," Balfe, 18
"La Caduta de' Giganti," Gluck, 101
"La Cambiale di Matrimonio," Rossini, 269
"La Chambre Gothique," Massé, 169
"La Colombe," Gounod, 117
"La Coupe du Roi de Thulé," Massenet, 174
"La Dame Blanche," 48; outline of, 49–51
"La Double Echelle," Thomas, 340
"La Ebrea" ("The Jewess"), 127
"La Favorita," outline of, 76–79

"La Fille Coupable," Boieldieu, 48
"La Fille de Madame Angot," outline of, 147–149
Lafont, M., 194
"La Forza del Destino," Verdi, 350
"L'Africaine," outline of, 205–208
"La Gioconda," outline of, 251–255
"La Grande Tante," Massenet, 174
Lagrua, Mlle., 365
"La Jolie Fille de Perth," Bizet, 43
"La Jolie Parfumeuse," Offenbach, 236
"Lakme," outline of, 69–72
"La Langue Musicale," Halévy, 126
L'Allemand, Miss Pauline, 282
L'Allemand, Mme., 69, 107
"La Marjolaine," Lecocq, 144
"La Marocaine," Offenbach, 236
"L'Ame en Peine," Flotow, 91
"L'Amico Fritz," outline of, 166–168
Lammert, Frl., 410
"La Muette de Portici." See "Masaniello"
"La Nonne Sanglante," Gounod, 117
"La Perichole," Offenbach, 236
"La Petite Mariée," Lecocq, 144
"La Princesse de Trebizonde," Offenbach, 236
"La Princesse Jaune," Saint-Saëns, 287
"La Reine de Chypre," Halévy, 126
"La Reine de Saba," Gounod, 117
"La Reine Topaze," outline of, 171–172
"La Rinegata," 86
"L'Arlesienne," interludes, Bizet, 43
Lasalle, M., 290
"La Savojarda," Ponchielli, 251
Laschi, Signora, 213
"La Sonnambula," 30; outline of, 34–36
"La Source," ballet, Delibes, 69
"La Statue," Reyer, 262
"La Stella del Monte," Ponchielli, 251
"La Straniera," Bellini, 30
"Last Will and Testament," Merz, 469
"La Tempête," Halévy, 126
"La Tentation," Halévy, 126
Lathrop, George Parsons, 62
"La Tosca," outline of, 259–261
"La Traviata," outline of, 358–361
"La Vallière," Bartlett, 468
Lavelle, Calixo, 469
"La Vendetta," Hamerik, 469

INDEX

"La Veuve Grapin," Flotow, 91
"La Vie Parisienne," Offenbach, 236
"La Vierge," Massenet, 174
"Lawn Tennis," Woolf, 470
"La Zingara," Balfe, 17, 18
Leavitt, W. J. D., 469
"Le Barbier de Trouville," Lecocq, 144
"Le Brasseur de Preston," Adam, 1
"Le Chalet," Adam, 61
"Le Cid," outline of, 177–179
"L'Eclair," outline of, 129–131
Lecocq, Charles, sketch of, 144
"Le Comte Ory," Rossini, 277
"Le Dilettante d'Avignon," Halévy, 126
"Le Duc d'Albe," Donizetti, 78
"Le Duc Gemelle," Ponchielli, 251
"Lee-li-nan," Stahl, 470
Lee, William H., 107, 282
Lehmann, Frl. Lilli, 110, 113, 398, 410
Lehmann, Frl. Marie, 410
"Leichte Cavallerie," Suppé, 333
"Leila," Shelley, 469
"Le Juif Errant," Halévy, 126
"L'Elisir d'Amore," outline of, 84, 85
Lely, Durwar, 319
Lemaire, Ferdinand, 288
"Le Mariage aux Lanternes," Offenbach, 236
"Le Médecin malgré lui," Gounod, 117
"Le Naufrage de la Méduse," Flotow, 91
"Le Nozze di Figaro." See "The Marriage of Figaro"
Leoncavallo, Ruggiero, sketch of, 150
"Leonello," Fairlamb, 469
"Leonora," Fry, 468
"Léonore." See "Fidelio"
"Le Pardon de Ploermel." See "Dinorah"
"Le Petit-Duc," Lecocq, 144
"Le Pré aux Clercs," outline of, 135, 136
"Le Prophète." See "The Prophet"
Lerda, M., 186
"Le Roi de Lahore," outline of, 175–177
"Le Roi d'Yvetot," Adam, 1
"Le Roi l'a dit," Delibes, 69
Leroux, Mlle., 9
"Les Bavards," Offenbach, 236

"Les Brigands," Offenbach, 236
"Les Cent Vierges," Lecocq, 144
"L'Esclave de Camoens," Flotow, 91
"Les Cloches de Corneville," Planquette, 248
"Les Contes d'Hoffmann," Offenbach, 237
"Les Deux Journées," outline of, 59–61
"Les Diamants de la Couronne." See "The Crown Diamonds"
"Le Sélam," Reyer, 262
"Les Mousequetaires de la Reine," Halévy, 126
"Les Noces de Prométhée," Saint-Saëns, 287
"Le Songe d'une Nuit d'Été," Thomas, 340
"Les Pecheurs de Perles," Bizet, 43
"Les Rosières," Herold, 132
"Les Souvenirs," Halévy, 126
"Les Tours de Mercure," Florio, 469
"Le Talisman," Planquette, 248
"Le Timbre d'Argent," Saint-Saëns, 287
"L'Etoile du Nord." See "The Star of the North"
"Le Val d'Andorre," Halévy, 126
Levasseur, M., 127, 186, 194, 277
"Le Villi," Puccini, 256
"L'Impresario in angustié," Ricci, 266
Lind, Jenny, 74, 76, 186, 191, 194, 195, 350
"Linda de Chamouni," outline of, 88–90
Lipiner, Siegfried, 114
"Lischen et Fritzchen," Offenbach, 236
"L'Italiana in Algeri," Rossini, 269
Lockroy, Mr., 171
"Lodoïska," Cherubini, 59
"Lohengrin," outline of, 393–398
Lolli, Sig., 218
"L'Ombre," Flotow, 91
Loomis, Harvey W., 469
"Lord Buncombe's Daughter," Adamowski, 468
Lorenz, J. M., 469
Lörtzing, Gustav Albert, sketch of, 154
"Love's Stowaway," Henschel, 469
Lucca, Mlle., 205
Lucca, Mme., 344

INDEX

"Lucia di Lammermoor," outline of, 81-83
"Lucille," Pratt, 469
"Lucio Silla," Mozart, 212
"Lucrezia Borgia," outline of, 86-88
Ludwig, Mr., 282
"Luisa Miller," Verdi, 350
"Lurline," 441; outline of, 446-448

M

"Maid Marian," outline of, 66-68
"Maid of Artois," Balfe, 17
"Maître Griffard," Delibes, 69
"Maître Wolfram," Reyer, 262
Malibran, Maria Felicia, 27, 34, 126
Mallinger, Mlle., 402
"Mam'zelle Quat'sous," Planquette, 248
Mandini, Signor, 213
Mandini, Signora, 213
"Manila Te Deum," Damrosch, 62
Manners, Charles, 319
"Manon Lescaut," Halévy, 126
"Manon Lescaut," Puccini, 256
"Manon," outline of, 180-182
"Manru," outline of, 244-247
Mansuède, M., 262
"Maometto Secondo," Rossini, 270
Marai, Mlle., 6
Marchisio, Barbara, 274
Marchisio, Carlotta, 274
Maretzek, Max, 469
"Margarethe" ("Faust"), Gounod, 118
"Margherita d'Anjou," Meyerbeer, 185
Mariani, Mme., 274
Mariani, Sig., 252, 274
Mariano, Sig., 34
"Marie Magdaleine," oratorio, Massenet, 174
Marini, Sig., 187
"Marino Faliero," Donizetti, 73
"Marion Delorme," Ponchielli, 251
Mario, Sig., 9, 77, 79, 81, 86, 187, 354, 361
"Maritana," outline of, 442-446
Marschner, Heinrich, sketch of, 157
"Martha," outline of, 92-95
"Masaniello," outline of, 9-12
Mascagni, Pietro, sketch of, 161
Massé, Felix Marie, sketch of. 169
Massenet, Jules E. F., sketch of, 174

Massol, M., 9, 277
"Masters of French Music," Arthur Hervey, 181
"Ma Tante Aurore," Boieldieu, 48,
"Matilda of Hungary," Wallace, 441
Maurel, Sig., 372, 375
May, Miss Alice, 309
"Mazeppa," Tschaikowsky, 347
"Medea," Cherubini, 59
Medini, Sig., 368
Meier, Herr, 26
Meilhac, M., 44, 237, 239
Meisslinger, Miss Louise, 138
Meister, Herr, 26
Mélesville, M., 132
Menasci, Sig., 162
Mendelssohn, quoted, 195
"Mephistopheles," 52; outline of, 53-55
"Mercedes," Leavitt, 469
"Merlin," outline of, 113-116
Merten, Wilhelm, 62
Merz, Karl, 469
Meyerbeer, Giacomo, sketch of, 185
Micelli, Signora, 218
"Mignon," outline of, 340-344
Milde, Herr, 394
Milder, Frl., 26
"Miles Standish," Franciulli, 469
"Miles Standish," Kielblock, 469
Millard, Harrison, 469
Millöcker, Carl, sketch of, 209
Miolan-Carvalho, Mme., 118, 122, 123, 171, 172, 198, 354
"Mireille," Gounod, 117
"Miss Fauvette," Massé, 169
Mitle, M., 288
"Mitridate, Rè di Ponto," Mozart, 212
Mitterwurzer, Herr, 389, 398
"Mizpah," Burr, 468
"Mlle. Maie et M. de Lembre," Harris, 469
"Mlle. Modiste," Herbert, 469
"Mlle. Wagner" (Massenet), 184
"Mme. Favart," Offenbach, 237
Mollenhauer, Edward, 469
Mongini, Sig., 368
"Montezuma," Gleason, 469
Mori, Mlle., 277
Mosenthal, 56, 110, 233
"Moses in Egypt," Rossini, 269
Mozart, Johann C. W. A., sketch of 212
Muhlmann, Mr., 245
Müller, Frl., 26

INDEX

N

Nachbauer, Herr, 402
"Naïda," Flotow, 91
"Nanon," outline of, 98–100
Nantier-Didiée, Mme., 354
Nardi, Mlle., 182
Naudin, M., 205
Navarrini, Sig., 372
"Nero," outline of, 282–285
Nessler, Victor E., sketch of, 229
Neuendorff, Adolph, 469
"Newport," Goldbeck, 469
Nicolai, Otto, sketch of, 233
Niemann, Herr, 398, 410
Niering, Herr, 410
Nilsson, Mme. Christine, 52, 344, 345, 359
"Nina," Eggers, 468
Ninth Symphony, Beethoven, 25
Noblet, Mlle., 9
Nohl, Dr. Ludwig, quoted, 413
"Norma," 30; outline of, 31–33
Nossig, Alfred, 244
"Notre Dame de Paris," Fry, 468
Nourrit, M., 127, 186, 194, 277

O

"Oberon," outline of, 456–460
"Oberto," Verdi, 350
Obin, M., 205, 274
Occheley, Sig., 213
Offenbach, Jacques, sketch of, 236
"Onganita," Young, 470
"Opritchnik," Tschaikowsky, 347
"Orphée aux Enfers," outline of, 241–243
"Orpheus," outline of, 102–105
"Orpheus and Eurydice," Gluck, 101, 102
"Ostrolenka," Bonawitz, 468
"Otello," Rossini, 269
"Othello," outline of, 372–375
"Otho Visconti," Gleason, 469
"Our Flats," Holst, 469
Oxenford, Mr., 39

P

Paderewski, Ignace Jan, sketch of, 244
Page, N. C., 469
"Paille d'Avoine," Planquette, 248

Paine, John K., 469
"Pamurge," Planquette, 248
Pantaleoni, Signora, 372
"Paolo," Jakobowski, 142
"Papa's Wife," De Koven, 468
"Paragraph III," Suppé, 333
Parepa-Rosa, Mme., 171, 214
"Parisina," Donizetti, 73
Paroli, Sig., 372, 375
"Parsifal," outline of, 430–436
Pasqua, Signora, 375
Pasta, Mme., 30, 31, 34, 73
"Patience," outline of, 316–319
Paton, Miss, 456
Patrie overture, Bizet, 43
Patti, Mme., 76, 359
"Paul and Virginia," outline of, 169–171
"Pauline," Danks, 468
"Paul Jones," Planquette, 248
Paul, Mrs. Howard, 309
Paulton, Mr., 142
Pelagalli-Rossetti, Sig., 375
Pellesier, Victor, 468
Penco, Mme., 361
Pepoli, Count, 36
Perotti, Sig., 386
Persiani, Mme., 81
"Peter Schmoll and his Neighbors," Weber, 449
"Philémon and Baucis," outline of, 123–125
Phillips, Mr., 442
"Phryne," Saint-Saëns, 287
"Phyllis," Rowe, 469
Piave, M., 266, 351, 354, 358
Piccini's rivalry with Gluck, 102
Piccolomini, Marie, 18, 359
"Pierre and Catherine," Adam, 1
Pierson, Miss Bertha, 282
Pillet, M. Léon, 386
Pini-Corsi, Sig., 375
"Pipe of Desire," Converse, 468
"Pique Dame," Suppé, 333
"Pique Dame," Tschaikowsky, 347
Planard, M., 129, 135
Planché, J. R., 456
Plançon, Pol, 177
Planquette, Robert Jean, sketch of, 248
"Polyeucte," Gounod, 117
Ponchielli, Amilcare, sketch of, 251
Ponziani, Sig. Felice, 218
Poole, Miss, 442
"Pounce & Co.," Woolf, 470
Power, Mr., 311

INDEX

Pozzoni, Signora, 368
Pratt, Silas G., 469
"Preciosa," outline of, 463-465
Prévost, Eugene, 469
Prévost, M., 277
Prévot, M., 277
"Prince Ananias," Herbert, 469
"Princess Ida," outline of, 321-324
"Prinz Methusalem," Johann Strauss, 296
"Priscilla; or, the Pilgrims' Proxy," Susette, 470
"Proserpine," outline of, 293-295
"Psyche," Thomas, 340
Puccini, Giacomo, sketch of, 256
"Puritania," Kelly, 469
Pyne, Eliza, 13, 24
Pyne, Louise, 13, 15, 198
"Pyramus and Thisbe," Weil, 470

Q

"Quinto Fabio," Cherubini, 59

R

Rameau's influence on Gluck, 101
"Rat Catcher of Hamelin," Neuendorff, 469
"Raymond," Thomas, 340
"Red Feather," De Koven, 468
Reeves, Mr., 13
Regnal, M., 118
Renaud, M., 262
"Requiem" by Mozart, 213
Reyer, Louis E. E., sketch of, 262
Ricci, Luigi, sketch of, 266
"Richard Cœur de Léon," cantata, Benedict, 39
Richard, Mlle., 290
Richings-Bernard, Mrs., 76
"Rienzi," outline of, 380-386
Righetti, Mme. Giorgi, 270
"Rigoletto," outline of, 354-358
Rinaldini, Sig., 386
"Rip Van Winkle," Bristow, 468
"Rip Van Winkle," Jordan, 469
"Rizzio," Massenet, 174
"Robert the Devil," outline of, 194-198
"Robin Hood," outline of, 64-66
Robinson, Herr, 110, 113
Robinson, Mr., 398
Robjohn, W. J. *See* Florio, Caryl

"Rob Roy," De Koven, 64
"Roderico, Rè de'Goti," Ponchielli, 251
Roger, M., 201
"Romance of a Summer," Butterfield, 468
"Romani," 31, 34, 84, 86
"Roméo et Juliette," outline of, 121-123
Romer, Miss, 18, 442
"Romilda e Costanza," Meyerbeer, 185
Ronconi, Sig., 6, 354
Rosa, Carl, 56, 386
"Rosalie et Myrza," Boieldieu, 48
Rossi, Mlle., 270
Rossini-Colbran, Mme., 274
Rossini, Gioacchini A., sketch of, 269
Ross, Sig., 88, 273
Rothe, Herr, 26
Rowe, G. F., 469
Royal Carl Rosa Opera Company, 138
Royer, M., 76
Roze, Mme. Marie, 52
"Rubezahl," Flotow, 91
"Rubezahl," Weber, 449
Rubini, Sig., 34, 36, 73
Rubinstein, Anton G., sketch of, 281
Rubinstein, Herr, 451
"Ruddygore," outline of, 326-328

S

Sainte-Foy, M., 198
Saint-Saëns, Camille, sketch of, 287
"Sakonntala," Reyer, 262
"Sakuntala" overture, Goldmark, 110
"Salammbo," Beck, 468
"Salammbô," Reyer, 262
"Salome," Richard Strauss, 303, 307
"Samson and Delila," outline of, 288-290
Sanderson, Miss Sybil, 182
Santley, Mr., 386
Saporitti, Signora Teresa, 218
"Sappho," Gounod, 117
"Saratoga," Goldbeck, 469
"Satanella," Balfe, 17
Saxe, Mme. Marie, 205
Scaria, Herr, 430
"Schach dem König," Brüll, 56
Schack, Herr, 223
Scheff, Miss Fritzi, 245
Schefzky, Frl., 410

INDEX

Scheidemantel, Herr, 245
Schickaneder, Emanuel, 223, 224
Schlosser, Herr, 402, 410, 411
Schloss, Herr, 389
Schnorr von Carolsfeld, Herr Ludwig, 398
Schnorr von Carolsfeld, Mme., 398
Schröder-Devrient, Mme., 380, 386, 389
Scottish descent of Donizetti, 81
Scotti, Sig., 259
Scribe, M., 6, 9, 12, 49, 127, 185, 186, 190, 194, 195, 201, 205
Seidler, Frau Caroline, 451
Seipelt, Herr, 461
Sembrich, Mme., 245
"Semiramide," 270; outline of, 273–276
Senneck, O. G., quoted, 467
Shelley, Harry R., 469
"Siege of Rochelle," Balfe, 17
"Siegfried," outline of, 422–426
Sieg itz, Herr, 113, 437
"Sigurd," outline of, 262–265
"Silvano," Mascagni, 162
Silvestre, M., 290
"Simon Boccanegra," Verdi, 350
"Simplicius," Johann Strauss, 296
Sinclair, Mr., 274
Srandin, M., 147
"Sir Roger de Coverley," Crouch, 468
"Sleepy Hollow," Maretzek, 469
Smith, Harry B., 64, 66
"Soldiers' Return," Goldbeck, 469
Somma, M., 365
Sonnleithner, M., 26
Sontag, Frl., 76, 461
Sousa, John P., 470
"Stabat Mater," Rossini, 270
Stagno, Roberto, 162
Stahl, Richard, 470
Stalport, M., 262
Staudigl, Mme., 194
Steffernone, Signora, 361
Stehle, Frl., 407
Stehle, Mme., 375
Stehman, Gerhard, 62
Steller, Sig., 368
Sterbini, M., 270, 271
Sterling, Miss Agnes, 282
St. Georges, M. de., 12, 74, 92, 129
"Stiffelio," Verdi, 350
Stoddard, Alonzo, 107, 282
Stolz, Mme., 76
Storace, Signora, 213

"Stradella," outline of, 95–97
Strauss, Johann, sketch of, 296
Strauss, Richard, sketch of, 303
Stretton, Mr., 18
Stritt, Herr, 110
Stümer, Herr Carl, 451
Suaratoni, Sig., 166
Sucher, Frau, 288
"Sulda," Florio, 469
Sullivan, Arthur A., sketch of, 309
Suppé, Franz von, sketch of, 333
"Surcouf," Planquette, 248
Susette, Thomas W., 470
"Suzanne," Florio, 469
"Sylvia," ballet, Delibes, 69

T

"Tabasco," Chadwick, 468
Tagliafico, Sig., 6, 187
Taglioni, Signora, 194
Talazac, M., 288
Tamagno, Sig., 372
Tamburini, Sig., 36, 79, 187
"Tancredi," Rossini, 269
"Tannhäuser," outline of, 389–393
Targioni-Tozzetti, Sig., 162
Taskin, M., 182
"Tcharavitchki," Tschaikowsky, 347
"Tcharodjeika," Tschaikowsky, 347
Teal, Jeannie, 162
Temple, Mr. R., 309, 311, 319
Ternina, Mme., 259
"Thais," Massenet, 174
"The Adventure Club," Leavitt, 469
"The Algerian," De Koven, 64
"The Ameer," Herbert, 467
"The Archers; or, the Mountains of Switzerland," Carr, 467
Théâtre Nationale, founded by Adam, 1
"The Barber of Seville," Rossini, 269; outline of, 270–273
"The Beautiful Galatea," outline of, 337–339
"The Beggar Student," outline of, 209–211
"The Begum," De Koven, 64
"The Black Domino," Auber, 5
"The Bohemian Girl," outline of, 18–22
"The Bride Elect," Sousa, 470
"The Bride of Messina," Bonawitz, 468
"The Brides of Venice," Benedict, 39

INDEX

"The Bronze Horse," Auber, 5
"The Burglar's Bride," Loomis, 469
"The Charlatan," Sousa, 470
"The Chimes of Normandy," outline of, 248-250
"The Commodore," Goldbeck, 469
"The Contrabandista," Sullivan, 308
"The Corsican Bride," Mollenhauer, 469
"The Country Wedding," Goldmark, 110
"The Crown Diamonds," outline of, 12-16
"The Crusaders," Benedict, 39
"The Daughter of Jephtha," Meyerbeer, 185
"The Daughter of the Regiment," outline of, 74-76
"The Demon," outline of, 285, 286
"The Disappointment; or, the Force of Credulity," Barton, 467
"The Enchantress," Balfe, 17
"The Fencing Master," De Koven, 468
"The Fifth of November," Crouch, 468
"The First Lieutenant," Page, 469
"The Flying Dutchman," outline of, 386-389
"The Fortune Teller," Herbert, 469
"The Free Lance," Sousa, 470
"The Gate of Brandeburg," Meyerbeer, 185
"The Golden Cross," outline of, 56-58
"The Gondoliers," outline of, 330-332
"The Grand Duchess of Gerolstein," outline of, 237-239
"The Highwayman," De Koven, 468
"The Huguenots," outline of, 186-190
"The Idol's Eye," Herbert, 469
"The Jewess," outline of, 127-129
"The Knickerbockers," De Koven, 468
"The Knight of the Leopard," Balfe, 18
"The Light Keeper's Daughter," Blake, 468
"The Lily of Killarney," outline of, 39-42
"The Little Duchess," De Koven, 468
"The Love Spell" ("L'Elisir d'Amore"), 84

"The Lyre and the Sword," Weber 449
"The Magic Flute," outline of, 223-228
"The Maid of Athens," Loomis, 469
"The Maid of Orleans," Tschaikowsky, 347
"The Mandarin," De Koven, 468
"The Marriage of Figaro," outline of, 213-218
"The Marriage of Jeannette," outline of, 172, 173
"The Masked Ball," outline of, 365-368
"The Mastersingers," outline of, 401-406
"The Merry War," outline of, 297, 298
"The Merry Wives of Windsor," outline of, 233-235
"The Mikado," outline of, 324-326
"The Old Guard," Planquette, 248
"The Paris Doll," De Koven, 468
"The Pearl of Bagdad," Lorenz, 469
"The Pet Dove" ("La Colombe"), Gounod, 117
"The Phantom" ("L'Ombre"), 91
"The Pirates of Penzance," outline of, 314-316
"The Postilion of Longjumeau," 1; outline of, 2-4
"The Prophet," outline of, 201-205
"The Puritan's Daughter," Balfe, 17
"The Queen of Hearts," Sousa, 470
"The Queen of Sheba," outline of, 110-113
"The Queen's Lace Handkerchief," outline of, 299-301
"The Ring of the Nibelung," outline of, 406-430
"The Robber of the Abruzzi." See "La Caverne"
"The Rose of Castile," outline of, 22-24
"The Rose of Tyrol," Eichberg, 469
"The Roundheads and Cavaliers," Arthur, 468
"The Royal Children," Humperdinck, 137
"The Runaway Flirt," Merz, 469

"The Scarlet Letter," outline of, 62, 63
"The Serenade," Herbert, 469
"The Singing Girl," Herbert, 469
"The Smugglers," Sousa, 470
"The Sorcerer," outline of, 309–311
"Thespis," Sullivan, 308
"The Star of the North," outline of, 190–194
"The Student King," De Koven, 468
"The Talisman," Balfe, 18
"The Taming of the Shrew," outline of, 106–109
"The Three Dragoons," De Koven, 468
"The Traveler," Hamerik, 469
"The Trumpeter of Sakkingen," outline of, 229–232
"The Two Cadis," Eichberg, 469
"The Two Caliphs," Meyerbeer, 185
"The Tzigane," De Koven, 468
"The Venetian Maskers," Trajetta, 470
"The Viceroy," Herbert, 469
"The Vintage," Pellesier, 468
"The Water Carriers," Arthur, 468
"The Water Carrier." See "Les Deux Journées"
"The Widow," Lavelle, 469
"The Wizard of the Nile," Herbert, 469
"The Yeomen of the Guard," outline of, 328–330
"The Zoo," Sullivan, 308
Thillon, Mme. Anna, 12, 74
Thomas, Charles A., sketch of, 340
Thomas, Theodore, 102, 172, 282
Tichatschek, Herr, 380, 389
Toccani, Mme., 34
"Tommaso Chatterton," Leoncavallo, 150
"Torquato Tasso," Donizetti, 73
"Tovelille," Hamerik, 469
Trajetta, Philippe, 470
"Treasured Tokens," Fairlamb, 469
"Trial by Jury," Sullivan, 308, 309
"Tristan und Isolde," outline of, 398–401
"Triumph of Columbus," Pratt, 469
Tryon, G. W., 470
Tschaikowsky, Peter I., sketch of, 347

U

"Ulysse," Gounod, 117
"Un Ballo in Maschera." See "The Masked Ball"
"Uncle Tom," Florio, 469
"Undine," cantata, Benedict, 39
"Undine," Lörtzing, 154
"Une Nuit de Cléopâtre," Massé, 169
Unger, Herr, 410, 411

V

"Vakoula, the Smith," Tschaikowsky, 347
"Valerie," Fairlamb, 469
Van Cauteren, Mme., 245
Van der Stucken, Frank, 470
Vanloo, M., 144
Van Zanten, Miss Cornelia, 282
Varesi, M., 358
"Vasco da Gama," Bizet, 43
Verdi, Giuseppe, sketch of, 350
Vestris, Mme., 456
Vestvali, Signorina, 361
Vianesi, Sig., 252
Viardot-Garcia, Mme., 102, 201, 288
Viardot, Mme. Pauline, 187
"Villiers," Page, 469
Vittarelli, Sig., 270
Viviani, Sig., 259
"Vlascla," Van der Stucken, 470
Vogl, Frau, 407
Vogl, Herr, 407, 410
Von Chezy, Helmine, 461
Von Grün-Sadler, Frau, 410
Von Milde, Herr, 113
Von Müller, Mlle., 288
Von Reichenberg, Herr, 410, 411
Von Wolzogen, Ernest, 304
"Voyevoda," Tschaikowsky, 347

W

Wachtel, Herr, 4
Wachter, Herr, 380, 386, 389
Waëtz, Herr, 76
Wagner, Frl., 389
Wagner, Richard, his influence on Bizet, 43; on Boito, 52; relations with Meyerbeer, 186; influence on Ponchielli, 255; sketch of, 379
Wagner, Siegfried, sketch of, 138, 437

INDEX

"Waldmeister," Johann Strauss, 296
Wallace, William V., sketch of, 441
Waner, Herr, 451
Warwick, Mrs. G., 309
Weber, Carl Maria von, sketch of, 449
Weckerlin, Frl., 411
Weil, Oscar, 470
Weinkoff, Herr, 26
"Werther," Massenet, 174
"Westward Ho," Woolf, 470
Wette, Adelheid, 138
Whitney, Mr., 282
Widmann, Joseph Victor, 107
Wiedemann, Herr, 451
"William Penn," Baker, 468
"William Tell," 270; outline of, 277-280
Winckelmann, Herr, 430
Wiskowatoff, M., 285
Wolff, Pius Alexander, 463

Woolf, Benjamin E., 470
Wüst, Frl., 380

Y

Young, Corinne, 470

Z

"Zaira," Bellini, 30
Zamboni, Sig. Luigi, 270
"Zampa," outline of, 132-134
Zelger, Sig., 6
Zell, M., 98, 209, 297, 333, 336, 337
"Zenobia," Pratt, 469
"Zerline," Auber, 5
Zerr, Mlle. Anna, 92
Zilli, Signora, 375
Zottmayer, Herr, 398
Zucchi, Mme., 205
"Zum Grossadmiral," Lörtzing, 154

INDEX OF PRINCIPAL NUMBERS

[The following index contains a list of the principal numbers in the various operas described in this volume which have become popular, whether in their original setting, or by frequent performances upon the concert stage:]

A

"Abscheulicher," aria, *Fidelio*, 28
"Adamastor, re dell' onde profondo," *L'Africaine*, 207
"Addio, speranza ed anima," duet, *Rigoletto*, 357
"Addio sublimi incanti," *Othello*, 373
"Ah, che la morte" (Miserere), *Il Trovatore*, 364
"Ah! chi mi dice mai," aria, *Don Giovanni*, 221
"Ah! e' strano poter" (Jewel Song), *Faust*, 120
"Ah! fors e lui," scena, *La Traviata*, 360
"Ah! mon fils," aria, *The Prophet*, 203
"Ah! non giunge," *La Sonnambula*, 36
"Ah! per stassera," polacca, *Mignon*, 344
"Ah! que j'aime les militaires," air, *The Grand Duchess of Gerolstein*, 239
"Alas! those Chimes so sweetly pealing," alto aria, *Maritana*, 445
"Allmächt'ge Jungfrau, hör mein Flehen," prayer, *Tannhäuser*, 393
"Allmächt'ger blicke gnädig," prayer, *The Jewess*, 128
"Allmächt'ger Vater," *Rienzi*, 385
"Al mio pregar," prayer, *Semiramide*, 276
"A lovely Arab Maid," arietta, *Oberon*, 458
"Al suono dell' ora," *The Star of the North*, 192
"Amor, misterioso angelo," Habanera, *Carmen*, 46
"An jenem Tag," aria, *Hans Heiling*, 159
Anvil Chorus, *Il Trovatore*, 363
"A rosy Crown we twine for Thee," chorus, *Der Freischütz*, 455
"As the Heron calls in the Reeds," *The Queen of Sheba*, 112
"A terra! si, nel livido," aria, *Othello*, 374
"Ave Maria, plena de' grazia," *Othello*, 374
"Ave Maria," *The Huguenots*, 189

B

Ballet Music, *Nero*, 284
Ballet Music, *Queen of Sheba*, 112
Ballet, "The Hours," *La Gioconda*, 254
"Batti, batti," aria, *Don Giovanni*, 221
"Bei Männern, welche Liebe fühlen," duet, *The Magic Flute*, 226
"Bella figlia dell' Amore," quartet, *Rigoletto*, 358
"Bella siccome un angelo," romanza, *Crispino*, 266
Bell Sextet, *Fatinitza*, 335
"Bel raggio," aria, *Semiramide*, 275
"Bist du mein? Hab' ich dich wieder," duet, *Tristan und Isolde*, 400
"Blissful Tidings, reassuring," waltz song, *Boccaccio*, 337

C

"Call me thine own," romance, *L'Eclair*, 131
"Caro nome," *Rigoletto*, 357
"Catalogue Song," *Don Giovanni*, 221
"Céleste Aïda," romanza, *Aïda*, 369
"C'era un re di Thule," folk-song, *Faust*, 120
"Che faro senz' Eurydice," *Orpheus*, 105

INDEX PRINCIPAL NUMBERS

"Chi mi frena," sextet, *Lucia di Lammermoor*, 83

"Cielo e mar," romance, *La Gioconda*, 253

"Com' e bello," aria, *Lucretia Borgia*, 86

"Com' e gentil," serenade, *Don Pasquale*, 80

"Comme il tient ma pensée," *Esclarmonde*, 183

"Conosco un Zingarello," *Mignon*, 343

"Coronation March," *The Prophet*, 204

"Credo in un Dio crudel," mock credo, *Othello*, 373

"Crowned with the Tempest," sextet and chorus, *Ernani*, 353

D

"Das schöne Fest, Johannis-Tag," *The Mastersingers*, 404

"Das Todesurtheil sprich," scena, *The Jewess*, 129

"Deh vieni alla finestra," serenade, *Don Giovanni*, 222

"Deh, vieni, non tardar," *The Marriage of Figaro*, 218

"Del Tago sponde addio," ballad, *L'Africaine*, 207

"Deponiam il branda," march, *Faust*, 121

"Der Hölle Rache kocht," aria, *The Magic Flute*, 226

"Der Vogelfänger bin ich ja," *The Magic Flute*, 225

"Deserto sulla terra," *Il Trovatore*, 363

"Die Hoffnung," aria, *Fidelio*, 28

"Dies Iræ," *Faust*, 121

"Dio dell' or," drinking-song, *Faust*, 119

"Di pescatore ignobile," romanza, *Lucrezia Borgia*, 87

"Di Provenza il mar," andante, *La Traviata*, 360

"Di quella pira," aria, *Il Trovatore*, 364

"Dites lui," romanza, *The Grand Duchess of Gerolstein*, 239

"Dove guardi splendono," mandolinata, *Othello*, 373

"Dove sono," aria, *The Marriage of Figaro*, 218

"Dream Music," *Hansel and Gretel*, 140

"Durch die Wälder, durch die Auen," melody, *Der Freischütz*, 454

E

"Eccomi sola ormai," aria, *The Huguenots*, 190

"Ecco ridente il cielo," cavatina, *The Barber of Seville*, 271, 272

"E danzan su lor tombe," monologue, *La Gioconda*, 252

"Eily Mavourneen, I see thee before me," *The Lily of Killarney*, 42

"Ein Mädchen oder Weibchen," *The Magic Flute*, 227

"Einsam in trüben Tagen," *Lohengrin*, 396

"Ernani, involami," aria, *Ernani*, 352

"Erstehe, hohe Roma, neu," *Rienzi*, 383

"Euch Lüften, die mein Klagen," *Lohengrin*, 397

"Evening Star," *Tannhäuser*, 393

F

"Fare thee well, my Flandrish Maiden," romanza, *Czar and Carpenter*, 156

"Farewell, the Dream is over," *Lakme*, 72

"Filina nelle sale," rondo gavotte, *Mignon*, 343

"Fin ch' han dal vino," *Don Giovanni*, 221

Flower Girls' Scene, *Parsifal*, 434

"Flow on, flow on, O silver Rhine," romanza, *Lurline*, 447

"Frau Holda kam aus dem Berg hervor," *Tannhäuser*, 392

"Freudig begrüssen wir die edle Halle," march and chorus, *Tannhäuser*, 392

"Froh grüss ich dich, geliebter Raum," recitative, *Tannhäuser*, 392

"From the Valleys and Hills," quartet, *The Bohemian Girl*, 20

G

"Gerechter Gott," *Rienzi*, 384

"Glöcklein im Thale," cavatina, *Euryanthe*, 462

"Good Friday Music," *Parsifal*, 435
"Good Night Quartet," *Martha*, 94
Gypsy March, *Preciosa*, 464

H

"Hark, the Lark in yonder Grove," romanza, *The Merry Wives of Windsor*, 234
"Hat man nicht auch Geld daneben," *Fidelio*, 28
Hunters' Chorus, *Der Freischütz*, 455
Hymn to the Virgin, *Stradella*, 97

I

"I am the Monarch of the Sea," *Pinafore*, 314
"I am the very Pattern of a modern Major-General," *The Pirates of Penzance*, 316
"I boschi, i monti," hymn, *William Tell*, 279
"I dreamed I dwelt in Marble Halls," *The Bohemian Girl*, 20
"I have lost my Eurydice," *Orpheus*, 105
"I hear it again, 't is the Harp in the Air," romanza, *Maritana*, 445
"Il balen del suo," aria, *Il Trovatore*, 364
"Il cavallo scalpita," whip-song, *Cavalleria Rusticana*, 163
"Il segreto per esser felice," drinking-song, *Lucrezia Borgia*, 88
"I'm called Little Buttercup," *Pinafore*, 314
Incantation Music, *Der Freischütz*, 455
"In diesen heil' gen Hallen," aria, *The Magic Flute*, 227
"Infelice! e tuo credevi," bass solo, *Ernani*, 353
"In fernem Land, unnahbar euren Schritten," scena, *Lohengrin*, 398
"In happy Moments, Day by Day," ballad, *Maritana*, 445
Intermezzo, *Cavalleria Rusticana*, 164
Intermezzo *L'Amico Fritz*, 167
"In the deep Ravine of the Forest," duet, *The Crown Diamonds*, 14
"In these sacred Halls," aria, *The Magic Flute*, 227

"Invano il fato," aria, *Robert the Devil*, 197
"Io dico no, non son paurosa," aria, *Carmen*, 46
"Io grembo a me," slumber-song, *L'Africaine*, 207
"I want to ask you," drinking-song, *Martha*, 94

J

"Jerum, jerum, halla, halla, he," folk-song, *The Mastersingers*, 404
Jewel Song ("Ah! e' strano poter"), *Faust*, 120
"Johohoe! träfft ihr das Schiff im Meere an," ballad, *The Flying Dutchman*, 388
"Jours de mon enfance," aria, *Le Pré aux Clercs*, 135
"Joy to the high-born Dames of France," allegretto. *Oberon*, 458
"Jungfrau Maria! Himmlisch verklärte" (Hymn to the Virgin), *Stradella*, 97

K

"Komm Hoffnung," adagio, *Fidelio*, 28

L

"La Calunnia," aria, *The Barber of Seville*, 273
"Là, ci darem la mano," duet, *Don Giovanni*, 221
"La donna e mobile," aria, *Rigoletto*, 357
"La gloria inflammi," trio, *William Tell*, 279
"L'Air du Sommeil," slumber-song, *Masaniello*, 11
"La luna immobile," duet, *Mephistopheles*, 55
"La nuit sera bientôt venue," *Esclarmonde*, 183
"La parlate d' amor," ballad, *Faust*, 120
"Largo al factotum," buffo aria, *The Barber of Seville*, 272
"La rivedra nell' estasi," romanza, *The Masked Ball*, 367
"La vendetta piu tremenda," duet, *Ernani*, 353

INDEX PRINCIPAL NUMBERS

"Le bruit des chants s'eteint dans la forêt immense," aria, *Sigurd*, 264
"Le crede il padre," aria, *Dinorah*, 200
"Leggiadre rondinelle," duet, *Mignon*, 343
"Leise, leise, fromme Weise," scena and prayer, *Der Freischütz*, 454
"Liebes-Tod" ("Mild und leise wie er lächelt"), *Tristan und Isolde*, 401
"Like a Dream bright and fair" ("M' appari"), *Martha*, 95
"Lost, proscribed, an humble Stranger," aria, *Martha*, 93
"Love Scene," *Feuersnot*, 306

M

"Mab, regina di menzogne" (Queen Mab song), *Roméo et Juliette*, 123
"Ma dall arido," aria, *The Masked Ball*, 367
"Madamina! il catalogo," buffo aria, *Don Giovanni*, 221
Mad scena, *Hamlet*, 346
March of the Grail, *Parsifal*, 433
"March of the Guilds," *The Mastersingers*, 405
"Mein Herr und Gott, nun ruf' ich Dich," prayer, *Lohengrin*, 397
"Mi chiamano Mimi," duet, *La Bohème*, 258
"Midnight sounds," quartet, *Martha*, 94
"Mira, O Norma," duet, *Norma*, 33
"Mir ist so wunderbar," quartet, *Fidelio*, 28
Miserere, *Il Trovatore*, 364
"Mit Gewitter und Sturm," *The Flying Dutchman*, 388
"Moorish Rhapsody," *The Cid*, 179
"Morgenlich leuchtend in rosigem Schein," prize-song, *The Mastersingers*, 405
"Morning Dawn," *Die Gotterdämmerung*, 427

N

"Nelle fatal di Rimini," aria, *Lucrezia Borgia*, 86
"Nobil donna e tanto onesta," romanza, *The Huguenots*, 189
"Non conosci il bel suol," romanza, *Mignon*, 342
"Non mi dir," aria, *Don Giovanni*, 222
"No, no, no, no," allegretto, *The Huguenots*, 189
"Non più andrai," aria, *The Marriage of Figaro*, 216
"Nothung! Nothung! neidliches Schwert," *Siegfried*, 423
"Notte e giorno faticar," aria, *Don Giovanni*, 221
"Nume del Ciel," prayer, *Masaniello*, 11
"Nun sei gedankt, mein lieber Schwan," *Lohengrin*, 397

O

"O casta fior," aria, *Le Roi de Lahore*, 176
"Ocean, thou mighty Monster," *Oberon*, 459
"O, che volo d'angello," cavatina, *I Pagliacci*, 153
"O cieli azzurri," romanza, *Aïda*, 371
"O dolcezzo perdute," aria, *The Masked Ball*, 367
"O, du mein holder Abendstern," *Tannhäuser*, 393
"O Elsa! nur ein Jahr an deiner Seite," *Lohengrin*, 398
"O'er Mountain steep, through Valley roaming," *The Crown Diamonds*, 13
"Of Herne, the Hunter, a Legend old," ballad, *The Merry Wives of Windsor*, 235
"O figlio, mio, che diro," aria, *The Prophet*, 203
"Oh! Araby, dear Araby," *Oberon*, 459
"Oh! gioja che si senti," *Lucia di Lammermoor*, 83
"Ohimè! morir mi sento," *Aïda*, 371
"O Himmel last dich jetzt erflehen," hymn, *Tannhäuser*, 392
"Oh, jours de première tendresse," duet, *Le Cid*, 179
"Oh, Stars that guide my fervent Love" ("O luce di quest' anima"), aria, *Linda de Chamouni*, 90
"Oh! 'tis a glorious Sight," scena, *Oberon*, 458
"Oh! 'tis pleasant," *Oberon*, 459
"O Isis und Osiris," aria, *The Magic*

INDEX PRINCIPAL NUMBERS 561

Flute, 226; chorus of same name, 227
"O Lola, c'hai di latti," Siciliana, *Cavalleria Rusticana*, 163
"O, luce di quest' anima," aria, *Linda de Chamouni*, 90
"O mio Fernando!" aria, *La Favorita*, 78
"O namenlose Freude," duet, *Fidelio*, 29
"On a Tree by a River a little Tomtit," ballad, *The Mikado*, 325
"On the Banks of sweet Garonne," duet, *Oberon*, 460
"On yonder Rock reclining," romanza, *Fra Diavolo*, 7
"O Paradiso," aria, *L'Africaine*, 207
"Or sai, chi l'onore," aria, *Don Giovanni*, 221
"O sink' hernieder, Nacht der Liebe," duet, *Tristan und Isolde*, 400
"O Sommo Carlo," sextet and chorus, *Ernani*, 353
"O susse Nacht," duet, *Tristan und Isolde*, 401
"O terra, addio," duet, *Aïda*, 371
"Over the dark blue Waters," quartet, *Oberon*, 458
Overture, *Der Freischütz*, 453
Overture, *Euryanthe*, 462
Overture, *Fidelio*, 27
Overture, *La Dame Blanche*, 51
Overture, *Mignon*, 342
Overture, *Oberon*, 458
Overture, *Preciosa*, 464
Overture, *Rienzi*, 383
Overture, *Semiramide*, 274
Overture, *Tannhäuser*, 391
Overture, *The Flying Dutchman*, 388
Overture, *The Water Carrier*, 61
Overture, *William Tell*, 278
Overture, *Zampa*, 134
"O zittre nicht, mein lieber Sohn," aria, *The Magic Flute*, 226

P

"Parigi, o cara," duet, *La Traviata*, 361
"Parisian Bacchanale," *Tannhäuser*, 391
"Per la fè, per l'onore," *The Huguenots*, 189
"Piangea cantando" (Willow Song), melody, *Othello*, 374
"Piccolo casetta bianca," romanza, *Manon*, 181
"Piero mio, go qua una fritola," *Crispino*, 267
"Pietà! pietà!" aria, *The Prophet*, 203
"Pif, paf, pouf," *The Grand Duchess of Gerolstein*, 239
Pilgrims' Chorus, *Tannhäuser*, 393, 394
"Piu bello sorse il giorno," barcarole, *Masaniello*, 10
Polacca, *Mignon*, 344
Postilion's Song, *The Postilion of Longjumeau*, 3
"Presso il bastion de Seviglia," seguidilla, *Carmen*, 46
"Pretty Gitana, tell us what the Fates decree," chorus, *Maritana*, 445
"Printemps qui commence," aria, *Samson and Delila*, 289
"Prithee, pretty Maiden," duet, *Patience*, 319
"Proudly and wide my Standard flies," *Fra Diavolo*, 8
"Pura siccome un angelo," cantabile, *La Traviata*, 360

Q

"Qual cor tradisti," duet, *Norma*, 33
"Quand Diane descend dans la plaine," hunting-song, *Orphée aux Enfers*, 243
"Quand j'étais roi de Beotie," *Orphée aux Enfers*, 243
"Quando rapita in estasi," aria, *Lucia di Lammermoor*, 83
"Questa o quella," aria, *Rigoletto*, 356
"Qui la voce," *I Puritani*, 37

R

"Recondita Armonia," aria, *La Tosca*, 260
"Regnava nel silenzio," aria, *Lucia di Lammermoor*, 83
"Regnava un tempo in Normandia," *Robert the Devil*, 197
"Rheinfahrt" (Rhine journey), *Die Gotterdämmerung*, 428
"Rheingold! leuchtende Lust! wie

INDEX PRINCIPAL NUMBERS

"lachst du so hell und hehr," *Das Rheingold*, 414
"Rhine Journey," *Die Gotterdämmerung*, 428
"Ride of the Valkyries," *Die Walküre*, 421
"Ritorna vincitor," *Aïda*, 370
"Robert! toi que j'aime," aria, *Robert the Devil*, 197
"Robin Adair," ballad, *La Dame Blanche*, 50
"Roland! tu m'as trahie," bravura aria, *Esclarmonde*, 184

S

"Salve dimora casta e pura," aria, *Faust*, 120
"Scenes that are brightest," *Maritana*, 446
"Selva opaco," romanza, *William Tell*, 279
"Sempre amar," duet, *Faust*, 120
"Sempre libera," *La Traviata*, 360
"Ser per prender," aria, *Dinorah*, 199
"Se vuol ballare, Signor Contino," *The Marriage of Figaro*, 216
Sextet, *Crispino*, 267
Sextet, *Lucia di Lammermoor*, 83
"Shadow Song," polka mazurka, *Dinorah*, 200
"Si, carina, caprettina," slumber-song, *Dinorah*, 199
"Siegfried's Tod," *Die Gotterdämmerung*, 429
"Si la stanchezza," duet, *Il Trovatore*, 364
"Silver Tinkling, ringing brightly," sextet, *Fatinitza*, 335
"Si puó, Signore," prologue, *I Pagliacci*, 152
"Soldiers' March," *Faust*, 121
"Son vergin vezzosa," polacca, *I Puritani*, 37
So rief der Lenz in den Wald," *The Mastersingers*, 404
Spinning Song, *The Flying Dutchman*, 388
"Spirit Dance," *Merlin*, 116
"Spirto gentil," romanza, *La Favorita*, 78
"Stride la vampa," aria, *Il Trovatore*, 364
"Su! del Nilo," ensemble and chorus, *Aïda*, 370

"Summ' und brumm du gutes Mädchen," spinning-song, *The Flying Dutchman*, 388
"Suoni la tromba (" Liberty Duet"), *I Puritani*, 37
"Sweet Spirit, hear my Prayer," *Lurline*, 448
Symphonic movement, *Feuersnot*, 306

T

"Take this Cup of sparkling Wine," drinking-song, *Lurline*, 448
"The Colleen Bawn," *The Lily of Killarney*, 42
"The Cruiskeen Lawn," *The Lily of Killarney*, 41
"The Flowers that bloom in the Spring, tra la," duet, *The Mikado*, 326
"The Gondolier, fond Passion's slave," barcarole, *Fra Diavolo*, 7
"The Heart bowed down," *The Bohemian Girl*, 21
"The merry Maiden and the Tar," *Pinafore*, 314
"The Moon has raised her lamp above," serenade and duet, *The Lily of Killarney*, 41
"The Rataplan," duet, *The Daughter of the Regiment*, 74
"The Witches' Ride" (instrumental), *Hansel and Gretel*, 139
"The Work that we're beginning," sextet, *Czar and Carpenter*, 156
"Three little Maids from School are We," trio, *The Mikado*, 325
"'T is sad to leave your Fatherland," *The Bohemian Girl*, 19
"'T is the last Rose of Summer," ballad, *Martha*, 94
"Tomba degl' avi miei" (Tomb Song), aria, *Lucia di Lammermoor*, 83
"Toreador, attento," aria, *Carmen*, 46
"Toreadors' March," *Carmen*, 47
"Treulich gefuhrt, ziehet dahin," bridal song, *Lohengrin*, 397
"Triumph! die Rache, die Rache gelingt," bass aria, *Der Freischütz*, 454
"Tu, che fai l' addormentata," serenade, *Faust*, 121
"Turn on, old Time, thine Hour-glass," trio, *Maritana*, 445

INDEX PRINCIPAL NUMBERS

U

"Una furtiva lagrima," romanza, *L'Elisir d'Amore*, 85
"Una Vergine," aria, *La Favorita*, 78
"Una voce poco fa," aria, *The Barber of Seville*, 272
"Und ob die Wolke sie verhülle," aria, *Der Freischütz*, 455
"Unter blühenden Mandelbaümen," romanza, *Euryanthe*, 462

V

"Vedrai, carino," aria, *Don Giovanni*, 222
"Veglia dal ciel su lor," prayer, *The Star of the North*, 193
"Vissi d' arte e d'amour, no feci," *La Tosca*, 261
"Voi, che sapete," romanza, *The Marriage of Figaro*, 217
"Voici, le sabre de mon père," sabre song, *The Grand Duchess of Gerolstein*, 239
"Volta la terrea," *The Masked Ball*, 367
Vorspiel, *Das Rheingold*, 414, 416, 423, 428
Vorspiel, *Die Walküre*, 417
Vorspiel, *Hansel and Gretel*, 139
Vorspiel, *Lohengrin*, 396, 431
Vorspiel, *Parsifal*, 431
Vorspiel, *The Mastersingers*, 403
Vorspiel, *Tristan und Isolde*, 400

W

"Wahn! wahn! Ueberall wahn," *The Mastersingers*, 405
"Waldweben," *Siegfried*, 424
Waltz arietta, *Roméo et Juliette*, 123
Waltz, *Faust*, 120
"Was gleicht wohl auf Erden dem Jägervergnügen" (Hunters' Chorus), *Der Freischütz*, 455
"Wass muss ich hören," duet, *The Flying Dutchman*, 389
Wedding March, *Lohengrin*, 397
"Welding of the Sword" ("Nothung! Nothung! neidliches Schwert"), *Siegfried*, 423
"We will dance a Cachuca," *The Gondoliers*, 332
"What Time the Poet hath hymned," *Patience*, 319
"When at Night I go to sleep," lullaby, *Hansel and Gretel*, 140
"When other Lips and other Hearts," *The Bohemian Girl*, 21
"When the fair Land of Poland," *The Bohemian Girl*, 21
"When the Foot the Wheel turns lightly," quartet, *Martha*, 94
Where strays the Hindoo Maiden?" aria, *Lakme*, 71
"Where the Buds are blossoming," madrigal, *Ruddygore*, 327
"Willow Song," melody, *Othello*, 374
"Winterstürme wichen dem Wonnemond," spring song, *Die Walküre*, 419
"Wir winden dir den Jungfern-Kranz," chorus, *Der Freischütz*, 455
"Wlastla la santa," rondo, *The Star of the North*, 192
"Wo berg ich mich," recitative and aria, *Euryanthe*, 463
Wotan's Farewell and Magic Fire Music, *Die Walküre*, 421

Y

"Yes, let me like a Soldier fall," *Maritana*, 445
"You may put 'em on the List and they never will be missed," *The Mikado*, 325
"Young Agnes," serenade, *Fra Diavolo*, 7

Z

"Zephyr Duet," *The Marriage of Figaro*, 218
"Zitti, zitti," trio, *The Barber of Seville*, 271, 273
"Zu dir wall, ich, mein Herr und Gott," chorus, *Tannhäuser*, 392, 393